Borderless Empire

Early American Places is a collaborative project of the University of Georgia Press, New York University Press, Northern Illinois University Press, and the University of Nebraska Press. The series is supported by the Andrew W. Mellon Foundation. For more information, please visit www.earlyamericanplaces.com.

ADVISORY BOARD
Vincent Brown, *Duke University*
Cornelia Hughes Dayton, *University of Connecticut*
Nicole Eustace, *New York University*
Amy S. Greenberg, *Pennsylvania State University*
Ramón A. Gutiérrez, *University of Chicago*
Peter Charles Hoffer, *University of Georgia*
Karen Ordahl Kupperman, *New York University*
Mark M. Smith, *University of South Carolina*
Rosemarie Zagarri, *George Mason University*

Borderless Empire

Dutch Guiana in the Atlantic World, 1750–1800

Bram Hoonhout

The University of Georgia Press
ATHENS

Paperback edition, 2022
© 2020 by the University of Georgia Press
Athens, Georgia 30602
www.ugapress.org
All rights reserved

Most University of Georgia Press titles are available from popular e-book vendors.

Printed digitally

The Library of Congress has cataloged the hardcover edition of this book as follows:
Names: Hoonhout, Bram, author.
Title: Borderless empire : Dutch Guiana in the Atlantic world, 1750–1800 / Bram Hoonhout.
Other titles: West Indian web
Description: Athens : University of Georgia Press, [2020] | Series: Early American places | Revision of author's thesis (doctoral)—European University Institute, 2017, titled The West Indian web : improvising colonial survival in Essequibo and Demerara, 1750–1800. | Includes bibliographical references and index.
Identifiers: LCCN 2019010723 | ISBN 9780820356082 (hardcover : alk. paper) | ISBN 9780820356075 (ebk.).
Subjects: LCSH: Essequibo—History. | Demerara—History. | Netherlands—Colonies—America—History. | Netherlands—Colonies—History—17th century.
Classification: LCC F2351 .H66 2020 | DDC 988.1/2—dc23
LC record available at https:// lccn.loc.gov/2019010723

Paperback ISBN 978-0-8203-6258-8

For my parents

Contents

	List of Maps, Tables, and Figures	xi
	List of Abbreviations	xiii
	Acknowledgments	xv
	Introduction: Borderless Societies	1
1	The Borderland	19
2	Political Conflicts	43
3	Rebels and Runaways	74
4	The Centrality of Smuggling	111
5	The Web of Debt	136
6	Borderless Businessmen	162
	Conclusion: The Shape of Empire	189
	Appendix 1	193
	Appendix 2	195
	Notes	197
	Bibliography	245
	Index	267

Maps, Tables, and Figures

Maps

I.1	Essequibo and Demerara, their neighboring colonies and their major connections	5
I.2	Detail from a 1737 map of Suriname	7
I.3	Essequibo and Demerara around the turn of the century, with details of their plantation infrastructure and points of control	8
1.1	The Orinoco-Essequibo borderland	23
2.1	Detail from the mouth of the Demerara River, 1784	56
3.1	The three main desertion routes from Essequibo to Venezuela	89
3.2	Plantations and planters involved in the 1772 revolt in Demerara	99
3.3	Plantations involved in the 1789 *bomba* insurgency	103
3.4	Uprisings, desertion, and maroon attacks in 1795	108
5.1	Caerte van de rivier Demerary van Ouds Immenary, gelegen op Suyd Americaes Noordkust op de Noorder Breedte van 6 Gr. 40 Min, 1759	158
5.2	Carte de la Colonie de Demerary, 1784	159
5.3	Generale en speciale kaart der Colonien van de republicq der Ver. Nederl., geleegen in Guyana, langs de Zeekust der rivieren Poumaron, Essequebo, Demerary; van de grensen van Berbice tot de rivier Morocco aan de grens in de Spaansche Bezitting Oronoco, 1796	160

| 6.1 | Estates of the individuals mentioned in the text | 177 |

Tables

2.1	Number of plantations in Essequibo and Demerara, 1716–1800	50
3.1	Enslaved Africans in Essequibo and Demerara, 1735–1832	82
4.1	Vessels arriving in Essequibo and Demerara, 1700–1799 (annual average)	116
4.2	Exports from Essequibo and Demerara, March 1784–February 1785	121
5.1	Overview of mortgage funds active in Essequibo and Demerara	142
A1.1	Missions of the Reverend Father Capuchins of Catalonia of the Province of Guiana, 1788	193
A1.2	Goods ordered for 1,000 Amerindians, 1803	195

Figures

2.1	Origins of the Demerara supporters for the 1785 petition	62
4.1	Population of enslaved Africans in Essequibo and Demerara, actual numbers compared to counterfactual numbers based on registered slave imports, 1769–1795	133
5.1	Exports from Essequibo and Demerara, 1745–1801 (in lbs)	156
5.2	Registered exports from Essequibo and Demerara, 1798–1802 (in pounds sterling)	157

Abbreviations

ACA	Amsterdam City Archive, Amsterdam, the Netherlands
BGBB	British Guiana Boundary Books
—BC	—British Case
—BCC	—British Counter Case
—VCC	—Venezuelan Counter Case
BL	British Library, London, United Kingdom
BPL	Boston Public Library, Boston, United States
BT	Board of Trade
CO	Colonial Office
CUST	Boards of Customs, Excise, and Customs and Excise, and HM Revenue and Customs
IISH	International Institute for Social History, Amsterdam, the Netherlands
LRS	Liverpool Record Office, Liverpool, United Kingdom
MCC	Middelburgse Commercie Compagnie (Middleburgh Commercial Company)
MHS	Massachusetts Historical Society, Boston, United States
NAG	National Archives of Guyana, Georgetown, Guyana
NL-HaNA	Dutch National Archives, The Hague, Netherlands
NRS	National Records of Scotland, Edinburgh, United Kingdom
NYHS	New York Historical Society, New York, United States

RAB	Raad der Amerikaanse Bezittingen (Council of American Possessions)
RdK	Raad der Koloniën (Council of the Colonies)
RBML	Rare Book and Manuscript Library, Columbia University
S-G	Staten-Generaal (States-General)
TASTD	Trans-Atlantic Slave Trade Database
TNA	The British National Archives, Kew, United Kingdom
UA	Utrecht Archives, Utrecht, Netherlands
VOC	Vereenigde Oostindische Compagnie (Dutch East India Company)
VWIS	Verspreide West-Indische Stukken (Unsorted West Indian Papers)
WIC	Dutch West India Company
ZA	Zeeuws Archief (Zealand Archives), Middleburgh, Netherlands

Acknowledgments

Writing a book inevitably involves incurring many debts. As this project has its origins in my dissertation, I would like to thank my advisers at the European University Institute (EUI) in Florence, Jorge Flores and Regina Grafe. Jorge's support and flexibility allowed me to shape my own project. At the same time, his encouragement to go beyond my comfort zone of economic history and incorporate more social history helped to make this a more balanced work. Regina made sure that I did not forget about the economic side. Her cheerfulness and willingness to discuss chapters over Skype or over pasta are much appreciated, and her incisive comments and broad knowledge of Atlantic history have been enormously helpful. I owe a Deutz-sized debt to my academic mentor, Cátia Antunes. While it cannot be recounted in full here, suffice it to say that her unfaltering faith as well as the many talks and rounds of feedback have been fundamental to my academic development over the past seven years. Her dedication to "her" PhD students (broadly conceived) is a model for any adviser.

At Leiden University, "Team Catia," among others, always offered me a warm welcome. I have spent many hours thinking or drinking with Kate, Joris, Erik, Éli, Julie, Kaarle, Edgar, Hasan, Noelle, Miguel, Susana, João Paolo, Karwan, Jeannette, Sanne, Matthias, Aniek, and Marion, which helped develop our projects as well as our friendship. Similarly, many people at the EUI made life enjoyable, whether in academic settings, in town, or on the Schifanoia calcetto pitch; thanks to

Roel, Matthijs, Martijn, Florian, Sanne, Diana, Marijn, Bouke, Niccolò, Bartosz, Jonas, Esther, Stephanie, and Miquel.

I have benefited from the generous advice and support of many others, whom I like to thank here. Gert Oostindie read the entire manuscript and gave very useful comments. Marion Pluskota, Michiel van Groesen, Karwan Fatah-Black, and Damian Pargas provided valuable input for the book proposal. Wim Klooster offered helpful advice during his stay at the NIAS, as well as when we met in the years afterward, just like Marjoleine Kars. Several participants at the FEEGI, CHAM, BGEAH, ISCECS, Itinerario, and ESSHC conferences provided valuable input. I am grateful as well to Paul Koulen, Johan van Langen, Roelof Hol, Ben ter Welle, and Syeade and Jerry Lagra all of whom contributed in one way or another to research in Guyana. In addition, David Alston has been very supportive in tracking Scots. I would also like to express my gratitude to the Prins Bernhard Cultuurfonds for generously funding my research in Guyana, Barbados, and the United States. Finally, I want to thank the many archivists who have helped me in my quest for the few and scattered sources that deal with Guyanese history.

Parts of this book have been published previously, as Bram Hoonhout and Thomas Mareite, "Freedom at the Fringes? Slave Flight and Empire-Building in the Early Modern Spanish Borderlands of Essequibo–Venezuela and Louisiana–Texas," in *Slavery & Abolition* (2018); and as "Smuggling for Survival: Self-Organized, Cross-Imperial Colony Building in Essequibo and Demerara, 1746–1796," in *Beyond Empires: Global, Self-Organizing, Cross-Imperial Networks, 1500–1800*, ed. Cátia Antunes and Amélia Polónia (Leiden: Brill, 2016), 212–35. I would therefore like to thank Taylor & Francis and Brill for their permission to reuse parts of this material.

At the University of Georgia Press, I have been happy to work with Walter Biggins, Jordan Stepp, and Bethany Snead, who saw the potential for the book and always responded quickly to queries. In addition, I am grateful for the excellent copyediting of Sheila Berg. I am also thankful to the two great reviewers commissioned by the Press, who saw more clearly what the book was about than I could myself and whose suggestions were pivotal in reframing the book.

Finally, I would like to thank friends and family. I have been privileged with fantastic and supportive parents and a wonderful sister, as well as with friends who show there is more to life than academic work. Ultimately, though, my greatest thanks to my dearest Anouk.

Borderless Empire

Introduction: Borderless Societies

When in 1796 the British invasion fleet approached the Demerara River, its commanders were in for an unpleasant surprise. The expedition, arriving from Barbados with some thirteen hundred men, aimed to take possession of the Dutch colonies of Essequibo and Demerara, situated on the Guiana coast of South America. Theoretically, the British came to offer "protection" to the colonies in the name of the Dutch Stadtholder. In practice, they were keen on taking these lucrative colonies for themselves. The Dutch colonies of Essequibo and especially Demerara already had a high percentage of British planters, and their fertile soils carried the promise of great riches. Their coffee, sugar, and cotton could fuel the unfolding Industrial Revolution in Britain with the raw material for its machines and the stimulants for its workforce.

Yet the shallow mouth of the Demerara presented an unforeseen obstacle to the invaders. Even though the heavy warships deliberately kept their distance, the lighter landing vessels failed to reach the shore. The English surgeon George Pinckard was traveling with the fleet and described the unfortunate situation. Instead of going ashore with the earliest tide in the morning, by five o'clock the entire advanced fleet had run aground, frustrating any plans of a quick invasion. The troops, neither able to attack nor able to retreat, became sitting ducks and were forced to await the next tide. The British thus had to change course. Their large ships were ordered to block the river mouth and to anchor within firing range of Demerara's fort, to prepare for a possible Dutch counterattack.[1]

However, the Dutch officials preferred to avoid confrontation. In fact, they were happy to surrender, as long as personal property remained intact. The scenario of a foreign takeover was familiar to the colonists: in the 1780s they had been occupied twice, first by British and then by French forces. After some initial confiscations of ships, the colonists had actually profited from those foreign occupations. Being part of the British or French empire had provided access to more commercial opportunities than they could ever hope for under the Dutch. Consequently, exporting to London or buying enslaved Africans from British slavers had greatly stimulated the expansion of the plantation economy in the 1780s, and the colonists expected similar opportunities now that the British were at their doorstep again.

Another reason for this positive attitude toward a British takeover was the large number of British settlers already present in Essequibo and Demerara. Throughout the eighteenth century, Essequibo and Demerara had welcomed many foreign planters. With the offer of generous ten-year tax breaks, many colonists had been enticed to move from islands like Barbados and Antigua, to abandon these increasingly depleted lands for fertile virgin soil. By the time of the takeover, British and North American colonists probably made up at least half of the planter population.[2]

Consequently, the British took control of the colonies peacefully the day after the initial standoff.[3] Thereafter, except for a short intermezzo in 1802–3, the colonies would remain in British hands, and in 1814 the Netherlands officially ceded them to Britain. In 1831 the two colonies, together with neighboring Berbice, would be merged to form British Guiana. As a newly acquired part of the empire, many British planters, slave traders, and investors jumped on the opportunity to get rich quickly. The slave trade soared and investment boomed. While throughout the Atlantic world the system of slavery was increasingly challenged by abolitionists, it accelerated and intensified in newly acquired regions like Guiana. In fact, in the decade after the takeover, Demerara was the fastest expanding region in the world of slavery.[4] A dream for absentee planters, a nightmare for the enslaved and abolitionists, British Guiana became the site of one of the greatest slave uprisings—the Demerara rebellion of 1823—and a source of fabled riches.[5]

However, the eighteenth century, under Dutch rule, was a profoundly different period. In the first quarter of the century there were just a handful of plantations in Essequibo, while Demerara was not even opened for colonization until 1746. Rather than being stimulated by the metropolis, the two colonies were largely neglected by the governing body—the

Dutch West India Company (WIC)—which led to a situation of constant near-collapse. Irregular supplies from the Dutch Republic meant that food and building materials were almost always in short supply. In addition, the planters were perennially frustrated by the lack of enslaved Africans for sale, most of whom died young because of the terrible conditions in which they lived and worked.[6] Furthermore, the colonial administrators lamented the vulnerability of the colonies, which was the result of a lack of military support. Without sufficient troops and adequate fortifications, the colonists were helpless against external invaders as well as internal insurgencies in the form of slave uprisings.

Nevertheless, the plantation economy grew quickly. In 1735 only thirty plantations existed in Essequibo, and in 1745 Demerara was just a river running through virtually impenetrable rainforest. Yet afterward especially the Demerara colony expanded rapidly. Within fifty years the two colonies had grown to include 2,000 whites and over 42,000 enslaved Africans, toiling on some four hundred plantations.[7] By this point, the Demerara colony had eclipsed Berbice, as well as Essequibo, its former overlord colony, and was rapidly catching up with Suriname, the jewel in the crown of the Dutch plantation empire.[8]

This book seeks to understand how Essequibo and Demerara could survive and expand in this period. It does so by underlining the importance of local improvisation and connections across cultural and imperial borders. In other words, it posits that Essequibo and Demerara were borderless colonies.

There were five remarkable aspects in Essequibo's and Demerara's development: a borderland with Venezuela, which allowed enslaved people as well as soldiers to escape thereto; a heavy reliance on Amerindian allies as bounty hunters and as shock troops during revolts; a strong dependence on private initiative and local improvisation; smuggling as the basis for all domains of colonial trade (the import of provisions, the export of cash crops, and the slave trade); and a high number of non-Dutch planters. These characteristics—as the chapters that follow demonstrate—were interrelated, as they were the result of the open nature of the colonies. Individually these elements might be visible in other empires, but together they resulted in a unique mix that made Essequibo and Demerara into borderless societies.

This "borderlessness" was especially noteworthy because it was manifested in the second half of the eighteenth century. The process of improvised empire building is normally associated with the seventeenth century, as during the eighteenth century European states became more involved and tried to enforce their mercantilist systems. France and Britain tinkered with their exclusive systems by making smuggling centers into free ports and by being strict toward the rest.[9] Portugal had a period of mercantilist revival, initiated by the Marquis of Pombal, and Spain also tried to get a firmer grip on its vast empire through the Bourbon Reforms.[10] Even the Dutch Republic tried to bind its colonies more strictly to itself by constructing a system of plantation mortgages that tied planters to investors in the metropolis.[11] Although these initiatives might be ineffective or even counterproductive (in the case of the Thirteen Colonies), the interesting aspect of Essequibo and Demerara is that the metropolitan authorities did not even try. With the state at a distance, the colonies retained their borderless nature, both in a geographic and in an institutional sense.

The geographic context is visible in map I.1, which shows that the colonies were located at the fringe of the Dutch empire. To the west, they faced the Spanish empire. The borderland separating Essequibo and Venezuela stretched far and wide and was mostly covered in dense rainforest, but rivers like the Cuyuni offered a way of connecting the two European colonies. The Cuyuni was used to facilitate trade but also allowed enslaved Africans to escape from the Dutch to the Spanish side, where they hoped to be declared free.[12] In addition, the borderland was home to a great and diverse number of Amerindian groups several of which became allies of the Dutch. Looking east from Demerara, we find the other Dutch Guiana colonies, Berbice and Suriname. Berbice was similar to Essequibo and Demerara in geographic openness, although it did not expand as quickly, possibly because it attracted fewer foreign settlers. Being run by a private society, it had its own dynamic and still awaits a thorough modern study for the Dutch period.[13] Suriname, on the other hand, is well studied and serves as a mirror for Essequibo and Demerara throughout this book.

The four Dutch colonies of Essequibo, Demerara, Berbice, and Suriname all shared a pattern of development that was dictated by water. In an area covered by forests, the plantations were laid out along the coast or riverbanks, after enslaved people had cleared the grounds. Each plantation then became an island in itself. Building on the Dutch knowledge of reclaiming land through *polders*, a plantation needed a system of waterworks to make the cultivation of the fertile Guianese soil possible. An estate had a system of front, side, and back dams to keep out water, from the river or sea as well as from the rainforest. Within this enclosed

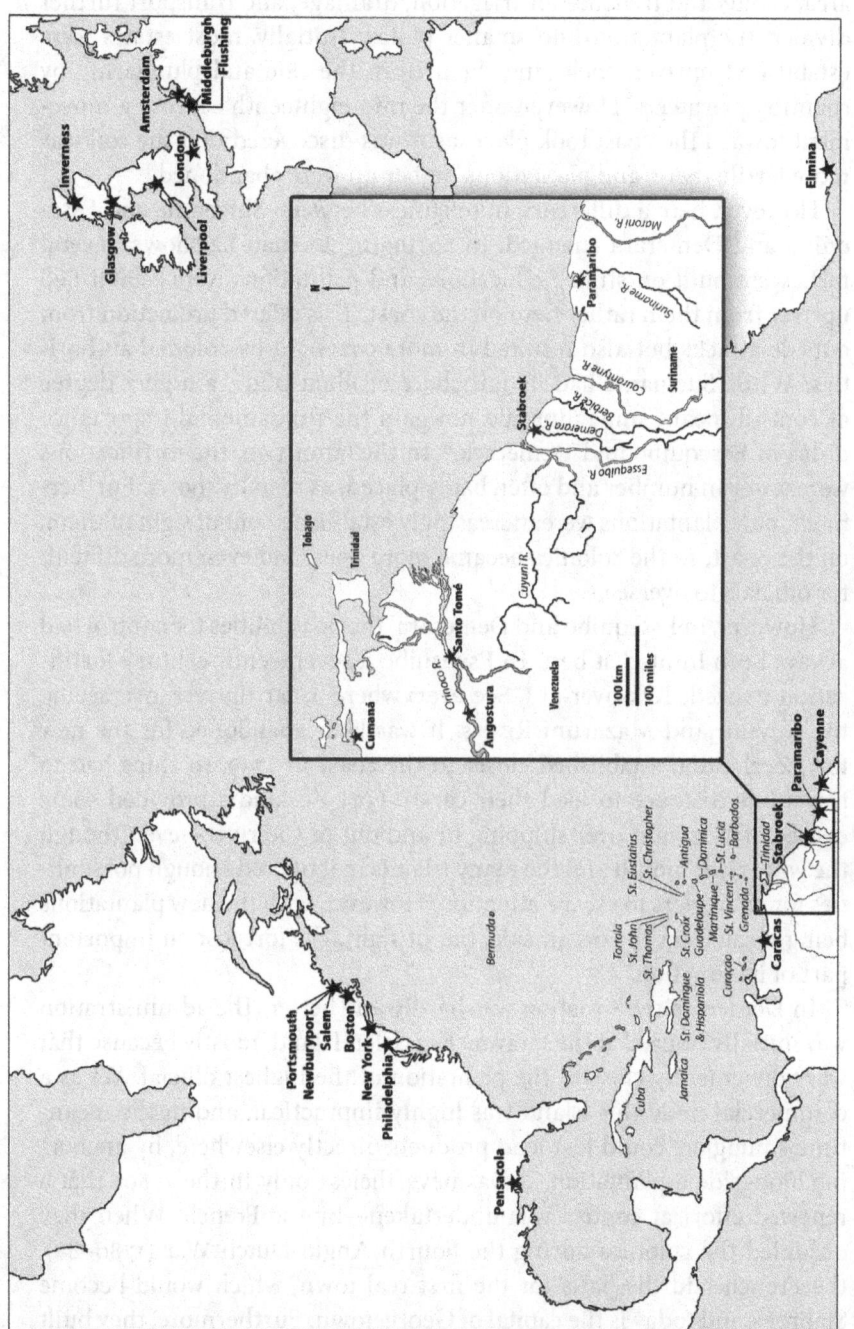

MAP I.1. Essequibo and Demerara, their neighboring colonies and their major connections by the end of the eighteenth century.

area, canals and trenches for irrigation, drainage, and transport further divided the plantation into smaller plots.[14] Initially, most estates were established upriver, sheltering them from the tide and plundering by roaming privateers. However, after the mid-eighteenth century a movement toward the coast took place, as it was discovered that the soil was more fertile there, and plantations higher up were abandoned.[15]

However, here a difference in openness between Suriname and Essequibo and Demerara emerged. In Suriname, as map I.2 shows, several forts were built on strategic locations and plantations were established upriver from them rather than on the coast. This offered protection from outside attacks but also resulted in more oversight by colonial authorities. While Suriname had its fair share of illicit trade, a higher degree of control meant smuggling did not gain the fundamental importance it did in Essequibo and Demerara.[16] In the latter two, the fortifications were fewer in number and often badly placed, as map I.3 shows. Furthermore, new plantations were increasingly established out of sight of them, on the coast, so the colonies became more open and even more difficult for officials to oversee.

However, in Essequibo and Demerara, the possibilities for control had always been limited at best. In Essequibo a seventeenth-century fortification existed, Kyk-over-al ("See everywhere"), far upriver, overseeing the Cuyuni and Mazaruni Rivers. It was later abandoned for the new fort, Zeelandia, established closer to the coast in 1739, so ships had to travel less distance to load their cargo. Fort Zeelandia provided some degree of oversight over shipping in and out of the river—even though the wide river mouth and the many islands in it offered enough possibilities for smugglers to escape attention. However, with the new plantations being located on the ocean side, out of sight, the fort lost an important part of its function.

In Demerara the situation was hardly any better. The administration was initially housed at the faraway Borsselen Island, mostly because that was conveniently close to the plantation of the highest official. Yet as a commercial node this island was highly impractical, and in the meantime smugglers could just load products directly elsewhere, by anchoring alongside a plantation. It was nevertheless only in the 1780s that a renewed effort at control was undertaken—by the French. When they occupied the colonies during the Fourth Anglo-Dutch War (1780–84), the French laid the basis for the first real town, which would become Stabroek and today is the capital of Georgetown. Furthermore, they built fortifications at both sides of the mouth of the Demerara River, although

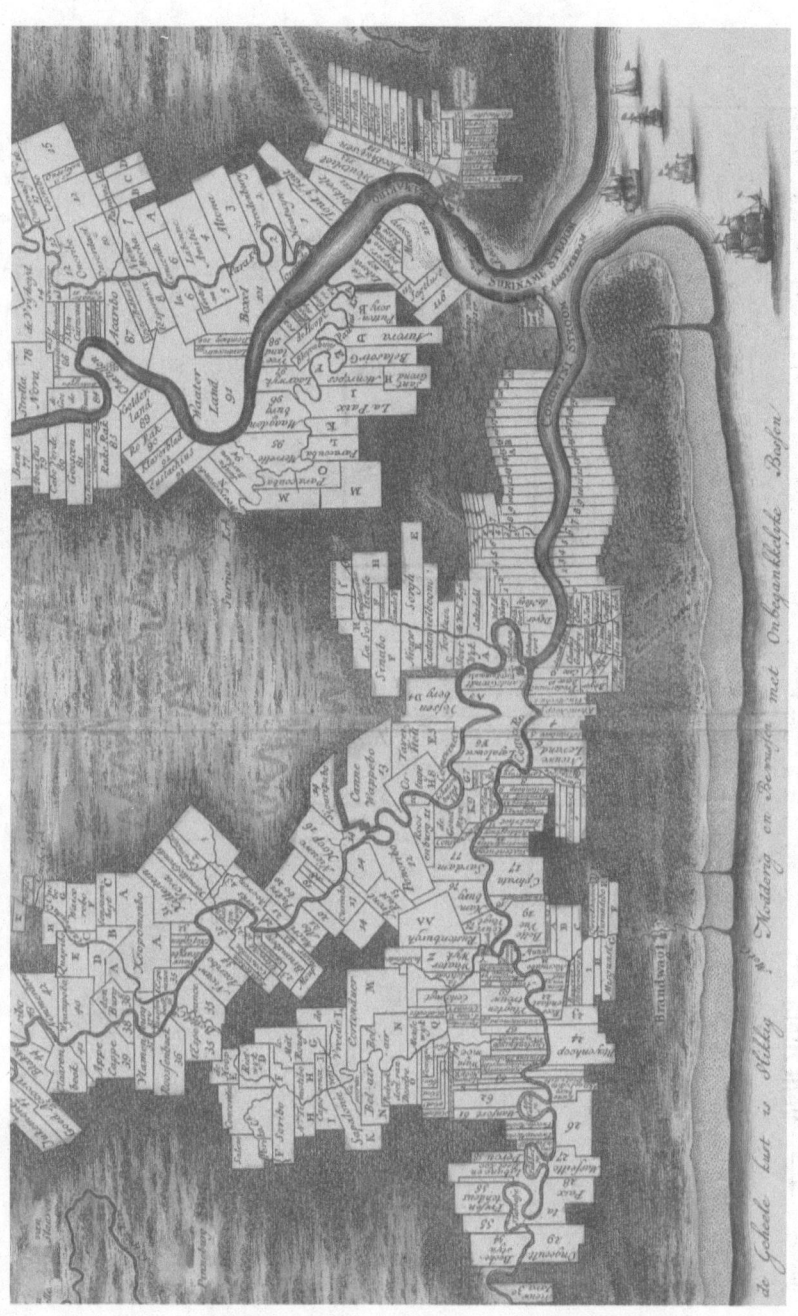

MAP I.2. Detail from a 1737 map of Suriname (south-up orientation). Sailing up the Suriname river, one would encounter Fort Nieuw–Amsterdam first, before reaching Fort Zeelandia and the city of Paramaribo. While Suriname's plantation sector expanded afterward, it did not take the coastal form of Essequibo and Demerara. Source: Algemeene kaart van de Colonie of Provintie van Suriname, Alexander de Lavaux, 1737, Rijksmuseum Amsterdam, NG-478.

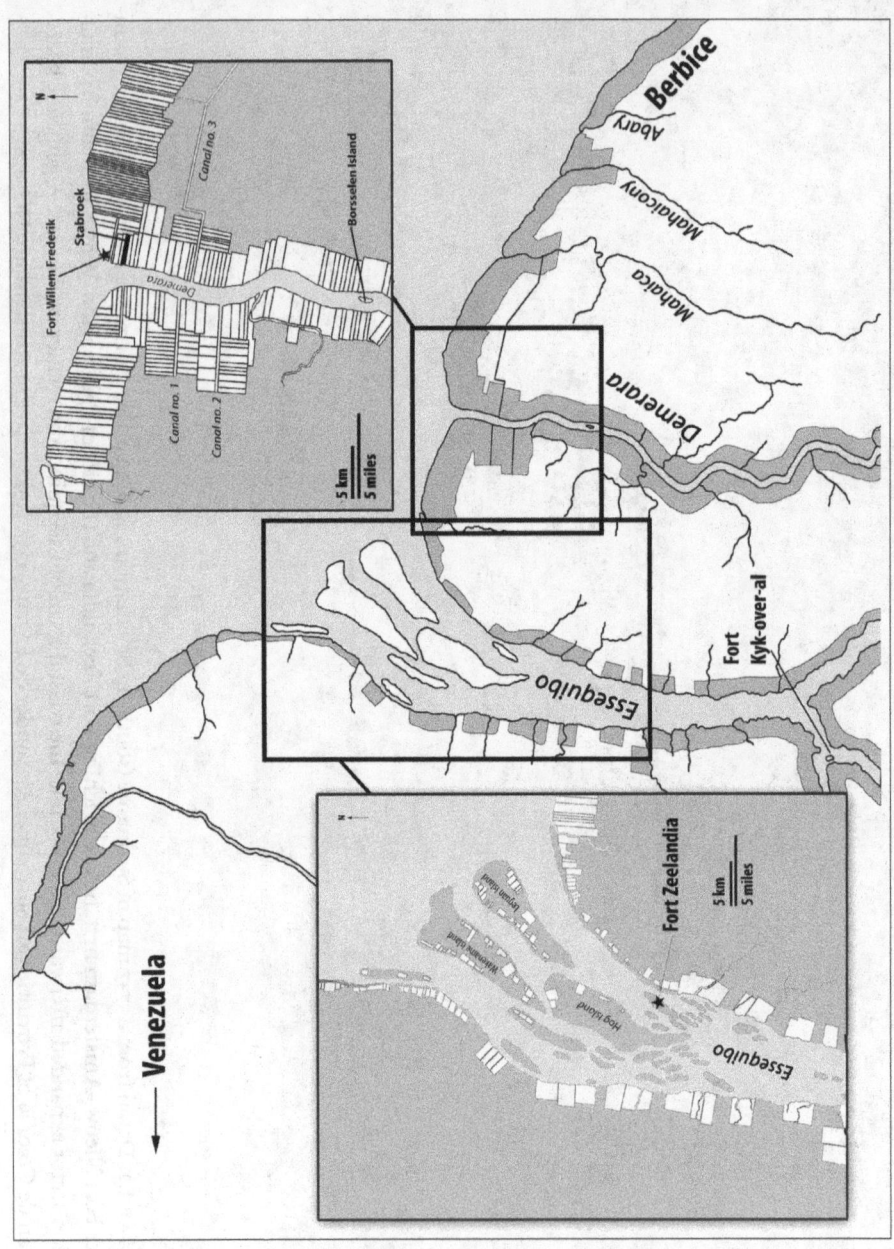

MAP I.3. Essequibo and Demerara around the turn of the century, with details of their plantation infrastructure and points of control.

the Dutch quickly abandoned one side once they regained possession of the colonies.[17] Regardless, a fort at the entry of the river was of little use to prevent illicit trade from the coastal plantations. Even the mud banks favored smugglers, as they made it hard for the deep patrol ships to pursue the lighter smuggling craft that could get closer to the shore.

Smugglers profited not just from the geographic conditions but also from the institutional openness. Essequibo and Demerara were open to foreigners who were willing to try their luck. These might be planters abandoning exhausted soils elsewhere for fertile virgin soil, particularly in Demerara, or adventurers starting in the provision trade and diversifying into plantation ownership later. In any case, these immigrants brought their commercial connections with them. As a result, they often continued their previous business practices, for example, by buying captives from British slavers or exporting cotton via Barbados. This was illegal under Dutch rule, but in these weakly governed colonies they often got away with it. Indeed, in Essequibo and Demerara openness and institutional weakness went hand in hand, as lack of oversight allowed local actors to develop their own initiatives. The reason that the institutional structure remained underdeveloped was because the WIC was both unwilling and unable to develop it. More specifically, the fact that the colonies were ruled by the Company posed three problems.

First, the Company itself was a strange animal. The first WIC had been a weapon in the Dutch War of Independence (1568–1648) against Spain, had obtained the slave fortress of Elmina, and had temporarily occupied Brazil (1630–54) but went bankrupt in 1674. Its successor, the "second WIC," owned small free-trade emporiums like Curaçao and St. Eustatius but otherwise had ambivalent goals. It held the monopoly on the slave trade but voluntarily gave these rights away in 1738 as it could not turn a profit. But while it abandoned the idea of a trading organization, the Company did not become particularly enthusiastic about empire. The grand ambitions of wrestling large territories from others were gone, but now the WIC had to deal with the problems of governing colonies on the Guiana coast, in a period in which its debts accumulated rapidly.[18] In other words, it lacked the means to facilitate the expansion of empire, leaving a vacuum in which local actors could develop their own initiatives.

The second problem was that the WIC was too divided to rule Essequibo and Demerara effectively. Governing proved much more complicated than in Suriname, in which the Company also had a share but which was dominated by Amsterdam interests.[19] In contrast, Essequibo and Demerara became a battleground for the rivalry between Amsterdam and Zealand. Considering that the WIC's governing board (the Assembly of Ten, or Gentlemen Ten) included representatives from the various provincial chambers, decision making was often thwarted by provincial interests. As Zealand had taken the initiative for the colonization of the Essequibo River in the seventeenth century, it claimed sole authority over it, in particular, the exclusive right to trade. Amsterdam maintained that the changes in the later WIC charters had opened the trade to all Dutch citizens. Furthermore, the WIC's income from the colonies was low—it operated three plantations itself and otherwise only levied customs and colonial taxes—and the Amsterdam chamber bore most of the frequently incurred losses, being the largest contributor to the Company.[20] Amsterdam thus desired more influence in the colonies' administration, but Zealand opposed it. This rivalry barred any plans for development. Only in 1770, after two decades of infighting, could an uneasy compromise be made, to be revised into a marginally less uneasy compromise two years later.[21] While the Company was willing to invest for its part in the governance of Suriname, even after the compromise Essequibo and Demerara remained deprived. Supplies, military protection, patrol ships, and infrastructure all received minimal if any attention.

These issues were connected to the third problem: the lack of a proper legislative framework. No charter existed on which colonization was based, and the laws in force were the same laws as in Holland, insofar as they were applicable. By-laws, rather than laws, thus proved the basis for much of the colonial administration, signifying its improvised nature. These by-laws and proclamations were issued by the Council of Policy, one of the two councils (also called courts) responsible for the administration, the other one being the Council of Justice. The former unified legislative and executive powers; the latter wielded judicial power. In practice the division was not as clear-cut, since the Fiscal (the prosecutor, or bailiff), had a say in both councils. The Council of Policy was the most important body for the colonists as its by-laws had the force of law once they were approved by the Company directors in the metropolis. In both councils planters were represented, although the precise constellation changed over time and was a source of friction.

In this legislative limbo, without a clear metropolitan plan, the shape of empire was determined by those on the ground. While all empires were improvised to some extent, improvisation was really at the core of Essequibo's and Demerara's development.[22] With too few provision ships coming from the Dutch Republic, the colonists bought their fish and flour from North American traders. Considering that there were almost never more than one hundred soldiers—most of them sick or eager to desert—the colonists looked for military solutions locally. Internal stability (rather than a foreign invasion) was their biggest concern, so they recruited the Amerindian population as bounty hunters and soldiers, to capture runaway slaves and quell slave uprisings. Furthermore, when the Dutch slave traders did not arrive, the colonists were quick to breach the mercantilist rules and buy their enslaved laborers from foreign traders instead. And if illegal trade was the best way to settle such business, the planters were only happy to comply and the local officials to consent. Consequently, a substantial amount of the plantation produce disappeared into the Atlantic network rather than going to the metropolis. While these haphazard solutions could not solve all the planters' problems, they worked well enough to allow colonial expansion to take place.

While these conditions created a unique society in Essequibo and Demerara, similar elements of borderlesness were visible elsewhere in the Atlantic world. The story of Essequibo and Demerara thus has a lot to offer to scholars of Atlantic history. Indeed, historians of the Spanish empire will see many parallels. Improvisation was a key feature of Spanish governance too, epitomized by the famous phrase *obedezco, pero no cumplo* (I obey but do not comply), used by governors to indicate they would ignore or alter a specific metropolitan decree to fit the local circumstances.[23] The large Spanish empire also had many borderlands, where authority was thinly spread and developments were "entangled" with that of a neighboring empire.[24] Furthermore, illicit trade was fundamental to the existence of the Spanish empire too, as smugglers filled the gap that the unreliable fleet system left open.[25] In fact, as in Essequibo and Demerara, Spanish colonists often did not consider smuggling to be opposed to the empire itself. In eighteenth-century Venezuela, a moral economy of smuggling existed, as colonists reasoned they were right to trade with foreigners because the lack of Spanish supplies left them no other choice. Furthermore, they were willing to rise up for this "right."[26] And when the British mistook this willingness to engage in contraband trade for disloyalty in the War of Jenkins' Ear (1739–48), they were quickly proven wrong.[27] As this book shows, in Essequibo and Demerara a similar moral economy of smuggling was at work.

For historians of North America or the British empire, this book might offer different parallels, namely, in a similar openness during the seventeenth century. In the early phases of English colonization, legal supplies were scarce, prompting colonists in the West Indies and the Chesapeake to trade with the Dutch, across imperial boundaries. Furthermore, they lobbied to legalize these exchanges—prohibited by the Navigation Acts—as they considered open trade to be in the empire's best interest.[28] However, colonists gradually realized they had more to gain from mercantilism, to the disadvantage of the Dutch. Although illegal trade persisted, imperial control increased and the mercantilist system largely worked.[29] Therefore, while stricter enforcement of the rules after the Seven Years' War (1756–63) provoked resistance in the Thirteen Colonies, the British West Indies preferred to stay within the empire, being dependent on metropolitan protection and the protected home market.[30] The Dutch had thus lost their role as middlemen, a function that was taken over by US traders. By the end of the eighteenth century, the roles were completely reversed: Dutch colonies, like the ones in Guiana, relied on foreign shipping, while US merchants turned toward global trade and became crucial connectors between different regions and empires.[31]

This book also emphasizes that the image of the Dutch as quintessential inter-imperial brokers is only valid for the seventeenth-century "Dutch Moment," when they were instrumental in jump-starting other empires.[32] Afterward, the Dutch had to carve out a new role for themselves in the increasingly mercantilist Atlantic world. Free-trade hubs like Curaçao and St. Eustatius generated substantial profits, but this does not mean the Dutch were ideological free traders. The Dutch favored open inter-imperial commerce when they could profit from other empires but instated mercantilist regulations when it came to their own plantation colonies on the Guiana coast. However, this book shows that the borderless nature of Essequibo and Demerara made enforcement of such laws virtually impossible. Consequently, the two colonies drifted away from the Dutch Republic and became increasingly connected to the rest of the Atlantic world.

This study thereby also integrates the story of Essequibo and Demerara into Dutch imperial historiography, which has more or less forgotten about them as a result of the dual Dutch-British legacy. In fact, the most elaborate accounts for this part of Guiana date from the nineteenth century.[33] Since most seventeenth- and eighteenth-century documents are in Dutch, British historians faced a language barrier while Dutch historians tended to write about bigger or more economically successful parts of the empire, such as the East Indies, the Caribbean islands, or Suriname.[34]

Over the years, this focus has produced many thorough studies, often with an emphasis on trade. Recently the literature has branched out to more diverse and more transnational topics.[35] By analyzing Essequibo and Demerara in a similar transnational light, this book contributes to a fuller understanding of the early modern Dutch empire.

Historians of Suriname, and historians of slavery in general, might therefore be interested to see how the borderland conditions of Essequibo and Demerara shaped their regime of slavery. As the Spanish, like on many of their imperial fringes, promised freedom to runaways from Protestant countries, the most daring from Essequibo (and to a lesser extent Demerara) had an attractive escape option.[36] In contrast, in Suriname they might have become maroons.[37] Furthermore, in Suriname such maroon societies proved to be a powerful counterforce to the plantation hierarchy, while in Essequibo and Demerara marronage was both less common and less viable. There, Amerindians cooperated with the plantocracy to destroy most incipient maroon societies while also crushing resistance in the form of revolts. This study thus contributes to discussions on how regimes of slavery were shaped by geographic conditions and the power balance between the different actors involved. Elsewhere, maroons and indigenous peoples might cooperate to resist the colonial regime, but in the Guianas, Amerindian groups were vital in upholding the slavery regime.[38]

In general, this book highlights how empire building was a process that transcended "national" or ethnic boundaries. It thus aligns with recent studies that focus on connections and argue against the balkanization of the Atlantic world into separate "national" or "linguistic" Atlantics (i.e., Spanish, French, and British).[39] Instead, like in the minds of contemporaries, it makes more sense to speak of a "Greater Caribbean" in which similar societies were connected with each other across imperial borders.[40] This attention to connections will likely lead historians to appreciate the importance of intercolonial commerce, slave trading, and smuggling more.[41] The case of Essequibo and Demerara demonstrates how those linkages were formed and how they contributed to the integration of the Atlantic world.

To understand how this web of connections emerged in Essequibo and Demerara, it is necessary to look at the colonial level. Especially considering the underdeveloped institutional structure, the most important decisions were improvised in the colonies rather than formulated in metropolitan boardrooms. Furthermore, a local vantage point can more easily uncover the transimperial networks that proved indispensable. Of course, this research cannot ignore the effects of developments in the metropolis or within Europe, as the colonies were caught up in several wars and metropolitan money financed much of the colonies' expansion. Therefore, the analysis alternates between different scales when needed.

The source base is varied, by necessity, as many manuscripts have been lost. The core body of sources consists of the WIC archives, both those remaining in the Netherlands and those that ended up in the British Colonial Office (CO) archives after the takeover. Although part of the WIC archive in the Netherlands was sold to a rag dealer in the nineteenth century, sufficient duplicates remain available in London.[42] The National Archives of Guyana and a variety of reports and requests constitute an additional source, for both personal and judicial perspectives, although much of the material is heavily damaged. The Amsterdam City Archives (ACA) reveal information about financial flows and the States-General (S-G) archive in the Netherlands provides insights about the highest echelons of administration. This material is combined with other sources, such as trade statistics from the British Caribbean and correspondence of various merchants, spread out across British and North American archives. The British-Guiana boundary dispute books—produced in the arbitration of the borderland conflict between Britain and Venezuela—contain additional material and allowed me to use Spanish sources, in translation.

Taken together, this body of sources forms the basis for a multilayered story but one that nevertheless focuses on the colonial level. To investigate how the borderless nature of empire in Essequibo and Demerara affected the different dimensions of colonial development, this book takes a thematic approach, in six chapters.

The first chapter focuses on the geographic openness, investigating developments in the borderland between Essequibo and the Spanish empire, later to become Venezuela. It demonstrates how precarious the presence of both the Dutch and the Spanish colonists was in the early phases of colonization. Dutch traders had originally arrived in the seventeenth century to trade with the Amerindian population, whereas the Spanish, especially in the eighteenth century, aimed to establish missionary villages. Amerindian resistance to the mission process led several groups to ally with the Dutch, who on the other hand also bought enslaved Amerindians. The latter typically came from the areas farther away from the Dutch settlements, including areas claimed by Spain. The fact that Amerindians could not be enslaved under Spanish law resulted in tense relations. Furthermore, after 1750 the Spanish authorities promised freedom to enslaved Africans who managed to escape from the Dutch side and convert to Catholicism. Nevertheless, the borderland dynamics were not only characterized by tension and animosity; especially before 1750, relations between Dutch and Spanish authorities were fairly good, resulting in a lively trade as well as exchanges of runaway slaves.

Chapter 2 looks further into these local improvisations, by examining how the people on the ground influenced the system of colonial governance. It first explains how the institutional structure came about by looking more closely at the political interactions on the Dutch side. It therefore examines rivalry in the metropolis, as well as in the colonies. Considering that local proclamations constituted an important form of governance, colonists were adamant about retaining influence in the Council of Policy. So when the WIC tried to curb this influence, the colonists rose up in protest. Several cross-"national" coalitions were formed to reclaim these rights, and it even seems that a coup was within the realm of possibilities. The end of the century brought further political polarization as pro-British and pro-France factions debated constitutional renewal in the colonies while worrying about whether Britain or France would invade first. Once the pro-British governor deserted on a British ship, the colonists had to improvise again to devise a new practice of administration, although they were soon subjected to the British invasion.

The third chapter shows how openness and local initiative also shaped the regime of slavery. It focuses on runaways and revolts. The former aimed to seek asylum in the Spanish areas, as noted above, but had to deal with Amerindians who acted as trackers and bounty hunters for the Dutch colonists. This improvised alliance between the colonists and indigenous groups (particularly the Caribs) was crucial for maintaining a hold over the large number of enslaved people. Furthermore, the flight of potential rebels alleviated the pressure on the slavery regime. Such desertion thus contributed to stability. This also applied to the military: disgruntled soldiers could defect to the Spanish—reducing the chance of mutinies—and sometimes did so together with the enslaved. The option of running away, together with the role the Amerindians played, explains the lack of maroon communities in Essequibo, for which neighboring Suriname is so well known. In Demerara marronage was more common, as it was more difficult to get to the Spanish areas. Consequently, the few revolts that took place all occurred in Demerara. Again, the Amerindians proved crucial in upholding the slavery regime, as they were decisive in quashing these insurgences.

After this local perspective, chapter 4 looks toward the Atlantic to investigate the crucial trading connections. It demonstrates that openness to Atlantic commerce was vital for the colonies' expansion and that local officials played an important role in facilitating many of the often unofficial exchanges. Due to the conflict between Amsterdam and Zealand, Essequibo and Demerara were typically ill supplied with regard to almost everything. Food and other basic provisions like candles, planks, and stones were imported from the intra-American network, while enslaved Africans were smuggled in on a large scale. The Dutch slave trade was declining by the end of the eighteenth century, and most slave traders preferred to sell their captives in Suriname rather than in Essequibo or Demerara. It is likely that this slave trade was paid for by plantation products. These cash crops could be marketed in Amsterdam, to remit the proceeds to Britain, but an alternative illicit circuit existed as well. Many of the intra-American ships carried small or medium cargoes of cotton, sugar, or coffee, which probably found their way to Britain via Barbados or any of the other British islands. This commercial trade network proved vital for the two colonies' survival and integrated Essequibo and Demerara into the wider Atlantic trading systems.

The fifth chapter analyzes more direct ties with the metropolis in the crucial domain of credit. While the lack of institutional support explains the late start of Essequibo and Demerara, the system of credit explains why it could rapidly expand after 1750. However, while credit typically tied a colony closer to the metropolis, in Essequibo and Demerara the planters abused the system and retained local control over the unwinding of it. This intricate system of plantation mortgages greatly stimulated the growth of the plantation sector throughout the Guianas, especially after 1760, but proved to be a bubble. However, creditors encountered a host of difficulties when they tried to reclaim their money from the indebted planters. While those investing in Suriname also sustained large losses, it proved possible to execute estates and restructure loans there. In Essequibo and Demerara, because of the vague legal framework and influence of key administrators, investors managed to postpone execution for a long time. Local officials had a good reason to do so. As planters were indebted to each other, executing one part of the chain would lead to a string of subsequent defaults. Furthermore, the preference order was so unclear in the colonies that virtually all possible claimants could claim that their debts were preferential. This obscurity seems to have provided the two colonies with an unintended form of stability. While the financial entanglement likely inhibited additional Dutch investments, there were enough non-Dutch people willing to come and invest in the colonies. Those from Britain and North America were particularly interested, and because they used both their personal credit lines and the Dutch mortgages, they were apparently able to exploit larger estates.

Chapter 6 draws the various strands together by looking at case studies of non-Dutch individuals and how they made use of the borderless nature of Essequibo and Demerara. It thereby shows how the process of Atlantic integration worked in practice and highlights its "self-organized" character. The Atlantic economy was not just shaped by top-down imperial measures from states but also emerged out of the myriad interactions between individuals. This bottom-up process of self-organization was particularly important in the undergoverned societies of Essequibo and Demerara.[43] The borderless businessmen analyzed in this chapter illustrate this process and showcase the broader developments discussed in previous chapters, such as the welcoming attitude to foreigners, the pervasiveness of smuggling, and the connection between trade and plantation ownership.

These chapters add up to a story of empire building as an Atlantic-wide process. They show that borderless colonies could still exist by the late eighteenth century and that improvised connections across cultural and imperial borders were at the heart of Essequibo's and Demerara's development.

1 / The Borderland

The history of the borderland between present-day Guyana and Venezuela is relevant today.¹ The large swath of Guyana west of the Essequibo River, forming about two-thirds of the country, has historically been a zone of contention and interaction. When the borders solidified in the nineteenth century, British Guiana rather than Venezuela came to control most of this former borderland (see map 1.1). Yet this division remained a source of political tension afterward and was fueled recently by the discovery of oil reserves off the coast of the contested area, attaching a major economic element to the issue. While this chapter focuses on borderland relations during the early modern period, it makes use of the sources generated by the border conflict itself.

Luckily for the historian, the border dispute prompted both parties to go back to historical sources to prove their claims. The British, having officially taken possession of the Dutch colonies in 1814, were quick to extend claims over the borderland as well. The Dutch had never been very interested in doing so, but in 1825 the British commissioned the German naturalist and explorer Robert Hermann Schomburgk to establish clear limits. Perhaps unsurprisingly, after several years Schomburgk came up with a demarcation line that allocated British Guiana most of the contested borderland. This "Schomburgk line" would be the basis of negotiations for the rest of the century.² Venezuela, on the other hand, advanced a different demarcation line: one that pushed Venezuela's border as far east as the Essequibo River, rejecting all British claims. Diplomatic relations deteriorated further toward the end of the nineteenth century, and in 1895 they agreed to arbitration by the United States. To substantiate their claims, the two countries reproduced several volumes of archival material, going back to the first phases of settlement. In these so-called British Guiana Boundary Books (BGBB), reports and correspondence from missionaries, governors, and other officials were reproduced insofar as they related to the borderland, thus giving access to archival material that is often unavailable otherwise. While these selections are obviously biased, they still offer vital information as Dutch-British and Spanish sources can be compared and contrasted.

The opposing countries based their claims on their different imperial traditions. In a nutshell, the Venezuelan case relied on the Spanish claim of discovery, which—by the time the Dutch arrived in the late sixteenth century—had "ripened into Spanish title by occupation."[3] The British case, in brief, sidestepped the settlement issue and based its argument on trade: the Essequibo-based Dutch had been active as traders and smugglers well into the Orinoco. After these (multivolume) opening arguments, each country could reply to the other's case and put forward a counter case. In appendixes they reproduced the source material. The final result was proclaimed in 1899 and largely followed the Schomburgk line, although Venezuela received sovereignty over the mouth of the Orinoco. Venezuela felt mistreated and opposed the treaty. In 1962 they brought the issue before the United Nations and in 1966 the UN established the Mixed Commission to settle the dispute. However, until today no agreement has been reached.[4]

In the terminology of Jeremy Adelman and Stephen Aron, then, the transition from borderland to "bordered land" is still not entirely complete. Adelman and Aron observed that in eighteenth-century North America a situation of overlapping territorial claims slowly gave way to the system of sovereign states and international diplomacy that we know today.[5] While previously European and indigenous powers balanced each other out, once the British (and later the United States) became strong enough, they started to enforce borders and overrule indigenous land claims. The borderland thus became a "bordered land".

In the case of Essequibo and Demerara, the British plans to draw demarcation lines in the early nineteenth century can be seen as an effort in this direction. Previously, neither the Spanish nor the Dutch made any specific claims as to how far its territory extended. Both powers had a general idea, but could not enforce borders even if they wished. While in 1750 the Spanish king sent out the Real Expedición de Limites (Royal

Boundary Expedition), it was mainly concerned with enforcing Spanish control over the Orinoco region. In fact, the European powers hardly had an idea of what transpired in the interior or what it looked like, as attested by the continual attempts to find El Dorado up until the 1770s.[6] Furthermore, Amerindian groups were still players of importance well into the nineteenth century.

The region thus remained a borderland, or in the concepts of other historians, a "contact zone," "middle ground," "zone of transculturation," or space of "entanglement."[7] In these places, overlapping European and indigenous claims had to be worked out on the ground rather than adjudicated on a metropolitan drawing board. This chapter investigates how the resulting balance of power evolved over time and why different groups cooperated or came into conflict with each other. By zooming in on the local level, it showcases how the open geography of the borderland shaped the colonial societies of Essequibo and Demerara.

A short first section provides the necessary historical and geographic context. The next sections demonstrate what the borderland meant to various actors. It starts with the Spanish side, moves on to the Dutch, then analyzes the role of the Amerindians, before ending with a discussion on how the British approached the borderland.

Situating the Borderland

During the seventeenth and eighteenth century, four main groups of actors confronted each other. In the west there were Spanish settlers along the Orinoco River in Venezuela, while in the east the Dutch colonists settled along the Essequibo River. In between these Europeans and around them lived various Amerindian groups. Finally, African runaways crossed the borderland from the Dutch to the Spanish side.

The Spanish were the first Europeans to settle in the area. Their incursions into the interior, with its large and diverse population of Amerindian societies, often led to conflict. Many Amerindian groups effectively resisted Spanish efforts to resettle them in missionary villages. During the seventeenth century, the Dutch often proved willing to join this fight, as they were still in a war to acquire independence from Spain. After the peace was concluded in 1648, the relations changed somewhat, and Dutch and Spanish settlers saw the need to support each other's colonial project, because their presence was still weak. An important point of conflict, however, was that Carib Amerindians often made inroads into Spanish-claimed territory to capture other Amerindians and sell them as "red slaves" to the Dutch. Under Spanish law these captives were free, but the Dutch were eager to buy these people and support the Caribs, who became increasingly important for the Dutch.

In the seventeenth century the Dutch had sought to establish relations with Amerindians in order to trade in exotic products, but in the eighteenth century this dynamic changed. As the plantation complex expanded, the Caribs (as well as several other groups) could acquire European goods by capturing enslaved African runaways and returning them for a reward. This Dutch-Amerindian cooperation became all the more important when in 1750 the Spanish instated a religious sanctuary for runaways. In other words, enslaved Africans who fled from the Dutch to the Spanish side and converted to Catholicism were to be declared formally free. Many Africans seized this opportunity, putting more strain on the relationship between the Spanish and the Dutch while strengthening the bond between the Dutch and their Amerindian allies.

Map 1.1 gives geographic context to the borderland. Three routes of contact existed: via the ocean, via the coastal stretch, and via the inland rivers, particularly the Cuyuni. Running from the Spanish areas toward the Dutch in Essequibo, the Cuyuni River proved to be a vital part of the borderland infrastructure. The Spanish established missionary villages along the river, and the Dutch placed outposts as well, in an effort to have some oversight. Such posts were manned by a "postholder" and sometimes a few soldiers and could function as contact points with the Amerindian population as well.

The Dutch colonists discerned five principal groups: in additon to the Caribs (today called Kalina), there were the Arawak (today called Lokono), living along the coast and river mouths; the Akawaio, residing more inland around the Demerara and Mazaruni Rivers; the Warao, on the seacoast between the Orinoco and the Pomeroon; and the Macushi, living on the savannah and mountainous areas in the interior. While the Caribs had the most warlike reputation, the Arawak and Akawaio and—to a lesser extent—the Warao were also involved as military allies, for both the Spanish and the Dutch.[8] It is important to note, though, that more Amerindian groups lived farther inland, that the ethnic groups lived in separate groups with their own leaders, and that these ethnic distinctions were reported through European eyes and therefore probably more complex in practice.

MAP 1.1. The Orinoco-Essequibo borderland.

The Spanish Side

The Spanish view of borderlands, as Tamar Herzog has argued in her recent insightful book, centered on claim making. Rather than through warfare or the defense of previously drawn lines, claims could best be extended in peacetime by means of gradual penetration. The issue then was whether such lands were "vacant" or not and whether the Amerindian inhabitants made "proper use" of the land. Since Europeans defined "proper use" according to their own norms, they could legitimize the subsequent appropriation. Furthermore, this process was more similar across empires than is often assumed. Notions of English colonists preoccupied with control over land and Spaniards with control over people are overstated, as both groups were concerned with legitimizing their presence and securing their power over land and over indigenous peoples.[9]

Nevertheless, in Iberian claim making, conversion was a vital instrument, for baptised Amerindians could be portrayed as vassals of the crown and hence would extend the royal claims. Thus religious orders like the Jesuits could present themselves as conquistadors: by forcibly converting indigenous peoples and relocating them to missionary villages, the orders turned Amerindian lands into European lands. This attitude changed in the second half of the eighteenth century, as Amerindians were seen as possessing "natural freedom." Therefore, their allegiance had to be secured through treaties rather than forced baptism. However, such negotiations, involving extensive improvisation and expensive gift giving, were still fraught with problems and could result in violent interactions.[10] Indeed, the Spanish approach to the Guiana borderland contained all of these elements: a focus on subverting or relocating, through gifts or through force, and treaty making with some Amerindian groups, sometimes to solicit their help against others. While the Jesuits were present as well, the two orders most heavily involved were the Capuchins and the Franciscans.

However, the missionaries managed to gain control over the Guiana borderland only in the eighteenth century, for in the seventeenth century the Spanish colonial presence remained fragile. In fact, the colonists were often attacked and beaten back, as the Guianas had been an area of imperial competition ever since Sir Walter Raleigh arrived in 1597 on his quest to find El Dorado. While the early European presence was small, the number of Amerindian groups was relatively large: an estimated one hundred thousand people.[11] Consequently, after his return in 1618,

Walter Raleigh could solicit the help of local Amerindians to destroy Santo Tomé, which was the center of Spanish colonization in the Orinoco area. The settlement was rebuilt but would suffer the same treatment three more times in the following decades. It is important to note that between 1568 and 1648 the Spanish and the Dutch were involved in a prolonged conflict over Dutch independence. This fighting carried over to the Americas: Santo Tomé was destroyed once again in 1629 by an English-Dutch alliance and by a Dutch-Amerindian coalition in 1637 and 1639. The Peace of Münster in 1648 brought an end to Spanish-Dutch hostilities and recognized the Dutch presence in the region. For a decade there were peaceful trade relations between the Spanish and the Dutch. Yet when in 1658 a new governor attempted to stop these (illicit) exchanges, the Dutch again raided Santo Tomé and Carib attacks resumed as well.[12]

At this point the Spanish were not yet concerned with the borderland, as they focused on gaining control of the area north of the Orinoco River. The French had been forming relationships with the local Caribs there as well, which curtailed the possibilities for Spanish expansion. While the Spanish succeeded in establishing three missionary villages in the 1660s, within several years they were either abandoned or destroyed by the French, the Caribs, or both. And when Jesuit missionaries attempted to establish control over Amerindian groups in the Orinoco region in 1679 and again in 1684, they were pushed back by combined Carib forces. Subsequently, the Jesuits' efforts subsided and they withdrew from the region in 1694, not to return for four decades.[13] Thus the Amerindians were the dominant power in the Guianas during the seventeenth century and were able to dictate the terms on the middle ground.

The balance of power changed profoundly in the eighteenth century. After the War of the Spanish Succession (1701–13), the Spanish Bourbon monarchy started a new attempt to increase its control over Guayana. It took several years to entice the Jesuits and Capuchins to undertake a renewed attempt, but as control of the region north of the Orinoco increased, confidence grew that expansion might be viable in the direction of the Dutch as well. This attempt was supported by the monarchy through the sending of settlers and soldiers. For example, in 1725 thirty families, armed with tools and guns, were sent from the Canaries to Orinoco, accompanied by soldiers. Bolstered by this official support, raids against the Amerindians increased, and in 1728 a thousand people were captured. After 1732 the number of missionary villages grew, stimulated by competition among the three religious orders involved: the Jesuits of Santa Fé, the Franciscans of Piritu, and the Capuchins of Trinidad.[14]

Gradually, especially after 1750, the Spanish moved farther southeast from the Orinoco, penetrating the borderland and enlarging their presence at the expense of the Caribs. As the missionaries expanded, the Caribs found their room to maneuver increasingly restricted. For those opposing the new way of life in a missionary village, the choice narrowed to violent resistance or moving away. Both roads were taken. In 1751 and 1752 several Spanish settlements were overrun by Caribs, who killed several resident priests.[15] The Spanish nevertheless continued to push on. Indeed, in a later report the commandant of Guayana wrote, "The Orinoco was nearly deserted, or rather dominated by the savage Caribs, up until about 1755, when the Royal Boundary Expedition arrived, which was commanded by Commodore Don Joseph de Iturriage. He tamed the pride of the Indians, and subdued and handed over many of them to the missionaries."[16] This relocation of the Amerindian population was one of the prime objectives of the Boundary Expedition, and it gave the Spanish a strong footing in the borderland.

The Amerindians preferring migration over fighting had little choice but to move eastward, in the direction of the Dutch. As the three groups—Spanish, Amerindians, and Dutch—now came closer together, tensions increased. In 1758 a Spanish raid destroyed the Dutch post on the Cuyuni River, which was a major borderland connection.[17] It was used by the Caribs to sell Amerindian captives from the Orinoco to the Dutch and as an escape route for Essequibo slaves to the Spanish areas (see below); it could also be used by the Spanish to enter Dutch territory in case of conflict. The effect of the destruction was manifold. First, the Dutch lost control of a vital borderland gateway: the trade in "red slaves" would decline, and African slaves now had better chances to flee. This process was aggravated by the migration of the Caribs living in the area. Their presence had functioned as a buffer, both against the Spanish and against the desertion of slaves, so they left a void as they moved farther southeast. Finally, the Spanish established two missions on the Cuyuni, increasing their control over this crucial river and making it unlikely the Caribs would return.[18]

Consequently, the Dutch director-general, Laurens Storm van 's Gravesande (1704–75), was strongly aggrieved. He first sought redress from the Spanish governor, who, however, insisted that the Cuyuni was Spanish territory. Subsequently, Storm also sent copies of this discussion to the metropolis, urging resolution of the matter at the higher level of European politics. While this indeed inspired action—the States-General sent a "Great Remonstrance" to Madrid in 1759—it did not lead to a resolution of the problem, as the Spanish crown did not make any concessions.[19]

In fact, as the Spanish enlarged their influence in the borderland, they were emboldened to attack the Dutch Moruka post as well, in 1769 and 1774. This post guarded the coastal connection between the two empires. Its repeated destruction meant the Dutch had even less oversight over borderland movements, making it easier for runaways and deserters to flee.[20] These small-scale raids on Dutch posts could have large effects but at the same time showed that the Spanish were not strong enough to confront the Dutch directly, or establish permanent control over the borderland.

Meanwhile, the conquest of the Amerindian lands continued. Under Manuel Centurion, appointed governor of Guayana in 1765, Spanish power was consolidated in the new capital of Angostura (at the narrow stretch of the Orinoco), and missionary work continued. The expulsion of Jesuits from the empire, in 1767, had little effect on this process, as the Capuchins were the main drivers. In 1771 they founded their last mission, having effectively conquered all of the Carib groups living in the Spanish areas. Often the missionaries employed a divide-and-conquer policy, using previously resettled Warao or independent Akawaio Amerindians to attack Carib communities while later turning against those same groups.[21] Consequently, the population in the missionary villages continued to grow. The historian Neil Whitehead lists 4,786 Caribs in Franciscan missions in 1782 and 4,459 Caribs living in Capuchin missions in 1788.[22] By the latter year, the Capuchins had twenty-eight missionary villages under their control, including 14,012 Amerindians (see Appendix 1.1).[23]

This continued expansion into Amerindian territory was partly a result of the general expansion in Venezuela, particularly in the province of Caracas. The region, which had long been a relatively insignificant part of the empire, thrived after 1777. Trade reforms now allowed the inhabitants to trade with foreigners, under certain conditions. Furthermore, Spain emerged as a large market for cacao, Venezuela's main export during the eighteenth century. Consequently, Caracas became one of the most dynamic parts of the empire, and its population grew from 333,000 in the late 1780s to 427,000 in the first decade of the nineteenth century. While in Caracas the Amerindian population was still subject to loss of land because of encroaching haciendas, the process of relocating Amerindians had passed. In the province of Guayana, however, it continued.[24]

Nevertheless, it seems that many Amerindian groups had effectively escaped the mission system and maintained their autonomy, as became apparent during the revolutionary times at the end of the century. The Spanish governors greatly feared an attack by the British and calculated that the indigenous groups in the borderland would side with the invaders. In 1790 the fear was voiced that Guayana could become the gateway to dismantling the entire Spanish empire, as the Orinoco and its tributaries could carry the British to Cumaná and even to Santa Fé, and from there to Mexico and Peru.[25] However, this scenario would not come to pass. A British invasion indeed took place, but it was directed against the Dutch areas rather than the Spanish.[26]

The Dutch Side

From the Essequibo vantage point the borderland looked rather different. Rather than missionary control, the prime concerns of the Dutch were trade (in the seventeenth century) and preventing the escape of enslaved workers (during the eighteenth century). Consequently, in the nineteenth century the extent of the trade network would be the basis of the British claims to the borderland.

In the seventeenth century, the Dutch saw Guiana as a source of exotic products, particularly annatto, an orange-red food colorant and condiment. Foodstuffs and cotton hammocks were also traded in this early period, between 1630 and 1650. The Arawak were major trading partners, but the Dutch also entered the Orinoco area themselves, to trade with Amerindian groups there.[27] The Dutch also had plantations for the production of sugar, but between 1650 and 1680 Essequibo's main export was annatto rather than sugar.[28]

Besides trading forest products, a defining trade of the borderland was the one in enslaved Amerindians ("red slaves"). Slavery was practiced before the coming of the Europeans, although within Amerindian societies slavery was part of the social structure rather than of economic exploitation. For the Caribs, the word *pito* or *poito* is said to have carried a meaning that ranged from brother-in-law to client to slave, and the Arawak word *maco* had a similar connotation. In a raid the Caribs or Arawak sometimes chose to take the women as wives and the men as *poitos* or *macos*, possibly also assimilating the children as slaves.[29] There was thus an existing system that the Dutch could adapt to their needs.

Enslaved Amerindians were not usually employed as plantation hands but rather as domestic servants or for other tasks on the estates, such as hunting, fishing, and growing cassava, all to support the livelihood of the enslaved Africans.[30]

In 1686 the WIC prohibited the enslavement of the four major ethnic groups living close to the Dutch settlement—the Caribs, Arawak, Akawaio, and Warao—to ensure peaceful relations.[31] However, the directors were still content to acquire slaves from other groups living farther inland, and these "red slaves" were still sought after by the colonists. The Company was actively involved in buying enslaved Amerindians, for we find that in 1699 "Jotte, the old negro" was sent out from Fort Kijkoveral into the Mazaruni, coming back with "four female slaves, two children, and a boy."[32]

In their stance toward Amerindian slavery the Dutch diverged from the Iberian powers. In 1542 the Spanish New Laws outlawed the enslaving of Amerindians, and Portugal did the same in 1574, although it retained an exception for "cannibals" and slaves taken in "just wars."[33] And while the missionary villages still demanded labor from the Amerindians, it was of a different kind than chattel slavery. The French were somewhere in between. They also employed the "just war" rhetoric to legitimize taking indigenous slaves, even though after 1700 it was forbidden to enslave Amerindians in the French Caribbean. However, indigenous captives from French Canada were still sold into slavery in the Caribbean until the 1760s and indigenous slavery continued well into the 1790s in New France itself.[34]

The difference between the Spanish and Dutch views on Amerindian slavery proved to be a major influence on the borderland dynamics. Whereas the Spanish considered the Amerindians living in the Orinoco areas free vassals of the king, the Dutch bought these people as "red slaves." The slave traders in between were mainly Caribs, although the Arawak and the Akawaio were also involved.[35] Consequently, these specific Amerindian groups resisted Spanish efforts to close the slave trade and became natural allies of the Dutch. In fact, the Carib slave trade with the Dutch followed the same pattern as the regular trade, bringing enslaved Amerindians from the Orinoco region to Essequibo both via the Cuyuni and via the coastal route. This trade was part of the regular commercial network, and slaves were sold, in addition to quantities of balsam, cotton, hammocks, copaiba, annatto, wild animals, and horses.[36]

The Company seemed to have made the slave trade its own prerogative around 1712, and in 1723 a post on the Arinda River (a tributary of the Essequibo) was established, deep in the interior, which had the slave trade as its main purpose.[37] Because the slave trade could have wide-ranging political effects, the WIC tried to control this trade itself rather than leaving it in the hands of free-wandering adventurers who might provoke conflict. However, private traders ignored the prohibition and remained active afterward. In 1730 the local authorities noted that several planters were sending their own slaves or "free Indians" into the Cuyuni and Mazaruni to acquire red slaves". These ventures violated the Company's privileges, and offenders risked confiscation of all vessels, slaves, and goods, plus a fine of 50 guilders (presumably per slave).[38] Later, in 1752, it appears colonists were again allowed to go to Orinoco to buy "red slaves" but only to a maximum of six people and on payment of a fee of guilders per slave.[39]

The Early Cuyuni Trade Network

To get a better understanding of the complex borderland interactions during the seventeenth century, it is worthwhile to zoom in on the Cuyuni trade network. This heart of the borderland generated both cooperation and tension among the different groups. The Caribs and Dutch cooperated in the enslavement of Amerindians living in areas under the control of the Spanish, to the dismay of the latter two. In addition, the borderland dynamics were further complicated by warfare between different Amerindian groups, such as the Arawak or Akawaio versus the Caribs. And finally, as a last element of complexity, the Dutch also sent some of their African slaves into the borderland to procure Amerindian slaves. All of these issues are illustrated by a quotation from 1683 by Essequibo's *commandeur*. Because warfare had, for several years, disrupted trade in hammocks and foodstuffs, he reported that he had "sent a negro up in Cuyuni in order . . . to establish peace between the Akuways [Akawaio] and the Caribs, so as by this means to get hold of the wild-pig hunting there as formerly."[40]

The borderland trade was indeed a thoroughly cross-cultural affair. At the turn of the century peace apparently returned, for we find a very lively trade from Kijkoveral, involving a wide array of goods. The day journals of the fort for 1699 mention "negro traders" (whether they were enslaved or free is unknown) who set out to procure horses; a boy named Jan Antheunissen who brought "fourteen or fifteen bundles of poison wood" from the nearby Mazaruni River; and Jotte, "the old negro," who went into the Upper Cuyuni in a canoe to fetch a supply of bread. During the following year, "the old negro Big Jan" brought "10 quakes of oriane [annatto] dye, 30 quakes of bread, 8 quakes of pork, and 4 quakes of fish."[41] While bread, fish, and dye were regular goods, the pork seems somewhat unusual in this summation and might refer to the wild pigs mentioned above. During the remainder of 1700 the Africans Big Jan, "his boy Sam," Jan Swart, "Handsome Claesje," and Lieven made several trips into the interior, carrying specific trading wares to procure foodstuffs and annatto dye. Unfortunately, very little is known about these black intermediaries and their legal status. The same applies to the Amerindians who sometimes functioned as peddlers traveling back and forth with the African traders, receiving payment for their services.[42]

Probably the most vital among the merchandise listed above were the horses and other draft animals that were necessary to run the sugar mills. These draft animals could only be procured from Spanish Guayana, which was a tremendously arduous journey. From the Dutch side, it involved six weeks of traveling from Kijkoveral to the Cuyuni savannah, where the horses were brought from the Upper Orinoco, deep into Spanish territory. Here, then, we find a middle ground in both a physical and a metaphorical sense: the area was situated between the Spanish and Dutch settlements, while the exchange relied on African horse buyers, licensed white Company traders, and Amerindian transporters. The trade seems to have commenced in 1693 and continued in the following years, although in 1702 a great scarcity in the number of horses was noted in Essequibo, resulting partly from disease and partly from a Spanish prohibition on this trade.[43]

Indeed, the middle ground was no stable ground, and changes on either the Dutch or the Spanish side, like the installation of a new governor, could easily disrupt trade relations. However, under the precarious circumstances in the borderland, such prohibitions generally did not last long, insofar as they were effective at all. The horse trade certainly did not disappear after the Spanish ban. At this point the WIC still organized trading ventures for both the planters and its own interest, as attested by an announcement from 1706 calling any planter who wanted to buy horses from the Cuyuni to report to the fort with "men and trading wares." Nevertheless, it appears that the Spanish were able to seal off this route from 1707 on, as no further horse trading voyages via the Cuyuni were reported. The alternative route to acquire Spanish horses was less dependable, consisting of a coastal voyage that involved sailing up the Orinoco and past the Spanish fortress, for which permission was needed.[44] However, in this borderless world metropolitan policies were easily circumvented.

The gap left by the Spanish was quickly filled by English traders, using the coastal route. Apparently this trade was so effective that in 1731 the WIC urged the Essequibo inhabitants to trade with the Spanish again instead. The Company feared that the English traders would have much more merchandise on offer than could be procured in Orinoco. And while contraband trade with the Spanish was condoned, the WIC did not want to encourage it any further, fearing it would undermine Company authority.[45] In the preceding year the WIC had also prohibited private trade in the Cuyuni and Mazaruni regions, allowing only licensed Company traders. This move signified the transition from Essequibo as a trading colony to one where plantation agriculture dominated. The horses were vital as draft animals, but the free-roaming adventurers could become more of a liability than an asset. Their free agent behavior might provoke conflict, while it became important to maintain favourable relations with the Spanish as well as the Amerindians.[46]

The Eighteenth-Century Connections

Although it is unlikely that the trade with the English entirely subsided, the connections with Orinoco were strengthened in the decades afterward. The relations between the Dutch and Spanish governors seemed to be good in the 1730s, to mutual benefit. Both European powers were too weak to maintain a presence by themselves, so they were willing to help each other out. For example, in 1734 the Dutch dispatched two canoes with thirty hogsheads of bread, four half-barrels of rum, and four barrels of molasses to exchange for horses, and when the Spanish governor in 1735 requested a quantity of bread, the Dutch complied and received three horses and six mules in return.[47] In 1746 a plan was made to facilitate the trade in mules and oxen by cutting a road through the forest from Essequibo.[48] The Capuchins, administering large ranches with many thousand head of cattle, seemed in favor, but the Dutch were having second thoughts since a direct road would mean an easy flight route for runaway slaves.[49] In 1752 the Company directors went a step further in reducing contact, prohibiting the overland cattle trade.[50]

Nevertheless, an elaborate exchange network was in place, involving not just foodstuffs but also a diverse array of manufactured goods. An anonymous but well-informed source reports that in 1750 the Dutch brought to Orinoco white and blue cloths, Rouen linen, coarse britannias, white holland, striped stuffs for gowns, other common cotton goods and some hats; a large quantity of brandy, some white wine and implements, axes, picks, hatchet and cutlasses. And for the smugglers of the interior they convey spices, especially cinnamon and cloves in cases; fine new hats of good quality and first class white ones; velvets, silks, some lace, pieces of britannias and hollands, medium and fine; wax, flour, and wine. What the Dutch take back is money (usually in gold), tobacco from Barinas [Varinas], mules, a few heifers; and a small amount in hides, balsam of copaiba, hammocks, and other similar goods.[51]

The vessels employed were quite substantial—armed with swivel guns (*draaibassen*) and blunderbusses and "carrying twelve to sixteen men besides the Aruac [Arawak] Indians who act[ed] as rowers."[52]

However, as plantation agriculture became the prime focus of the colonists, the WIC became stricter about allowing foreign trade. In 1761 the Company engineered a change in the trade directions, aiming to end Dutch involvement in the Orinoco trade and allowing the Spanish to come to Essequibo instead, as they had been doing for several decades. The Company argued it wanted to transfer the risk to the Spanish, so no more Dutch vessels would be sent out. This explanation is not satisfactory, however. It is more likely that the Company was afraid that Dutch vessels would become embroiled in Spanish-English hostilities in the ongoing Seven Years' War, which could drag the Dutch into the conflict. This scenario was not farfetched, since Dutch traders were still active as smugglers. Regardless of the motives, the policy was so successful that in 1794 the Dutch governor was unaware that the direction of trade had ever been otherwise.[53]

This shift in trade patterns did not mean that the officials in Essequibo were passively awaiting what the Spanish would bring, even though the Company was now more dependent on the decisions of the Spanish governors. On 14 July 1772 the director-general wrote back to the WIC directors:

It is related here that a new Governor has arrived in Orinoco. Should that be true, I hope that he will not be such a Turk as his predecessor. With the latter there was not the least chance of getting anything out of Orinoco, and he even forbade the usual salting in the mouth of the river, and set a strong watch to prevent it. If the present one shows a little more tractability, as the former ones did, I will soon take advantage of it; there must now be abundance of cattle there.[54]

The fishing and salting in the mouth of the Orinoco had been a vital activity for the Dutch, for the salted fish provided a welcome addition to the diet of the enslaved.[55] However, fishing ventures were often used as covers for smuggling in the Orinoco. Consequently, the Spanish seized several ships in the 1760s, leading to the grinding halt of the fishing trade. As a result, the colonists turned to imports of North American fish to satisfy their needs.[56]

As the eighteenth century progressed, then, the trade connections became more complicated and of decreasing importance. The Spanish became stricter in their policies and less likely to connive as their reliance on the Dutch decreased. At the same time the Cuyuni trade declined because of the establishment of Spanish missions and the withdrawal of the Caribs. Nevertheless, the Amerindians, and the Caribs in particular, continued to play a crucial role in the development of the colonies.

The Amerindian Side

Already in the 1680s the Dutch solicited the help of Amerindian groups to retrieve runaway slaves, even though Essequibo was mostly a trading colony at this point.[57] Consequently, the number of "slave refugees" was comparatively small, which means that bounty hunting was not the dominant way of obtaining European goods.[58] During the seventeenth century the Amerindians could simply acquire such manufactures through trade. However, as we have seen, Essequibo's transition from trading colony to plantation colony meant that the Amerindians had to find other ways to tie the Europeans to them.

The most important changes were manifested in the second half of the eighteenth century. Not only did the plantation sector expand rapidly thanks to generous mortgage credit (see chapter 5), but in 1750 the Spanish monarchy implemented a major institutional change. It decided to grant freedom to all slaves from English or Dutch colonies seeking refuge in Spanish areas, as long as they embraced Catholicism and were baptised.[59] Although marronage had been a familiar phenomenon before 1750, this declaration nevertheless had a major impact on the intercultural relations in the border zone. It offered the possibility of a life of freedom, as opposed to an uncertain existence as a maroon in the forests. Understandably, this new rule motivated many Africans to flee. As this issue deserves much more attention, it is analyzed in depth in chapter 3. For now it is important to know how the flight of enslaved Africans gave a new dynamic to the role of Amerindian groups in the borderland.

Indeed, as chapter 3 shows, the Dutch lacked effective means to retrieve these runaways themselves. For example, a plan was made in 1758 to send officers of the militia (*burgerofficieren*) into the woods to chase the refugees, but that failed; most planters were very reluctant to perform military service, complaining that they already paid taxes to this end. Moreover, they were at a loss in the rainforest anyway.[60]

Trying to find a legal solution proved fruitless as well. In 1769 the officials in Essequibo and Demerara urged the States-General to establish a "cartel" with the Spanish authorities, agreeing to return each other's refugees.[61] Six years later nothing had come of it, as the Spanish court had not answered the plea of the States-General.[62] However, since refugees were solely a problem for the Dutch, the Spanish monarchy had little reason to comply, as the Dutch ambassador recognized.[63] Consequently, the colonial officials appealed to the metropolis for help. An often-repeated complaint was that the colony would fall to "total ruin" if the stream of runaways was not cut off. The colonists therefore turned to the Amerindian population for help.

The Postholder Structure

To mobilise these Amerindian troops, the Dutch used the pre-existing structure of outposts. There were four posts, on major strategic points: the Mahaicony River in the east (separating Demerara and Berbice), the Arinda (leading into the interior), the Cuyuni (the interior route to the Orinoco region), and the Moruka (to guard the coastal route between the Essequibo and the Orinoco). These posts had to project colonial authority inland and prevent incursions, but were also places where Dutch and Amerindian traders met each other, exchanging European goods for annatto and "red slaves".[64]

The local postholder (*posthouder*) traded on behalf of the Company and on his own behalf and was indeed expected to augment his otherwise meager salary with profits from his private trade. In addition, the postholder was supposed to control movement into the interior by detaining everyone who did not have the right passports. The *posthouders* were originally "respected soldiers," who would man the post together with several *bijleggers* (assistants) and preferably several Amerindians.[65] Nevertheless, these outposts controlled little outside their immediate vicinity: as some WIC officials explained, the refugees often took off in one of the plantation's boats and with the right tide could obtain a decisive head start.[66] The posts thus were mainly important because of their connecting function to the Amerindians.

However, not all postholders were able to maintain good relationships with Amerindian groups. On the one hand, postholders received specific instructions to "further peace and friendship with the Indian nations"; on the other, they had to demand payment, "through gentle means," in case the trade had put an Amerindian in debt to the Company.[67] In this light it is telling that the WIC had to issue many proclamations over the years stating that postholders or others must not beat or abuse or obstruct the trade of the Amerindians.[68] In case of such abuse, the Amerindians could take their case to the Dutch authorities, which indeed led to the replacement of postholder Hendrik Eeltjens in 1779. However, this change apparently only made matters worse: Eeltjens's successor, Daniel Sternbergh, about whom many accusations were made, was killed by Akawaios.[69] Slowly the Company realized it needed a different set of people for these functions, and in 1775 a "mulatto or native" named Schultz became postholder in Arinda, selected based on his years of travel in that region and his knowledge of the local languages.[70]

Maintaining good relationships with the various Amerindian groups became a key concern for the colonists. While they were upset by the murder of Sternbergh, they did not insist on a strong reprisal. Instead, if the perpetrator could be found, they wanted to know what his reasons had been, but no force was to be used to get him to come to the fort. In addition, the instructions for the new postholder stipulated that he abstain from violence, even if under attack by Amerindians, unless in utter need. Furthermore, to reduce friction, the new postholder should reduce trade with Amerindians as much as possible and refrain from buying "red slaves" from them. If others passed by the post, having bought enslaved Amerindians, the postholder had to send one of his men and a "free Indian" as interpreter with them to the fort to make sure no allies were enslaved.[71] In 1793 the colonial authorities prohibited the trade in "red slaves" altogether, for the same reason.[72] For instance, if a Carib person sold an Arawak as a slave without the Dutch knowing, the relation with the Arawak group could be severely damaged.

While the Amerindians made their own decisions about when and how to help the colonists, their interdependence increased as the century progressed.[73] The growing Spanish advancement into the borderland, as well as the concomitant decline in trade with the Dutch, meant that

Amerindian groups had to reorient their way of living. Instead of through trade, they could now acquire European goods by capturing runaways.[74] On the other hand, for the Dutch control of borderland desertion routes became more important even though their influence in the area waned. As a result, they had to rely more on their Amerindian allies. Interestingly, the reward for catching a runaway was the same for an Amerindian as for a postholder, which is important to note in such a racially divided society.[75] In fact, alliances with the Amerindians relations were valued so much that in 1789 the Council instructed the postholder to come to the fort twice a year, together with Amerindian leaders, so that they could "receive some veneration from the Honourable Company and Colony."[76] The bargaining position of the Amerindians had thus increased considerably throughout the century.

Growing Amerindian Power

The strong bargaining position for the Amerindians was visible in two ways, namely, the dispensing of gifts and access to guns. For example, the planters provided substantial rewards for Amerindian support when a slave insurrection in August 1772 appeared to get out of hand. (see chapter 3). Two plantations were pillaged, and while the local burgher-captain managed to hold his own against two attacks, a successful counteroffensive could only be launched with the help of two hundred Caribs. As a result, the Carib captains (called Owls, *Uilen* in Dutch) received rewards in the form of silver jewelry, and the soldiers received smaller gifts such as cloth, trumpets, and looking-glasses. These gifts were considered an improvement on previous rewards, which consisted of silver half-moon collars of breast pieces engraved with the WIC emblem.[77] The silver collars had apparently become less useful at this point, because "the Spaniards have made these things so common amongst them, that they now have some in gold which cover their whole chest."[78]

Faced with such European competition over Amerindian favors, the Dutch needed to increase their investment in the Amerindian alliances. Furthermore, the Amerindians themselves learned to make better use of this bond and realized they could demand that the Dutch reaffirm their friendship with presents. For example, in 1778 an Amerindian delegation (of unknown origin) came to the fort in Essequibo and promised to provide military aid in times of need while also enjoying the food and rum provided.[79] Indeed, the alliance was so crucial that the 720 gallons of *kiltum* (rum) from the WIC's own plantations were allocated as presents for Amerindians coming to Essequibo. Yet the director-general remarked that this amount was completely insufficient, noting that the Amerindians "are not received properly, if they do not leave drunk and take a pint or two of liquor..., wine bread, and *bakkeljauw* [salted cod] with them."[80]

The three wartime changes in power (from Dutch to English to French and back again to Dutch; see chapter 2) had further emboldened the Amerindians to increase their demands, prompting the director-general to ask the WIC for advice on how to handle such situations. While noting the mounting expenses, he also wrote that "we must gratify these people in every respect, for they, on our side, are our only resource against the negroes."[81] In fact, the number of gifts at this point was so large that the Company stores would no longer suffice. Consequently, the WIC had to buy goods from others at market prices. The director-general complained how expensive sending out an Amerindian search party was, because of "the manifold presents which we must [give] to the Indians, without which they will not move a step, and especially when we must here purchase goods therefore (as has happened on this occasion), but the entire welfare of the Colony depends thereon."[82]

Indeed, there was a real need to be forthcoming, as became apparent in 1785. Several Carib leaders threatened to abstain from helping the colonists and even to side with the Africans if they did not receive gits immediately. After "several days" of drinking in the capital town of Stabroek they were apparently satisfied and left again.[83] These situations did not occur just at the seat of government, for in the same year the postholder of the Arinda post was confronted with a group of 108 Amerindians seeking to pledge allegiance to the Company in exchange for presents, "upon which the Commanders each obtained a silver metal collar, a half piece of salampore [sic] two flasks gunpowder, and the others each 5 ells of salempore, besides salt fish, soopye [rum], and bananas, wherewith they all departed very satisfied."[84] In other words, the Amerindians made effective use of their powerful position vis-à-vis the Dutch.

This increased leverage was also visible in the ease with which Amerindians could acquire guns from the Dutch. In 1750 there still was an official prohibition on selling arms to indigenous groups, probably born out of caution that these weapons might be used against the colonists themselves.[85] However, by 1785 this situation had totally changed. When a group of seventy-five Amerindians were hired for an expedition on the east bank of the Demerara River, they received fifty muskets and a hundred shot cartridges, in addition to provisions for the search.[86] While at times a search party indeed returned with runaways, the Amerindians also received remuneration "for their effort" if they had pursued in vain. Moreover, the practice of borrowing weapons for an expedition must have been very convenient for the Amerindians; they could simply indicate they had found tracks of runways, upon which weapons would be supplied for the duration of the pursuit.[87] However, it is possible that these guns were used in inter-Amerindian warfare and slave raiding too.

The British Side

After the British takeover the bargaining position would only grow stronger. Initially, however, the Amerindians retreated into the interior, seeing that a different power had taken over. This move resulted from the inexperience of the British, who were unaware of the value of the alliance and hence did not provide the customary presents.[88]

This situation would change quickly enough: after the British took over for the second time, in 1803, after a one-year intermezzo, they developed an elaborate Amerindian policy. First, they retained the postholder system but revised it to address its weaknesses. An important step was to increase the postholders' salaries, as the British recognized that low-paid officials were more prone to abuse their position. While a postholder made 192 guilders per year under the Dutch, in the British period this increased to 1,200 guilders for a free colored postholder and 2,200 guilders in the case of the appointment of a Lieutenant Moore in 1803.[89] While the late eighteenth century saw considerable inflation, it would only explain a doubling or at best tripling of the salary, not an increase of 1,000 percent.[90]

Furthermore, the instructions for postholders were augmented in order to reduce conflicts. First, postholders were to summon the Amerindians from time to time and dispense a few small gifts, to maintain the friendship.[91] In addition, when a new postholder was appointed, he would be introduced to the Amerindians and the rules would be clearly laid out for all: the postholder could not demand unpaid labor from the Amerindians or confiscate the goods they carried from trading with the colonists. Several other stipulations highlighted some of the abuses that had taken place before. For example, article 12 stated, "He shall not take or appropriate to himself the property of the Indians, much less their wives and children, on pretence of their being indebted to him, even in case of an Indian having had goods from him on credit, and refusing to pay for the same. The loss arising there-from to be for the Postholder."

This article was a clear indication that the rights of the Amerindians needed to be protected against abuse, and indeed the British appointed several "Protectors of the Indians." The indigenous could voice any complaints they might have with their Protector, and the latter was to act as a mediator for any agreements postholders might make with the Amerindians. For example, if the postholder wanted to hire indigenous workers for woodcutting, fishing, or paddling, the Protector would check whether this agreement was voluntary and if the Amerindians received proper payment. Furthermore, if the postholder wanted to marry an indigenous woman, the Protector had to confirm that she was not already engaged to another man and had to obtain consent from her parents. If in doubt, the Protector could refuse their union.[92]

The Protectors (apparently two in Essequibo and two in Demerara) also had an important function in dispensing gifts. The list in Appendix 1.2 gives an idea of the variety of goods ordered for the Amerindians. Extending the Dutch tradition, the British engaged in an annual distribution of such presents to continually renew their bond with the Amerindians. However, as the colonists discovered, there was a disadvantage to holding a specific gift-giving day, namely, some Amerindians might miss it and thus feel offended.[93]

A bigger problem for the colonists was that the amount of money spent on gifts skyrocketed. In some years the Protectors advanced more than 15,000 guilders in presents.[94] Nevertheless, the colonists deemed the practice worthwhile. When in 1812 a decision was made to limit the annual budget for Amerindian gifts to 20,000 guilders, one of the Financial Representatives found a loophole, stating that it was not decided *when* this limit would have to be obeyed. In an argument to the Court of Policy, he stated that the maximum of 20,000 guilders should be seen as a lofty goal for the future rather than an actual limit.[95] Indeed, in the previous years, spending greatly exceeded that threshold. In 1811 a total of 82,250 guilders (or 6,904 pounds sterling) was accounted for, and in 1812 it was 61,348 (or 5,112 pounds sterling) even though further expenses were accrued afterward.[96] The fact that these sums had spiraled out of control only underlines the importance of the Amerindians.

Yet relations were not always smooth, as the issue in 1810 with the Carib leader Manariwan (or Manerwan/Manerwa) illustrates. When the British took over in 1803, trade in "red slaves" was still allowed, as long as they came from groups the Amerindians considered enslaveable—that is to say, the ones living in the interior.[97] However, the abolition of the slave trade in 1807 put a stop to this traffic. The prohibition was a concern for

Manariwan, a "King, or Chief" of one of the Carib groups who had taken many captives in a recent war. Initially Manariwan had sent an envoy to the British, hoping to acquire goods in exchange for not killing or selling his prisoners. Yet his envoy was sent away, as the British were not sure of the man's status and did not take him seriously. Subsequently, Manariwan himself came to the capital with a group of followers including "a suite of musicians and other attendants." After negotiations with the Court of Policy, it was agreed that Manariwan would keep his prisoners as domestic slaves and receive "such articles as he had demanded."[98]

The British were unsure of their case, however, and sent out informants to assess "the real strength" of Manariwan and to see whether he was really as important as he claimed to be (it was later established that he was).[99] The matter simmered on, for in 1812 Manariwan came back with three hundred men, demanding his annual tribute—indeed, "tribute" seems a better term than "presents" here. He brought several leaders of smaller Amerindian groups with him to show that they were on friendly terms and no longer subject to enslavement. Yet the new British governor, Hugh Lyle Carmichael, did not consider himself bound to honor an agreement made by his predecessor, although he was willing to give in on this occasion. Problematically, there were not enough goods in the warehouse to dispense, so the governor scrambled together what he could, apparently resulting in a satisfactory solution for both parties. However, soon afterward five Arawak leaders came down as well, demanding to be treated in the same way. Otherwise, they threatened, they would start a war and sell their prisoners. The governor was less forthcoming this time, dissuading them from waging war and promising presents in the future for "good behaviour."[100]

The British Amerindian policy thus aimed at preserving friendly relations at almost all costs. Only the acting governor, Codd, seemed to have really disagreed, as he wrote in 1813, "It is, however, obvious that our Colonies are tributaries to the Indians; whilst the proper system of policy would be to make them allies, looking to us for protection; and whilst living within our territories, affording them such aid as we might conceive they deserve, the quantity of rum and sugar issued tending to render them almost useless; for my part, I think the whole present Indian system requires to be reconsidered."[101]

As an alternative, to lessen the financial burden, Codd proposed to adopt a system modeled on that of the Spanish. In his view, the Amerindians should be brought together in larger communities where they would learn to rear cattle, in order to sell it to the colonists. Furthermore, he deemed instruction in dress and social life necessary, especially to reduce the vice of drunkenness "to which they are much attached."[102] However, his propositions went unheeded, and the gift-giving system continued. Only in 1831 did the system change, shifting to triennial presents; in 1838 it came to a complete stop. As slavery had been abolished in 1833, the need to maintain an alliance had vanished. There was no longer any need for trackers or bounty hunters. The result was that the Amerindians retreated back into the interior, away from the plantation society.[103]

It was only under British rule, then, that the slow and incomplete transition from a borderland to a "bordered land" was initiated. During previous centuries, the Guiana region was a borderless region, where cooperation could exist despite official sanctions and where the changing balance of power was determined by local improvisation rather than by official borders or open warfare.

For the Spanish, the borderland was a liability during the seventeenth century, when Amerindians could collaborate with European enemies to threaten the fragile Spanish presence. Yet during the eighteenth century, various indigenous groups were brought under control via the missionary system. In this process, the Spanish also extended their claim further into the borderland. For the Amerindians the borderland also had a dual function: for some, like the Caribs, it presented an opportunity to sell other Amerindians as slaves to the Dutch; for others, Spanish incursions posed a threat to their way of life. While indigenous groups gradually lost influence in the borderland, the enslaved Africans saw their opportunities increase. Escaping to Venezuela in the hope of being set free became easier. In the eyes of the Dutch, these escapes constituted a threat to their plantation system. Consequently, the Dutch, and later the British, relied increasingly on Amerindian groups to catch such runaways.

The colonial structure of the Dutch was thus rather underdeveloped. Therefore, the next chapter takes a look at the political interactions on the Dutch side to explain why and to see how the lack of political support affected colonial governance. It shows that political conflict was present at all levels: in the colonies themselves, in the Dutch Republic between the various WIC Chambers, and at the international level, leading to several foreign takeovers. However, the colonists actually profited from the weak governance, so they were keen to defend their interests when the Company tried to strengthen its grip.

2 / Political Conflicts

"What would you do with your handful of people, against 40,000 negroes which we can bring here at all times, most of whom are already prepared and . . . who could then cut you and your 80 soldiers to [Syrup] in case of the least resistance, if you would deny us the access to the councillors?"[1] It was late in the evening in early September 1787 in Demerara and Lieutenant Carel Ernest von Lasberg was having a strange meeting indeed. His conversation partners were the brothers Maurits Balthasar Hartsinck and Cornelis Hartsinck, two prominent Demerara planters who had come to his house and apparently planned to overthrow the colony's government.

The lieutenant found himself amid a larger conflict between the colonists and the WIC over the division of power in the local Council of Policy. As the WIC directors in the metropolis had little idea of what was going on in the colonies, the Council of Policy was the place where most of the colonial decision making took place, typically in an ad hoc and improvised fashion. For the planters this meant it was crucial to have a say in the Council, so they could thwart new taxes and frustrate enforcement of mercantilist rules. The planters had seats on the Council, which was made up of both Company officials and planter representatives (so-called civil councillors), yet the balance of power was subject to change.

Throughout the eighteenth century the number of civil councillors increased to four, equal to the number of WIC officials. However, in 1784 the Company had tried to shift the balance in its favor. Civil councillors would henceforth be appointed from above rather than nominated from below, and their number would be reduced to three, making the Company dominant again. In subsequent years the resentment against this decision increased, involving large-scale petitions and a refusal to pay colonial taxes. By 1787 tensions had reached a boiling point. A group of planters considered the new Council, filled by top-down appointments, an illegitimate form of government. To end this "tyranny," they wanted to have the councillors replaced—peacefully if possible, through force if necessary.

Hence Lieutenant Lasberg found himself approached by the brothers Hartsinck, who were desperate to gain his support. First they tried to convince him through reasoning, but when their attempts proved unsuccessful they resorted to threats. And while they wildly exaggerated the number of enslaved Africans they could mobilzse, the threat of armed resistance was not to be dismissed lightly: the military garrison was small, the slave population was large, and the planters were angry. The administration by the WIC had never been very effective, but by 1787 the opposition had become so great that the administrative system was on the brink of collapse.

When the two planters came to the lieutenant's house they were perfectly honest about their intentions. Claiming to speak for the majority of the planters, they explained their aim of overthrowing Demerara's Council of Policy by forcing the councillors to step down or perhaps even take them prisoner. However, to do so, they wanted Lasberg's help. The military inevitably would have to take sides, and the two planters claimed to have the support of Lasberg's superior, although the lieutenant doubted this.[2] So the Hartsincks seemed to put the fate of the colony in the hands of the young lieutenant: would he order his soldiers to stand aside and allow the coup, or would he command them to intervene and shoot?

The lieutenant hesitated. He had some sympathy for the revolutionary reasoning. Maurits Balthasar Hartsinck, one of the dissenters' leaders, made a compelling case that the director-general was a tyrant and the Council of Policy plainly unconstitutional.[3] Yet even though Lasberg was willing to concede that the Council was formed illegally, he had doubts about the actions that would follow from this conclusion. Since he had taken an oath to serve the WIC and had a duty to protect civilians, Lasberg declared he would not allow any bloodshed. For Hartsinck this hesitation was an opening, and he jumped on the opportunity: if the lieutenant did not have any *principal* objections to the coup, Hartsinck reasoned, they were now just negotiating practicalities.

Subsequently, several scenarios were presented to allow Lasberg to look away with a clean conscience. The revolutionaries could, for example, stage fake slave revolts in remote parts of the colony, drawing all the soldiers away from the government center. Alternatively, if the officers would give their men double rations of rum, the revolutionaries would act when everyone was drunk. A third option was to kidnap the director-general, put him on a ship, and send him out of the colony, thereby removing the only legitimate authority left to issue military orders. In the subsequent state of anarchy the change of government could be easily accomplished. Yet all of this was too radical for the lieutenant. He finally made up his mind and declared he would fulfill his military duty. Attempts to bribe him with a piece of land and slaves did not change his mind, and when Hartsinck resorted, as we just saw, to threats, Lasberg did not give in either. He replied by saying he would order that the ringleaders be shot, after which the rest would probably back down quickly. So while he had flirted with the idea of supporting the dissenters, in the end Lasberg's sense of duty prevailed. The revolutionaries would have to manage without the military.[4]

We will never know what would have happened if Lasberg had chosen to defect, but the above story reveals that violent overthrow of the colonial government was a real possibility in this divided colony.[5] Rivalry occurred on multiple levels, not just in Demerara. Officials in Essequibo and Demerara sometimes came into conflict with each other, just as the Amsterdam and Zealand Chambers of the WIC argued over the administration of the two colonies. And the colonies also became involved in international rivalry, as they were occupied by both the British and the French during the Fourth-Anglo Dutch War and again by the British in 1796–1802 and 1803, during the French and Napoleonic Wars. The end of the century in particular proved a hectic period during which the two colonies were divided between pro-French and pro-British factions; the conflict was ultimately resolved by the British takeover. Indeed, after 1803 the colonies would remain in British hands, and in 1814 they were officially ceded by the Netherlands to Great Britain.

Nevertheless, the political history of the two colonies involved more than just conflict and in fact depended on continuous negotiation. WIC and civil councillors cooperated to improvise solutions to emerging problems, and violence was shunned. This negotiation could take various forms, such as petitioning, defying Company regulations, or refusing to pay taxes. In the end it was through bargaining rather than bloodshed that the colonists had their despised councillors replaced.

In this respect these Dutch colonies were no different from the other European empires. Many historians have noted the limited power of early modern states to enforce top-down legislation and demonstrated how this weakness led to bargaining between different levels of government.[6] Colonists could express their opinions in various ways, ranging from informal to formal. Examples are petitioning, tax evasion, and evading trade restrictions but also outright revolt.[7] All empires were thus "negotiated empires."[8] Nevertheless, differences remained in the specifics of power sharing. For example, the Spanish empire can be seen as a "stakeholder empire" in which local elites and merchants were co-opted, smoothing out many of the difficulties of running the empire.[9] In the Portuguese case the king ruled by attempting to guide a "nebula of power" in his desired direction, consisting of competing councils, judges, governors, viceroys, and religious orders.[10] The Iberian empires thus were polycentric, but their juridical complexity actually increased their stability, as overlapping authorities—colonial and central, religious and secular—balanced each other out.[11] Although the Dutch Atlantic empire was both different and smaller, it was also characterized by overlapping authorities. For the case of Essequibo and Demerara, the so-called legal pluralism resulted in tensions between the jurisdictions of the WIC and the States-General (where appeals of the colonial court were heard), between the councils in the two different colonies, and between the colonial councils and the WIC directors.[12]

This chapter, then, looks at how conflicts between different layers of government affected colonial administration. The many opposing interests led to indecisiveness and a weak institutional structure. On the one hand, this meant that the colonists could not count on solid metropolitan support; on the other, they paid hardly any taxes and were not restricted in their borderless commerce. The chapter proceeds chronologically in four parts, starting with the rivalry over who was to govern in and over the colonies, both in the metropolis and in Essequibo and Demerara themselves. Second, it outlines the effect of the foreign takeovers on the colonies in the Fourth Anglo-Dutch War, before delving into the political issues that inspired the near-revolution described above. And third, it discusses the transition to British rule in 1796 in light of revolutionary developments occurring at the time.

Internal Institutional Bickering (1750–1780)

The Dutch Republic was characterized by fragmentation. Sovereignty ultimately resided in the individual provinces rather than with the States-General, which meant that taking decisions at the highest level proved difficult if one of the provinces would be harmed. Vested provincial interest could thus obstruct decisions that would have been in the "national" interest. Since the WIC was also divided into provincial chambers, the political bickering found its way into Company governance as well. Amsterdam and Zealand, the two provinces most dependent on maritime trade, vied with each other for commercial success, at the level of both the States-General and the WIC. Regarding Essequibo and Demerara, the main point of contention was whether Zealand possessed exclusive trading rights. Zealand claimed these rights on the basis of its early involvement, while Amsterdam, which bore the brunt of the financial expenses both in the Company and in the Republic as a whole, argued that trade should be open.[13]

Zealand indeed had had an important role in the early colonization. The first ventures to the Guiana coast had been made in the late sixteenth century by private traders, before the establishment of the WIC in 1621, but afterward Essequibo became a Company colony. When the exploitation proved unprofitable, plans to abandon it were voiced in 1632. The Zealand Chamber, however, desired to keep the colony under its special care, provided it would have exclusive trading rights. This issue was not officially resolved, but in practice Zealand became the dominant actor with regard to Essequibo. In 1658, when the financial burden became too great, the Zealand Chamber transferred its authority to the three towns of Middleburgh, Veere, and Flushing. This transfer was not successful either, so in 1670 Zealand's WIC Chamber took responsibility again—which was based on the informal acquiescence of the other chambers rather than a formal arrangement.[14]

The issue of colonial authority only became pressing when the plantation sector started to develop in the eighteenth century and shipping connections became both more profitable and more important for the colony's survival. Therefore, in 1750, the Gentlemen Ten aimed to encourage private trade and urged all chambers to stimulate their merchants to sail to Essequibo. The Zealand Chamber, still claiming exclusive trading rights, was strongly opposed to this move. Immediately it forbade the commander in Essequibo from allowing any ships that did not carry a special permit from the Zealand Chamber.[15] This ban would set off a dispute between Amsterdam and Zealand that dragged on for decades. Amsterdam, with its large mercantile fleet, wanted free trade for all Dutch citizens, while Zealand held on to its claim for fear of being outcompeted.[16]

Here we find a clash between the unwritten rights claimed by Zealand and the formal-legalistic interpretation of Amsterdam. In 1674 the first WIC had been dissolved and the second WIC established. Zealand claimed that its previous rights remained intact, while Amsterdam noted that the Company had never formally granted the colony to Zealand and that the charter of the second WIC did not mention any exclusive rights for Zealand.[17]

In the 1750s the two parties engaged in long but fruitless negotiations, and afterward Amsterdam let the issue rest until 1765. By then the situation had changed dramatically and the region was no longer a money-devouring backwater. The plantation sector was booming, made possible by the huge sums of credit that Amsterdam investors had lent to new planters (see chapter 5). Moreover, much of this expansion had taken place in neighboring Demerara, which was still a dependency of Essequibo. Amsterdam favored splitting the two, which would likely make Demerara a colony open to all Dutch traders. Zealand, in contrast, remained strict in referring to "Essequibo and dependent rivers," to keep Demerara within its self-proclaimed exclusive sphere. Yet no solution was found and only after extensive lobbying did both parties agree to arbitrage by the Prince of Orange.[18]

On 25 October 1770 the prince made his decision, which was a compromise: he denied exclusive trading rights to the Zealand Chamber but gave it the right to allocate the first sixteen permits to sail to the colonies each year. If fewer than sixteen ships were outfitted, as was usually the case, other merchants could apply. However, their ships would have to load and unload in Zealand, supporting the provincial economy, much to the dismay of Amsterdam. This solution did not satisfy anyone, so the ruling was revised in 1772. Again, it was far from straightforward: only the Zealand Chamber was allowed to issue permits during the first half of the year, after which the other chambers could do so as well, provided they loaded and unloaded in Zealand. Moreover, the first nine ships from Zealand would be allowed to load cargo in the colonies first, as long as they arrived there before November.[19]

It thus proved difficult to redesign the trading structure, and the same applied to the administrative system. By the late 1760s the number of plantations in Demerara was more than double that of Essequibo (see table 2.1), yet Essequibo was officially still the seat of government, from where Demerara was administered.[20] Hence some institutional changes were required. As mentioned above, Amsterdam wanted to split the two colonies, while Zeeland preferred to keep the overarching structure intact and only dig a communication canal. Typical of the institutional deadlock, neither proposal was enacted. Essequibo remained the dominant colony, where the director-general resided, as the highest authority over the combined rivers. The highest authority in Demerara, the commander, was subject to the director-general in Essequibo. While lower court cases could be processed in Demerara, any appeals or cases involving more than 150 guilders were to be brought before the Council of Justice in Essequibo.[21] Thus the old-fashioned institutional structure was retained because no agreement could be reached regarding a more appropriate structure.

This continued imbalance between Essequibo and Demerara was impractical, yet a more fundamental problem persisted: the government of the colonies was effectively still based on a seventeenth-century model of Company exploitation. Previously, the colonies had revolved around Company plantations and trade with Amerindians, but in the eighteenth century private plantations formed the backbone of the economy. However, the Council of Policy, ruling both rivers, still looked more like a body of pioneers than one of professional administrators. Besides the director-general, Demerara's commander and the secretary, the council consisted of Essequibo's military commandant and the managers of the three WIC plantations.[22] The latter three especially had little to do with the general affairs of the colonies and were a remnant of the previous century. The expanding plantation economy demanded a more effective administrative body, but that proved to be a slow and painful process.

Increasing the Planter's Voice

The first attempts at reform were made in 1767. The power of the WIC was diminished in favor of the planters by granting seats to civilian (non-WIC) representatives. The longest-serving WIC plantation manager kept his seat, but the other two were replaced by planter representatives. These civil councillors (*burgerraden*) would be nominated by the officers of the burgher militia, to which all male planters belonged. Subsequently, the director-general would choose from among the nominees. A similar change was made to the local judicial branch, the Court of Civil and Criminal Justice.[23] Still, the planter interest was in the minority.

Table 2.1. Number of plantations in Essequibo and Demerara, 1716–1800

Year	Essequibo	Demerara	Total
1716	20		20
1735	30		30
1762	68	93	161
1766	70	121	191
1767	69	141	210
1768	84	160	244
1769	92	206	298
1777	118		
1779	129		
1780	140	240	380
1788	182	287	469
1795		284	
1798	111–53	320	431–73
1800			490

Source: See note 20.

In 1773 a major reorganization took place that gave the planters an equal number of seats in the Council of Policy. Previously, the administration of both colonies had relied heavily on Director-General Storm van 's Gravesande, who at times combined almost all relevant offices. In 1771 he wrote that because many offices had been vacant for years, he was filling the roles of secretary, bookkeeper, receiver, and auction master in Essequibo, as well as commandership of Demerara.[24] It is likely that the WIC, after Storm retired in 1772, rethought their system of governance and took a step toward professionalization of the administration. It was decided to split the administration of the two colonies and to give Demerara more autonomy, by granting the colony its own Council of Policy. There, just as in Essequibo, the interests of the planters and the WIC would be balanced. In both colonies the new Council of Policy would consist of four WIC functionaries (the commandant, the auctioneer, the fiscal, and either the director-general or the commander as president) plus four civil councillors elected by the planters.[25] The president would have the casting vote.

Even though in theory the WIC officials still dominated the voting process, in practice matters were more complicated. The president, like most of the other Company officials, was both a Company official and a planter himself and thus had double loyalties. With slow lines of communication and little intricate knowledge of the situation in the colonies, much of the decision making in Essequibo and Demerara fell to the local council. The councillors would improvise solutions to pressing issues and ask for approval later. On the one hand, the WIC officials had to maintain a good reputation in the eyes of the directors if they wanted to make a career. On the other hand, there were so few people available for administrative posts that in practice officials were not easily dismissed. It is illustrative that Storm van 's Gravesande at times received strong criticism from the Company, yet was not discharged even though he wanted it himself: he pleaded for his discharge at least in 1746, 1763, and 1766, yet was only allowed to retire in 1772.[26] In short, it was far from certain that the loyalty of the president to the Company would trump the allegiance to his fellow planters.

While the reform of 1773 was a step toward a more professional and impersonal bureaucracy, it created considerable uncertainty because the rules remained vague about the relationship between the two colonies.[27] Both now had their own council, but these were not completely autonomous. Twice a year a combined council would be convened to address issues of mutual importance.[28] Here the overlapping jurisdictions came to the fore. For the new director-general, George Hendrik Trotz, it was unclear how this divided government should work in practice and how far his powers reached: could he, as the highest authority over both rivers, intervene in matters of his neighboring colony? And would Demerara's commander be allowed to act independently, or would he have to seek approval first?[29]

An additional problem was that an entire new administrative apparatus had to be built in Demerara, which presented many practical difficulties. First, for instance, all the minute books of Essequibo had to be analyzed for rules and resolutions pertaining to Demerara, which then would need to be copied.[30] Second, housing had to be found for the new officials, and since even the director-general was living in a "sad, bad lodging," this task proved difficult.[31] In the unforgiving tropical climate the wooden houses deteriorated faster than new ones could be built.

The experience of Frederick Roetering, one of the new officials sent out from the metropolis, illustrates the problems of a colony in the process of development. His job as secretary was hindered by the commander, who declined his rather basic requests for paper and ink. In addition, when he received the copied documents from Essequibo, they were in such a sorry state that he exclaimed, "Had there never been a Secretariat I would have seen better chances to bring everything in order than I do now." Furthermore, he ran out of money quickly because he had to rent his own lodgings, supply meals for the assistant scribes, and make do without the customary food rations or enslaved African servants. Appealing to the director-general did not help: Roetering had almost closed the secretariat for want of paper, and although the secretary had received a barrel with meat and one with rye flour, he had to return the latter because it was infested with worms.[32] So, despite the WIC's intentions, the 1773 reforms did not immediately establish a satisfactory colonial administration.

In fact, the reforms created new problems: they fostered competition over appointments, personal status, division of resources, and income. Regarding appointments, the institutional conflict between Amsterdam and Zealand was mirrored in the selection of the new governors. Zealand had appointed the new director-general (Trotz), while Demerara's new commander (Paul van Schuylenburg) was chosen by Amsterdam. Perhaps unsurprisingly, the two did not get along very well.[33] And in the small colonial world, where one man's death meant another man's promotion, many were preoccupied with their own position. Such rivalry was visible in formal disputes about precedence of authority but also in social settings, such as the personal order in funeral processions.[34] Sometimes it became violent, such as in the council meeting of April 1778 when the military commandant spoke out against Trotz, who dealt him a blow. The commandant hit back, and purportedly the council was so divided that the meeting "almost ended in a free fight."[35]

Yet the rivalry within the administration went further than personal conflicts, as the colonies faced genuine problems on how to divide scarce resources, and each colony accused the other of holding onto European supplies for itself.[36] Similarly, the rations of *kiltum* (rum) produced on the WIC plantations in Essequibo did not always find their way to Demerara.[37] Another issue was the division of forced labor, for which the Company had two sources: the enslaved Africans on its own plantations and the "chain negroes" ("kettingnegers"). The latter were convicted slaves who had been sentenced to work for the Company, often for life. They lived at Fort Zeelandia in Essequibo, under the supervision of the soldiers, but they were also set to work on infrastructural improvements such as constructing roads and repairing buildings. However, as seen in the lacking and leaking houses, this group of convicts could not perform all the desired work, so the two colonies often argued over who needed the labor the most.[38]

Competition also took place over entitlements. Several official positions generated extra income, a welcome addition to the meager Company salary. For example, when a ship entered the colony, it not only had to pay customs but also faced many other WIC charges, payable to the head of government, the secretary, and the surgeon. However, with the duplication of functions, several functionaries in Essequibo found their side earnings severely reduced. Since economic activity in Demerara was much greater, its officials received far higher sums in emoluments. Understandably, officials in Essequibo therefore argued for a system of pooling the revenues and splitting them equally, whereas those in Demerara strongly opposed this idea, arguing that they had rightfully earned their share.[39]

All in all, the WIC did not succeed in establishing a well-functioning institutional structure, and even though it generally spent more on Essequibo and Demerara than it earned, it could not shoulder the protection costs. The fortress in Essequibo fell into disrepair, Demerara had no defense structure whatsoever, and the soldiers were often sick and without guns.[40] In essence the WIC remained a trading company. Administering an empire was a completely different enterprise—and one that the ailing WIC could not accomplish. The position of the Company only deteriorated during the eighteenth century, and it is therefore no surprise that Essequibo and Demerara were so easily conquered in the Fourth Anglo-Dutch War.

War and Occupation (1780–1784)

The Fourth Anglo-Dutch War led to three years of foreign occupation, first by the British (from 23 February 1781 to 1 February 1782) and later by the French (from 1 February 1782 to 6 March 1784).[41] These occupations proved rather benign. Although thirty-one ships were captured by the British forces, all the other private property was left undisturbed and the legal structure was left intact. For the colonists the occupation was probably even beneficial, because they were freed from Dutch trading restrictions and became part of the vast British empire. Suddenly they had official access to the huge British slave trading network, allowing them to acquire many more enslaved Africans than they previously could. In this way, Essequibo and Demerara saw an expansion process similar to what French and Spanish colonies experienced during the Seven Years' War: French planters on Guadeloupe (in 1760) and Martinique (in 1762) had more or less welcomed the British because of the capital and slave trade they brought, and in Cuba the British occupation set off the sugar boom that made the island one of the dominant sugar producers of the nineteenth century.[42]

Likewise, the British occupation of Essequibo and Demerara was generally a smooth affair; the main problem for Dutch colonists was the oath of allegiance. They were required to swear loyalty to the British king but feared this might compel them to take up arms against the Dutch Republic.[43] The colonists took great pains to convey how abhorrent the oath was, and although the British lieutenant governor, Kingston, doubted the sincerity of the protesters, he was willing to come to terms with them. The oath would be adapted, just as it had been after the occupation of Martinique. The colonists only had to take up arms against the Dutch if the colonies were to be officially ceded to Britain, which relieved their concerns. However, Kingston also reminded the colonists about the advantages the British empire could bring, advantages they could see on the previously conquered French islands.[44]

The British also tried to improve the colonial structure by establishing a town in Demerara. However, they were driven out by French forces before they could realize this project. The French were allies of the Dutch at the time, so the planters were not amused when their ships (five men-of-war and thirteen merchant vessels) were once again subjected to confiscation. Yet afterward, the same procedure was repeated: the French replaced several key officials, left property intact, and gave everyone the same privileges as French citizens.[45]

An important difference between Dutch and French rule was that the latter realized the potential of Essequibo and Demerara and immediately undertook major infrastructural developments. The first step was to go ahead with erecting a central town, which the French, like the British, saw as a crucial step.

> It is considered necessary, from the great extent of this river and its banks, to have a Capital, which will become the business centre; where Religion will have a temple, Justice a palace, War its arsenals, Commerce its counting-houses, Industry its factories, and where the inhabitants may enjoy the advantages of social intercourse. This is perhaps the only instance of a European colony, among thousands throughout the world, which has arrived at some magnificence without the establishment of either town or village.[46]

Previously, social, religious, and political life was spread out over the colonies. Essequibo had a church on Fort Island, while church services in Demerara took place in one of the administrative buildings on Borsselen Island, 30 miles upriver. Essequibo had an arsenal at Fort Zeelandia; in Demerara the few military supplies were deposited at the watch post (*brandwagt*) near the coast. And while the social life in colonies like Saint-Domingue or Suriname revolved around the major port city, in Essequibo and Demerara it was dispersed, taking place on individual plantations instead (see chapter 6). In order to merge these social, religious, and administrative dimensions, the French set to work constructing a town, which would be called Longchamps. They levied several slaves from every plantation, and to the dismay of the planters, the "colony tax" (Colonie Ongelden) was also increased to pay for the infrastructural works. Much of this money was used for the two fortifications, La Reine on the west bank and Le Dauphin on the east bank of the river mouth, close to Longchamps (map 2.1). These forts made it easier to monitor the incoming and outgoing ships, making smuggling at least somewhat more difficult.[47]

The French also introduced other innovations, such as setting exchange rates between guilders and the foreign currencies in circulation (such as the "Portuguese Joe's"), the issuance of 150,000 guilders in paper money, and the institution of a postal service. In March 1784, six months after the peace of Versailles, the French returned the colonies to the Dutch, who immediately sought to undo several of the reforms. Trade restrictions were reinstated, La Reine was abandoned, and the postal service was abolished.[48] In addition, Longchamps was renamed Stabroek, and the fortress would thereafter be called Willem Fredrick.

In the meantime the WIC directors had drawn up their own plan to remodel the administration of the two colonies. The main aim was to enhance the Company's grip on the local administration. One of the basic tenets was to increase salaries. It was decided that officials should have sufficient income to make them independent of other activities, and since there had been many complaints about the meager remuneration before, the WIC was willing to pay. The director-general would see his basic salary increase from 1,800 to 18,700 guilders, that of the captain-commandant of the forces would go from 900 to 4,000 guilders, and even ordinary soldiers were to receive 300 instead of 96 guilders per year.[49] Although this seemed an ingenious idea in theory, in practice the WIC had absolutely no money to pay for it all. The extra annual expenses of the reforms would more than double the Company's expenses, and it

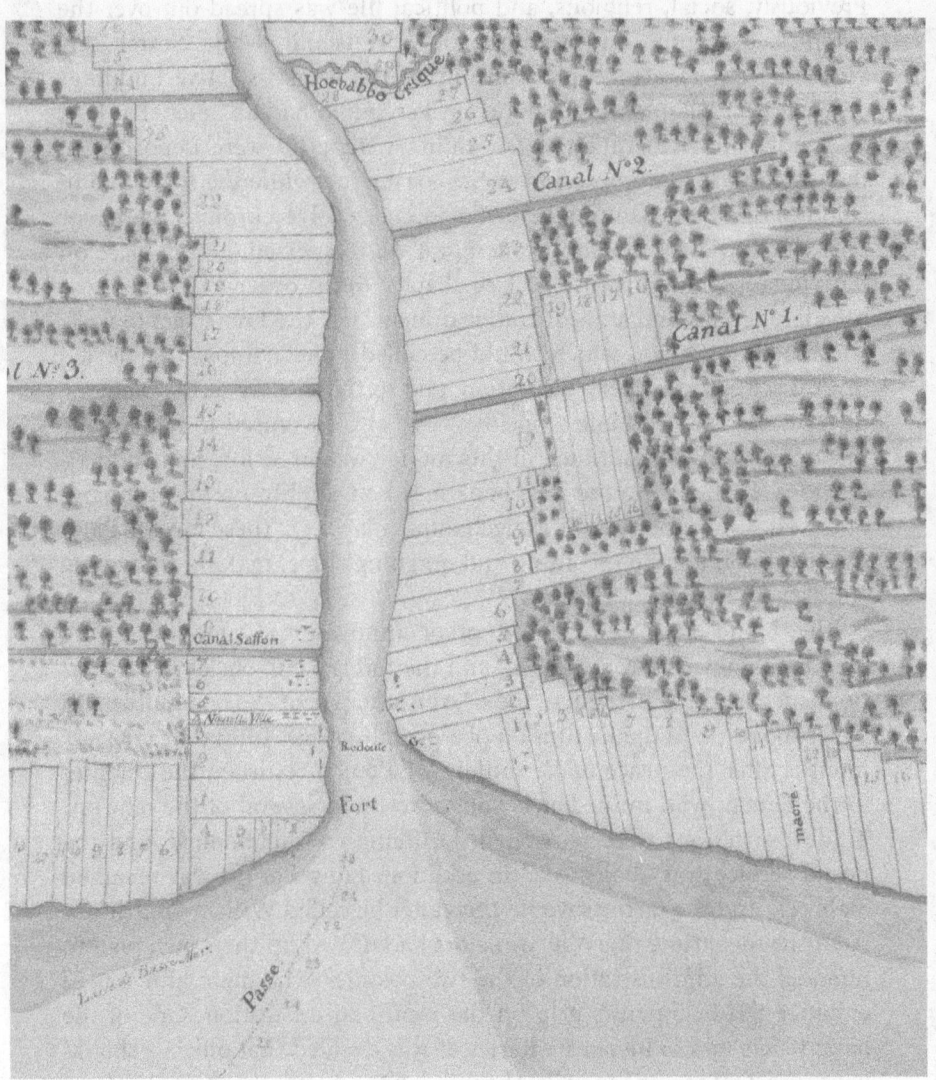

MAP 2.1. Detail from the mouth of the Demerara River, 1784. From D. Pruimelaar, "Carte de la colonie de Demerari en 1784," NL-HaNA, Verzameling Buitenlandse Kaarten Leupe (herafter Kaarten Leupe), 4.VEL, inv. nr. 1498. Longchamps is labeled "Nouvelle Ville" under no. 4, the fortress Le Dauphin under no. 1 on the left side (which is the eastern side, as it is a south-up map), and La Reine under "Redoute" on the right (thus western) coast.

already had huge losses. The Company therefore asked the States-General for a loan of three million guilders but was granted only 800,000. As a result, the WIC had to let go of its grand ambitions and backtracked on the salary increases. While in the May 1783 edition of the plan the WIC had still budgeted to spend 250,000 guilders per year, this sum was later trimmed to 187,550 and subsequently to 116,800 guilders per year.[50]

The second set of reforms was constitutional. The economic dominance of Demerara was recognized by making it the administrative center. Henceforth, Essequibo would be administered by a commander, subordinate to the director-general, who would reside in Demerara, where the future Combined Council meetings would be held as well. In addition, the idea was to professionalize the judicial system by appointing European lawyers or judges as the presidents of the Courts of Civil and Criminal Justice. Considering that almost no one in the colonies had any legal knowledge, this plan would have been a great step forward. However, it proved too expensive, again. The sole source of legal knowledge would remain the fiscal. He would continue in his double executive and judicial role, being both the public prosecutor (and hence a member of the Council of Policy) and the legal adviser to the Council of Justice.[51]

A similar revision, but of much greater importance, would take place in the political domain: the influence of planters over the local administration would be reduced. The new Councils of Policy would consist of the head of government and the next four Company functionaries in rank, in addition to just three civilian councillors.[52] So while previously the balance between planters and the Company had been equal, the planters were now in the minority. Moreover, the planter representatives would no longer be nominated by their peers but be appointed by the director-general. It was this implementation that would stir the outrage in planter society and lead to the revolutionary talk of the brothers Hartsinck.

The Dutch Revolutionary Moment (1784–1787)

The planters' discontent was partly an outgrowth of the political dissatisfaction that had arisen within the Dutch Republic itself, especially after the loss of the war against Britain. The Dutch Republic had effectively become a second-rate power in Europe after the War of the Spanish Succession, yet it continued to enjoy a comfortable political and economic position, as its neutrality was protected by Britain. When this protection disappeared in the Fourth Anglo-Dutch War, the weaknesses of the Dutch were clearly exposed. Furthermore, the war had led to large economic losses due to confiscations of ships and merchandise. And the WIC had been deprived of its income during the foreign occupations, pushing it further into debt. Finally, the Dutch slave trade had come to a virtual standstill and did not revive afterward, hampering the prospects of the colonies.[53] Thus the defeat in the war served as a wake-up call for those who had not realized the Dutch had lost their international prominence.

The externally imposed problems were compounded by internal strife, as the Dutch Republic experienced increased polarization between pro-British royalists on the one hand and pro-French reformists on the other. The former, the so-called Orangists, supported Stadtholder William V of Orange and had a support base in both the wealthy rentier class of regents and in the lower strata. The rival pro-French, Patriot faction, coming from a more middle-class background, essentially wanted to end the regents' hold on positions in the city councils. These Patriots desired a bottom-up way of electing officials, as opposed to top-down appointments. While the Patriots drew inspiration from the American Revolution in their rhetoric, their democratic ideals did not stretch that far. Their aim was essentially to broaden the existing elite to include their own "enlightened elite."[54]

Through their own popular press, the formation of their own militia, and mass demonstrations, the Patriots gained political prominence, jeopardizing the stability of the Dutch Republic. By summer 1786 the Patriots had managed to take over the councils in many cities, and in May 1787 a battle was fought between Orangist and Patriot forces, resulting in eighty casualties. The Patriots movement was aborted after their militia arrested Princess Wilhelmina in June 1787: she called on her brother, Frederick William II of Prussia, for help. Soon afterward, an army of 26,000 Prussian soldiers marched into the Dutch Republic and restored the Orangist order. The Patriot militia was disbanded, their clubs were forbidden, and many of them fled to seek refuge in France.[55]

Preoccupied as the Patriots were with metropolitan politics, they never formulated an elaborate view of the position of the colonies. Nevertheless, in 1784 a specific magazine was founded, *De Oost- en West- Indische Post* (the *East and West Indian Post*), to comment on situations in the colonies. In this short-lived publication, several letters were printed from Demerara planters wherein they voiced complaints about the WIC's administration of the colonies.[56]

More important, a twelve-volume work espousing Patriot ideas appeared between 1785 and 1788, called *Brieven over the bestuur der colonien, gewisseld tussen de heeren Aristodemus en Sincerus* (Letters regarding the administration of the colonies, exchanged by the gentlemen Aristodemus and Sincerus). The author of this fictional exchange remained anonymous but was clearly well aware of the problems with the governance of Essequibo and Demerara. Using Patriot rhetoric, the author criticized the WIC's policy on a host of issues, including the slave trade, taxes, and mortgages. The most relevant one for now, however, was the relationship between the colonies and the Dutch Republic.

The author of the *Brieven* compared the development of the two colonies to the breeding of horses: one had to invest before any results could be had. While trading colonies like Curaçao could generate immediate profits, "agricultural colonies" like Essequibo and Demerara could not. Still, agricultural colonies also generated trade, so a financial loss to the Company did not have to mean a loss for the Dutch Republic as a whole. However, the burden had to be divided fairly. At present only the colonists contributed, the author argued, while the rest of the country reaped the benefits.[57] Therefore, the author argued, a monopolistic company like the WIC was not fit to rule the two colonies. It looked primarily after its own interests, while "the sovereign"—by which he alternately meant the States-General, the inhabitants of the Dutch Republic, "the people," or "the nation"—would look after the greater good. Hence the colonies should fall under the sovereign, who would also take care of protection costs. If cities in the republic did not have to pay for their protection against foreign armies, why should the colonies?[58]

Delving deeper into financial matters, the author noted that the sovereign and the Company had divergent interests, as the latter had an annual loss of 100,000 guilders on Essequibo and Demerara. The Company had an incentive to increase taxes, while the sovereign would keep taxes low to foster development. In addition, the current taxes on enslaved people were not conducive to the colonies' development anyway, the author reasoned: the death of an enslaved person posed a great financial risk to a planter, so it would make more sense to tax the plantation's output instead of "input." A tax on the crop would ensure each planter paid to capacity, uninfluenced by droughts or bad harvests. And otherwise, if Essequibo and Demerara were really such a burden to the Company, why would the WIC not hand them over to the States-General?[59]

The *Brieven* contained more policy suggestions, such as the liberalization of the slave trade. Dutch slave traders delivered too few captives, who therefore were expensive, so the author proposed several measures: allow buying from foreigners if the Dutch did not deliver a certain quota or in case the price rose above a certain threshold; or just allow direct trade with West Africa. The latter would have the added benefit of providing an outlet for the rum produced on sugar estates. Consequently, it would improve the financial position of the planters, which would benefit the financiers in the Dutch Republic. Thus liberalization of the slave trade would be for the greater good. Even though planters might pay foreign slavers clandestinely with plantation products, the author argued, it would be a small price to pay for the survival of the colonies.[60]

All in all, the *Brieven* offered a comprehensive critique of Company rule rather than a coherent alternative theory of empire. In fact, the author's strongest convictions, and most likely the occasion for publishing the *Brieven*, involved the position of the colonial council. The issue was the same as the one that led the Hartsinck brothers to plot a coup: the postwar change from an equal number of Company and civil councillors to a situation in which civil councillors were outnumbered and only appointed by the WIC.[61] To understand how the colonists reacted to this change, it is necessary to return to the colonial level.

Demerara in 1785: No Taxation without Representation

When, after the war, the new director-general, Jean L'Espinasse, arrived in the colonies he immediately noticed the tense political climate. His first mission was to form a new Council of Policy, because according to WIC rules all officials were automatically dismissed once a foreign power took over. The prewar civil councillors found this automatic dismissal hard to swallow, for they felt they had done the Company a valuable service by keeping the colonies running during the war. In fact, they were expecting a reward or promotion rather than dismissal. Moreover, the idea that the civil councillors would now also be appointed through the WIC was an affront to the planter community. According to the planters, the new procedure was an infringement of their traditional rights and arbitrary and unjustified interference with the local order. The planters vehemently objected to the new way of governing and closed ranks to prevent its implementation.

In practice this boycott meant that L'Espinasse had trouble finding volunteers to fill the seats, especially for the Demerara council. He first asked three of the prewar councillors to take up their positions again. Yet one died and the other two refused. Interestingly, two of the men who would later plot the coup were also asked to serve as councillors—not as civil councillors, but in the name of the Company. These were Hermanus Jonas and Maurits Balthasar Hartsinck. However, both refused to sit, considering the new way of forming a council illegitimate.[62] This process of refusal continued: one planter was persuaded to sit in as civil councillor for the first meeting but later sent his letter of refusal, like two others had done before him.[63] Since the problem was getting more serious, the fiscal proposed to go back to the previous method of selecting civil councillors, namely, asking the officers of the Burgher Militia for nominees from which L'Espinasse would then choose. However, L'Espinasse insisted on asking more people. The planter community seemed united in their resistance, however, for the next three people declined as well.[64] Subsequently, the director-general resorted to asking foreign planters. Their appointment would have been a breach of WIC rules, but David Breton (French) and J. Brotherson (colonial-born English) could not be persuaded anyway.[65] Seemingly out of options, the next move was to make refusal an offense: persons who refused to sit on the council without a lawful excuse were liable to a fine of 3,000 guilders.[66] This measure might have helped, because Christopher Johan Hecke and François Changuion were finally convinced to accept the position. Now the rest of the Demerara planter society rose to action.

Five of Demerara's prominent planters took the lead: Bernard Albinus, Bartholomeus van den Santheuvel, Louwe Idsert Douwe van Grovestins, Hermanus Jonas, and the already familiar Maurits Balthasar Hartsinck. These were prominent men who all performed or had performed functions as councillor, receiver, president of the Orphan and Estate Chamber, or fiscal.[67] On 25 February 1785 they handed a petition to the director-general (followed by a similar one on 18 March) that called for restoration of the "traditional" rights of representation.[68] It was signed by 159 planters, of whom 125 signed in Demerara.[69]

This petition drew support from across "national" boundaries. A different document from 1785 supposedly listed the names of all the planters in Demerara, numbering 109. Of those, only three did not sign the petition.[70] Interestingly, the origin of these 109 people is known. Combining these figures leads to figure 2.1, which shows that the petition enjoyed support from all quarters, in what was a very diverse plantation society. Both the Dutch and those labeled "British" (which included those from the British Caribbean and the United States) rallied behind the protest.[71] The "other" group listed a Russian, a Prussian, two Swiss, two Flemish, and one Italian. Clearly, the planter community was united

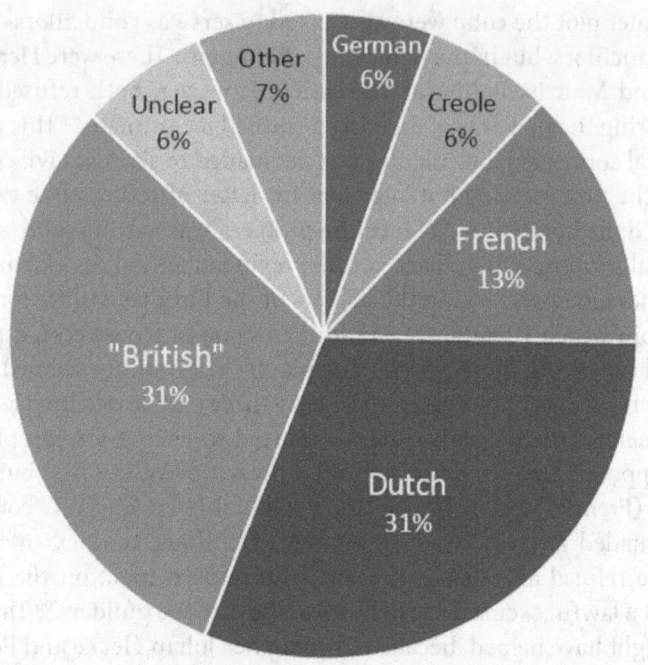

FIGURE 2.1. Origins of the Demerara supporters for the 1785 petition. Source: NL-HaNA, VWIS, 1.05.06, inv. nr. 59.

enough to launch a major political protest against the WIC, and national origin presented no barrier to political cooperation.

The arguments in the petition varied in nature, from practical objections to theoretical reflections. Just as in other cases around the Atlantic, this protest had both a constitutional and a taxation element. The colonists argued that legislative and judicial powers should be kept separate and that the fiscal, as prosecutor and member of the Council of Policy, could not be an adviser in the Court of Justice. Another more practical point was that the WIC had always made a distinction between councillors and employees. And since the *burgerraden* were not employees, the Company simply had no right to dismiss them.

The planters' key issue, however, was the right to choose their own representatives. The petitioners referred to the reforms of 1773 and questioned the Company's right to change this "constitution." Here the colonists encountered a fundamental problem: there was nothing like a constitution. Unlike Suriname, there was no charter on which the colonization in Essequibo and Demerara was based other than the charter for the WIC, so without such an overarching document the WIC could indeed unilaterally change the "rules of game."[72]

Rather than having a clear legal basis, colonization in Essequibo and Demerara was an improvised affair based on a continuously expanding set of WIC rules, proclamations, and by-laws. This ad hoc nature of decision making went so far that everything that was put to paper in council meetings or official correspondence functioned as a form of jurisprudence. Such notes could then be used to stage later claims, which is exactly what the petitioners did. For example, during the war, on 28 October 1783, the WIC had written a letter to the "then functioning Council" in the colonies, encouraging the councillors to continue in their role. This phrasing implied that the Councillors were not automatically dismissed after the invasion. How then, the petitioners asked, could the Company claim such a dismissal afterward? The petitioners considered the prewar council the only legal one and therefore urged the director-general to allow Joseph Bourda, Anthony Pieter Swaen, Willebordus Ramaeckers, and Pieter van Helsdingen to take up their seats again. However, the director-general found their proposals too radical, and he considered himself not authorized to judge. To give in would have been tantamount to letting the planters choose their own government, so L'Espinasse instead referred the planters to the Company directors.[73]

The colonists also simply protested against increased taxes. In the improvised tapestry of regulations, the taxation structure had always remained ambiguous. The main taxes were the poll taxes and the colony tax, both based on the number of enslaved persons a planter "owned." The poll tax went to the WIC headquarters in Europe, whereas the colony tax could be spent locally. Yet it was not stipulated when the latter could be levied and how high it could be. For instance, to pay for their improvements, the French had instated a colony tax of 2.50 guilders per enslaved person over twelve years old. Combined with the existing 2.50 guilder poll tax, the result was a tax of 5 guilders per enslaved worker per year. However, when they returned the colonies to the Dutch, the French repaid these sums. After the war the colonists therefore expected the taxes to go down. Yet the expensive reform plans of the WIC meant that taxes actually went up, to a total of 6 guilders per slave.[74]

Lacking the formal political power to change this increase, the planters adopted another tactic: defiance. In the petition the planters flatly refused to pay the new rate, offering to pay only the old poll tax of 2.50 guilders per slave instead. Since the WIC did not formulate a reply to their petitions, the issue remained unresolved. The result was that many planters simply decided to pay no poll taxes at all in the next three years.[75] While these taxes were relatively small expenses for the planters, the problems with levying them showcase the planters' resistance to metropolitan control.[76]

In fact, it was also very *convenient* for the planter community to portray the council as illegal and unconstitutional: if there was no legal government, they reasoned, there were no legal restrictions that could be broken. By subsequently declaring the colony to be in a state of anarchy (*regeringloosheid*), the colonists legitimized their own defiance. Officially, the colonists were held by WIC rules to ship all their produce to the Dutch Republic, in line with the prevailing mercantilist doctrine. Yet in the supposed state of anarchy, the planters claimed they were not breaking any rules if they sold their produce to foreigners or bought enslaved Africans from foreigners. And because the Dutch Republic was tied up in its own political problems (discussed below), no solution was forthcoming. The colonists were quite content with this situation. During the war they had experienced relative commercial freedom, and they were reluctant to relinquish it. If the Company did not provide any public goods but rather stood for taxes and restrictions, they preferred free trade and anarchy.

Demerara in 1787: The Escalation

The colony enjoyed stability as long as this situation lasted. Only when a renewed attempt was made to curb smuggling did the political fight continue in earnest. Since 1784 warships had been sent to the colonies to prevent illegal trade, but it was only in 1787 that a particularly zealous captain, Frans Smeer, took serious steps to do something about it (see chapter 4). He managed to convince L'Espinasse to issue a proclamation forbidding any ship to sail out of the river after sunset, with the idea of making illegal trade considerably more difficult.[77] This measure seemingly pushed the planters over the edge: as long as "anarchy" meant freedom to smuggle they were perfectly content with it, yet now they wanted to end it and rose to action.

By September 1787 L'Espinasse had heard the rumors: he would receive a petition drafted by Albinus, Van den Santheuvel, Jonas, and Hartsinck carried by armed civilians to back up the demands. At first he dismissed the talk, considering the men incapable of organizing any substantial resistance. Yet when he heard from Lieutenant Lasberg about Hartsinck's effort to stage an armed uprising, L'Espinasse changed his mind.[78] He took his precautions but had to be careful, for he had been told that the planters were looking for a provocation. If the planters could portray the director-general as a military despot, they would later be able to claim they had no other choice than to dispose of him. So L'Espinasse was on guard; he had extra artillery placed and posted sentinels in Stabroek to watch out for any armed civilians. On 12 September he informed the WIC, "The people here are not used to anything other than anarchy and they do not want to be ruled." He reported that the situation was "utterly precarious" and that the directors "should not be surprised about anything, whatever happens."[79] L'Espinasse's concern is understandable, for it was not easy to draft a petition with such broad support in a decentralized colony like Demerara.

Indeed, the names of the petitioners reflected the social, economic, and geographic structure of the colony. Geographically, canvassing a petition was complicated by the lack of an urban center (Stabroek was still very small) and by the dispersed plantations along the various rivers and creeks. In other words, there was no central location where the resistance could be organized and a petition had to be carried from the first plantation to the last, several days' sailing distance from each other. Thus there could be no deliberation over the text once it had been drafted: the choice was simply to sign or not to sign. With the planters unable to coordinate their decisions, the person carrying the petition had a crucial role, as he could persuade people directly.

Consequently, the names on a petition were also in part a reflection of the social network within the planter society: if the most prominent planters put their names down, the others were more likely to follow. This mechanism applied not just to the Dutch planters but also to the non-Dutch signers; the leader of the English faction appears to have been Thomas Cuming, and for the French it probably was J. P. Cuche. Indeed, when the "revolutionary" petition was finally brought to L'Espinasse on 15 October 1787, an interesting coalition presented itself: among the 130 colonists we find not only Dutch but also many British, as well as the majority of the French planters. So while these foreign planters could have no representation in the WIC structure, they could still be politically active through petitioning.[80]

The planter society was far from united though, for L'Espinasse soon received a counter-petition, from over sixty inhabitants, supporting him. These planters stated they were very content with the director-general, and essentially wanted to have it noted that they had been on the loyal side in case the crisis would blow over.[81]

In addition to the geographic and social dimensions, there was an economic element to the petitioning. Importantly, the four leaders of the dissenting faction were at the same time agents of mortgage funds in the Dutch Republic. Because as agents they held the gateway to much-needed credit, the four men had a powerful leverage instrument since many planters were deeply indebted to the mortgage funds (see chapter 5). The danger of being cut off from credit would surely have pressured planters into signing, even if they did not entirely agree with the political message.[82] It is therefore not unthinkable that true support for the petition was not as great as the 130 names would suggest.

Nevertheless, the coalition of protesting planters made stern demands, desiring an overhaul of the political structure. They either wanted to reinstate the prewar council or reform the administrative structure as was outlined in the WIC's own Concept Plan of Redress. Indeed, it must be noted that the WIC had tried to resolve the problem. In 1786 a committee was formed, which presented a concept plan to the States-General in March 1787. It contained many desirable elements for the planters, including a proposal to collect taxes for the previous years only at the old rate, a plan to dig a communication canal between the two colonies, and advice to establish a proper code of laws. Furthermore, several changes in the composition of the Council of Policy and the Council of Justice were proposed, the vital one being a return to nomination of councillors by the colonists themselves, through an Electors College. The Dutch Republic was tied up in its own Orangist-Patriot struggles, however, and its overseas problems had a very low priority.[83] It was in this context, without an immediate solution in sight, that the petitioners pushed their agenda forward. No longer would they tolerate the governor's tyranny, nor would they "willingly lay down their free necks on the chopping block of arbitrary lust for power." In a thinly disguised threat the planters urged L'Espinasse to comply, so they would not be obliged to take "a stronger, to everyone more undesirable measure."[84] Interestingly, L'Espinasse believed that the tenth volume of the *Brieven* had been the inspiration for this "violent manifesto."[85]

This petition triggered a serious political crisis in Demerara. Upon reading the request, two councillors immediately resigned, feeling that their position had become untenable.[86] Since three other seats had been vacant for a while, there was suddenly little of a council left. L'Espinasse could only rely on the receiver of taxes (Jacques Andriessen) and the fiscal (Anthony Meertens). However, the former was unavailable because he appeared to be terminally ill, and the latter quickly defected to the dissenters (even though he repented soon afterward).[87] The whole institutional framework had thus fallen apart and the director-general had to deal with the situation entirely on his own.

While later historians have looked unfavorably upon L'Espinasse, he actually handled the situation rather skillfully.[88] By immediately offering to give up his own position, he removed the fuse from the powder keg, depriving the planters of an excuse for violence. The dissenting planters seemed to have hoped for a provocation by the director-general and hence were not satisfied with his move. For the moment they urged L'Espinasse to remain in his position, and with the danger of violence out of the way, the two parties returned to the negotiating table. In this situation, L'Espinasse understood that his best bet was to accommodate the planter's wishes now and face the judgment of his superiors later. His improvised solution was that the planters would nominate seven candidate representatives among themselves, within "twelve to fourteen" days. Continuing the previous tradition, he would then choose three civilian councillors from these nominees to form a new and legitimate council.[89]

This proposition was more or less accepted by the planters, although discussions ensued on the practical implementation. Who would be allowed to vote for the nominees, all colonists or only planters with a certain number of slaves? L'Espinasse's proposal named "the Burghers" as the ones with the right to vote—yet, his opponents replied, there had never been an official explanation of who would qualify as a Burgher. In addition, the period of twelve days was deemed too short to consult everyone, and indeed no nominations were made in this period.

L'Espinasse therefore improvised again: considering that in the 1785 petition the majority of the colonists had asked for the reinstatement of Bourda, Swaen, Ramaeckers, and Van Helsdingen, the director-general deemed this desire "the general will" of the colony and decided to ask them to take up their seats again.[90] Since this move would mean a return to the older practice of having four instead of three civil councillors, the parity between WIC and colonists' votes would also be restored. After some more details had been hammered out between L'Espinasse and the four main dissenters, this solution was agreeable to all and put an end to the political crisis.[91] Without any interference, and even without any correspondence with the metropolis in these precarious weeks, the local actors had thus both created and solved a serious political crisis.

For the moment these changes were enough to quiet the political situation. Since the Orangist-Patriot crisis in the Dutch Republic was resolved (for the moment), more attention could be paid to colonial matters. Indeed, it was now just a matter of waiting for the ratification and implementation of the Plan of Redress, which followed in 1789. To implement this plan, two commissioners were appointed, Willem Cornelis Boeij and Willem August Sirtema, baron of Grovestins. In their report they neatly summarized the source of the problems: the WIC officials had wanted to "execute resolutions and orders with a blind zeal," pitting the director-general against the fiscal and the colonists, who, "characteristic of Colony Councillors, favoured the system of planters over the government." They concluded that this clash between metropolitan dogma and the desire for colonial autonomy, among other grievances, had brought the colony to a "complete state of anarchy [regeeringloosheid] and that except for the public order and safety, which fortunately remained intact, nobody reckoned himself obliged to comply with any of the established laws or orders, or to pay any dues."[92]

After arriving in Demerara on 26 May 1789, the two commissioners formalized the changes in the administrative structure by discharging the old councillors and administering the oath to the new ones. The Councils of Policy of the two colonies were merged, and henceforth each colony would send its fiscal and two chosen representatives to the General Council, with the director-general acting as president. The councillors would be chosen by an Electors College (Collegie van Kiezers) comprising seven electors, who were also responsible for nominating the members of the Councils of Justice. The colonial apparatus was not merged entirely, for each colony retained its own judicial council; these would not be combined until 1812.[93] And while the members of the council had to be Dutch, electors could be of non-Dutch origin. Indeed, the names of the electors reveal the growing influence of French and British planters: in both colleges at least two of seven electors were not Dutch. The entire situation was sealed when Grovestins and Boeij returned to the Dutch Republic in August 1789, together with L'Espinasse, whose requested resignation they had provisionally granted.[94]

So the Plan of Redress put a definite end to the political turmoil, and no further major changes were made afterward, as in 1791 the WIC met its inexorable demise when its charter expired without being renewed. The result was that on 1 January 1792 the colonies passed into the hands of the Dutch state, which governed them through the newly created Council of Colonies (Raad der Kolonien). The new governor of the two colonies was already familiar: Willem August van Grovestins. Under his rule Essequibo and Demerara became part of the revolutionary turbulence spilling over from Europe.

The International Revolutionary Moment (1795–1803)

Although the political turmoil seemed to have come to an end in 1787, it had only just begun. When the Patriots were ousted from the Dutch Republic in 1787, calm initially returned to the colonies too, but the Dutch were soon caught up in international politics. In 1795 the French revolutionary army marched into the Dutch Republic, with many Patriots at their side. The French replaced the Dutch Republic with the new "Batavian Republic," effectively a puppet state. Suddenly the simmering battle between the pro-British Orangists and the pro-French Patriots was settled decisively in favor of the latter. These battle lines between opponents and supporters of the new regime were drawn even starker in the colonies.

In fact, the overthrown Stadtholder, William V of Orange, fled to Britain, where he asked King George III to take the Dutch colonies into "protection." The British were all too eager to comply with these so-called Kew Letters, fearing that the French would otherwise annex the Dutch possessions, both in the East and the West Indies. The Stadtholder's order to accept British "protection" caused considerable confusion in the colonies, for it seemed closer to military occupation—or at least that is what the governor of Dutch Ceylon experienced. There, it took seven months for the local Dutch authorities to sign a capitulation treaty with the British, after the latter had captured a strategic harbor. The Dutch governor of Ceylon believed protection could consist of a British garrison, while the British fleet started from the idea of a temporary occupation.[95]

Even greater confusion arose in Essequibo and Demerara. The new governor, Grovestins, was an outspoken Orangist, and his pro-British stance had brought stability to a colony where the majority of the planters were British. Indeed, after the start of the French Revolutionary Wars (1792–1802), Essequibo and Demerara had initially taken a pro-British stance. The colonies had refused to accept any French refugees and had shipped their produce in British convoys via Barbados.[96] Yet this position became untenable with the establishment of the (pro-French) Batavian Republic, which immediately summoned Grovestins to break ties with British ports and seek French protection instead. Furthermore, the governor was warned about a possible British invasion. The local council complied with these orders and on 27 April 1795 banned all armed ships except Dutch and French ones.[97]

Yet soon afterward Grovestins received the Kew Letters: on 3 May the British frigate *Zebra* arrived with instructions from William V to seek *British* protection, against a possible *French* invasion. In addition, an accompanying British message offered six hundred British men to protect the colonial government. However, the local council chose to follow the orders coming from the Dutch Republic and rejected the British offer. This decision seems to have been too much for the Orangist in Grovestins: on 5 May he left the colony on board the *Zebra*, never to return. Since he had given no warning, or taken any precautions for after his flight, Grovestins's hasty departure left the colonies in disarray. He wrote a letter to the council explaining that he felt he had to leave and was going to Martinique (and possibly on to London). Interestingly, he gave a precise account of the cash and bills of exchange in the various colonial chests, possibly to prevent later accusations of fraud. Nevertheless, the sudden political vacuum in this tense period triggered a political crisis.[98] The British, unlike in Ceylon, left without taking the colonies by force—for the moment at least.

With unreliable communications in this crisis atmosphere, the colonists had to improvise again. No successor for Grovestins could be found immediately: Essequibo's commandeur was abroad, and the acting fiscal of Demerara refused, as did Demerara's secretary, Anthony Beaujon. While Beaujon had been mentioned by Grovestins as a possible successor, he did not want to accept the responsibility in this difficult time. Yet developments moved quickly. The next day, 6 May, the acting commandeur of Essequibo, John Plettner, was persuaded to take command.[99]

Yet this makeshift solution was only the start of further conflict, as French-British rivalry became intertwined with the struggle for the older Patriot ideals. Indeed, the local Patriot faction seized the opportunity to push for more democratic control of the colonies. On 8 May an angry mob gathered outside the secretary building, rallying behind the cries of "Liberté, Egalité, Fraternité." The group demanded access to the documents because a rumor was going around that Beaujon had secretly asked the British to intervene, and the Patriots wanted to see if the allegations were true.[100]

Even though the mob was calmed, the Patriots continued to push for reform but this time through petitions. They argued that after Grovestins's flight, authority fell back to the Council of Policy. Furthermore, they demanded that the position of president of the council be filled by planter representatives. This position was to be shared between one planter from Essequibo and another from Demerara and was to rotate every eight days. In addition, it was decided that in the new council the three vacant councillor seats were to be filled with planters as well, solidifying a planter majority in government. In fact, at this point there was little government left, and after the acting fiscal resigned in protest, it came down to John Plettner to formally represent the metropolitan authority in the new council. While the period of this planter-dominated council has been called the "Demerara Republic," it is probably better to see it as an improvised and temporary form of crisis government.[101] Indeed, when the new council received instructions on 27 June 1795 to install Antony Beaujon as the new governor, they did so without protest.[102]

When the internal colonial disputes were settled, then, the colonists could worry again about international issues. Even the pro-French faction did not want the colonies to be taken over by French forces, especially not after the French abolition of slavery in 1794. So when Victor Hugues arrived in the Caribbean, the planters had reason to fear. In order to keep the enemies of France occupied, Hugues's aim was to disturb their plantation societies by encouraging slaves and free coloreds to revolt. This incitation inspired, among others, rebellions in Guadeloupe in 1793, St. Vincent and Grenada in 1795, and Jamaica in 1796 while creating unrest in many other places.[103]

Consequently, when the colonists in Essequibo and Demerara heard rumors that Hugues had arrived in French Guiana, they were frightened. Not only did it signify a possible French invasion, but it also invoked fear of a slave revolt. These fears were not unfounded, for in the chaotic early weeks of May, a mulatto woman named Nancy Wood had apparently attempted to encourage the enslaved Africans to revolt, although without success. Regardless, in early June, a large-scale revolt broke out on Demerara's west coast, although probably unrelated to any French activity.[104]

In the end there would be no French takeover, however, because the British came first. Historians disagree over whether this British invasion in April 1796 was solicited by Antony Beaujon; nonetheless, it is clear that local initiatives played a major role. British planters had recognized the opportunity for political change and had been making requests to the British Colonial Office in London to take Essequibo and Demerara for the British crown. A French capture would be detrimental to their business interests, they argued, so it would be better to strike first. And this scenario was indeed what came to pass. After brief negotiations, the British force of thirteen hundred men ensured the quick surrender of the Dutch. The council did not have a problem with capitulation, as long as property remained intact, the extant laws remained in force, and no new laws would be made. An interesting detail here is that one of the councillors who signed the capitulation, Thomas Cuming, was British himself, and one of the foremost planters in the colony (see chapter 6).[105] The British agreed to the council's demand and retained Antony Beaujon in his post, although Lieutenant Hislop would be the supreme authority.[106] The situation was thus more or less a repetition of the takeover of 1781 and was similar to the "protection" that was offered to Ceylon.

The coming of British rule brought many advantages to the colonists, as they gained (renewed) official access to British networks of finance and trade. Indeed, the colonies entered a whole new phase under British rule. In the following years, large amounts of capital flowed into the colonies, while especially slave traders from Liverpool brought in thousands of African captives. The colonies became increasingly anglicized with the arrival of many British planters, financers, and traders; however, the official language of the courts remained Dutch, although proclamations were now bilingual.[107]

The colonies were in a peculiar situation now: since no peace treaty had been signed, the Dutch Republic still had a claim to the colonies even though they were in the hands of the British "protectors." And since British interests far outnumbered Dutch ones by the turn of the century, the peace of Amiens in 1802 made little sense: the colonies were restored to the Dutch, who now essentially had to administer a rapidly expanding British colony without the means to do so. It would not be long, therefore, before the British retook the colonies, and from 1803 they would remain in British hands. Although the official transfer of sovereignty occurred only in 1814, Essequibo and Demerara were effectively under British control from 1803.

This takeover would probably have occurred without the institutional instability in the colonies. The Dutch Republic was at the end of its life and unable to resist the increasingly powerful French and British states, and incorporation in the British empire might be seen as the logical outcome of the growing anglicization of the colonies. Institutional weakness thus did not cause the invasion, but it was influential in shaping the colonies' trajectory by allowing for self-organized expansion.

Through a metropolitan lens, the institutional structure of the two colonies was decidedly weak: the colonies were essentially defenseless and governing often came down to muddling through. In the eyes of the planters, however, this weakness instead enabled the development of the colonies. With ample room for local initiatives, the colonists had little reason to rise up against the Company and seek independence, like many of their Latin American neighbors would do later. As long as there was not too much metropolitan intervention, the colonists just muddled and smuggled along as they liked. When the Company tried to increase its influence, the colonists voiced loud protests, and when the Company's administration was the most fragile—during the supposed state of anarchy between 1785 and 1787—the political system actually proved very stable. Only when the metropolis initiated new control measures, with renewed efforts to curb smuggling, did the situation escalate. Nevertheless, negotiation at the colonial level prevented a coup. In the end, there was even a certain resilience in the improvised structure that arose: despite becoming British, the colonies retained the Dutch Plan of Redress as the basis of governance until 1928.[108]

All in all, colonists were less concerned with external invaders and more concerned with the "internal enemy"—the enslaved population. The lack of support from the metropolis rendered the plantation hierarchy vulnerable to uprisings. The few Company soldiers could do little, and many of them were eager to desert to the Spanish, which weakened the garrison even more. As the next chapter demonstrates, however, the brutal slave regime nevertheless was quite stable, and desertion was a key factor in explaining why.

3 / Rebels and Runaways

Maddelon was a young enslaved woman in Demerara who found herself caught up in a perilous situation. On 14 August 1772 a rebellion took place on her plantation on the west coast and she became embroiled in it against her will. Her sister's partner, the *bomba* (driver) Jacob, had been plotting a revolt, together with several of the other *bombas*. Apparently Jacob had said, "The new master treats us so badly, let us put a knife in his throat." A change of owner was always a moment when the existing negotiated balance was disrupted, and the new planter—Pieter Cornelis Hooft—had increased both the workload and the whippings. Yet Maddelon did not support the violent plans and apparently reported them to her master's wife. Consequently, Jacob received a flogging or beating (*maling*), and Maddelon must have been viewed with suspicion afterward. Therefore, when the revolt finally broke out, she felt trapped.[1]

She wanted to leave, but the rebels threatened to kill her if she dared to do so. Therefore, she was forced to witness the violent events that followed: how Hooft was called out from his house with news that a deserter had been caught, how he was subsequently attacked and beheaded by the *bombas*, and how his house was raided for clothes, guns, and ammunition. She saw or heard how Hooft's wife tried to escape, how she fell and was killed, and how the rebels cut her belly open to use her blood for an apparent obeah ritual, to find her unborn child inside. Yet somehow she managed to escape, making her way to the nearby plantation of J. B. Struys. However, although she was free from the violence of the rebels there, she soon was captured by the whites. Deemed a potential rebel, she was brought to the fort for questioning.[2]

In her testimony she made conscious choices about who to blame and who to absolve. She only incriminated the leaders of the revolt—the *bombas* Jacob, Daniel, and Quamina—while also mentioning that the *bomba* Felix had defected after the whites were killed. In general, she mentioned the actions of others, not of herself. When she was questioned about a golden ring she might have stolen in the chaos, she denied the accusation; it had been a gift. It was nevertheless taken from her upon capture. Furthermore, she emphasized that the rebels were Hooft's people, not those of her previous master, Pieter Callaert, thereby protecting the people she knew. In addition, she confirmed the interrogator's suspicions that Callaert had been behind the revolt: he had encouraged the *bombas* to take action against their cruel new master. Maddelon had little reason to protect her former master: Callaert had threatened to kill her if she revealed that he had delivered a weapon, powder, and shot to Jacob. Furthermore, she confirmed that Callaert had raped her, stating that he "was with her and used her in his bedroom on a plank before they were sold."[3]

In the end, together with other stories, Maddelon's account was deemed reliable enough to prove that she had not actively participated in the uprising and to convince the authorities that Callaert was guilty. Furthermore, most of the convicted rebels were indeed from Hooft (and other planters), not from Callaert.[4]

For the historian, accounts like Maddelon's provide unique insights into the lives of the enslaved, despite their interpretational problems. The enslaved only answered questions, which were clearly aimed at seeking confirmation rather than entertaining divergent perspectives. Hence, those being interrogated might follow these leads, in order not to draw suspicion onto themselves. In addition, the testimonies of the enslaved were written down by a white clerk, who might introduce his own layer of interpretation, especially when translating from a creole language to the bureaucratic language. Furthermore, the enslaved had their own motives to lie or bend the truth, such as protecting their loved ones or incriminating their enemies. For example, Maddelon was accused by others of having been the one who lured Hooft outside before he was killed. In the end, however, the authorities believed the larger number of accounts that pointed to another woman, called Clarissa, who was burned alive with exceptional cruelty.[5] Nevertheless, with careful reading and cross-referencing, these statements have a lot to offer to the historian.[6]

Normally, testimonies by enslaved Africans and Amerindians against whites were not admitted in court, yet now the local court made an exception. If the rebels had not been stopped, the court reasoned, "nothing less than the ruin of this entire colony and the premature death of so many white Christians" would have been the result.[7] Still, statements like Maddelon's were not enough to convict Callaert. They only served as legitimation for his torture, in order to procure a confession. And while Callaert denied any involvement after the first session, just before the second day of his torture his memory suddenly returned to him and he confessed to having been the instigator of the revolt.[8]

The revolt will be discussed in more detail below. For now it is useful to note that Maddelon's experience captures crucial elements of the slavery regime in Essequibo and Demerara. A constant tension between accommodation and resistance, fight or flight, pervaded the lives of the enslaved. As Marjoleine Kars has recently and wonderfully demonstrated, most people tried to avoid violence from any side and simply wished to dodge rebellions like this one. They might plead for mercy, surrender, or try to carve out a living as a maroon nearby.[9] My purpose here is to investigate the various ways in which the borderless nature and improvised alliances in Essequibo and Demerara affected the enslaved.

The question, then, is how the slavery regime could survive. If control by the West India Company was so weak, as argued in chapter 2, why were the enslaved not able to overthrow the plantation hierarchy? And how did the possibility of acquiring freedom in the Spanish areas, as discussed in chapter 1, influence the slave society on the Dutch side? What was the role of other groups, such as soldiers and Amerindians, in stabilizing or destabilizing the regime? This chapter focuses on the two main mechanisms used to challenge the plantation hierarchy: running away and staging revolts. I argue that running away was in fact a stabilizing factor and that revolts had little chance as long as the Dutch could rely on Amerindian support.

This first point is that the existence of an "escape option" in the Orinoco region significantly increased the stability of the slave regime. Indeed, "desertion"—fleeing from an oppressive labor regime—proved key. The open border allowed the most daring to get away, who might otherwise have chosen violent resistance. Furthermore, WIC soldiers—neither completely bonded nor completely free—also fled to the Spanish areas and might otherwise have sided with the enslaved or caused unrest by staging a mutiny. Last, the viability of running away was one of the reasons that few maroon societies were formed in the forest. While maroons in Suriname often attacked plantations, the relative absence of maroon communities in Essequibo and Demerara contributed to the stability of the slavery system.

The second pillar of the slavery regime was support from the Amerindians. Rather than rely exclusively on European soldiers, the colonists formed alliances with indigenous groups. This assistance could take the form of commando groups that searched the forests for incipient maroon hideouts but also of auxiliary troops to put down rebellions. This help was necessary because European soldiers were of little use in the jungle and were eager to defect to the Spanish. Because of the Amerindians, revolts thus barely had a chance to succeed.

The stability of the slavery regime therefore depended on local conditions and local alliances. The next sections situate the slavery regime of Essequibo and Demerara in a wider context, then discuss desertion (of both Africans and soldiers) and rebellions.[10]

Situating the Slavery System

Full-scale plantation slavery arrived relatively late in Essequibo and Demerara. While they had known slavery since the seventeenth century, the plantation sector only started to grow quickly after the mid-eighteenth century. In this respect, Essequibo and Demerara were less like Barbados and more like the many islands conquered by Britain during the Seven Years' War. During this period the British had occupied (among others) Martinique, Guadeloupe, and Cuba, and in all of these places a sudden openness to British slave traders had fueled the rapid expansion of plantation exploitation. Similarly, the so-called Ceded Islands—Grenada, Dominica, St Vincent, and the Grenadines and Tobago—saw a major influx of British capital after they were ceded to Britain by France and Spain in 1763.[11] Similarly, British capital and slave trading stimulated the expansion of the plantation complex in Essequibo and Demerara.

While Brazil and the southern United States also experienced expansion of plantations in the eighteenth and nineteenth centuries, they had a longer tradition of plantation slavery. In contrast, in other colonies such as Mexico and Peru, plantation slavery was less prominent, and recurrent growth within the indigenous population meant that enslaved labor became less important.[12] In yet another group the growth of slavery had halted as soil exhaustion had taken its toll, for example, in Barbados and perhaps Suriname.[13] Suriname had known plantation exploitation for longer, while Essequibo and Demerara were largely undeveloped in this respect.

These temporal differences in the arrival of large-scale plantation slavery had a profound effect on the demography of the enslaved. The death toll among the enslaved in Essequibo and Demerara was enormous. Clearing the environment was backbreaking work anywhere but worse on the Guiana coast. The cutting down of the dense rainforest was arduous in itself, but the enslaved also had to dig an elaborate system of waterworks to make the plantation into a *polder*. An intricate system of dams, canals, and sluices was needed to control the water level on the plantation. The front dam protected against the tides, the back dam prevented excessive rainfall from the forest from overrunning the estate, and the side dams completed the system. In between, trenches and canals had to be dug to allow for adequate irrigation and transport of products in small punt boats.[14]

So labor demands were higher, but, in addition, slavery was also deadlier in new areas because of the low percentage of creolized slaves. The American-born enslaved had more resistance to local diseases, yet new areas could not be developed without a large influx of African captives (although in the United States the internal slave trade offered an alternative). In Suriname the demographic decline was 4.7 percent per year in the period between 1750 and 1775, when it experienced a rapid expansion of both its plantation sector and its trade in enslaved Africans. Afterward, the expansion halted and the slave trade dwindled, and the rate of demographic decline dropped to 2.4 percent.[15]

It is well known that the demography of (Caribbean) slavery became less negative in the nineteenth century, partly as a result of creolization, partly because expansion had stopped, partly because of amelioration measures. Barbados and Antigua, for example, had experienced positive growth of the enslaved populations since the late eighteenth century. For Suriname a similar trend is visible. Yet Essequibo and Demerara remained at the forefront of expansion, at least until the abolition of the slave trade in 1807, and therefore still had the associated harsh working conditions and negative demographics.[16]

On a more general level, the demographic conditions in Essequibo and Demerara were consistent with the Caribbean model, with its negative growth, as opposed to the North American mainland model, in which positive growth was the norm. Caribbean colonies typically had higher death rates than births and thus continually imported new African captives to make up for the deficit. Historians have not yet fully explained this regional difference, although currently the onus seems to be on explaining low Caribbean fertility rates rather than high death rates; the fertility of enslaved women on the North American mainland was 80 percent higher than in the average Caribbean colony.[17] In any case, a vicious cycle might have emerged: African-born slaves had lower chances of survival than American-born ones, as the former lacked disease resistance and were usually malnourished from the horrific transatlantic crossing. Consequently, to make up for this loss, planters imported even more Africans, further inhibiting the process of creolization.[18]

A final influence on demography was the type of crop produced, and here Essequibo and Demerara were in line with most of the Caribbean. Sugar was the worst crop for survival rates: whereas coffee plantations saw a demographic decline of 3 percent, for sugar estates this was closer to 5 percent.[19] Sugar cultivation entailed more intensive production: the large investments in mills, draft animals, and boiling houses necessitated a large scale of operation. Furthermore, sugarcane spoiled rapidly and had to be processed as quickly as possible. As a result, the workload for the enslaved increased greatly during harvest time because the mill had to be kept running throughout the night. In addition, crushing cane in the mill was a dangerous job, for if a limb became caught in the cane crushers it would quickly be amputated by an overseer with a machete. The cultivation of coffee was less intensive as the berries did not need as much processing; cotton, in turn, required less labor than coffee.

In Essequibo and Demerara the crop that delivered the most value at the end of the century was cotton. Many planters decided to focus on this crop as its price was, although volatile, generally on the rise in the last quarter of the eighteenth century, partly because of the unfolding of the Industrial Revolution in Britain.[20] Nevertheless, sugar and coffee remained in demand because of the collapse of the Saint-Domingue economy after the 1791 revolution there. As the island had been the biggest producer of coffee and sugar in the world, a sudden stop meant that world prices rose and other colonies saw opportunities to fill the gap. All around the Greater Caribbean, particularly in Brazil and Cuba, planters profited from this development. The enslaved in Essequibo and Demerara, then, produced a mixture of crops but with a focus on cotton. Yet another outside influence altered this structure. After Eli Whitney invented the cotton gin in 1793, it suddenly became lucrative to grow cotton in the United States. A rapid expansion ensued and US planters would quickly outcompete other cotton producers, lowering prices and forcing planters in Essequibo and Demerara to revert to sugar in the early nineteenth century.[21]

So crop regimes mattered a great deal for the structure of the slavery regime and explains to a large extent the difference with neighboring Venezuela, which focused on the cultivation of cocoa. In contrast to sugar, cocoa was less labor-intensive and could be produced on smaller plots. It had been cultivated in Venezuela since the sixteenth century but only became a prominent crop in the eighteenth century, stimulated by the formation of the Caracas Company, which received a royal monopoly on trade with Venezuela in 1728. At the end of the century Venezuela had about 64,000 enslaved workers, of whom at least 60 percent worked in cocoa cultivation.[22]

Slavery in Essequibo and Demerara differed from many other regimes in an additional aspect, namely, the comparative lack of urban slavery. In most societies in the Americas, a large share of the enslaved population worked in urban settings rather than on the plantations. Both on the Caribbean islands and on the North and South American mainland, enslaved people could be found in jobs ranging from dockworker to cleaner and from road builder to saleswoman.[23] However, since an urban settlement did not even exist before 1784, urban slavery hardly played a role in Essequibo and Demerara. In the capital, Stabroek, there were 466 enslaved persons, 238 whites, and 76 free people of color in 1786. Around 1800 these figures had nevertheless increased significantly, to 1,500 whites, 200 free coloreds, and 5,000 enslaved persons.[24]

The comparative lack of urban environments reduced the options for enslaved people to escape from the plantations. Around the Americas, free people of color lived in urban settings, where dark skin was not necessarily equated with slavery. There, runaways could try to pass as free to carve out a new living for themselves. In Essequibo and Demerara, much like in Suriname, passing proved virtually impossible. In fact, in Suriname manumission rates were well below one percent between 1760 and 1820 and the number of free colored people was low. Only later in the nineteenth century did manumission and the share of free coloreds rise.[25] This situation was no different in Essequibo and Demerara: the British, after the takeover, explicitly aimed to limit manumission in order to prevent the creation of a group of free coloreds that did not fit into the racially based plantation hierarchy.[26]

In Essequibo and Demerara, then, the ratio of black to white persons was highly skewed and the numbers of enslaved people continued to grow quickly (see table 3.1).[27] This imbalance meant that the plantation hierarchy was vulnerable, and administrators were well aware of it. For instance, in 1784 Essequibo's Council of Policy instated a rule that every planter should have one white person for every fifty slaves that he paid taxes for. For every lacking white person a fine of 1,000 guilders would be assessed. However, since the number of whites was so small, a two-year grace period was granted.[28] In the end such measures had little effect, and on average a plantation had only three white persons.[29] Heavily outnumbered, many a planter engaged in cruel punishments to maintain discipline.

In fact, Dutch colonial law hardly offered the enslaved any protection: nothing like a Slave Code, or Code Noir, existed, neither in Batavia, nor the Cape of Good Hope, nor the Guiana coast. And while on the Cape in 1754 at least an attempt was made to standardize the various local decrees pertaining to slavery, it took much longer before something of the sort was done in Essequibo or Demerara.[30] There, in 1770, the director-general described the depravity of the situation:

> In the English islands no one may upon his own authority give a slave more than forty lashes and so, to keep on the safe side, no one ever gives more than thirty-nine; it is true that this may be done two days running, but what is that compared with what goes on here? We have no laws, concerning the matter (at least none is known to me) and when I remonstrate I am told that everyone is master of his own slaves and that as long as he does not kill them (i.e. if they but come from the stocks alive) it is no business of the Fiscal's.[31]

On paper the situation improved somewhat in the following years. In 1771 the Council of Policy in Essequibo reacted to complaints from the Dutch Republic about the cruel treatment of the enslaved by publishing a new by-law. It forbade work on Sundays and prohibited masters from meting out "undeserved punishments." If they needed to discipline someone, then it had to be with "a Christian mind" instead of cruelly.[32] No specific limits were set to the chastisements, however. In 1773 the WIC published a by-law for Demerara too, which stated that masters were no longer to abuse their enslaved people or withhold necessities from them. Such cases could be investigated in the future, but the by-law remained vague regarding possible fines.[33]

In 1784 the rules became clearer. Work on Sunday was still prohibited, punishments would be limited to twenty-five lashes, and planters had to provide adequate clothing for the enslaved, as well as sufficient plots to cultivate their own food (one acre per five persons). However, it also stated that the enslaved were forbidden from trading cash crops on their own account, that they had to carry passes if they wanted to

Table 3.1. Enslaved Africans in Essequibo and Demerara, 1735–1832

Year	Essequibo	Demerara	Total
1735	2,600	—	260
1755		920	
1762	2,571	1,648	4,219
1763			
1764	2,915	2,214	5,129
1765	2,918	2,458	5,376
1766	2,978	2,569	5,547
1767	3,119	3,245	6,364
1768	3,284	4,145	7,429
1769	4,543	5,967	10,510
1777	8,289		
1776		More than 9,639	
1779		More than 12,620	
1782	8,700	12,559	21,259
1788	9,574	16,773	26,370
1795	10,612	27,865	38,477
1796	12,678	30,141	42,819
1797	13,579	33,992	47,571
1798	12,360/14,567	36,651/37,431	49,011/51,998
1802			49,451
1817		77,867	
1832		65,556	

Source: See note 27.

leave the plantation, and that tougher castigations were possible but had to be carried out by government officials. The penalties for the planters ranged from 30 guilders (if a slave was sent out at night without a pass) to 900 guilders. The latter related to the gruesome situation when an enslaved person had committed suicide. In such cases the planter had to ask a physician to inspect the body, just as when an enslaved person had died shortly after a punishment.[34] However, sometimes after a suicide the planter put the head of the person on a stick, to interfere with the person's life after death and to terrorize others.[35] The new rules did not prohibit this practice, but it required the approval of a councillor of the Court of Policy first.[36]

One the one hand, these developments can be seen as a step toward awarding legal rights to the enslaved, who could take their complaints about violations of these rules to the fiscal. Indeed, some historians viewed the fiscal as a precursor of the later "Protector of slaves" under the British and therefore argue for a tradition of legal activism by the enslaved. On the other hand, they also acknowledged that the fiscal was a slave owner himself whose main allegiance resided with the plantation hierarchy. Consequently, fiscals dismissed most cases and punished the complainants for "ungrounded accusations."[37] While the sources do not allow such a detailed reconstruction as for the British period, the legal protection for the enslaved should not be exaggerated. Planters remained the masters of their domains, where no one checked the torture they inflicted, nor are there indications that the fiscal actively looked for mistreatment himself. Neither would the planters have been eager to provide a mistreated person with a pass to voice a complaint in Stabroek. An enslaved person might go himself, but such a journey could take several days with little chance of success. And even in case the fiscal would rule in favor of an enslaved person, he or she was unlikely to receive a warm welcome upon returning to the estate.

In short, Essequibo and Demerara were among the worst places to be an enslaved African in the late eighteenth century. With high death rates, a population that was continuously in flux, little legal protection, and the exhausting labor demands of an expanding colony, it is quite remarkable that the plantation hierarchy was able to survive. Desertion proved one of the main ways in which the pressure on the system was released.

The Deserters

Other than everyday resistance in the form of destroying tools and slowing the work pace, running away was the most common way of opposing the slavery regime. Historians have discerned various forms of marronage, including *petit marronage* (temporary absence), *grand marronage* (a definitive escape from the plantation), and step-by-step marronage (hiding near the plantation to stay in contact with loved ones but possibly leading to grand marronage later).[38] This last form is similar to the recent conceptualization of "borderland maroons," in contrast to "hinterland maroons," who sought refuge in inaccessible places farther from the plantation.[39]

For this chapter, I distinguish between "maroons" who formed (either nearby or further removed) societies in the forests in search of "informal freedom" (de facto but not de jure freedom), and "slave refugees," who tried to escape Dutch territory in order to reach the Orinoco, in the hope that the Spanish would grand them "formal freedom"—freedom under the law.[40] Furthermore, this chapter employs the concept of desertion, defined as "unpermitted absence from work."[41] Defined this way, it applies to enslaved runaways as well as to soldiers. In the case of Essequibo and Demerara, soldiers fled in substantial numbers to Orinoco too, sometimes in collaboration with the enslaved. By fleeing, they relieved the pressure on the plantation hierarchy, reducing the likelihood of a mutiny or rebellion.

Indeed, during the eighteenth century the line between free labor and slave labor is best seen as a continuum.[42] Soldiers and sailors were theoretically free to leave *before* and *after* their contract period (although press gangs and imposed debt burdens severely limited this freedom), yet *during* their contract these laborers were far from free.[43] And while their situation was obviously better than that of the enslaved, they were also confronted with poor rations, arduous work, and corporal punishment. For example, on Paramaribo's waterfront and on Suriname's rivers, sailors and slaves performed very similar tasks, and desertion was common among both groups.[44]

While desertion was a characteristic of any plantation society throughout the Americas, the specific manifestation could be said to depend on three types of geography, natural, social, and political, as well as on the stance of the indigenous groups. Natural geography is the most straightforward. For a viable maroon society to establish itself, there had to be a space beyond the reach of the colonial arm, where the maroons would not be discovered easily, where they could plant crops, and where they could hold their own through guerrilla warfare in case of an attack. This space could be the dense Amazon rainforest or the mountains of Jamaica or St. Vincent.[45]

Social geography refers to the extent and nature of the slaveholding settlements: the more widespread the white presence was, the fewer pockets of freedom existed and the greater the chance of discovery for the runaway. Consequently, in the developed colonial society of North America, the enslaved in Virginia and North Carolina were forced to seek refuge in places like the "Great Dismal Swamp" on their border.[46]

Alternatively, they might hide in plain sight, that is, in the urban society of the southern United States. There, the large free black communities that arose in the nineteenth century could harbor the majority of escapees from slavery.[47] In Essequibo and Demerara, with hardly any urban infrastructure to speak of, this was not a realistic possibility.

The third crucial characteristic, political geography, refers to jurisdiction. A runaway might obtain informal or even formal freedom by crossing jurisdictions. Because of their religious sanctuary policy, this opportunity existed particularly if the other side was Spanish. Examples are the borderland of Florida and the later United States, as well as the borderland between the United States and Mexico.[48] Maritime borderlands could offer the same prospect, such as between the Danish Virgin Islands and Spanish Puerto Rico or between Dutch Curaçao and Spanish Tierra Firme.[49] In the case of the latter, slaves from Curaçao could work as sailors, sometimes with a "temporary manumission" for the duration of the journey. Such papers gave them ample opportunity to desert once on Spanish ground and apply for formal freedom there.[50]

The final component to consider is the nature of the relationship with indigenous groups, insofar as those (still) existed. While on Dominica the Caribs remained a separate group, on St. Vincent they merged with the maroons into the so-called Black Caribs. By basically joining forces, the Black Caribs proved to be more than a match for the British colonists in the rebellion that broke out in 1795.[51] Similarly, groups like the Seminoles in North America absorbed black refugees to form powerful communities that could resist white incursion for a long time.[52] On the other end of the continuum, we find situations in which the indigenous collaborated with the colonists to return runaways or divulge their hiding places. Much depended on who the indigenous considered the biggest threat to their livelihood, the runaway Africans or the white settlers. For example, in the Cape Colony in southern Africa, the local Khoi and San groups were hostile to black runaways during the eighteenth century and sometimes worked as trackers. However, as they themselves became subject to the often oppressive labor regime of the Vereenigde Oostindische Compagnie (VOC), the Khoi changed their allegiance and cooperated with the enslaved in a major revolt in 1808. Hence we see that subaltern solidarity emerged against a common enemy.[53]

Taken together, these four elements can also explain the different desertion patterns in Suriname, on the one hand, and Essequibo and Demerara, on the other. In Suriname marronage was a familiar phenomenon since the seventeenth century, and maroon communities still exist today. The remarkable fact was that in Suriname maroon communities could hold their own against colonial forces. In the 1750s military expeditions to subdue them failed, leading to peace treaties in the 1760s with the most numerous groups (the Ndyuka and the Saramaka), on the promise that they would return future runaways.[54] Afterward the Boni Maroon Wars (named for their leader, Boni) would keep the authorities in Suriname occupied and cash-strapped for over two decades.[55] In Suriname, marronage was thus a viable strategy, also because there was no possibility to escape to a different jurisdiction and because passing as free in the small free colored community in Paramaribo was unfeasible.[56] Furthermore, the geography was favorable and the declining Amerindian population refused to aid the colonial society by tracking or fighting maroons, which played out in the favor of the latter.[57]

The situation was markedly different in Essequibo and Demerara. While the exact size of maroon societies remains unclear, they were small in comparison to Suriname. Alvin Thompson mentions that three hundred maroons were living northwest of the Essequibo by 1744 and that Demerara had at least eight maroon settlements in 1795, but these statements are hard to verify.[58] In 1788 the authorities nevertheless noted that 23 maroons were living in the forests of Essequibo and 58 in Demerara.[59] Demerara likely had more maroon societies than Essequibo for it proved much harder to escape to Venezuela from Demerara because of the distance and lack of direct connections such as the Cuyuni River. Regarding Essequibo,, it is interesting to note that the Aripaeño, a present-day group of maroon descendants in Venezuela, claims to descend from slave runaways that came from Essequibo in the eighteenth century.[60] All in all, however, maroon societies had little chance of survival in Essequibo and Demerara because they were frequently destroyed by Amerindian forces, as I discuss below. Moreover, such societies were less likely to be formed in the first place, because (especially in Essequibo) it was more attractive to try to obtain formal freedom in Orinoco.

The Orinoco Escape Option

Already before the Spanish instated their religious sanctuary in 1750, deserters arrived from the Dutch side. Hoping to find informal freedom, many runaways must have abhorred the possibility that they might be sold back into slavery. The Dutch tried to claim the runaways, yet typically without success.[61] Therefore, the Dutch authorities placed their hope in the establishment of a "cartel," a treaty that obliged both parties to return each other's runaways. The Spanish ostensibly had little to gain from such an agreement, for they did not have any people deserting to the Dutch side. Nevertheless, because the Spanish still valued friendly connections with the Dutch at this point in time, they were sometimes willing to accommodate the Dutch requests, although this depended on individual governors.[62]

This cooperation, however, took the form of financial compensation: when a runaway was sold back into slavery the Dutch sometimes received the proceeds of the sale. While a disaster for the runaway, it worked out well for both the Dutch and the Spanish, as Storm wrote in a letter in 1749: he stated that he connived with the Spanish traders coming to Essequibo and that the governor of Cumaná would pay for two deserted slaves from a WIC plantation. At that time a cartel seemed possible too, although the Spanish insisted that the Dutch deliver any deserters in person, while they themselves were only willing to offer monetary compensation.[63] In fact, the exchange agreement would not come to pass until 1791, but the practice of reimbursements continued during the 1750s. For example, in 1754 Storm wrote of three deserters for whom they would receive 400 guilders, minus expenses. One of those was from the Company plantation Agterkerke, sold for 150 pesos or 300 guilders, "which sum he would certainly not be worth here, being one of the greatest rascals that we had."[64]

Yet the situation changed after 1750, and the Spanish sanctuary policy characterized the change in relations between the two European powers: from mutual cooperation to sustain their incipient empires to a more confrontational stance now that the Spanish presence had grown stronger. During the 1760s the Spanish stopped returning the proceeds of sold refugees, making the situation worse for the Dutch planters.[65] The refugees still arrived, but according to Storm the Spanish commandants simply kept the money for the auctioned runaways themselves.[66] Unfortunately, at present it is unclear how many of the slave refugees received freedom and how many ended up in slavery or another form of forced labor. Several Capuchin fathers testified that some were sold but that those looking to embrace Catholicism were set free.[67] At least some went on to live among Amerindians or started small cotton plantations.[68] By the early nineteenth century, apparently close to two hundred refugees lived in Angostura.[69]

All the Amerindian slaves received freedom as well since they were legally free according to Spanish law, or in the words of a friar, "[The Amerindians] being subjects of the King criminally enslaved by the

Dutch, who maintain this inhuman traffic with the Caribs contrary to all law, we cannot and must not restore them to slavery when they have the good fortune to escape it."[70]

The question then arises why not all of the enslaved Amerindians on Dutch plantations chose to desert. After all, they were in a better position than many of the African runaways, being familiar with the terrain and surviving in the forest. Yet, aside from a case in 1727 when twenty-three "red slaves" deserted, there seem to be few instances of enslaved Amerindians running away.[71] The reason might be that Amerindians on Dutch plantations enjoyed a relatively good status and sometimes had the freedom to visit their free relatives.[72] Their skills as hunters, fishermen, and cassava growers were of vital importance for the plantation's food supply, and their labor was not as easily replaced as that of the Africans since a plantation typically had only a very small number of enslaved Amerindians, if any.[73] Furthermore, enslaved Amerindians were mostly from groups living farther into the interior, meaning that fleeing would entail traveling through a region of possible enemies, such as the Caribs. Finally, it is likely that the image of life on the Spanish side was not one of living as free vassals but rather as forced converts in a missionary village.

The Spanish missionary activity, on the other hand, created opportunities for African runaways. The Caribs were vital allies of the Dutch and were rewarded for returning runaways, so their presence in the borderland between the Spanish and the Dutch formed a major hurdle for slave refugees. Hence as the Caribs were forced to retreat at the Spanish advances, more room opened up for African runaways.

The route via the Cuyuni River (map 3.1) became open to slave refugees after the Spanish destroyed the Dutch post there in 1758 and in the process uprooted the local Caribs, who migrated elsewhere. The post was seemingly not reestablished until sometime between 1765 and 1767, and because of the two Spanish missions founded farther upriver, the Caribs did not return. Thus both the Dutch and Carib guards had disappeared. Storm summarized the situation in 1762: "No negroes can get away unless the Indians connive at their escape or unless they go over to the Spaniards, which, since the occurrence at Cuyuni, can scarcely be prevented." Even the reestablishment of the post would not provide any relief for the Dutch planters without the Caribs. Storm wrote, "The road for the runaways is now quite open and free, it being impossible for the Post in Cuyuni to stop them, there being a number of inland paths; nor can we be warned in any way by the Indians, there being no more of these in that river."[74]

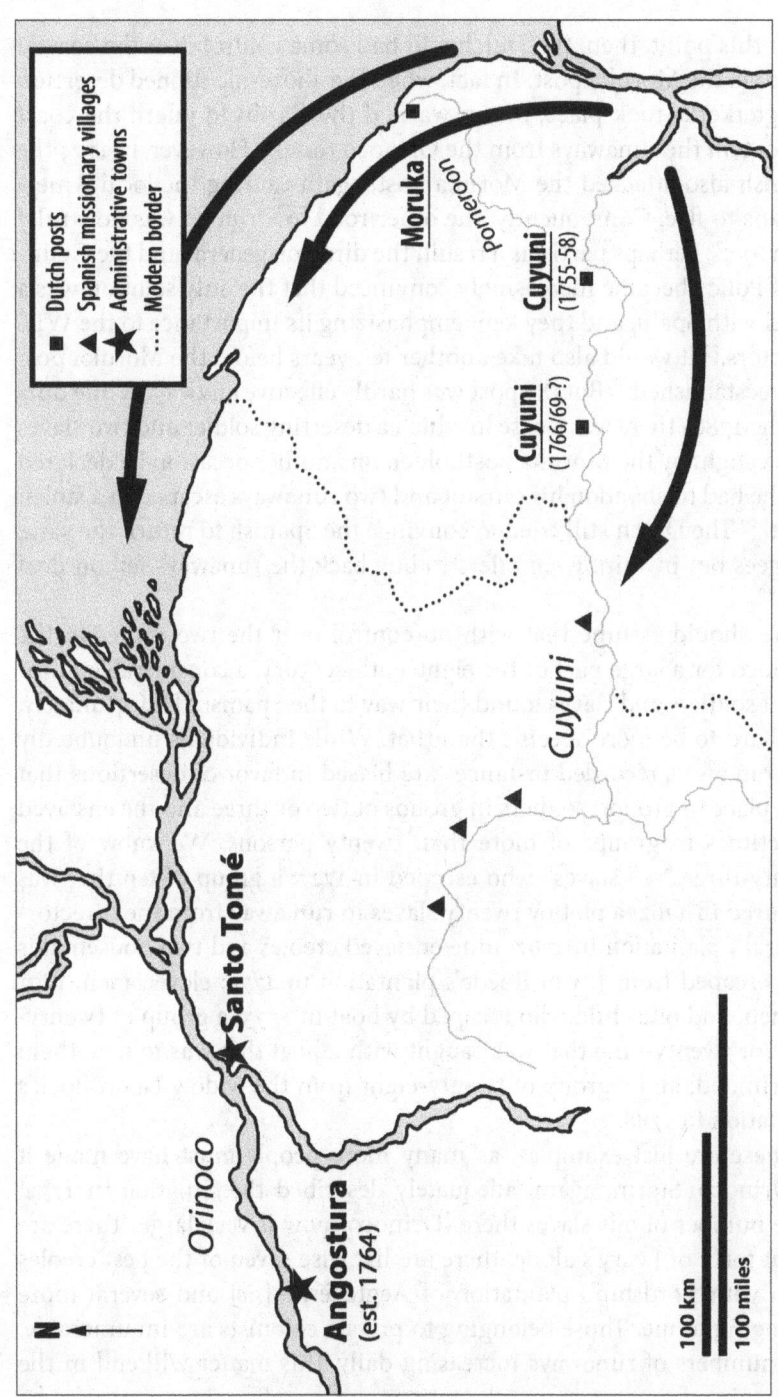

MAP 3.1. The three main desertion routes from Essequibo to Venezuela.

At this point, then, the Dutch still had some control over the coastal route via the Moruka post. In fact, when the above-mentioned desertion at Agterkerke took place, Storm warned the Caribs to guard the coast and cut off the runaways from the Orinoco route.[75] However, in 1774 the Spanish also attacked the Moruka post, again causing the local Amerindians to flee. Consequently, the other road to Orinoco was now fully open too.[76] Perhaps partly as a result, the director-general and the Council of Policy became increasingly convinced that the only solution was a cartel with Spain, and they kept emphasizing its importance to the WIC directors.[77] It would also take another ten years before the Moruka post was reestablished.[78] But the post was hardly effective anyway. While during the 1780s there was a case in which a deserting soldier and two slaves were caught by the Moruka postholder, on another occasion he declared that he had to abandon his pursuit and two runaways escaped in a stolen vessel.[79] The Dutch still tried to convince the Spanish to return the slave refugees but in vain. Even offers to buy back the runaways fell on deaf ears.[80]

We should assume that with no control over the two routes to the Orinoco for a large part of the eighteenth century, a considerable number of soldiers and slaves found their way to the Spanish. Unfortunately, it is hard to be more specific than that. While individuals undoubtedly also ran away, recorded instances are biased in favor of desertions that took place in groups: soldiers in groups of two or three and the enslaved sometimes in groups of more than twenty persons. We know of the twenty-three "red slaves" who escaped in 1727; a group of ten that was captured in 1762; a plot by twenty slaves to run away from the director-general's plantation in 1767; nine enslaved creoles and two housemaids who escaped from J. van Roede's plantation in 1770; eleven men, four women, and one child who escaped by boat in 1773; a group of twenty-eight or twenty-nine that was caught with a boat that was to take them to Trinidad; and a group of twenty-eight from the widow Noordhoek's plantation in 1788.[81]

These are just examples, as many more people must have made it to Orinoco. Storm, again, adequately described the situation in 1772: "The number of our slaves there [Orinoco] now is very large. There are about forty of Leary's alone; there are likewise seven of the best creoles from your Lordship's plantation of Aegtekerke [sic] and several more belonging to me. Those belonging to private colonists are innumerable. The numbers of runaways increasing daily, this matter will end in the total ruin of a great many plantations, unless efficacious remedies be adopted."[82] His successor would echo these sentiments, stating that "no week passes" without desertions, which would soon lead to the "total ruin" of the colony.[83]

In the 1780s the rate of desertion may have declined. During the French occupation, a French envoy to Orinoco had apparently taken several enslaved persons on his trip who witnessed the situation of the slave refugees there. Upon their return, they could disprove any hopes of a free and leisurely life, and this news spread throughout the colonies to deter further desertions. In addition, the story that a recaptured runaway in Essequibo was sold to a merchant from Orinoco seemingly also served to underline that Africans were slaves in the Spanish areas as well.[84] Without additional evidence, it is hard to judge the real effect of these stories, and as discussed above, desertions continued to take place afterward.

In 1784 the WIC thought a similar campaign of deterrence would be useful. A Mr. Perpignan had gone to Orinoco and found a former slave of Mr. Ramaeckers there, who had informed him that refugees were indeed baptised and declared free. However, he reported that their situation was still miserable, as "they are starving, to prevent which they are given, on behalf of the King, their food and drink, or 5 stivers per day."[85] They also had to work on the fortifications or in the mines, a fate not much better than slavery, and indeed some had been reenslaved. Thus the Gentlemen Ten proposed to set up a fund of 10,000 guilders to buy back several Orinoco slaves, to be taken over by their former masters or otherwise by the Company itself. These unfortunate reenslaved Africans would then spread the word about the dreadful Orinoco, after which the absconding would surely cease.[86] However, like all of the WIC's grand plans, the idea was shelved and forgotten.

Regardless, a significant difference in the forms of desertion between Essequibo and Demerara existed, due to geographic circumstances. While the enslaved in Essequibo were close to the Orinoco area, those in Demerara had to travel much farther afield. Furthermore, they could not just steal a boat and sail up a river like the Cuyuni or the Moruka. They either had to go via the ocean, which would be dangerous in an unseaworthy raft, or travel through the forests to Essequibo, with all the risks of getting lost or getting caught. Consequently, it seems that deserters in Demerara more often chose to become maroons as opposed to becoming slave refugees. An additional element that contributed to this development was that Demerara quickly became the dominant colony with the most enslaved laborers and hence more deserters.

Consequently, while the role of Amerindians in preventing desertion became less prominent in Essequibo, it only increased in significance in Demerara. As the Spanish gradually took over the borderland, fewer Caribs remained to act as bounty hunters. Various indigenous groups continued to return deserters in exchange for goods like cottons and rum, yet it did not seem to occur often, and they seemingly never brought back large groups.[87] A possible explanation is that it took time, usually several days, to warn and recruit the Amerindians, giving the deserters the chance to put more distance between themselves and their pursuers.[88]

The Amerindians nevertheless remained vital to the colonists in destroying incipient maroon hideouts. In Demerara it seemed that "step-by-step" marronage was more prevalent, where individuals would try to carve out an existence within reach of their former plantation. This practice seemed to have grown during the 1780s, probably because of the war (1780–84) and subsequent withdrawal of the Amerindians. To counteract this development, it became more common from 1785 on to actively recruit and send out Amerindian search parties to scout the forests for maroons. The director-general reported that there were not many maroons, yet he also stated that their numbers were increasing because the colonists had neglected the problem.[89] These search parties would destroy any huts and provision grounds they encountered, but they usually returned empty-handed or with only a few of the runaways they were expected to capture.[90]

An example of how such small groups of "borderland maroons" could continue to exist is provided by the case of the community living only 150 yards behind the Velserhoofd plantation. In 1789 two enslaved workers from Mr. B. Nugent reported to the Court of Policy that they had encountered two houses while they had been "lost in the forest." There were ducks and fowl walking around, and the men estimated that about a dozen people were living in the hideout. As they approached the houses they set off a bell alarm, after which they were confronted by the maroons and ran away. The fact that the houses were well built and the ground raised to keep out the water suggests that these maroons had been living there for a quite a while and did not intend to make the step toward grand marronage farther into the jungle. Yet now that the discovery was made, they probably had to, for the council decided to send an Amerindian commando "to capture or kill them."[91]

Thus, because of the Amerindians, maroon societies could exist in Demerara but could not easily develop into long-standing and independent groups as in Suriname. Furthermore, while marronage grew with the expansion of the plantation sector, maroon groups did not become a large threat to the plantation society, except during the general chaos of 1795, which I address below. First, however, it is instructive to see what influence the other enforcers of the slavery regime had, namely, the military.

The Other Deserters: Soldiers

Soldiers were expected to safeguard the boundaries of the slavery regime but often undermined them instead. While the living conditions of soldiers were not as bad as those of the enslaved, their status was still far below that of the planter class. Hence desertion was rampant among the military recruits. Karwan Fatah-Black has put the annual rate of slave desertion in the "Dutch Atlantic" at 0.5 percent, compared to 5 percent for soldiers in Suriname.[92] Soldiers, bound by their contracts and the accompanying debts, had the same motive as the enslaved—seeking freedom—but more opportunities to desert.

The precarious equilibrium in which partially unfree soldiers were supposed to keep totally unfree Africans in check could be abruptly destabilized, as became clear in the great uprising in Berbice. There, during an epidemic that severely weakened the white population, the enslaved rose in rebellion in early 1763. The rebelllion spread quickly, and within a month the insurgents, led by an Akan named Cuffy (or Kofi), had overrun most plantations and taken Fort Nassau. The retreating colonists had lost control of the colony and were trapped at an upriver plantation. With reinforcements from St. Eustatius, Suriname, and the Dutch Republic only arriving slowly, the outlook for the colonists was bleak.[93] On 3 July, a mutiny among two-thirds of the soldiers broke out. Their grudges had been building up in the previous months, discontent as they were with the heat, the insects, the bad food, the low wages, and the possibility that at any moment they could succumb to tropical diseases. The many French mercenaries felt intimidated by the anti-French atmosphere, and the situation was made worse for those stationed at the Auriarie post, who had been compelled to clear forests and cut wood. The soldiers considered this slave labor. Yet their commanders had added insult to injury: the local Amerindians were not employed in these tasks, relegating the soldiers to a low spot on the social ladder. Captain Canitz declared that he would "rather see a European than an Indian killed."[94]

In this situation the mutinous soldiers decided to run off and tried to reach Orinoco. However, as it is a long and arduous journey from Berbice, they ran out of provisions and got lost, after which they decided to join the black insurgents. Understandably, the slave rebels were suspicious of the soldiers, and twenty-eight of them were immediately killed, while the remaining thirteen were brought to Cuffy's headquarters. Ironically, for several of them capture meant they would be engaged in slave labor, the very reason for their desertion. In short, as Marjoleine Kars concluded, soldiers were not simply enforcers of colonial boundaries; they also challenged and crossed them.[95] Hence it is worthwhile to see how the behavior of the military influenced the stability of the slavery regime in Essequibo and Demerara.

Desertion among soldiers was in fact a recurring source of concern, and it was one of the main reasons the garrison was always understaffed and functioning below standard. Many soldiers did not even make it to the colony, as the death rate on board could reach 30 percent.[96] And when the recruits arrived, they were generally so indebted that their normal service time of four years was insufficient to clear their debt, despite the fact they still only had a paltry sum to live on. Their outfits were typically ragged as they could not afford new clothing, and their living quarters resembled a sheep's pen, one official wrote.[97] Consequently, many recruits choose to run off. Soldiers were in fact so prone to deserting that Storm had great reservations about employing them in pursuit of slave deserters: "We do not dare to send any one after them, not only on account of the smallness of our numbers, but because it is feared that those who are sent would join the runaways, especially if they have a good boat and provisions."[98]

The main problem in Storm's view was the high percentage of Catholic recruits, who would be tempted to join the Spanish forces on the Orinoco. Storm regularly urged the directors to send Dutch or at least Protestant soldiers, but it proved in vain. In 1768 a group of twelve recruits arrived, none of whom was French according to the accompanying report. However, once disembarked, only three turned out to be non-French: "The others are all French deserters, so that I conclude that your Lordships have been scandalously deceived by the recruiting agents, who are infamous scoundrels."[99]

It even appeared that the Amerindians protested against Frenchmen, whom they would not accept as postholders. When Storm had finally found a suitable candidate, Pierre Martin, to occupy the renewed Cuyuni post, he refrained from appointing him because of Amerindian protests. He contemplated making Martin postholder in Mahaicony, although there the Warao "came to the Post in great numbers and well-armed with the openly expressed intention of murdering a French Postholder had they found one there."[100]

Storm was so fed up with getting French recruits that he told the directors he would send all new French soldiers back on the first departing ship. He also firmly agreed with his son, the commander of Demerara, after another four French soldiers and a sailor deserted together: "The Commandeur of Demerary made a very good guess when he wrote to me on the arrival of the last transport, 'There are again some good recruits for Orinoco.' In this way they will not require any recruits from Europe, if they are so well provided by us." Moreover, in Spanish service these deserted soldiers could become a liability, as Storm observed in the same letter. He heard that some of them planned to attack the Moruka post and perhaps even the plantations below: "Certainly not to pay their respects to the owners."[101]

Sometimes soldiers and slaves joined forces to escape together, and there are even cases of postholders themselves deserting. In 1766 a plot was discovered involving three or four soldiers who wanted to run away to the Spanish with a group of enslaved women, and in 1768 the Moruka postholder, his assistant, and two other whites sought refuge in Orinoco.[102] An interesting case of this subaltern cooperation came before the Court Martial of Demerara on 14 August 1786. Apparently, in July the soldier Flinck had, while drunk, left his rifle at his post and had gone to help two slaves steal a boat from the plantation Vlissingen. The boat was fully rigged, with sails and oars, and the plan was to make off together to Orinoco. However, Flinck was caught; the fate of the two slave refugees is unknown. He tried to defend himself by saying that the enslaved had got him drunk and that his desertion was the result of the harsh punishments he had received as a soldier. The case was a serious one, as mutinous soldiers were a direct threat to the stability of the colony. Desertion was punishable by death. However, while that seemed to have been the original sentence, it was altered to service for life at the fortress. Flinck was thus put on par with the "chain negroes" and was to subsist on a slave ration, although he would receive more clothing and would eat bread instead of bananas.[103]

In short, desertion was a common phenomenon, particularly in Essequibo. Perhaps counterintuitively, it probably increased stability in the long run. By offering an escape route out of the plantation hierarchy, the most daring of the enslaved could get away, who might otherwise have chosen other forms of resistance. In addition, the option of desertion for soldiers reduced the chance of a mutiny, which would otherwise be a good moment for the enslaved to rise up. Yet desertion was less viable in Demerara: lacking a direct connection to the Orinoco region, marronage was the only option, but the Amerindians prevented maroon societies from establishing a permanent presence. Therefore, resistance to the slavery regime took another form in Demerara: insurgency. It is probably no coincidence that the three known revolts, in 1772, 1789, and 1795, all took place in Demerara.

The Rebels

Historians have offered various motives and typologies to explain when, why, and with which goals the enslaved rose up. Eighteenth-century revolts might have been more "restorationist" than revolutionary in character. Rather than aiming to overthrow the system of slavery itself, the rebels sought to rectify a particular wrongdoing, such as an increase in work hours or infringement of "customary" rights.[104] The explanation might be the involvement of mostly African-born men, who sought to regain personal freedom. In contrast, societies with many people born locally, in slavery, were perhaps more likely to spur revolts aimed to overthrow the system of slavery itself. Nevertheless, we must also note that rising up against the plantation class was tantamount to suicide, and as more examples of brutally oppressed revolts spread, the enslaved might have become more cautious.[105] Indeed, violence was part and parcel of the plantation system.[106]

However, most people were primarily concerned with just staying alive rather than initiating rebellions based on revolutionary ideals.[107] As the case of Maddelon already showed, even during uprisings many people focused on their personal survival, for example, by avoiding violence or seizing the opportunity to escape. The resistance in 1795 possibly had more of a revolutionary character, but the previous two revolts, in 1772 and 1789 in Demerara, were more restorationist.[108]

The Callaert Crisis of 1772

From the accounts of Maddelon and others we already know that the immediate causes for the rebellion in 1772 were P. C. Hooft's cruel treatment and Pieter Callaert's incitement to rise up. A transition of ownership was always a potential source of unrest, as a new balance between the master and the enslaved had to be negotiated.[109] Hooft had undermined the existing situation by bringing in enslaved people of his own and increasing the workload and the punishments. Callaert made use of the growing resentment, and when the *bomba* Jacob secretly complained to him about their treatment, he encouraged Jacob's feelings of hatred.[110]

For Callaert, the resentment against Hooft had an economic origin. A thirty-three-year-old Catholic man from Dendermonde in the southern Netherlands, Callaert had only recently acquired the estate (Anna Catharina), yet had apparently overstated his credit facilities. A petition from 1771 suggests that his creditors took possession of the plantation, after which Hooft—the neighbor—apparently acquired it.[111] Previously, mortgage funds in the Dutch Republic had been liberal with granting credit, and dispossessions had been highly uncommon, although times were changing in the early 1770s (see chapter 5). Nevertheless, Callaert still hoped that he would be able to sort out his finances and obtain new credit from the republic. Hence, if Hooft could be removed, he might be able to get his estate back.

In the meantime, Callaert himself, with his Amerindian wife, Juno, went to live on the estate where Mr. Pilleman/Belleman was director. He had taken a gun with him, likely the one he would later hide on the Company road for Jacob to pick up. In an alternative version, Callaert delivered several guns directly, as well as one or more barrels of powder and lead.[112] Regardless, the revolt broke out on 12 August 1772 and Hooft was killed and his weapons' storage plundered. Hooft had planned to sell the guns that now found their way into the hands of the rebels, making them a serious threat to the safety of the colony, especially because the memory of the 1763 revolt in Berbice was still fresh.[113]

At this point the entire plantation was in chaos, and many of the enslaved now faced the terrible decision of choosing sides. Joining the revolt was highly risky, a decision that seemed to entail an inescapable and painful death, as the Berbice rebellion had shown a few years earlier. However, not joining was dangerous too: several of the enslaved testified that the ringleaders Quami and Jacob threatened to kill them if they refused to cooperate or if they ran away. The enslaved woman Lea even mentioned Jacob saying, "We are at war with the whites & from now on you will be our slaves," upon which she responded, "We are not your slaves, we will stay with the whites."[114] The same thing had happened in the 1763 Berbice uprising, where revolutionaries sometimes reenslaved people to continue production on the plantations. Similarly in this case, many people tried to "dodge" the rebellion and, like Maddelon, Hester, and Pierro, chose to flee to the nearby plantation of Struys (probably Zeelugt), which was not overrun. One "Angolan" man named Febus even stated that the loyalty to the whites was spread along ethnic lines, with the Angolan slaves "crying" when they heard of their master's death. In reaction, the enslaved from Amina (Akan from Elmina) threatened to kill them, upon which the Angolans ran off. However, this story is not consistent with other accounts that portray Angolans among the rebels.[115]

After having pressed the enslaved population into this life-defining choice, the rebels went to Edward Martin Bermingham's plantation, De Haag (see map 3.2).[116] There, a firefight ensued with several whites. Callaert was present in the house, although his role in the defense was disputed: according to some he crawled on the floor refusing to fire his gun, while Callaert claimed he shot someone. The insurgents urged Callaert and his wife to come out, assuring the two they would not be harmed. However, Callaert urged them to go away. Some witnesses stated that Callaert gave his gun through a window to Jacob, which would explain why one of the guns of the Bermingham household was missing afterward. Callaert denied the accusation, just as he denied encouraging the rebels to take a boat (*corjaar*) to sail to Amerindian territory (Bokkenland, "Buck country"). Callaert seemed surprised by the turn of events, having apparently hoped the rebels would act later so he could get away together with his wife. Now he was caught in the crossfire, as he had not envisioned the magnitude of the forces that were set loose by his scheme.[117]

Indeed, the genie was out of the bottle, and the colonists were frightened by the rapid spread of the revolt. The rebels attacked other plantations and much of Demerara's west coast was in turmoil. The burgher militia had trouble organizing itself: when two owners of nearby estates, Johann Boode and C. J. Hecke, tried to make a plan with six others to organize their defenses, half of them ran off. Boode and Hecke got into an argument, as each wanted to entrench himself on his own estate rather than leave it unattended. Soon afterward, at least Boode's estate, Uitvlugt, was attacked and burned.[118]

In the meantime, a command center was set up at Zeelugt, where the burgher militia, "Company creoles," and Amerindian reinforcements were assembled. The "Company creoles," presumably enslaved people from the WIC's own long-standing plantations, were important to the colonists' cause, but this applied even more to the far larger number of Amerindians. Storm van 's Gravesande noted that he immediately sent "a sergeant, a corporal, and fifteen men to the coast, together with fifteen armed creoles" and another fifteen men the next day. Indeed, a motley

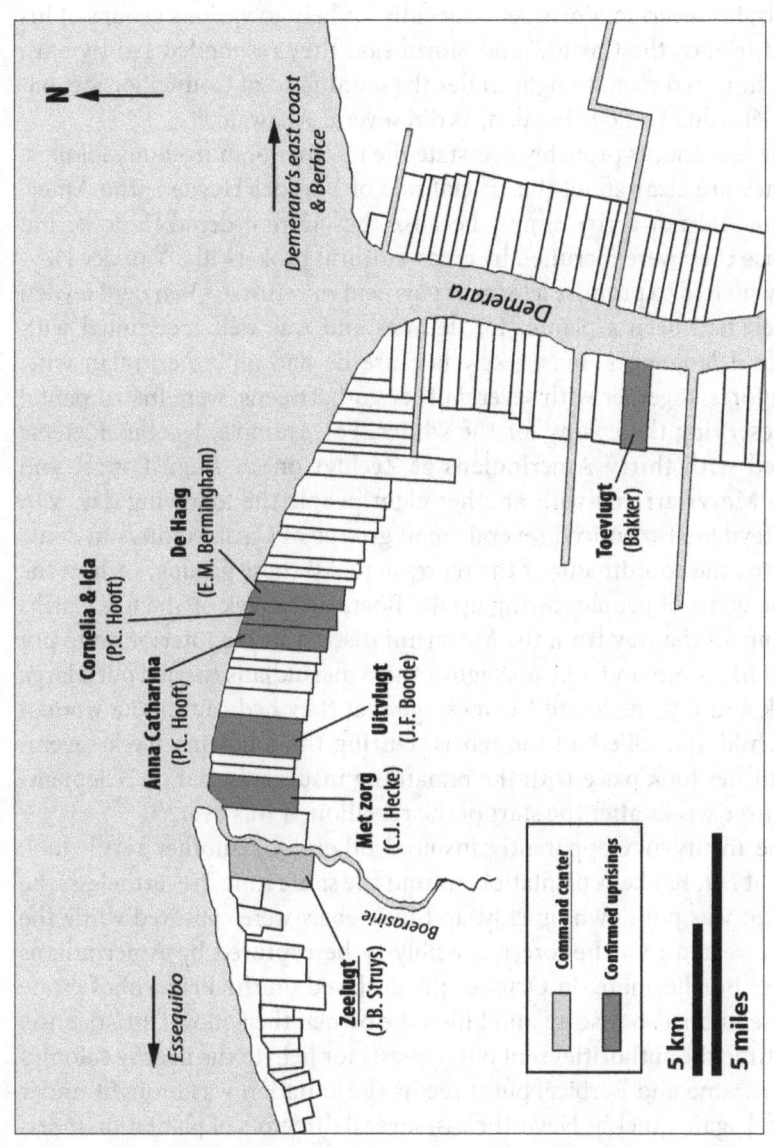

MAP 3.2. Plantations and planters involved in the 1772 revolt in Demerara.

crew of soldiers, civilians, and WIC creoles managed to reconquer Hooft's plantation and kill fourteen insurgents. The rest had retreated into the woods, however, so Storm sent out calls for help to various groups of his "good friends the Caribs," and Storm said they responded swiftly with three hundred men, to fight under the command of Councillor Stephanus Gerardus Van der Heyden, as did several Akawaio.[119]

These accounts probably overstate the number of indigenous soldiers, yet they are clear about the crucial role of Van der Heyden. The Amerindians did not arrive simply because they were ordered to do so but because they were recruited by cross-cultural brokers like Van der Heyden, who had to promise a form of payment in return.[120] Van der Heyden himself had been a planter for decades and was well acquainted with the local languages, most likely because he had an Amerindian wife. His efforts, together with several other go-betweens, were instrumental in preserving the colony for the whites. For example, Jacobus Pieterse arrived with thirty Amerindians at Zeelugt on 19 August 1772, and Jacob Meyer arrived with another eight people the following day. Van der Heyden also enticed several small groups of Carib soldiers to come and was the coordinator of the repression. All these groups, such as the twelve boats of people rowing up the Boerasirie creek or the five Caribs coming all the way from the Mazaruni district in the interior, were put under his command. On 30 August, the Amerindians carried out a large attack and returned with the message that they had captured a woman and child and killed all the rebels. During the following week several skirmishes took place with the remaining insurgents, but on 6 September, three weeks after the start of the rebellion, it was over.[121]

The insurgency apparently inspired others, for another revolt took place at Mr. Bakker's plantation around the same time. Nevertheless, the attempt was put down quickly, and five rebels were captured while the rest retreated into the forest, possibly to be captured by Amerindians later.[122] Furthermore, in October the enslaved on the Princenhof estate in Essequibo also rose up and killed the owner, the widow Christiaanse. This time the authorities sent out requests for help to the nearby colonies of Suriname and Berbice, but it seems the situation was brought under control again quickly. Nevertheless, several directors of plantation mortgage funds in the republic voiced their concerns to the States-General that it was paramount to finally put the colonies' defenses in order.[123]

In the subsequent trials of the captured rebels, the colonists devised a range of cruel punishments to set an example, clearly differentiating between different roles in the insurgency. The harshest verdicts were for those who shot at whites or used obeah to incite others: Howard was to be beheaded, Cobina and Louis were to be broken on the wheel and beheaded, and Neeltje and Gratia were to be strangled on a pole. Afterward, their heads were to be put on stakes and their bodies burned. Others, who were not charged with active participation in violence but had, for example, carried ammunition, at least made it out alive: Hendrik and Bienvenue were sentenced to lifelong work in chains for the colony, Spadille received a flogging in addition, and for Vulcanus "harsh" (*streng*) flogging and branding were added to the same lifelong labor in chains. Similarly, Susanna, Claartje, and Bella were sentenced to chain labor and a flogging, as they had remained with the rebels until the final moment and would not have returned if not captured. Prins and Cocqueray, who "several times" deserted from the whites to the rebels, would be auctioned off at the first possibility, possibly because they were deemed uncontrollable. Finally, the "English negro" Felix would have his ears cut off and would be sent—together with Caesar and Carel—to North America and banished for life; the authorities judged them likely to encourage further rebellions within the colonies and thus too dangerous to remain.[124] Perhaps most interestingly, when Callaert was finally convicted in 1774, he was ordered to be broken on the wheel, beheaded, and burned. In other words, he received treatment similar to that of the slave rebels, so this might be the only time in the colony that white and black were treated equally.[125]

All in all, this was a peculiar revolt, but it speaks to broader themes such as the ease with which a revolutionary spark could be ignited and the importance of Amerindians, both in their role as shock troops far outnumbering the regular military and in their role as scouts in retrieving the rebels that had retreated into the woods. Furthermore, most of the enslaved preferred to dodge the rebellion, trying to stay alive rather than face cruel punishment when the revolt, almost inevitably, was quelled.

The *Bomba* Plot of 1789

Demerara's west coast remained a hotbed for insurgencies, as the familiar plantation belonging to Boode, Uitvlugt, was at the center of a joint rebellion in 1789. It started on 23 September and was organized by seven *bombas* from four different plantations (in addition to Uitvlugt, Vrees en Hoop, Leonora, and Groeneveld; see map 3.3). The motive seems to have been the recent demotion of one of the *bombas*, who then concocted a plot for a larger rebellion against the whites. The leaders had apparently fomented their bonds by drinking from a calabash filled with blood, water, and lemons.[126]

Around nine in the evening, thirty to forty insurgents from the three other plantations arrived at Uitvlugt, armed with cutlasses and machetes, and they proceeded to kill the white servants. Boode himself was having dinner with the plantation's director and was alarmed. The two men grabbed their pistols and managed to deter the rebels from coming upstairs. The insurgents briefly retreated and killed three of the slaves high up in the plantation hierarchy—the crop supervisor (*tuinbaas*), the scribe, and the boiling supervisor (*stookbaas*). The second and third waves of attack on the house also proved unsuccessful. One of Boode's own *bombas* cunningly tried to acquire weapons, by asking his master for guns to defend the estate. His request was denied, however, and a stalemate ensued.[127]

Again, the WIC structures could not cope with the revolt and the authorities cobbled together an improvised coalition of soldiers, burghers, sailors, "mulattoes," and Amerindians.[128] First, about thirty burgher militiamen came to guard the neighboring estates in order to prevent the revolt from spreading. Ships were ordered to anchor in front of the fortress and prepare for action, and the crew of the ship *Galathé* was already involved in tracking down the rebels. In the meantime Jacobus Pieterse and Daniel van der Heyden (the son of Stephanus Gerardus) had to summon as many Amerindians as they could.[129]

The familiar cross-cultural brokers were able to recruit Amerindians swiftly, and from all four "friendly" groups. Already on 26 September, three days after the revolt started, Van der Heyden returned with twenty Caribs and eighteen Arawaks, in addition to two "free mulattoes." Two days later Pieterse reported back with thirteen Caribs, twelve Arawaks, and a "free mulatto." These soldiers were sorely needed, as the burgher soldiers were fatigued and new ones were forsaking their duty. Moreover, another plot was discovered on the plantation of Mr. Sartorius, although the insurgents apparently hid themselves in the woods. In the subsequent weeks additional Amerindian soldiers were recruited until they numbered at least seventy-nine in total. Besides the Caribs and Arawaks, four Akawaios, and five Waraos participated.[130]

Subsequently, the makeshift commando unit set out daily to hunt for rebels in the forest and managed to capture or kill several of them, thinning out the ranks of the insurgents. After a week the colonists felt secure enough to send some of the soldiers back to Essequibo, convinced that only two or three rebels had escaped. One of the leaders, the *bomba* from

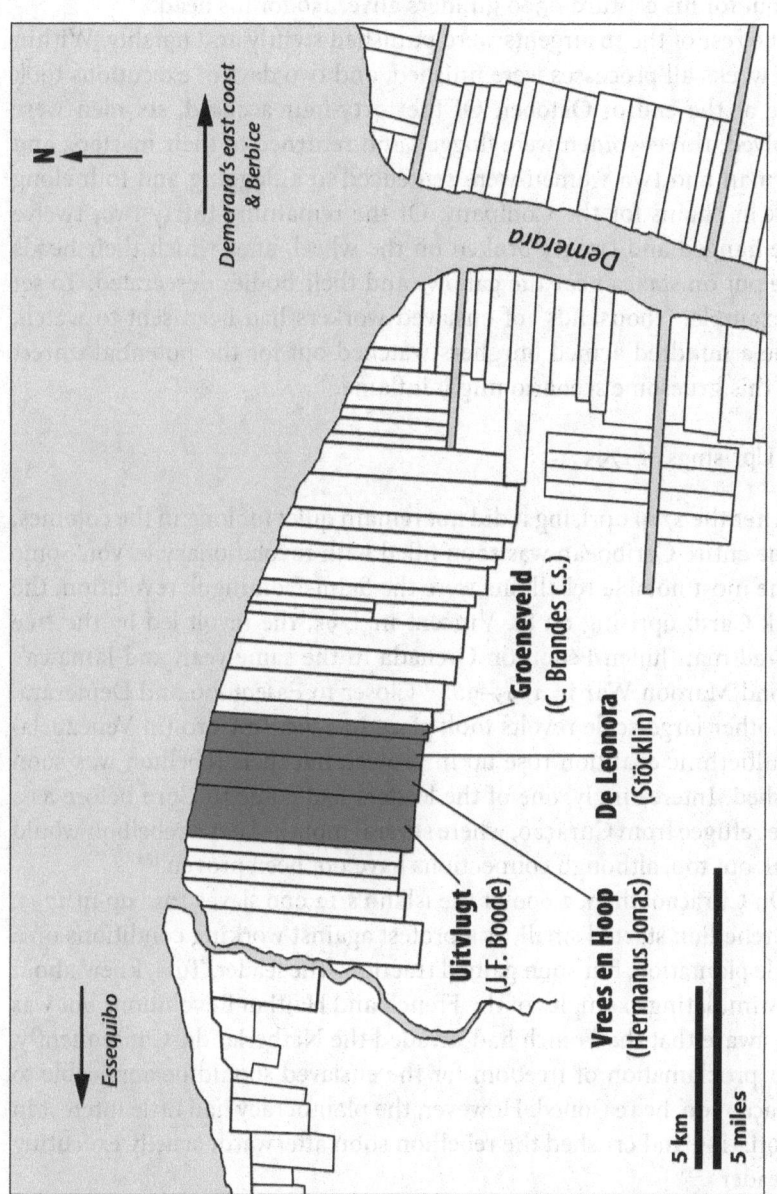

MAP 3.3. Plantations involved in the 1789 *bomba* insurgency.

De Leonora, Jack Nickols, had managed to get away, and a reward was put out for his capture—300 guilders alive, 150 for his head.[131]

The rest of the insurgents were punished swiftly and harshly. Within four weeks all processes were finished, and two days of executions took place at the end of October. Of the forty-four accused, six men were absolved, three women were flogged and returned to their masters, and one man and two women were sentenced to a flogging and to lifelong work in chains for the Company. Of the remaining thirty-two, twelve were hanged and twenty broken on the wheel, after which their heads were put on stakes near the gallows and their bodies desecrated. To set an example, "thousands" of enslaved workers had been sent to watch, while a hundred armed burghers watched out for the potential unrest that this gruesome scenario might inflame.[132]

The Uprisings of 1795

After the 1789 uprising it did not remain quiet for long in the colonies, as the entire Caribbean was soon filled with revolutionary fervor. Some of the most notable rebellions were the Saint-Domingue revolution, the Black Carib uprising on St. Vincent in 1795, the revolt led by the free colored man Julien Fédon on Grenada in the same year, and Jamaica's Second Maroon War in 1795–96.[133] Closer to Essequibo and Demerara, two other large-scale revolts took place in 1795. In Coro (in Venezuela) a multiethnic coalition rose up in protest, but their rebellion was soon crushed. Interestingly, one of the leaders had come to Coro before as a slave refugee from Curaçao, where several months later a rebellion would break out too, although connections have not been proven.[134]

On Curaçao, then, 2,000 of the island's 12,000 slaves rose up in 1795. The rebellion started small, as a protest against working conditions on a single plantation, but soon gained traction. The leader, Tula, knew about the stimulating examples of the French and Haitian Revolutions but was also aware that the French had invaded the Netherlands. Consequently, their proclamation of freedom for the enslaved should be applicable to Curaçao too, he reasoned. However, the plantocracy had little interest in negotiating and crushed the rebellion soon afterward, cruelly executing its leaders.[135]

The exact influence of the French and Haitian Revolutions on the many Caribbean uprisings nevertheless remains debated. While the enslaved did not need abstract ideologies to inform them that freedom was preferable to slavery, planters saw clear connections between the various rebellions and dreaded the spread of revolutionary ideas or people.[136] The fear applied even more strongly to French agitators like Victor Hugues who were sent to the British Caribbean to incite nonwhites to rise up and possibly support them in their effort. Declaring emancipation was a powerful tool to this end, and on many British islands revolts indeed broke out.[137]

Rumors of freedom could be even more important.[138] A persistent rumor circulated around the Caribbean, already before the Age of Revolutions, that the king had declared emancipation but that local planters withheld it. Considering that the French emancipation was declared in 1794, it is understandable that in the next years enslaved people elsewhere also believed they were free.[139] For the enslaved in Dutch colonies, the fact that the French had taken over the Dutch Republic must also have been important, even though this news was reported as a pact of friendship rather than as an annexation.[140]

While the exact reasons for the uprisings in Essequibo and Demerara in 1795 remain unknown due to a lack of sources, it is easily imaginable that the circumstances were favorable. The planters were terrified by the news of Hugues's arrival in nearby French Guiana, as rumors traveled that the two colonies were subject to an impending attack, while the colonists were heavily divided along pro-French and pro-British lines. And after the governor himself had deserted on 5 May 1795, chaos reigned within the colonial apparatus. There might be rumors about an emancipation declaration too, as the timing (May) was similar to the uprising on Curaçao. In this tense situation, the plantation hierarchy was as close to collapsing as it ever was.

In contrast to the revolts of 1772 and 1789, which had a clear immediate cause, the situation in 1795 developed gradually. The planters first noted that their enslaved workers increasingly deserted to the maroon communities living nearby in the forest. For the enslaved, the situation of political chaos might have seemed like the right moment to run away. Further, if emancipation was indeed around the corner, it might be wiser to hide and wait rather than run the risk of being sold or sent elsewhere in the meantime.

Regardless, as in previous cases, the revolt took place in Demerara. There, marronage had increased because of the growth of the plantation sector, while the planters had ceased to fit out enough Amerindian patrols to counter the development. Consequently, by 1795 sizable maroon communities had established themselves behind the plantations (step-by-step, or borderland, marronage). Apparently, the maroons were sometimes even bold enough to trade their produce at the local market. Rumors about a possible insurrection on the west coast traveled around the colony. Consequently, the planters received instructions to keep their enslaved workers away from the back dams, where they would be able to make contact with outsiders.[141]

The colonists were thus in a state of alert. On 14 May 1795—nine days after the governor's flight—the local courts decided to recruit seventy to eighty Amerindians and as many free black and "mulattoes" as possible to send out a large expedition into the forest. The maroons were getting bolder, raiding estates during the night for cattle and other supplies. On 9 June, the idea arose to demand that all free coloreds report for duty, at Stabroek or their militia captain, under punishment of a 50-guilder fine. It took several days to organize this, as the authorities had no idea where these people lived, but in the end it apparently succeeded. The Council of Policy also wanted forty "trustworthy slaves," who several prominent planters promised to provide.[142]

The initial attempts to subdue the maroons proved ineffective. On Saturday, 13 June, the "free mulattoes" Cornelis Karel and Jan van Ersbeek came back with a group of Amerindians, who were lodged and treated to bananas, fish, and rum from the colony's warehouse. On Sunday a group of whites and free coloreds went into the woods, but they were driven back and returned wounded. Subsequently, the nearby ships were asked to supply crewmembers to guard the back dams of the plantations, and the Amerindian squad went into the forest, armed with guns. They returned in vain, stating it was impossible to undertake such a venture during the rainy season. The colonists saw the need to wait, as wet ammunition was useless, meanwhile asking the postholders and several free blacks to recruit more Amerindians. The blacksmith was ordered to produce two hundred to three hundred arrows and repair the broken guns of the Amerindians.[143]

The following week must have been one of growing anxiety for the planters. A large group of maroons emerged on the west coast, behind Haarlem; four armed maroons had tried to convince the guards on La Resource to let the enslaved escape; and on 28 May a rumor emerged that an attack was imminent on La Retraite and the plantations at Canal no. 2 (map 3.4). Yet the attacks did not materialize, and meanwhile the "free mulatto" Benjamin Pieterse (probably related to the Jacobus Pieterse who played a key role in the revolts of 1772 and 1789) arrived with twenty-five Amerindians, promising that seventy more would follow. The colonists struggled to supply all these people with guns, so the authorities bought secondhand guns to be repaired.[144]

There was substantial enthusiasm for the expedition, which is explained by the large rewards that were offered: 400 guilders for a maroon taken alive and 200 for a severed right hand.[145] During the first two weeks of July, some volunteers brought back several maroons, as well as the severed hand of one that was killed. The forest commando unit under Major Louis De Mellet, including the "mulatto" Van Ersbeek and several indigenous soldiers, also brought back a hand and reported to have burned "3 or 4" maroon houses. How their reward was to be divided was not specified, to the later dismay of the Amerindians.[146]

Despite this growing coalition willing to fight the insurgent maroons, the colonists could not yet get a grip on the situation. The rebels managed to raid Windsor Forest and kill the owner, Mr. Clark. Furthermore, two *bombas* of Ruimsigt beheaded a soldier. In fact, the enslaved of Ruimsigt, Haarlem, and Waller's Delight decided to join the insurgents, swelling their ranks. Major de Mellet found his troops so stretched (see map 3.4) that the colonists decided to ask for help from Berbice and Suriname. They wanted a warship and three hundred to four hundred men, but any number would do, they implored. In the meantime the burning of plantations continued, at Rotterdam and Union. On the former plantation the enslaved joined the revolt, on the latter they apparently preferred to dodge the rebellion.[147]

As the army of rebels could thus continue to grow, the planters realized the insurgency could quickly spiral out of control. On 24 July they ordered all plantations on the west bank and west coast of Demerara to pierce their back dams, in order to flood any territory behind where the rebels might be hiding. In this proclamation, the authorities noted that a broad attack was necessary and quickly. While the plantocracy's number would decline—because people got exhausted and Amerindians might wish to return home—the insurgents would only increase in strength. Thus, if they waited any longer, they "might be obliged to evacuate that part of this Colony entirely."[148]

The situation thus seemed critical, but during the remainder of July the colonists regained some of the initiative. The capture of individual or small groups of maroons continued to the extent that the fort became too small, so some were kept in custody on a ship. Daniel van der Heyden and a group of Amerindians together prevented a group of slaves from joining the rebels. Indeed, contrary to their fear, the number of Amerindian soldiers continued to increase, while the ship *de Zeemeeuw* arrived from Berbice to lend support. Sailors from other ships were already serving as volunteers, so the colonists assembled a diverse group to start a

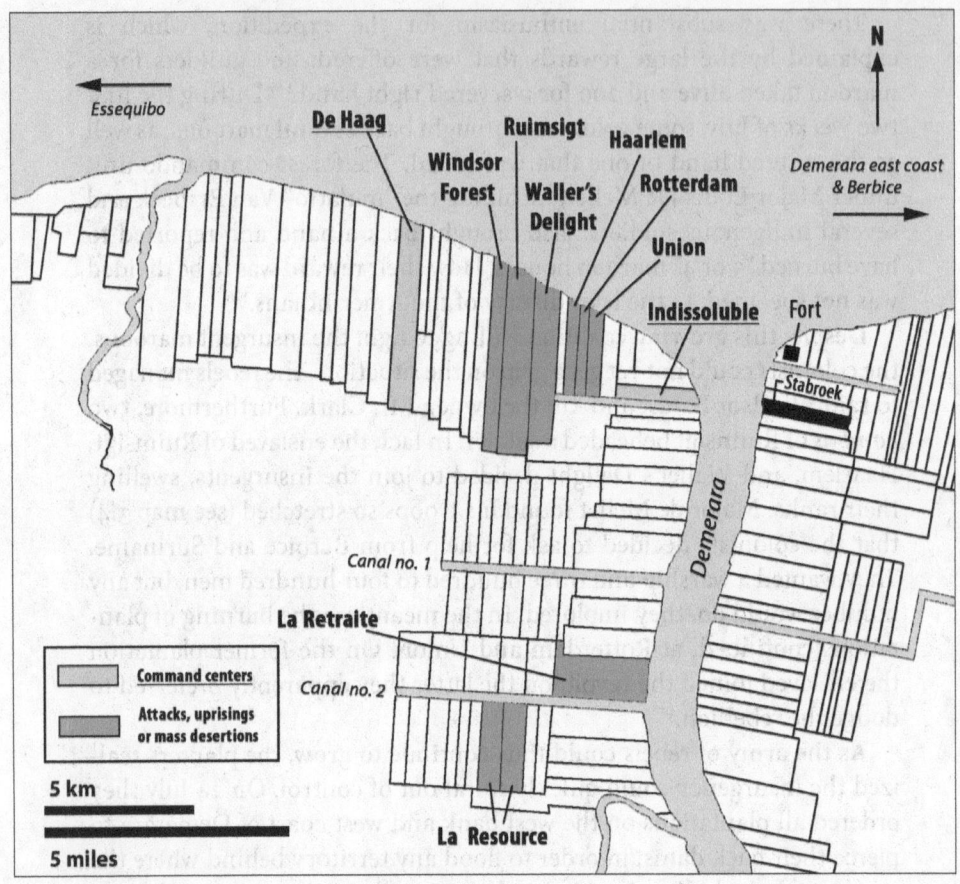

MAP 3.4. Uprisings, desertion, and maroon attacks in 1795.

large-scale counter offensive.[149] A rule was instated that every planter had to sell one slave for every fifty he possessed, and those would be bought by the authorities to form a Black Corps. Similar to elsewhere, freedom was promised to these men and thus finding volunteers proved easy enough.[150]

The aim was to encircle the maroons and launch a big offensive. Therefore, the colonists sent out two commando groups, each composed of Amerindians, fifty soldiers of the Black Corps, and several burghers and white volunteers. The Amerindians proved essential as scouts, preventing the commandos from being ambushed and discovering the multiple hideouts of the maroons. Most of the insurgents were apparently shot; women and children were taken prisoner. After this violent clash the groups returned, and "seventy black arms were displayed on the points of their bayonets." Afterward, the resistance was broken and the trials began. Thirteen rebels were broken on the wheel, and the ringleader was burned at the stake while his flesh was pinched out with red-hot tongs.[151]

The commando troops, on the other hand, were handsomely rewarded, for the expedition is said to have cost 154,000 guilders.[152] The commando leader, Major de Mellet, received a ten-year tax exemption, and the captains Le Blanc and Van der Heyden each received 1,500 guilders. The Amerindians received 5,500 guilders' worth of goods.[153] A total number of 357 Amerindians were eligible for rewards, which consisted of "rations" and one-half Portuguese Joe (worth 11 guilders) for the common soldiers, with higher payouts for their commanders. Yet the Amerindians were dissatisfied with this remuneration, since they claimed they had not received anything for their help in the previous uprising. Moreover, as the planters had been so desperate when calling for their help, the Amerindians were not expecting such stinginess now. Promises were therefore made to exchange the Amerindians' heavy rifles (which they had probably received for the expedition) for smaller hunting rifles and powder and shot.[154] Whether these promises were kept is unknown, but the colonists nevertheless recognized the importance of Amerindian support in upholding the slavery regime.

The slavery regime in Essequibo and Demerara, then, was an unstable and oppressive system that nevertheless managed to survive until Emancipation in 1833. Ten years earlier, in 1823, Demerara was the site of another uprising that ranks among the major slave revolts in the Caribbean.[155] During the eighteenth century, however, the stability of the slavery regime was sometimes challenged but never threatened. In contrast, in Berbice the enslaved were able to liberate a substantial part of the colony in the 1763 revolt, and in Suriname the colonists had to sign peace treaties with maroon groups that proved too powerful. In Essequibo and Demerara, the situation was markedly different.

Desertion and Amerindian involvement were crucial in this trajectory. Desertion functioned as a safety valve: it reduced the likelihood of a mutiny by the soldiers (as occurred in Berbice), and it offered the enslaved an alternative to violent insurrection. Unfortunately, it is impossible to quantify desertion in Essequibo, or the extent to which runaways received full freedom once they reached the Spanish. Nevertheless, the promise of "formal" freedom (as opposed to the "informal" freedom" of marronage) must have acted as a powerful incentive to flee from the brutal regime of bondage.

For those in Demerara, the long road to Venezuela made formal freedom an all too distant promise. Hence both borderland and hinterland marronage were more frequent in Demerara, when compared to Essequibo. Furthermore, the three revolts discussed above all took place on Demerara's west coast. It remains to be seen why this particular area was such a hotbed of resistance. Crop regimes might offer only a partial explanation: the west coast was dominated by coffee, as opposed to cotton on the east coast, but that fails to explain why the more inland sugar estates—the crop with the toughest labor regimes—were not at the center of resistance. Other explanations might be particularly cruel masters (as in the case of P. C. Hooft in 1772) and possibly the remembrance of previous uprisings on a plantation and the martyrs who died in them.

Regardless, uprisings had little chance in Essequibo and Demerara because of the support of Amerindian soldiers (particularly the Caribs). Their role was crucial during periodic raids against incipient maroon villages as well as during uprisings. Without them, rebels might have settled in the forest as maroons after a failed uprising. There, they might hide and launch new attacks later. This scenario the colonists feared the most, as they did not want to end up like in Suriname. In Essequibo and Demerara, however, the Amerindians made sure any remaining insurgents had nowhere to hide. As a result, there was little chance that an alternative power base to the plantation hierarchy could develop. Hence the plantation complex proved more stable than might otherwise be expected.

Importantly, this stability was shaped by local factors and local actors and their interethnic alliances on the ground rather than metropolitan military support. Nevertheless, broader developments and connections also influenced the lives of the enslaved: vital provisions often came from the wider Atlantic network, with all the risks that it entailed; in times of war, food shortages were likely. The next chapter looks into these and other trading networks, including the slave trade itself.

4 / The Centrality of Smuggling

> *Concerning [your plan] to place sentinels on incoming vessels to prevent fraud, which comes across to us as, to use that manner of speech ["]to tie a blind horse["], as no clandestine imports of unpermitted products occurs here, nor is anything brought in that pays incoming duties, which has to remain this way, in order not to hamper the import of provisions which is their only cargo and in order not to subject us and our slaves to shortage, and even if such [clandestine import] takes place a sentinel even if he never slept would not be able to prevent it.*[1]
> —Essequibo Council of Policy to WIC, 31 January 1774

In the above long-winded sentence Essequibo's government accurately captured the trading situation in the colonies: the provision trade, conducted in foreign ships, was essential for the survival of the colonies and should be left alone, free from duties. While the council knew these provision traders sometimes exported plantation products illicitly, it reassured the WIC. In Orwellian doublethink, the councillors denied that illegal trade took place while confirming it was impossible to prevent it.

The commercial web in which Essequibo and Demerara participated had a unique, interimperial shape. It was a local renegotiation of the inapt legislative framework that constituted a Dutch version of mercantilism, as I argue below. Officially, as in most of the other European empires, the two colonies were bound to the Dutch Republic: supplies had to come from the metropolis in Dutch ships, and products had to return via the same route. Yet in practice these connections proved insufficient, particularly with regard to colonial imports. Therefore, in 1742 the WIC allowed foreign traders to bring building materials into Essequibo—an exception that quickly grew into the standard practice of allowing foreign provisions as well.[2] These suppliers were only allowed to take bills of exchange and secondary products in return, such as wood, rum, and molasses. The primary products—the cash crops sugar, coffee, and cotton—were only allowed to go to the Dutch Republic. Similarly, the slave trade remained restricted to Dutch traders as well, despite their inability to meet the demand in the colonies. This official framework increasingly grew out of touch with the situation in the colonies, and illegal trade filled the gap. Though many cash crops still ended up in the metropolis, the commercial web that sustained the colonies was firmly rooted in contraband trade.

This chapter investigates how the colonists reacted to the mercantilist trade regime and how their improvised interactions created a trade network that allowed the colonies to survive and expand despite the circumstances. The chapter begins with a discussion of the trade regulations and demonstrates how Essequibo and Demerara were disadvantaged by a Dutch version of mercantilism. It then returns to the colonial level and in three sections analyzes the main branches of commerce: the imports of basic necessities, the exports of cash crops, and the trade in enslaved Africans. Here the borderless nature of the colonies affected both the commercial and the slavery regime. It made smuggling relatively easy, but it was also condoned by local officials who recognized the importance of unofficial trade.

Making Sense of Dutch Mercantilism

The phrase "Dutch mercantilism" may sound strange, as the Dutch are more typically depicted as the "antithesis of mercantilism" or "the champions of free trade."[3] With an unprotected home market and a history as interimperial brokers, the Dutch might seem like the opposite of a mercantilist country like Britain. There was indeed a period when Dutchmen played a disproportionally large role in the Atlantic. They contributed to the start of the plantation complex in the French Caribbean, to the slave trade for the Danish and the Swedes, and to the Jewish diaspora in the Americas.[4] However, this "Dutch Moment" was over by the late 1670s.[5]

By that point, as many historians have noted, the Dutch were increasingly pushed aside by the mercantilism of the French and the British, whose *systeme d'exclusif* and Navigation Acts aimed to reduce their reliance on the Dutch and favor their own states' interest.[6] Furthermore, Brazil, the biggest imperial possession of the Dutch, was lost in 1654. After the "Dutch Moment", then, a new phase started, in which the Dutch territorial empire was confined to the Guiana coast and their middleman role substantially reduced.[7]

Nevertheless, the island colonies of Curaçao and St. Eustatius still performed important brokerage functions. As free ports, they proved lucrative entrepôts where traders from all nations could buy and sell goods they could not legally exchange within their own empire. St. Eustatius fulfilled this role of illicit hub mainly for the nearby French and English possessions, while Curaçao looked mainly toward Spanish America, supplying tens of thousands of enslaved Africans. As one historian summarized it, "Dutch Caribbean transit trade was largely an illicit affair. Smuggling was so important to the Dutch Antilles that it was almost their *raison d'etre*."[8] Atlantic commerce thus remained important to the Dutch economy—even more important than the trade with Asia—as large amounts of foreign sugar and coffee was channeled to the republic via Curaçao and St. Eustatius.[9]

Yet the Dutch struggled to formulate an answer to the mercantilism of others and in the process ended up with their own version of mercantilism. While "mercantilism" is a contested concept, in the eyes of both contemporaries and historians, here it is sufficient to note that the Dutch tried to have their cake and eat it too, by trying to combine free trade and a closed system. On the one hand, the Dutch diverged from the British and French path by keeping their home market open, having only negligible tariffs.[10] By welcoming foreigners to bring their tropical commodities to the Republic, the Dutch secured a maximum input of raw materials for their sugar and tobacco refineries and kept prices low. Furthermore, Curaçao and St. Eustatius fulfilled the same role: they funneled raw materials from foreign empires to the Republic that could then be sold back to them at a profit, once refined. These exchanges contributed to the image of the Dutch as free traders. They even made mercantilist sense, as they would stimulate the Dutch industry and boost its balance of trade.

On the other hand, the Dutch tried to follow a closed model when it came to their own colonies. The plantation economies in the Guianas also had to serve the interests of the refiners by providing raw materials. Therefore, they were prohibited from trade with foreigners, like planters in most other empires. Over time, however, foreign traders were allowed to bring in provisions, as the Dutch failed to satisfactory fulfill this function. For example, since 1704 North Americans were allowed to bring horses, foodstuffs, and sundries like candles into Suriname, and after 1742 the import of foreign building materials was allowed in Essequibo as well.[11] Importantly, the cash crops still had to go exclusively to the Dutch Republic. These partial openings to imports are thus best seen as efforts to improve the Dutch version of mercantilism rather than in contradiction to it.

Instead, the Dutch version of mercantilism reserved an important place for monopolistic companies.[12] The Asia trade was completely controlled by the Dutch East India Company (VOC), and the WIC had a strong influence in the Atlantic world, controlling Curaçao, St. Eustatius, Essequibo, and Demerara and a part of Suriname.[13] The WIC held the slave trade monopoly too, although it was frequently circumvented.[14] However, in 1738 the WIC deemed the slave trade unviable and opened it to private traders. This privatization did not entail relinquishing the monopoly, for the slave traders had to pay the WIC a "recognition fee" of 20 guilders per enslaved African.[15] The WIC thus became an administrative rent-seeking body, taxing the trade of others rather than engaging in trade itself. While it taxed too much in the eyes of colonists, it taxed too little for effective governance.

Therefore, Dutch planters lacked the benefits of mercantilism that colonists in other empires enjoyed, such as a strong navy and high prices for their crops. The WIC had to ask the States-General to provide protection for merchant ships, and indeed convoys were sent out to Suriname in 1748.[16] However, by then the Republic had become a second-rate power and had trouble financing its naval commitments.[17] The convoys therefore soon became infrequent and Essequibo or Demerara was excluded anyhow.[18] Furthermore, while British colonists received inflated prices for their tropical commodities on their protected home market, Dutch planters were paid the lower prices of their competitive open market.[19]

Essequibo and Demerara were thus caught in an uncomfortable mercantilist straitjacket. They were seen as producers of cash crops and generators of trade but only as long as it was Dutch trade. The Dutch Republic favored free trade when it meant siphoning off the produce of other empires but preferred restrictions when it came to its own colonies. But as in other empires, a closed system proved a chimera, as supplies from the metropolis were inevitably more expensive than those procured from North Americans.

During both peace and war, North Americans eagerly exported building materials and foodstuffs to colonies in the Greater Caribbean and imported cash crops and molasses.[20] In fact, North American skippers completely outcompeted Dutch in the trade to Suriname by the late eighteenth century. In 1789 the slave trade to Suriname was opened to non-Dutch traders, and Americans quickly seized this opportunity.[21] In contrast, the slave trade to Essequibo and Demerara remained closed to outsiders, probably because Zealand, as the main slave trading province, considered it its own prerogative.

In other words, Essequibo and Demerara were not allowed to rely on foreigners but could not count on Dutch shipping either. As discussed above, the WIC Chambers of Zealand and Amsterdam competed with each other over preferential trading rights. The compromise of 1772 was complicated and did not solve the underlying issue, as in 1788 it apparently was necessarily to restate it.[22] Furthermore, as we shall see below, calls to ease or lift the mercantilist restrictions went unheeded. In the end, then, the reason Essequibo and Demerara nevertheless expanded so quickly was their improved intra-American web. Again, the borderless nature of the two colonies proved to be their greatest strength.

Provisions by the Barrel

As table 4.1 shows, the connections with the West Indies and North America were almost always more important than Dutch ones, not only in numbers, but also in tonnage. With an average size of 230 tonnes, the Dutch transoceanic vessels were about four times larger than the intra-American ones (average of 58 tonnes in 1792).[23] Yet these small sloops, snows, schooners, and brigantines had other advantages: they were fast and cheap and spent less time in ports, allowing them to make several voyages a year, in contrast to a single transatlantic voyage. Furthermore, because they could sail sharper to windward (45 degrees, as opposed to 60 degrees), these smaller vessels could outmaneuver bulkier patrol ships, a useful ability when on a smuggling voyage.[24]

The Dutch bilateral trade was nevertheless still important. Dutch shipping increased significantly after 1770, as the compromise between Zealand and Amsterdam now allowed the latter's merchant fleet to sail to the two colonies. Furthermore, during the 1760s and 1770s Amsterdam merchant-bankers also invested heavily in West Indian plantation mortgages (see chapter 5). One of the conditions was that a planter was obliged to send all his exports to the mortgage fund director in the metropolis and obtain all his imports through him too.

Yet for many of the provisions the latter obligation hardly made sense, and many chose to rely on the cheaper intra-American supplies instead. The fund directors were not particularly strict in enforcing this clause. Many provisions were hard to obtain from the republic, and regional imports lowered exploitation costs, reducing the likelihood of default. The overview of 1779–80 from an important mortgage fund illustrates this point: twenty of the thirty-one planters ordered goods worth less than 1,000 guilders, and seven of those would appear to get by with less than 100 guilders in goods for one year.[25] As these amounts were far from enough to run a plantation, let alone pay for the luxurious life

Table 4.1. Vessels arriving in Essequibo and Demerara, 1700–1799 (annual average)

	Total	Dutch Bilateral	Dutch Slavers	Intra-American	% Non-Dutch	Estimated Dutch Tonnage	Estimated Intra-American Tonnage
1700–1709	4.8	1.3	0.5	3	63	299	174
1710–19	7.9	1.5	0.4	6	76	345	348
1720–29	12.3	2	0.3	10	81	460	580
1730–39	16.4	1.9	0.5	14	85	437	812
1740–49	24.8	3.1	0.5	21	85	713	1,218
1750–59	47	4.2	0.3	43	91	966	2,494
1760–69	77.1	7.1	1.7	68	88	1,633	3,944
1770–79	141.2	14.6	2.4	124	88	3,358	7,192
1780–89	138.9	21	1.8	116	84	4,830	6,728
1790–99	228.6	16	0.5	212	93	3,680	12,296
Average	69.9	7.3	0.9	61.7	83	1,679	3,579

Source: Van der Oest, "Forgotten Colonies," 334; author's calculations.

many planters enjoyed, many of the provisions must indeed have come from the intra-American network.

There was an intricate web of intra-American suppliers. Although the archival material pertaining to Essequibo and Demerara generally does not permit a comprehensive breakdown of the different origins, a sample from the second half of 1775 offers a good indication.[26] It deals with forty-six intra-American carriers, as their cargo is listed in detail. (Other lists typically only refer to the wares of the large transoceanic ships as "general merchandise.")

The Greater Caribbean network provided both building materials and foodstuffs. Starting with the former, lime and bricks were regularly brought to Demerara: during the sample period, 835 barrels, 11 "small barrels," 600 bushels and 404 hogsheads of lime, 607 hogsheads of limestone, and 12,800 bricks were brought in.[27] While the colonists could obviously turn to the rainforest for wood, only a limited capacity existed to convert the logs into timber. As a result, Essequibo and Demerara exported timber and, to a lesser extent, planks for shipbuilding while simultaneously importing planks and shingles.[28] Some shingles (for roofs) were made locally, but the sample also shows that in the second half of 1775 no less than 324,000 shingles were imported, in addition to the large amount of 272,200 planks and 76,800 feet of planks.[29] This processed wood was said to be two-thirds cheaper from the intra-American network than if it was acquired via the metropolis.[30] Imported wood and metal products were also vital to construct the sugar and coffee barrels in which the cash crops were transported, and during the sample period intra-American traders delivered 12,000 pieces of stave wood and 2,000 hoops. Finally, to put everything together, nails were necessary. These probably came mainly from the metropolis, although in the sample we find 10 small barrels arriving via St. Eustatius.[31]

Food and drink reveal a similar dependence on intra-American trade, as metropolitan supplies were unreliable. Storm van 's Gravesande already reported in 1744 that he did not have enough flour in store to feed the military, and a year later he noted that without English provisions the entire colony would have been living on "a crust of dry bread."[32] Storm frequently complained about the situation and asked for more reliable provisioning from Zealand, such as in October 1766 when he noted that it had been 25 months since the colony had last been supplied. Rhetorically, he asked, "Is it possible to live 25 months with what had been sent for a year? The plantations and slaves have suffered the most because of this."[33] And in November 1769 he remarked that "if the English were not to come here, the Colony would be unfortunate indeed; this is very costly, too, both for the Company and the planters."[34]

Indeed, the enslaved were most vulnerable to food shortages, all the more because planters ignored the rules about allocating enough provision grounds (*kostgrondjes*) on their estates.[35] Securing supplies therefore became crucial to the colonies' stability. Fish was a staple of the enslaved workers' diet, so the fishing waters on the Orinoco mouth were of crucial importance. Yet the diplomatic difficulties outlined in chapter 1 disrupted this fish supply at times. The Orinoco region also supplied oxen and cattle, an important source of meat, although subject to the same uncertainties.[36] Similar fluctuations affected the salted fish, *bakkeljauw*, herring, and *stokvis* that North American traders brought, as their War of Independence made shipping more risky.[37]

Nevertheless, the sample illustrates the diversity of imported food and drink, including large cargoes of meat, fish, flour, butter, and drink. To be precise, the imports consisted of 391 barrels of "meat," 155 barrels of bacon, 600 pounds of ham, 19 live cows, 115 hogsheads of "fish," 380 barrels of herring, 22 barrels of mackerel, 19 small barrels of salmon, 76 hogsheads of dried fish, 2 barrels and 39 hogsheads of *bakkeljauw*, 710 barrels of flour (*bloem* and *meel*), 60 barrels of ship's bread, 115 barrels of butter, 2 baskets and 1 case (*kas*) of cheese, 11 small cases (*kisjes*) of oil, 60 cases of soap, 260 boxes of candles, 40 *kelders* of gin (*jenever*), 38 tierces of rice, 500 bushels of salt, 10 hogsheads and 20 barrels of tobacco, 30 barrels of green peas, 10 boxes of "wine," 23 barrels, 27 quarter casks, 11 hogsheads, and 1 pipe of Madeira, and 31 barrels and 4 hogsheads of porter.[38]

The origins of these products were diverse. Among the previous harbors that were listed by the captains, we find small islands like Martinique, St. Christopher (St. Kitts), and Bermuda, but the connections with the North American mainland proved more numerous. In order of importance, New York, Philadelphia, and "Georgia" were the three most frequented American ports and the principal suppliers of planks, shingles, and horses. The most frequent trading partners were St. Eustatius and Barbados, from where the main supplies of meat, butter, fish, limestone, flour and candles were brought. However, the ultimate source of these products was most likely the North American mainland.[39] Thus an important web of connections existed within the Americas, and all of this commerce had to be paid for somehow. The result was a lively contraband trade.

Clearing out Cash Crops

Unfortunately, export statistics are difficult to compile for Essequibo and Demerara. Until the British takeover, no customs house existed, which meant that the registration of the incoming and outgoing ships and cargoes was sketchy at best. Different officials recorded traffic in their own ways, sometimes in great detail, often just noting origins, vessel types, dates, and a general description of the cargo. No running series or annual overview of trade statistics seems to have been compiled, nor were the Company directors particularly interested in them. This improvised way of dealing with trade is in stark contrast to the standardized practices of the British, where the same forms recorded traffic in the North American as in the Caribbean colonies.[40]

Therefore, the forms from surviving port books can be used to reconstruct the smuggling network of Essequibo and Demerara, by looking at their British trading partners. For example, illicit exports of cotton would not show up in Demerara's books, yet it was apparently less of a problem for the same ship to declare these goods once arriving at Barbados. The entry and exit books of Antigua, Barbados, St. Christopher, Dominica, Grenada, and St. Vincent, although incomplete, thus constitute a valuable source. The data are scattered but seem relatively complete over the period between 1784 and 1789, with the best documented years from 1786 to 1788.[41] Few smugglers would have declared their contraband cargo, so the numbers presented below are an underrepresentation of the extent of the smuggling, but nevertheless give an indication of the patterns.

Like many intercolonial merchants, the traders in this network combined legal trade in provisions with illegal trade in cash crops and even in enslaved Africans.[42] For instance, on 29 January 1785 William Cunningham left Antigua for Demerara at the helm of the sloop *Betsey*, with eighty African captives on board according to the books.[43] Cunningham was a regular smuggler, for we find him arriving in St. Christopher in April and July, coming from Demerara with an illicit cargo of respectively 12 and 65 bales of cotton.[44] Up to 1789 another eight illicit slave voyages by other skippers can be identified via the foreign exit books, carrying an additional 343 slaves. Two of these ships came from Antigua, two others from Dominica, and the remaining four from Barbados. They all carried 10 to 60 captives, except for Benjamin Wright on the *Margarita*. Coming from Dominica and flying a Dutch flag, he had 130 enslaved Africans on board.[45] The most active smuggler was James Bisshop, who regularly traded between Demerara and Barbados. According to the entry books, he made seven voyages on the sloop *Good Intent* from Demerara to Barbados in 1786 and 1787 alone. On two occasions he included enslaved Africans among his inward cargo, which otherwise consisted of familiar items like porter, nails, beef, and candles. And on each of these voyages he illicitly exported cotton, in addition to his cargoes of hardwood. The total was 306 bales, varying between 8 and 81 bales at a time.[46]

If we look at the overall sample between 1784 and 1789, we can trace 67 ships departing from Demerara. Of these, only 19 did *not* declare that they were carrying contraband of some sort. The other two-thirds mainly carried cotton as their illicit cargo, on average 39 bales at a time (compared to an average of 96 bales for cotton-carrying vessels to the Dutch Republic).[47] Only one ship was active in the (legal) rum trade, while five smuggled small amounts of coffee out, to a total of 69 bags. In other words, the smuggling of cotton was much more pervasive than that of coffee. Considering that many of these small vessels visited the two colonies, the illicit network was impressive. Indeed, men like Cunningham,

Wright, and Bisshop were the ones who built a West Indian web by pursuing their own interests in both the legal and the illegal trade.

If we zoom out a bit, the picture arising from the above anecdotes can be confirmed using statistics of 1784 and 1785 that accidentally reveal the extent of smuggling. In 1783 the French returned the colonies to the Dutch, after their occupation during the Fourth Anglo-Dutch War. During both the British and French occupations, however, the colonists could trade within the more extensive British and French imperial networks, and it seems this practice continued afterward, when officially the Dutch mercantilist rules were in force again. Foreigners were thus no longer allowed to export cash crops. Nevertheless, for a while the register still showed the opposite, probably reflecting the practice of the previous years.

The data for the period between March 1784 and February 1785, shown in table 4.2, thus give a glimpse into the real trade network that otherwise remained hidden. Indeed, it seems the authorities gradually remembered the prohibition: after February 1785 we find fewer entries of foreigners exporting cash crops, and after May 1785 the books only recorded legal exports (rum, molasses, and wood). Undoubtedly, the export of cash crops continued but now illegally. Again, the figures in table 4.2 are an underrepresentation of the actual foreign trade, as for many ships the entries were left blank, and there were probably still smugglers who did not declare anything. Nevertheless, these numbers should give a rough indication of trade destinations and can be compared to figures for the bilateral Dutch trade.[48]

The majority of the sugar and coffee seemed to have found its way to the Dutch Republic, while almost all the rum was absorbed by the Greater Caribbean, particularly North America. There, the most frequent destinations were Boston, New London (Connecticut), and New York. Martinique was an important trading partner, and so was St. Eustatius, although the large amount of exported goods without a reported destination preclude the drawing of any hard conclusions.

Furthermore, the table shows that coffee was relatively unattractive to foreigners, whereas sugar and especially cotton disappeared into the intra-American network. Apparently one could get 25 percent more for sugar in North America, while cotton might be shipped to industrializing Britain, where it would command a higher price than in the Dutch Republic.[49] This image matches the anecdotal descriptions of sugar and cotton as the goods that were most often exported illegally.

Table 4.2. Exports from Essequibo and Demerara, March 1784–February 1785

Destination	Sugar (kg)	Coffee (kg)	Cotton (kg)	Rum (barrels)
Antigua		4,985	15,976	
Barbados	1,622	14,601	13,117	
Dominica	1,755		6,034	63
Guadeloupe		3,458	790	
Martinique	14,425	46,230	13,010	9
North America	71,505	63,324	8,178	992
St. Eustatius	3,236	15,975	27,424	95
St. Thomas	296	12,047	25,179	11
St. Vincent			16,126	10
Tobago	494	5,701	296	29
Tortola		296	3,829	3
Unknown intra-American	190,996	115,847	35,704	175
Amsterdam	386,901	1,424,573	191,178	9
Zeeland	812,334	774,051	110,261	
Total intra-American	284,329	282,464	165,663	1,387
Total Dutch Republic	1,199,234	2,198,624	301,439	9
Percentage intra-American	19	11	35	99

Source: NL-HaNA, VWIS, 1.05.06, inv. nrs. 150 and 151.

With *at least* 11 percent of the coffee, 19 percent of the sugar, and 35 percent of the cotton effectively exported illegally (and probably significantly more), smuggling was deeply ingrained in the colonial society of Essequibo and Demerara. And considering that this illicit trade was connected to the legal trade in necessary provisions, contraband connections proved fundamental to the survival of these borderless societies. Partially because of this importance, smugglers were hardly hindered by the authorities.

Vain Attempts at Curbing Smuggling: The Ordeal of Frans Smeer

The colonial authorities had few means and little interest in curbing the contraband trade.[50] The geography favored openness, as most of the new plantations were established along the long coastline, beyond the government's sight. However, the WIC was also not heavily invested in curbing smuggling. As it could not rely on the navy to patrol the coast, it had to pay for such ships itself, and it lacked the necessary means. The result was that before the Anglo-Dutch War controls were almost nonexistent and the extent of smuggling must have been even greater than described above. To be sure, the Company issued proclamations against illegal trade, including hefty fines, for example, in 1766, 1771, and 1773, but the repeated attempts only show they had little effect.[51]

The colonies had to wait until 1784 before the Company sent four large *hoeker* patrol ships to keep an eye on illegal trade.[52] Yet these had a limited impact, since the small and swift snows, sloops, and schooners easily outsmarted them. Indeed, as Lieutenant Wiggerts found out when he was patroling the Demerara coast with his vessel in March and April 1792, he basically played a game of cat-and-mouse with the smugglers. On many occasions Wiggerts tried to hail a suspicious ship, only to discover that it quickly sailed away. He would then chase it for hours, always in vain. Usually such ships turned toward the open ocean where they could not be caught. On another occasion, a cotton smuggler sped toward the shore simply to offload the illegal cargo where the deep patrol ship could not reach it.[53]

However, even if a smuggler were caught, securing a conviction could be hard, for the authorities were often on the side of the smugglers. Frans Smeer, captain of the patrol ship *De Maasnymph*, experienced this first-hand in 1787, and his reports give insight into how keen the colonial society was to continue smuggling.

Smeer was sent out to combat smuggling but quickly came into conflict with the Council of Policy, particularly the fiscal, Anthony Meertens. It started with an issue about status: Smeer was captain of his ship but only had the rank of lieutenant. He felt he was entitled to be received with the appropriate ceremony of an officer of the country, but the Council of Policy declined to honour him this way.[54] Matters deteriorated when Smeer asked to have the alleged smuggler Nicolaas Glad prosecuted, for the fiscal flatly refused. Glad was a resident trader and had transported 17.5 casks of sugar, 17 bales of coffee, and 17 bales of cotton from Essequibo to Demerara on behalf of the American captain Peabody. In such transport via the open sea, it was easy to transfer the goods to a foreign skipper. For Smeer, then, it was clear that Glad was facilitating smuggling. However, the council was of a different opinion.[55]

The councillors interpreted the rules in favor of the accused smuggler. They explained to Smeer that nothing illegal had transpired, as Dutch ships were allowed to transport plantation products between the two colonies. However, as the case seemed suspicious, the councillors decided to ask Peabody to take an oath and demand proper paperwork upon his departure, on threat of the forfeit of his deposited bond. This lenient reaction allowed Peabody to get rid of his contraband, and the products were indeed transferred to the first Dutch ship that departed. Smeer was perplexed. He considered it an insult to himself and to the council. Furthermore, he was irritated by the news that the council had apparently been blackmailed, as Meertens had threatened to resign as fiscal if Glad was prosecuted. Aware that this attitude made him look like an apologist for smuggling, Meertens made every effort to keep it out of the council's minutes.[56]

Thus, as the current rules failed Smeer, he tried to change them. He proposed to the council that all Dutch ships require a pass, specifying their cargo, before traveling back and forth between Essequibo and Demerara. Furthermore, the council should outfit small ships to cruise along the coast, which was dotted with cotton plantations that had a direct connection to the ocean and made smuggling all too easy. Again Smeer was disappointed. The councillors reminded him they were not allowed to make their own rules without the approval of the WIC. Tellingly, while the council had been eager to draft provisional laws in all other policy areas, they declined to do so in this case. Indeed, Meertens himself recognized that smuggling was probably widespread and that the existing laws left him little room to do anything.[57]

Consequently, Smeer went rogue and began his own surveillance operation, without the council's approval. He demanded that every ship passing *De Maasnymph* declare its goods and destination, and he announced that he would shoot at anyone who failed to comply. This proved no empty threat: at least two ships, claiming ignorance, found cannonballs flying in their direction. However, one of those balls landed on the estate of a planter, Maurits Balthasar Hartsinck, who was at that moment probably busy plotting the coup discussed in chapter 2. Smeer decided to be more careful afterward, which also meant that some ships just sailed past as they were under fire. Finally, the councillors issued a proclamation that ships must indeed declare their cargo at *De Maasnymph*. However, they initially issued it only in Smeer's name, not their own, indicating that they did not approve of it.[58]

Regardless of the rules, it was very difficult to get caught. Smugglers could choose between two options, depending on when and where the forbidden goods were taken on board. Nicolaas Glad apparently wanted to try the first option: to ostensibly transport products from one river to the other with the aim of transferring it to a foreign ship at open sea. The ocean was out of sight of the authorities and out of reach even for Smeer's patrol ship. This lack of oversight was the reason that many American ships could declare they left Demerara empty (in ballast) and that Smeer wanted every local ship to carry a passport with its cargo: that way he would be able check that no goods had disappeared en route between the two colonies.[59]

The second option was to buy the coffee, sugar, and cotton directly from a plantation while lying in the river. Foreign ships were allowed to have these cash crops on board, based on the idea that they would exchange them later for legal exports, such as rum and wood, or bills of exchange. Yet Smeer noticed a different habit: after having loaded, the ships would sail ten miles or more upriver, returning with molasses, rum, and wood but without proof that the other goods were unloaded. Subsequently Smeer declared, "They take a Westindian Oath, and with that they can sail out."[60]

Although the smuggler still faced the danger of inspection, illicit goods were never found, as Meertens himself confirmed. While the fiscal recognized the possibility of bribery—the inspectors received no share of the confiscated goods—it was also nearly impossible to discover hidden goods on a fully loaded ship. Besides, the fiscal himself had no desire to unload the goods at his own expense every time he suspected smuggling, even though he would personally receive one-third of the confiscated cargo and one-third of the additional fine.[61] Instead, he preferred to rely on a captain's word and honor when a foreign trader came to collect his clearance. Meertens would then ask the captain if he would be willing to declare under oath that the cargo manifest corresponded entirely with the actual cargo—Smeer's "Westindian Oath." Yet with some pride Meertens recalled several incidents when the captain changed his mind and came back a few days later after having sold his illicit goods (at a loss) to a local planter. Just as in the case of Peabody, the captain would face no further consequences afterward and was free to go.[62]

Ultimately, Meertens' colonial flexibility proved incompatible with the strict metropolitan views of Smeer. In fact, Smeer encountered opposition from all sides in the colony. He felt he was grossly overcharged for repairs on a ship anchor and complained that news of his discussions in the council reached the biggest smugglers within two hours.[63] Meertens, on the other hand, was most likely complicit in illegal trade himself—not necessarily by shipping contraband personally but rather by facilitating the exchanges for a bribe. For example, when a Bostonian brigantine arrived with provisions, its two merchants asked Meertens where they could pick up a return cargo. Meertens referred them to a Mr. Grant, where they loaded 42 hogsheads of sugar. Allegedly, when the merchants inquired about the legality, Meertens assured them they would not be visited. Perhaps new to the trade, the merchants did not trust this and unloaded most of the sugar but found several barrels deficient. Subsequently, in a drunken rage, the captain attacked one of the cooper slaves, for which he was arrested (which is why we know about this anecdote). Afterward, Meertens told this story to Smeer to prove he really was a man of the law and to prove he had taken no bribes at all, even though no one had mentioned such a thing.[64] Meertens role thus underlined the self-organized nature of the colonies and their borderless nature that resisted metropolitan control.

Indeed, the local authorities thoroughly disliked Smeer's meddling. They complained to the Company about his temper, his expressions, and his arbitrary methods.[65] Smeer felt the animosity clearly, noting, "Our country's officers (with a task like ours) are as welcome here as a pig in a Jewish kitchen."[66]

Nevertheless, Meertens was remarkably successful in his colonial career. Despite the States-General's alarm about the smuggling, Meertens was allowed to continue as fiscal for more than a decade. His habits remained the same. The British traveler Henry Bolingbroke would write how Meertens facilitated the smuggling of cotton to Britain and noted, "The fiscal's apparent indifference to what was going on never went unrewarded and if he did not absolutely smuggle his own produce out, he used to sell it to those who did." In 1799, after the British occupation, Meertens made his way to London to await a peace treaty and in 1802 returned as the new governor of the colonies—even though the colonies were soon taken over again by the British.[67]

Smeer, in the meantime, submitted his report to the Admiralty with several important policy recommendations, hoping to initiate change. For instance, he proposed that North Americans be allowed to export sugar, upon payment of a recognition fee of 6 or 7 guilders per hogshead. Similarly, the WIC could also allow foreigners to bring in African captives, upon payment of fee of 25 or 30 guilders. That way, the Company could improve its dire finances while simultaneously reducing the rampant smuggling.[68] While Smeer's suggestions made it to the States-General, they were not implemented, being too opposed to the existing mercantilist framework.[69] In the end, the most pressing issue, according to Smeer, was the slave trade. While the imports and exports might be regulated, the slave trade at present was plainly insufficient, as the Dutch slavers could not meet the demand. Changes were needed, because planters were importing captives on a grand scale, against the rules, as Smeer experienced.

Trading Enslaved Africans

Sometimes the same traders smuggled both cash crops and African captives, as the incident with the *Betsey* illustrates. On 12 June 1787 Smeer received word that the *Betsey* was about to clear out and after ordering an inspection learned that "six Negroes" were found on board. Meertens investigated the matter and found that they were slaves, two of them belonging to the plantation Belvedere and the other four to the captain, Henry Basden. For Meertens, the matter was settled, but Smeer pointed out that the slaves had not been registered when the ship had come in while the *Betsey* had illegally brought 57 African captives to Belvedere just two weeks before. Possibly, these six captives were part of the previous group of 57. Yet when Smeer offered to supply the evidence, the fiscal responded only, "Ha ha, is that so? Now I understand," and quickly departed, indicating he would investigate the matter further. However, that same afternoon the ship was allowed to depart.[70] Interestingly, as noted above in the British port books, Basden was a frequent trader to Demerara and an incorrigible smuggler. Indeed, he was back again in

Demerara by August, after which he went to Barbados, smuggling out 50 bales of cotton.[71]

While Basden received a fine, Smeer believed he was the one who was punished the most. The fine, at 1,200 guilders, was rather low and was probably part of Basden's normal operating costs. The division of the money proved more interesting: standard practice prescribed that one-third was for the fiscal himself, one-third for the colony's poor and orphanage fund, and one-third for the informer (*aanbrenger*), in this case Smeer. However, he strongly protested against this terminology. The *aanbrenger* was Jean Lavager, the captain of another vessel, as Smeer stated he was only doing his duty.[72]

Indeed, "informer" was a loaded term around the Greater Caribbean. While informers were generally promised a third of a prize, they rarely stepped forward. Mechanisms of social control often proved strong enough: informers were beaten, covered with tar and feathers, and dragged through the streets. Or they were intimidated, imprisoned, and ostracized. In Bermuda the word *informer* was even considered slander.[73] Being an informer signified a lack of loyalty to one's own community; it meant selling out to metropolitan powers that tried to suppress vital local smuggling circuits. By being called an informer, Smeer thus felt disrespected. Furthermore, it is telling that he could only acquire information from a foreign captain, as locals were unlikely to cooperate with him.

In fact, in Essequibo and Demerara officials had learned to be kind to slave smugglers because the regular Dutch slave trade proved so unreliable. As the WIC abandoned the slave trade in 1738, private traders took over. The Middelburgse Commercie Compagnie (MCC), established in 1720 in Zealand, became the most important actor. Between 1750 and 1795, more than 90 percent of the registered slave voyages to Essequibo and Demerara started in Zealand.[74] However, both the planters and the MCC were dissatisfied with the organization of the trade. Indeed, the limited Dutch slave trade meant that Essequibo, Demerara, and Suriname were in effect competing with each other. In this sellers' market, the few slave ships that set sail each year could simply choose the destination that offered the best terms, as was the policy of the MCC.[75] Suriname appeared most attractive, as securing payment was easier.

In Essequibo and Demerara the problem was the obligation to sell at auction.[76] The idea was to offer all buyers the same chance at acquiring enslaved laborers. Otherwise, the more well-connected planters might establish a "monopoly" by arranging slave imports via their contacts in the metropolis. While small planters now had a chance, the limited number of captives resulted in counterbidding, pushing prices higher and making it more difficult for anyone to actually afford any of the African captives. Moreover, in the frantic bidding process, planters sometimes offered more than they could pay, decreasing the security for the slave trader. In Suriname, on the other hand, the slavers could choose between auctions, contracts, and "out of hand" (*onderhands*, or *uit de hand*) sales. These latter two options allowed the captain to obtain more guarantees about the buyer's creditworthiness. Contracts could be drawn up in the metropolis with richer planters, while for local direct sales the captain could rely on the firm's correspondents in the colonies. Interestingly, Meertens was a correspondent for the MCC while also allowing foreign slavers to bring in captives clandestinely.[77]

Regardless, the rules in Essequibo and Demerara gradually offered more opportunity for slave traders: in 1776 "out of hand" became possible; in 1785 the rule stated that at most three quarters of the human cargo could be sold on contract, while at least one quarter had to be sold by public auction; and in 1789 all options were open.[78] However, especially after 1780 the Dutch slave trade declined sharply, so these changes could only have had a small effect.[79] In addition, they could not have solved the underlying payment issues.

Even very long credit lines failed to make Essequibo and Demerara attractive to slave traders. While they allowed up to 27 months' credit, in the 1760s the MCC reported outstanding claims of several hundred thousand guilders. Some of those claims were for unpaid deliverances, the majority for protested bills of exchange. Consequently, the MCC became even more reluctant to set sail to the two colonies.[80] The payment problems were partly the result of the widespread plantation mortgages. Planters in a mortgage fund were obliged to send their cash crops to the director in the metropolis, who would market the goods. This clause often prevented slave traders from taking in cash crops as payment, as they could in other empires. Chapter 5 discusses this issue in more detail, demonstrating the difficulty of reclaiming money in a colony mired in debt. The resulting insecurity further discouraged slave traders, even though there was a clear demand for enslaved laborers.

The reaction in the colonies was familiar: petitioning, improvising, and smuggling. In 1769 a group of English planters in Essequibo and Demerara sent their request to the Company (see chapter 6), which, however, dismissed it immediately as it refused to deal with a petition in a foreign language. The next year, a broader coalition was formed to present a petition in Dutch, with a supporting letter from Storm. The planters proposed to pay 10 guilders per slave in recognition fees to the WIC if they would be allowed to buy enslaved Africans from English traders. Foreign captives, they argued, were much cheaper than those brought by the Dutch. During the rest of the 1770s no more petitions are known; during the subsequent wartime occupations it was unnecessary as non-Dutch ships were welcome. Yet afterward, in 1786 and 1788, the planters again unsuccessfully asked to open up the trade to foreigners. And in the following year the commissioners Grovestins and Boeij made the same recommendation in their report to the Prince of Orange. In 1802, when the colonies were restored to the Dutch after the second British occupation, the same recommendation was put forward: it would be best if the trade was opened up, as long as the foreign slavers would pay a recognition fee of 10 guilders per captive.[81]

The reason these petitions had no effect is found in the conflicted mercantilism of the Dutch. On the one hand, it made sense to open up the trade to foreign slavers, if that would lead to more cash crops to refine and reexport. On the other hand, the WIC, especially the Zealand Chamber, favored a closed approach to protect its slaving sector. Consequently, the WIC struggled to remain consistent in its replies to the petitions. In its reaction to the 1770 petition the WIC first denied that slaves were too expensive, while it subsequently blamed the planters for bidding up the prices at the auctions. In the same fashion, the WIC refuted the claim that too few slave ships arrived, yet it also mentioned that the long credit terms were the reason that hardly any slavers were interested in coming. Clearly, while thus recognizing that Zealand's slave trade to the two colonies amounted to little, the WIC simultaneously maintained that opening up the trade would mean a great loss to the Dutch Republic in general and to Zealand in particular.[82]

Regardless, the colonists were not deterred and improvised their own solutions. For instance, in 1763, the colonial authorities attempted to reduce prices by instating a maximum price of 280 guilders per African. Yet this sum was far below the average price at the time of 430 guilders per person, thus antagonizing the slave traders further. Proving ineffective, the measure was only used once. The following year, the British planter Samuel Carter cooperated with the skipper Joseph Bragg and outfitted an illicit direct voyage to Africa, where Bragg sold rum in exchange for captives: 110 gallons for a man and 90 to 95 gallons for a woman. Yet the Company discovered the voyage, and no evidence appears of subsequent voyages.[83]

More effective was the flexible stance the Council of Policy adopted toward the foreign slave trade. For instance, in 1767 Storm wanted to condemn the slave smuggler John Birmingham, but the local council decided to let him off the hook, at the same time admitting that there was no way to prevent smuggling.[84] Even Storm himself was lenient when dealing with immigrating planters bringing their "previously owned" slaves. In January 1766 he wrote that he failed to see how he could stop those in Demerara "from sending slaves to their own plantations; not only those from Barbados totally insist on it, but those from St. Eustatius [as well].... I had to allow it provisionally."[85] He even sympathized with the planters, explaining to the WIC that foreign captives were markedly cheaper.

> My exactitude in preventing the importation of several foreign slaves, caused a general murmuring in both rivers and an open dissatisfaction; (and, spoken in private, [I] find that the inhabitants indeed are not quite wrong), they say, in Barbados the slaves cost around 320 guilders, in St. Christopher one can buy, as many as one desires, for 250 to 280 guilders, and here one has to pay an exorbitant price, and one cannot obtain half of what one needs.[86]

During the same year, 1766, the councillors decided to be strict regarding foreign slavers but to allow the transport of previously owned slaves from St. Eustatius, Suriname, and Berbice, although not from Curaçao.[87] Interestingly, the commander of St. Eustatius had already anticipated the ruling in 1765: he had sent eighteen enslaved people, including two children, to his own plantation, St. Jan, in Demerara, counting on Storm's flexibility. As the council put forward strict conditions, the Company assented to the practice. Planters had to gain prior consent from the WIC and provide proper paperwork citing names, ages, origin, and destination of the enslaved. They also had to submit a declaration under oath that the enslaved were brought by Dutch vessels and would not be sold within two years.[88]

The council clearly had the initiative in regulating the slave trade, as became clear in the prohibition of 1768. Suddenly, without consulting the WIC, it banned the trade from St. Eustatius. The reason given was that the paperwork was often deficient and the route was used as a smuggling loophole: planters on St. Eustatius would declare that they had brought slaves from their plantations on the free island of St. Croix and wanted to transfer them to Essequibo or Demerara. Considering that St. Croix was a free port, foreign slaves could be easily obtained if one had a contact at St. Eustatius willing to cooperate in the scheme. However, the more pressing reason was probably that the councillors feared importing diseases: recently several captives had brought the "Lazarus disease" and the "children's disease" with them. The councillors also wanted to prevent the arrival of "mutiny infected" (*muit zieke*) captives from Montserrat.[89]

The WIC later urged the council to reopen the St. Eustatius trade, as long as the rules were strictly obeyed. The WIC blamed Storm for the lax enforcement of the rules in the past, especially concerning the trade from the British islands. The directors had a point there, for that same year Storm had allowed two British planters to bring twenty-one enslaved Africans from Antigua. This incident had greatly embarrassed him, and he defended himself on the grounds that the slaves were only allowed to disembark because the death toll on board would otherwise soar. Interestingly, the WIC conceded and allowed the slaves to stay, as long as the paperwork was sound and the planters promised not to sell the slaves on within two years.[90]

However, the unofficial trade continued unabated. In a reaction to a petition to open the trade to foreigners, the WIC made some calculations. According to the WIC, between March 1763 and September 1769, Zealanders had delivered 2,619 enslaved Africans to the two colonies. In contrast, the enslaved population had increased from fewer than 5,000 to almost 10,000 slaves in this period. The population had thus grown far more quickly than the official trade would have allowed, even without taking the terrible demographic conditions into account. Speaking rhetorically, the directors remarked that "either the Zealand ships have delivered a fitting number of slaves and rather greater than the petitioners specify, or the people have taken little notice of our sharp prohibition of import, and have imported, secretly or by connivance, as many English slaves as they could possibly obtain."[91]

Despite these harsh words, little was done to counter the smuggling, nor could there be. The Dutch slave trade increased during the 1770s, but so did the illegal trade. In 1770 Storm remarked that he found that the inhabitants of Demerara were "openly & without the least restraint buying slaves from the English." The year after he lamented, "The importation of foreign slaves does not end. . . . [W]hen I notice it is too late or I lack the right and sufficient proof."[92] In 1774 the WIC proposed to place sentinels on ships to monitor the traffic. However, as quoted in the introduction, the council urged against it, stating that nothing illegal took place, nor could it be prevented from taking place.

The colony was simply too open and lacked the means of proper surveillance. A month later, in April 1774, two slave ships sailed straight past the fire watch (*brandwagt*) and lay anchored for several days without making their arrival known or undergoing the mandatory slave inspection. One of them even "got lost" as it sailed upriver. The Commandeur started a search, but only after several days was the ship discovered.[93] The council had been right: if illicit trade existed, it was impossible to prevent. Furthermore, the Dutch slave trade was past its peak after the 1770s and could not keep up with the insatiable demand for enslaved labor in the colonies.[94] Foreign slavers, mainly from Barbados, Antigua, and St. Christopher, eagerly filled this gap.[95]

To get an idea of the overall slave smuggling, it is instructive to follow the WIC's example and compare slave imports with the growth of the enslaved population. According to the figures from Suriname, the slave population would decline by 4.7 percent a year if no new African captives arrived, due to the low birthrates and the high death rates in the harsh conditions. Therefore, it is possible to estimate how many Africans would have been in the colonies if only registered imports had taken place (figure 4.1).[96]

I used two estimates, one of the presumed rate of demographic decline (4.7 percent per year) and one "optimistic" scenario, with a much lower rate of decline (2.4 percent, as in Suriname after its phase of expansion). As figure 4.1 shows, not even in the "optimistic" scenario could registered imports explain the rise of the enslaved population. In Essequibo the population would have actually declined without illegally imported captives, as most slavers went to Demerara. There, the difference between the official figures and actual population is dramatic, leading to the conclusion that only widespread unofficial trade can account for the rapid growth of the enslaved population.

This undocumented trade had two forms: the illegal slave trade; and the semilegal trade of foreign planters who brought enslaved people from their other plantations elsewhere with them. In some cases the latter would have been legal trade, if the planters had the required documents. In other cases, this semilegal trade would have been used as a loophole to bring in enslaved Africans brought from foreign slavers at one of the many Caribbean free ports. While the precise division between the semilegal and illegal slave trade is impossible to establish, it is clear that the Dutch slave trade cannot account for the population increase, by a great margin.

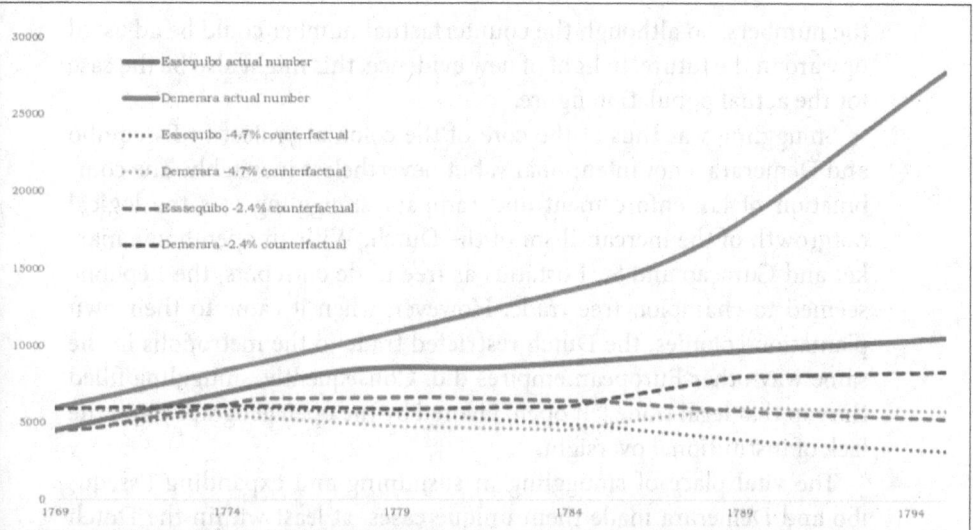

FIGURE 4.1. Population of enslaved Africans in Essequibo and Demerara, actual numbers compared to counterfactual numbers based on registered slave imports, 1769–1795. Source: see note 96.

The figure thus needs to be treated with care and provides an indication rather than hard numbers. For example, there may be slave voyages that have not been discovered, although the data used here, by Johannes Postma, already include estimates to make up for this element. Another caveat is that the majority of the voyages in the data set concern direct voyages from Africa, not their possible relocation to other empires afterward. In Venezuela, for example, this often clandestine trade was the biggest part of the slave trade.[97] Similarly, slave captains sometimes sold part of their human cargo in Suriname, before continuing to Essequibo or Demerara. Fortunately, Postma adjusted his figures for these partial sales. The condoned route via St. Eustatius to Demerara would fall in the same category, although Postma reckoned most of the registered captives from St. Eustatius were sold on nearby French islands, which probably represented a better market than the one in Essequibo or Demerara.[98] And as we have seen, the trade with St. Eustatius was often a cover for smuggling too rather than a large source of the legal slave trade.

On the other hand, the official number of enslaved Africans in the two colonies is likely too low as planters paid taxes based on the number of their enslaved workers. Planters regularly underreported the size of their enslaved population, and the authorities lacked the means to check the numbers. So although the counterfactual number could be adjusted upward in the future, in light of new evidence, this might also be the case for the actual population figure.

Smuggling was thus at the core of the colonial project in Essequibo and Demerara—not intentionally, but nevertheless inevitably. The combination of lax enforcement and rampant smuggling was the logical outgrowth of the mercantilism of the Dutch. With an open home market and Curaçao and St. Eustatius as free trade entrepôts, the Republic seemed to champion free trade. However, when it came to their own plantation colonies, the Dutch restricted trade to the metropolis in the same way other European empires did. Consequently, smuggling filled the gap that legal trade left open, favored by the open geography and the lack of institutional oversight.

The vital place of smuggling in sustaining and expanding Essequibo and Demerara made them unique cases, at least within the Dutch empire. While the Antilles were centers of illicit trade, this was basically their function in the Dutch mercantilist framework. On the other hand, the plantation colonies on the Guiana coast were supposed to be opposed to smuggling. And while in Suriname smuggling was rife too, it was less fundamental to the colonial project than in Essequibo and Demerara, where legal and illegal trade often were two sides of the same coin.[99] The case of these two colonies thus underlines the need to see smuggling as fundamental to the Atlantic world, not just for tiny trading islands, but also for the larger plantation colonies.[100]

Local officials recognized the vital role of illicit exchanges. Although Storm van 's Gravesande had a strong sense of duty and tried to convict smugglers—usually in vain—even he sympathized with the smuggling planters. While not in favor of total openness, he saw few problems allowing new planters to bring their previously owned captives. Furthermore, Storm was on good terms with several of the prominent British planters, who were actively engaged in smuggling. Being all too familiar with the infrequent supplies from the metropolis, Storm also recognized the need to accommodate when necessary. Yet he condoned only foreign *imports* (foodstuffs and enslaved Africans), deeming them necessary for colonial survival. Meertens, on the other hand, also facilitated the *export* of cash crops by foreigners. While blatantly illegal, these exports cemented the colonies' place in the Atlantic world.

In 1794 the centrality of this trade with foreigners was officially admitted. As war disrupted trade with the Dutch Republic, the local council chose to adopt unprecedented measures. It wanted to safeguard the imports of planks and provisions but recognized that rum exports were not valuable enough as return cargo to entice foreigners to come to the colonies. Furthermore, bills of exchange were often protested and the colonies were starved of cash. Therefore, the council decided to allow North Americans and other neutral ships to export cash crops, to the value of the provisions they brought and after payment of a recognition fee.[101] The following year the fees for foreign ships were abolished as well, to further stimulate the trade.[102] Finally, in 1795 temporary exemptions were granted to foreign slave traders to bring in captives.[103] With these measures, the practice of borderless commerce with the rest of the Atlantic world was recognized on paper.[104]

Nevertheless, one lifeline remained that tied the colonies to the metropolis: credit. A system of plantation mortgages developed after 1750 that aimed to remedy two problems in the Dutch Republic: the abundance of cash looking for profitable outlets and the desire to attract more plantation produce to the declining Dutch staple market. The solution was to make a mortgage conditional on the shipping of cash crops to the creditor. While this financial innovation facilitated the expansion of the plantation sector, it also hampered the slave trade and insisted on strict bilateral shipping. Chapter 5 demonstrates how this attempt to overcome the borderless nature of the two colonies fared.

5 / The Web of Debt

The previous chapters have shown how locally formed connections were crucial in explaining the development of Essequibo and Demerara, and this chapter completes this picture by looking at the financial lifelines. In other words, how could these ill-supplied, ill-managed, and indefensible colonies attract enough capital to enlarge their plantation sectors? Why could these colonies continue to expand rather than collapse under the mountain of debt? And how can we square the image of Guyana as a land of great riches for British planters in the nineteenth century with the eighteenth-century one of impending financial ruin?

This chapter proceeds in three steps. The first part provides a comparative contextual framework and introduces the Dutch system of plantation mortgages, or *negotiaties*. After this more metropolitan perspective, it analyzes how this structure played out in practice in the colonies. The mortgage frenzy became a bubble, yet no proper procedures existed to unwind the mountain of debt. However, the underdeveloped institutional structure proved yet again an element of strength. Different actors—local provision suppliers, the mortgage funds, and the auctioneer on behalf of the slavers—believed their debts would be preferential in case of a default. Furthermore, the messy and unpredictable process of execution likely deterred creditors from pursuing this route. For the investors the consequences were unfortunate, but the planters profited: as many colonists owed debts to each other, a single default could trigger a chain reaction. The directors-general, however, took pains to prevent that from happening. Local conditions thus stood in the way of metropolitan control, although it led to a web of debt that likely deterred future investments. The final part of the chapter therefore moves beyond debt and probes the question of profit, more specifically, why British planters were said to have attained enormous profits while the Dutch were caught in this web of debt.

Contextualizing the Credit Structure

Credit facilities were key in determining the pace of the expansion of the plantation complex. For instance, the plantation sector of Barbados could develop quickly thanks to loans from London financiers, while in Brazil growth was slower, as planters typically financed additional enslaved labor from current profits.[1] Similarly, new credit flows boosted the growth of the plantation complex of the Ceded Islands (St. Vincent and the Grenadines, Grenada, Dominica, and Tobago) when they came into British hands after the Seven Years' War.[2]

Yet money was only half of the story, as the conditions upon which it was lent proved crucial as well. Higher interest rates might compensate creditors for these inherently risky loans, but too high rates meant that planters would be pushed into default sooner, as their profits might be consumed by interest payments. In Britain itself, usury legislation put the maximum interest rate at 5 percent, although rates in the colonies could be higher. In Barbados the maximum rate was lowered in 1752 from 8 to 6 percent, but the average West Indian loan carried an interest rate of 6.98 percent. While this seemed high, it was perhaps not enough to compensate for the risks involved, such as war, crop failure, drought, and revolts.[3] The Dutch case illustrates this point. In 1736 the rate was capped at 8 percent in Suriname, but even at these high rates lending remained limited.[4]

The likelihood of reclaiming a loan was also important in determining the flow of credit. If creditors could not reclaim their money from defaulting planters, they were less likely to lend more in the future. Yet colonial development might be harmed if impatient creditors could all too easily put a plantation up for auction, trying to get (some of) their money back. A balance was therefore needed between protecting planters and supporting creditors.

Such rules differed across empires. Jacob Price distinguished between a British "creditor defense model" (in which colonial courts could be used to reclaim money) and the "Latin model" (which protected the integrity of the plantation, for example, by preventing creditors from selling slaves). In the end, the former model would be more beneficial to planters, as it resulted in lower interest rates.[5] However, these contrasts are likely overdrawn. For example, colonists in early Barbados could also frustrate debt collection and manage to disown creditors by simulating inflation with paper money.[6] Similarly, when in 1774 British creditors tried to seize debtors' estates in Grenada, the local House of Assembly prevented or at least postponed it. Parliament upheld the decision, effectively siding with the indebted colonists.[7] Even in the British case, then, it was not always clear who would shoulder the risk. As I show below, Suriname came closer to the creditor defense model, whereas in Essequibo and Demerara there simply was no model. The risk was nevertheless so diffused that it resulted in maintaining the integrity of the plantation.

In cases of reclaiming money the type of collateral (if any) was also important. Historians have debated to what extent mortgages (with the plantation and its enslaved population as collateral) were used. Although the topic is remarkably understudied, it seemed mortgages became more common in the second half of the eighteenth century.[8] The interesting point about the Dutch case is that mortgages, in the form of the *negotiatie* system, were hugely important and were in fact the main driver of the eighteenth-century growth of the Dutch plantation complex on the Guiana coast.

The Structure of the *Negotiaties*

The *negotiaties* provided a welcome stimulus to the Dutch economy. They pooled money from people in the Republic in an investment fund in order to lend it out to (would-be) planters in the colonies. The loans were secured by a mortgage on the estate, and the planters were obliged to ship all their cash crops to the fund director, who would act as merchant-banker and market the goods. Traders, refiners, planters, and investors all seemed to gain from this *negotiatie* structure. Channeling goods for refining and reexports made sense within Dutch mercantilism, and investors would receive a 5 to 6 percent return, which compared favorably to the 3 percent that could otherwise be had in the Republic.[9] Finally, the fund directors profited from the commission fees. Typically, a fund director charged a 2 percent commission for selling the cash crops, and some fund directors also charged 2 percent for arranging the planter's imports. While another 0.5 per cent for insurance might be added, the main benefit resided in the brokerage fees. Some, but not all, directors charged 1 to 2.5 percent of the mortgage sum to arrange the mortgage.[10]

This fee would constitute a considerable remuneration considering the large amount of money involved: by the 1780s, a typical sugar or coffee estate cost more than 100,000 guilders to establish (equivalent to 8,333 to 10,000 pounds sterling).[11]

To acquire the capital, a fund director sold bonds, typically of 500 or 1,000 guilders each. A planter or prospective planter could then apply for a mortgage if he could prove he (and his wife) were free from debts.[12] To spread the risk, a fund would extend mortgages to several plantations and only to "half, or ultimately 5/8," of the value of the estate. This value was determined by sworn appraisers (*priseurs*) and included the tools, buildings, and enslaved population.[13] To allow enough time to develop a profitable estate, the first ten years constituted an "interest-only" period, during which the planter only had to pay the 5 or 6 percent interest. During the next ten years, he would have to start repaying the principal, so that after twenty years everything should have been repaid and the mortgage could be terminated.[14]

Initially, the *negotiatie* structure seemed successful. During the second half of the eighteenth century, an estimated 80 million guilders was invested, which stimulated plantation expansion throughout the Guianas—41 million went to Suriname and 18 million to Essequibo, Demerara, and Berbice.[15] The heyday was the 1760s, when in Essequibo and Demerara the number of plantations nearly doubled.[16] However, the *negotiatie* system soon became a bubble.

The main problem was that the amount of credit was disconnected from the production or the profitability of a plantation and based solely on a subjective valuation.[17] And since a higher valuation meant that the planter could take out more credit, a speculative trend ensued. Rising prices for enslaved Africans meant that the value of this "collateral" increased, allowing for more credit. Furthermore, in Demerara the value of land skyrocketed. Storm remarked in 1769 that land prices stood at 30 to 36 guilders per acre, compared to 2 or 3 guilders ten years earlier, before the boom.[18] In 1771 a planter mentioned a price of 60 guilders per acre, which had risen from 4 guilders "several years" before.[19] The result was an upward cycle of debt that spiraled out of control.

In 1772–73 the optimism surrounding the *negotiaties* was overturned by an economic crisis in Amsterdam, which had spread from Britain.[20] A credit crunch ensued in which the practice of piling up ever more debt became impossible. While the stream of money did not dry up until 1776, the *negotiatie* boom had already peaked. Prices of coffee, as well as those for enslaved Africans, peaked in 1769, and so did the amount of new mortgage credit. In the following years millions of guilders were still extended in credit, but those who foresaw the impending crash had already stepped out and sold their plantations. A drought and renewed conflict with the maroons in Suriname further undermined the system. The financial crisis and subsequent downfall of a major mortgage fund sealed the fate of the *negotiaties* as popular investment instruments.[21]

In the development of the *negotiatie* system, three phases can be discerned. In the first, up to the credit crisis of 1772–73, the dominant form consisted of "general" (*generale*) *negotiaties*. In the prospectus, the fund director did not mention specific planters or plantations, only the broader colony. Investors thus made their decision based on the appeal of the general plan and the trust they had in the fund director instead of knowledge of the underlying specifics. At least forty general *negotaties* existed prior to 1772, often carrying generic names like L.a.A., L.a. B, and L.a.C (as in Littera A, sometimes called Letter A). After the credit crisis these types disappeared, as investors grew wearier and demanded more information. Supervision became stricter. After 1780 a final phase emerged, with mortgages almost exclusively granted to single estates, often those of prominent people. The idea of spreading risk by bundling ten or twenty plantations had collapsed after the crisis, but the *negotiatie* system apparently still proved attractive in this more restricted form.[22]

In Essequibo and Demerara the three phases are clearly visible while also displaying a clear shift from Zealand-based to Amsterdam-based creditors. The first major fund to extend mortgages to the two colonies was established in 1766 by Kornelis van den Helm Boddaert. This former mayor of Middleburgh and WIC director granted mortgages to at least thirty-five plantations, and by 1770 the capital involved was over a million guilders.[23] Other firms in this early phase were Tulleken de Vos & Comp, led by Mr. Ambrosius Tulleken (1728–84), who was an alderman in the Middleburgh City Council. This fund invested around 1.9 million guilders at the outset, and perhaps more later. A final fund was the one by De Bruyn & De Smit, which was also active in the slave trade. It invested half a million guilders in 1766, of which the city of Middleburgh contributed 25,000.[24] Only one fund from Amsterdam can be found among the early investors, the one of Daniel Changuion, which started in 1768 or 1769.[25] Amsterdam became involved mainly after 1770, because previously only ships from Zealand were allowed to sail to the two colonies, which made securing plantations products for Amsterdam rather difficult (see chapter 4).

Subsequently, in phase 2 many plantations went from an existing Zealand fund to an Amsterdam- (or Utrecht-)based one, as summarized in table 5.1. There were several fund directors overconfident enough to step in at exactly the wrong moment—just before the financial crisis. Dirk Wernard van Vloten, Jan van Rijneveld & Soonen, and Bartholomeus van den Santheuvel & Zoonen put millions of guilders into a system that was already on the verge of collapsing. In fact, Bartholomeus van den Santheuvel was so committed to the system that he injected over 60,000 guilders of his own money into the fund, advancing money to planters even though the revenues were insufficient. He went bankrupt, and the mortgages were taken over by Heemskerk Jr & Van Arp.[26]

Outside of such cases of default, it was generally good news for planters if they could transfer their mortgage to a new (and perhaps ignorant) fund director. Typically, they could use the new credit to pay off old debts and take out more credit based on increased valuations. Furthermore, a new mortgage could mean that the planter entered a new "interest-only" period of ten years, thereby postponing the problems of having to repay the principle. This debt pyramid inevitably collapsed. Phase 3 therefore witnessed only a few loans to prominent people such as Director-General L'Espinasse.

The *negotiaties* thus proved to be a financial fiasco, but the winding down of the debts took place along different lines in Suriname than in Essequibo and Demerara. In Suriname, it became common in the 1770s and 1780s for investors to convert a failing *negotiatie* fund into a society or limited liability company. They would sell the unprofitable plantations in the fund and buy the remaining ones themselves, to run them for a profit. They also tried to reduce the number of bonds or buy them back (so less interest had to be paid out) or convert them into shares (which only paid out if actual profits were available).[27] This way, the investors—if they did not insist on selling the plantations immediately for fire sale prices—could try to recoup some of their money. The popularity of this practice is attested by the fact that in 1796 probably around two-thirds of the Suriname estates were run by administrators for overseas creditors, with *negotiatie* funds as the main plantation owners in the colony.[28] Suriname thus came close to the creditor defense model.

In contrast, in Essequibo and Demerara this construction in which investors took back control seemed less prevalent, although few sources exist to provide the details. Nevertheless, two elements are clear. First, planters in Essequibo and Demerara were particularly bad at repaying their loans. The authoritative study estimated that in general less than

Table 5.1. Overview of major mortgage funds active in Essequibo and Demerara

Name of director	City	Capital Invested in Guilders (year known)	Estimated Number of Estates	Remarks
Kornelis van den Helm Boddaert	Middelburgh	More than 1 million (1770)	37	Many plantations later to Van den Santheuvel (and even later to Van Vloten)
De Bruyn & de Smit	Middelburgh	500,000 (1766)		At least one plantation later went to Van den Santheuvel; the city of Middleburgh invested 25,000 guilders itself; fund directors also active in the slave trade
Tulleken de Vos & Comp.	Middelburgh	ca. 1.9 million	At least 17	Taken over by Jan van Rijneveld & Soonen in 1770 or 1771
Daniel Changuion	Amsterdam	ca. 2 million	At least 13	Several plantations were later transferred to Van Vloten & Van den Santheuvel; started in late 1760s
Bartholomeus van den Santheuvel & Zoonen	Amsterdam	1.4 million (at the start, 1772)	At least 22	Took several estates previously at De Bruyn & De Smit, Changuion and, mainly, Boddaert. Itself taken over by Heemskerk Jr. & Van Arp in 1777
Dirk Wernard van Vloten	Utrecht	More than 2.5 million (1770s)	At least 11	Active mainly from 1772 onwards, took over several estates from Changuion and Boddaert
Van de Perre & Meijners	Middelburgh	100,000 (at the start, 1773)	5	Active in phase 2
Jan van Rijneveld & Soonen	Amsterdam	2.2 million (1780)	36	Provided the mortgages for Pieter Callaert and P.C. Hooft

Table 5.1. Overview of major mortgage funds active in Essequibo and Demerara (*continued*)

Name of director	City	Capital Invested in Guilders (year known)	Estimated Number of Estates	Remarks
Daniel Steven Schorer	Middelburgh		2	Middelburgh itself invested for 15,000 guilders; established in 1774 and 1775
Spoors & Sprenger	Middelburgh	90,000 (at the start, 1777)	1	Also an important trading firm
J. Heemskerk Jr. & J. W. van Arp	Amsterdam			Took over the fund of Van den Santheuvel in 1777
Turing & Comp.	Middelburgh	100,000 (at the start, 1791)	3	Only active in phase 3
Sebastiaan van Nooten Jansz.	Amsterdam	Ca. 1.4 million (1786–92)	8.5	Only active in phase 2, lending to L'Espinasse and Cuming, among others. Took over one estate from Van den Santheuvel, one from Van Vloten

Source: Van de Voort, Westindische plantages, 269–323; Hoonhout, "Subprime Plantation Mortgages in Suriname, Essequibo and Demerara, 1750–1800," 27; ACA, Notarissen, 5075, Notary Kier van der Piet, 13917/25.

25 percent of the original loans were paid back before 1800, but in Essequibo, Demerara, and Berbice by 1815 this figure was still below 15 percent.[29] Second, investors seemed to have encountered great difficulties getting rid of these indebted estates. In 1814 more than 500 plantations existed in Essequibo and Demerara, of which only 37 were still Dutch. However, 133 still carried a Dutch mortgage.[30] In fact, many bonds were only redeemed at some point in the nineteenth century, such as the *negotiatie* on De Herstelling plantation, which was paid off in 1845.[31] In Essequibo and Demerara, then, a web of debt inadvertently protected the integrity of the plantations.

Weaving the Web

The aim of the *negotiatie* system to regulate the colonial economy was cut short by the institutional chaos in the two colonies. Although the *negotiatie* conditions were elaborate, they generally failed to specify how to deal with defaults. As an improvised form of financial innovation, drafted in a time of overconfidence, the prospectuses were not interested in possible negative scenarios. This gap in the rules, exacerbated by the improvised nature of the colonial institutions, meant that it proved difficult for creditors to get their money back. On the other hand, it provided ample room for planters to game the system.

While the *negotiatie* system was controlled from the metropolis, colonial actors performed vital functions as *agendaris* (agent) and *priseur* (appraiser). An agent would look for reliable planters to grant credit, as well as monitor their behavior. Unfortunately, it is unclear how many agents were present in the colonies and how critically they examined the planters. What is known is that some (besides a salary) received a fee for bringing new planters into the fund. This fee would form a clear incentive for maximizing the loans extended, without close scrutiny of the underlying finances. Moreover, several prominent figures had a role as agents for a mortgage fund, giving them a clear stake in the continuation of the system. For example, Bernhard Albinus, councillor in the 1780s, was an agent for the fund of Dirk Wernard van Vloten in 1773. In the same year we can find Director-General G. H. Trotz acting as agent for the fund of Kornelis van den Helm Boddaert.[32] In addition, François Changuion Jr. was a councillor, president of the Orphan Chamber, and longtime agent for the fund of his brother, Daniel Changuion. He also worked as *priseur*.[33]

These *priseurs* had an even more important role than a fund's agents. Their estimates of an estate's value determined how much money a planter could borrow. In other words, the *priseurs* had the power to either inflate or deflate the property bubble. Being a *priseur* was not a specialized profession but rather a function performed on the side by prominent men. For example, between 1773 and 1775 the fund of Dirk Wernard van Vloten issued eight mortgages, worth 490,271 guilders, and used the same group of appraisers. Cornelis Overbroek and Thomas Cuming were responsible for most of the valuations, but Joseph Bourda and L. I. D. van Grovestins (brother of the later governor) were also involved.[34] All of these men were either councillors or would become councillors later in their careers, testifying to their social status. Furthermore, most of these men had mortgages themselves. Bourda was bound to Van Vloten in 1774; Cuming (together with Thomas Grant) had his estate mortgaged to Daniel Changuion, and so did Grovestins.[35]

Thus a serious principal-agent problem arose. Rather than act primarily on behalf of the mortgage funds, these men could further their own interests without immediate means of punishment. Bringing in a new planter would generate a bonus, and if the planter was unable to pay his debts, it was the fund's problem, not the agent's. Furthermore, the estate of an appraiser would also rise in value if he valued other estates higher and fostered the speculative trend.

Finally, there was a social dimension too. If a *priseur* would put a realistic value on an estate that would deny a fellow planter much-needed credit, he might push his colleague into default. Furthermore, in this small colonial elite, one man's debt was another man's asset. So the executing of one estate might trigger further bankruptcies because of the financial entanglement. The ledger of the Weilburg estate in the late 1760s demonstrates that plantations had transactions with a large number of people, both outside and inside the colony. Hoes, rope, butter, beef, pork, paint, tiles, lamp oil, and many gallons of rum all changed hands but usually without any transfer of cash. Instead, planters kept accounts of who owed what to whom. These exchanges bound planters to each other, particularly since the sums were substantial, as several of the British planters were also engaged in slave smuggling.[36]

Indeed, Storm also noted that smuggling made the financial entanglement worse. In 1770 he heard that planters were paying for illegal captives with bills of exchange payable in the Dutch Republic. He asked the Company for proof of such bills so that he could prosecute those involved. With such proof, he "had the thread & the clew would likely follow, because these must bleed when the others collapse & the whole matter would come to light."[37] Furthermore, during the following year, he discovered why such bills by highly indebted planters did not come back in protest; the planters simply tried to cash the bill again, including the 25 percent protest costs. While such an attempt might work if a planter's credit had increased in the meantime, often matters only got worse. After three such attempts to cash a protested bill, Storm emphasized, the original sum had doubled.[38] In 1771 the authorities therefore ordered everyone involved with the many protested bills to come to the fort to see if they could work out an agreement to prevent the "total ruin of the colony."[39] Obviously, the British smugglers shunned bills as soon as they discovered the problems with them. Consequently, in 1772 they insisted on payment in produce. In other words, one type of smuggling (in enslaved Africans) fostered more smuggling (in cash crops).[40]

Even if Storm had proof, he was reluctant to execute estates, fearing a colony-wide financial collapse. As many planters possessed protested bills of someone else, executing one would start a chain reaction that would ruin many others. Furthermore, because the *negotiatie* bubble was past its peak by that point, few buyers were interested, so prices at auction would be low. Execution would hurt a host of people: not just the planter and the workforce on his estate, but also the claimant (who probably would not receive the full amount) and all other potential creditors. Although Storm condemned planters who bought illegal captives, he deemed it too harsh to force them into financial ruin.[41]

Storm's successor, Trotz, also saw the need to prevent executions. When he was confronted in 1774 with protested bills of the widow FitzPatrick, he had two choices: be patient and hope she would be able to pay later or execute the estate to procure the money. He chose the former, as he considered execution of the estate "such a ruinous measure, that I am frightened when I count the multitude of our citizens that are nominated for that death sentence, because of the general discredit and weakening of prices of our products, which starts to generate a chaos of confusion here."[42] Interestingly, this reluctance to execute estates was paired with a belief that *if* it came to execution, the matter would be resolved in an orderly manner. However, this faith turned out to be mistaken. In general, "orderly" was an ill-fitting term to describe interactions in the two colonies, but the process of establishing debt preference proved particularly problematic. If an estate was auctioned off and the revenue was less than all the outstanding debts, who would be paid first?

If All Debts Are Preferential...

There were four groups that vied for preference of their claims: the Company, mortgage holders, provision traders, and those involved in the slave trade. The latter group consisted of the slave traders themselves but also the auctioneer in the colonies, who sometimes acted as guarantor for planters' slave debts, as we shall see below.

The interests of the slave traders and those of the fund directors were the most directly opposed. Although both groups had an interest in stimulating the plantation complex, they competed for the produce. The mortgage conditions obliged the planter to consign his cash crops to the fund director, while the slave traders also wanted cash crops rather than bills, which involved more risks. However, the slavers were prevented from doing so and also failed to get the right to reclaim enslaved Africans in case bills proved unreliable. Furthermore, there was an element of provincial rivalry involved. In cases of financial distress, a mortgage fund from Holland might put the payment of a bill in favor of slavers from Zealand last in line.[43]

During the 1760s and 1770s, the WIC attempted to regulate the financial side of the slave trade through mandatory auctions. The idea was that all planters had the same chance of buying enslaved Africans, while in theory the auctioneer (*vendumeester*) stood as security for the planters' debts to the slave trader. The planters would assign their bills of exchange to the auctioneer, so the slave traders did not have to deal with all the individual, potentially unreliable planters. To compensate for this risk, the auctioneer received a fee.[44] However, the auctioneer Adriaan Spoors seemingly refused to stand as security in at least 1763 and 1764, undermining the purpose. His refusal made the auction fees into an extra tax without providing any security to the slavers. They still had to deal with risky bills or take their human cargo elsewhere, which is what many of them did.

According to Storm van 's Gravesande, the rules offered ample protection for both the auctioneer and the slave traders. Disagreeing with Spoor on many issues, he thought that Spoor should accept his responsibility, which entailed little risk. Storm noted that the auctioneer could order the immediate execution of an estate if debts were not paid and had the right of preference.[45] Although Storm became increasingly opposed to executions, as the web of debt grew tighter, he still had enough faith in the system to follow his own advice, when he himself fulfilled the role of auctioneer (ad interim) in the late 1760s, as discussed below in the case of Callaert's estate.

Yet ideas about rights of preference proved fluid in the underregulated colonies. From a Council of Policy meeting in 1771 we can gather that execution was far from a straightforward affair. In this meeting the council had a heated discussion on the hierarchy of debts regarding the inventory of four deceased inhabitants. One of the estates belonged to the former auction master Nicholas Rousselet de la Jarie, who had died four years before.[46] The first proposal for a hierarchy of debt put the right of reclamation (*rei vindicato*) first, followed by "domestic debts" (*inlandse schulden*), including mortgages. Third came taxes (*landspenningen*), and fourth was wages and maintenance for the plantation. The last in line were protested bills, followed by salaries of scribes and those in charge of sequestration. In other words, it seems that mortgage holders and slave traders would be first in line.[47]

However, the council decided to improvise on its own order of preference, favoring the colonial interest. Taxes due to the colonial government came first; salaries, servants' pay, and advances were second; third, mortgages; and fourth, protested bills of exchange. In other words, the councillors made sure that all local interests were served before outside debtors would get anything. Two slaving firms had claims to the inventory of Rousselet de la Jarie, namely, Snouck, Hurgonje & Louissen for 17,599 guilders and De Bruyn & De Smit for 74,819 guilders—who were also mortgage fund directors. And these were only two of the forty-three claims on a total sum of 187,918 guilders. Yet the available capital comprised only 81,418 guilders. With insufficient funds and with the protested bills last in line, the slavers were unlikely to get their money. They intended to take the matter to the States-General, but no resolution is known. In addition, even though mortgage creditors were in a better position, they did not have any guarantee that they could get their money back either.[48]

In other situations different orders might be established, but that only underscores the unpredictability of the system. In 1773, when Trotz was jointly in charge of the sequestration of the Moerassie plantation, he delivered provisions to the estate to keep it running, but these claims ended up last in line. He had another claim that was awarded when the plantation was sold, but then the whole procedure started anew, and Trotz's previous claims were not even considered. Trotz suspected the new ordering had been arranged to avoid paying certain people. He contemplated bringing the case before the Court of Holland, but it is uncertain if this ever happened. Regardless, it is telling that even the director-general was unaware of how the system worked and suffered losses as a consequence. This case further underlines the arbitrariness and improvisation that characterized the colonies' institutions.[49]

Finally, Trotz attributed part of the financial chaos to the local Weesen Onbeheerde Boedelkamer (Insolvency Chamber). When the Court of Justice scrutinized its books, a host of irregularities turned up, ranging from deficient paperwork to sums that remained unpaid and apparently had gone into other pockets. Consequently, the president of the chamber, François Changuion Jr., was made financially responsible himself to pay outstanding claims. Instead of arranging an orderly settlement, Trotz remarked, the Insolvency Chamber had become a robbery chamber. Unsurprisingly, the chamber president could not pay for all debts and Trotz placed his estate under sequestration the next year.[50]

All of the above issues regarding mortgage claims, auctioneer's rights, and unowned estates came together in the case of Pieter Callaert. As chapter 3 demonstrated, Callaert's financial troubles were at the root of the large slave uprising in 1772. Callaert acquired the Anna Catharina estate, but his bills apparently came back protested. Storm, as auctioneer, was then left with 13,085 guilders in protested bills (around five-eighths of the 21,000 guilders Callaert paid for the estate). On 18 August 1772 Storm auctioned the estate and P. C. Hooft paid 48,600 guilders for it, using mortgage credit from the fund of Jan van Rijneveld & Soonen. Two other planters stood as guarantors for Hooft's debt. After Hooft's death in the revolt, however, the guarantors refused to pay anything. Thus the mortgage fund was now left as owner of the indebted plantation. Trotz, as auctioneer, had taken over 22,614 guilders in repeatedly protested bills from Storm, apparently convinced he had a solid claim. In the meantime, it turned out that Hooft also had a current account with the mortgage fund of Tulleken de Vos & Comp. in Amsterdam, of almost 10,000 guilders. The other fund, Rijneveld & Soonen, then proposed to ask the Insolvency Chamber to sell Hooft's *other* estate, Cornelia & Ida, to recoup the money. However, the financial entanglement proved so great that the matter ended up before the States-General in 1776. The States-General had already provided an instruction on debt handling in 1774, but the new one of 1776 explicitly dealt with insolvent estates and noninsolvent ones that were put up for auction.[51]

The States-General's ruling of 4 October 1774 was based on a proposal by the WIC. The Company basically acknowledged that there was no uniform basis for legal proceedings—as there were several different traditions—so it had asked the States-General to draft something tailored for Essequibo and Demerara. This new ruling favored the WICs interests:

poll taxes and other colonial duties owed to it became preferential to other debts (although these were small compared to mortgage debts). A claimant could bring his case before the court, after which an elaborate procedure had to be followed in which all claimants could step forward and contest any competing claims. To notify everyone, advertisements about the execution had to be placed—three times—in the Amsterdam, Rotterdam, and Middleburgh newspapers. Two curators, one of which had to be an agent of the mortgage fund, if applicable, would take care of the administration, for a fee of 10 percent of the crops. Nevertheless, the States-General instructed the local officials to arrange settlements in order to avoid lengthy procedures.[52]

The ruling was a typical product of Company reasoning: it took good care of its own affairs, yet failed to address the underlying issue of the preference problems. In fact, the same ruling noted that the legal system in the colonies would be based on the rules and criminal procedures of Holland of 1570, 1580, and 1599.[53] Neither the WIC nor the States-General apparently felt the need to formulate a more solid legal framework, leaving matters in the unpredictable, improvising hands of colonial actors. Only the chaotic situation surrounding Hooft's plantation spurred the States-General to expand on the rules about preference.

Indeed, the "new way of proceeding" of 1776 was explicitly aimed at rectifying the irregularities and malpractices that resulted from the lack of "fixed and certain ordinances" (*vaste en bepaalde ordonnantien*). The new rules aimed to lay out the procedure for the *judicium praeferentiae et concurrentiae*. Two curators had to assemble all claims, also through advertisements in the metropolis, after which the creditors had to reach an agreement. In case of conflict, the opposers could make a counterclaim within fourteen days, after which another two weeks were available for reply, and again for the counterargument. Two months later the local Court of Justice would pass the sentence. Real estate would be sold in four installments, and the buyer would acquire full ownership only after paying everything. Two guarantors had to commit themselves as well. First mortgages were preferential over second mortgages, and after a settlement had been reached the case was closed.[54]

Nevertheless, it still remained unclear how these rules would work in practice if several people considered their claims preferential. It was a (presumed) Barbadian, Alleyne Culpeper, who in 1777 asked the States-General to clear up the matter and provide future guidance. Culpeper had extended a mortgage for Mes Delices, which was about to be sold. He believed his claim was preferential but was unsure and asked if the preference ordering could be established *before* the execution. That way he could offer more at the auction and acquire the full estate. If most of his money would come back to him to settle his preferential claim, he could bid higher. Conversely, if others had preference, he would be more cautious. Earlier, he had tried to get an answer in the colonies but in vain.[55]

In the meantime the council had improvised a plan of its own: the bailiff would lay claim to all possessions of a debtor in case of a claim and settle the matter quickly, because prices could fluctuate greatly. Apparently, it also included a proposal to give preference to the first creditor pushing for execution. When this proposal reached the WIC, the directors shot it down. In this scenario anyone with even a petty claim would have an incentive to file a claim quickly and demand execution. The result would be financial chaos. Therefore, the matter went higher up, to the States-General.[56]

The debate in the States-General showed that the different provinces had difficulty formulating a workable solution. Interestingly, the most well considered reply came from the province of Utrecht rather than from Holland, the financial center. The deputies from Holland noted that executed estates drew much higher prices if the preference was established *before* the execution rather than afterward. Nevertheless, they refused to make this a standard policy, preferring to let the mortgage funds decide in each specific case. Apparently, the option of favoring first claimants was still on the table, as the deputies from Utrecht strongly argued against it. Instead, their preferred option was to let creditors compete with each other after the deduction of preferential debts. Furthermore, the one demanding the auction should pay for the execution costs. That way creditors would think twice before choosing this option and would also be deterred from making risky loans they could not easily collect.[57]

However, while the *procedure* in the colonies had become clearer, *preference* still remained a controversial subject. While WIC debts were at the top of the list, the rest of the order was less straightforward, as there often were no clear accounts of all the debts. For example, in the case of Hooft the colonial books showed no sign of a mortgage, even though the fund Rijneveld & Soonen did have clear proof in its own administration.[58] In addition, while mortgage funds believed their claims were preferential, other actors in the colonies thought differently.

The issue of plantation provisions proved particularly salient. Supplies were typically a local affair, which explains why the council in 1771 put such debts high in the debt hierarchy. Furthermore, as the enslaved were hit hardest by financial crises, colonial legislators realized that the provision trade should not be disrupted. The British Caribbean therefore witnessed an increasing number of laws giving preference to food and clothing for the enslaved, starting in 1798 and stimulated by debates about amelioration.[59]

The Dutch States-General considered similar legislation in 1778. In a debate about the rights of reclamation by mortgage funds, the States of Holland proposed to make mortgage debt preferential—after WIC debts—but on condition that the directors kept the plantation intact. If they did not, they themselves would be forced to honor bills from planters who supplied their estate. This condition included food, clothing, medication, and even enslaved Africans. Such spending had to be approved by the agents of the mortgage fund. If they refused, a planter could ask the court to intervene, which could rule to accept expenses for provisions but not for enslaved Africans. If the bills came back in protest, they would be preferential to all other debts, excluding Company debts. While it is unclear if this proposal was adopted, the other provinces seemed in favor.[60]

Actors in the colonies at least *believed* that claims for provisions were preferential, as we already saw with Trotz. When in 1780 Johan Bremer tried to collect a debt for goods delivered by his principal, Captain Jan Rousman, a local councillor told him he was out of luck, unless his cargo had consisted of the typical slave provisions of plantains and *bakkeljauw*.[61] A similar situation unfolded in 1800 concerning the Boston businessman Theodore Barrell (see chapter 6). He had delivered nearly 14,000 guilders in provisions to a recently deceased connection of his. Barrell feared there was not enough money in the estate to satisfy all claims, although he believed the executors would favor him. He likely only advanced such a large sum because he expected to be able to get it back: "As the chief of my demand is for plantation supplies I think in justice I ought to be among the first to be attended to," he stated. Nevertheless, nine days later he was no longer so sure and expressed his desire to quit life as a merchant and choose a less risky career as a commission agent.[62] Even by the end of the century, then, ambiguity and insecurity were still the norm.[63]

Indeed, while in Suriname many investment funds bought the indebted estates to have their administrators run them for a profit, in Essequibo and Demerara the situation remained convoluted. In 1788 mortgage funds had apparently taken over just 6 of the 182 plantations, while in Demerara none of the estates were registered as such. Nevertheless, of the 287 plantations in Demerara, 126 were confirmed as being burdened by a *negotiatie* mortgage, with 86 being free (but possibly mortgaged to British creditors) and the rest unknown.[64] While the colonial administration's accounting was not accurate enough to take these numbers as exact, they clearly indicate that many planters were heavily indebted and that an orderly winding down of those debts had not yet taken place.

All in all, in this hopelessly entangled web of debt it proved a nightmare to figure out who was to be paid first. All actors had a logical claim to preference: the WIC, as colonial authority; the mortgage holders, as they had lent on the idea of having the plantation as collateral; the slave traders, as they also believed they had extended credit on "human collateral," for without enslaved laborers a plantation was worth little; and finally the local provisioners, who reasoned that they should be first in line, for otherwise they would decline to deliver the provisions necessary for a plantation to survive. Inadvertently, this chaotic situation might have inhibited the number of executions, as no one could know the outcome beforehand. Furthermore, as long as all players believed they would be included among the preferential creditors, there was little need to push for execution, for nobody stood to gain anything from a fire sale auction. Finally, the colonial authorities had clear incentives to keep the web of debt intact, as untangling it would likely trigger a wave of defaults in which they might be caught up themselves.

Comparing Dutch and British Approaches

The question arises how this Dutch image of financial ruin and chaos compares to the later British image of Guiana as a land that offered planters "very rapid and splendid fortunes."[65] Indeed, many British owners of Guianese plantations became immensely rich and received large compensations when slavery was abolished in 1834.[66] Yet already under Dutch rule, foreign planters seemingly raked in large profits. For example, in 1761 Gedney Clarke Jr.—who I discuss more fully in the next chapter—claimed to have recouped the full sum of 12,000 pounds sterling (around 144,000 guilders) he had paid for his estate Het Loo in just one year. In subsequent years he apparently made a profit of 4,000 pounds (almost 50,000 guilders).[67] These are unusually large amounts, although his extensive smuggling business surely contributed.[68] Nevertheless, it prompts the question whether the divergent stories can be explained by the differences in time or if the British were simply more successful planters.

For later British writers the explanation was clear: the Dutch were lousy planters. The British traveler Henry Bolingbroke wrote at the turn of the nineteenth century, "[The Dutch] aspire only to a competency not to a fortune; and they waste labor [sic], under an idea of having their estates look like gardens. The Englishman makes more of his property; but the Dutchman leaves it a better inheritance." Bolingbroke deemed the Dutch good accountants, but as long as they did not expand their estates and fully exploit them, like the British, they would never become wealthy.[69]

Yet such large-scale plantations were mostly a phenomenon that developed *after* the British takeover. When Bolingbroke arrived in 1799 the colonies had already witnessed a transformation resulting from the large number of Africans brought in by British slavers after the takeover. Consequently, the average number of slaves per plantation had increased rapidly to more than one hundred in 1798.[70] This trend continued. In 1813 in Demerara 46 percent of the plantations had between 100 and 200 enslaved workers and another 40 percent had between 200 and 300 slaves.[71] In previous years, however, the average number of enslaved people working on an estate was surprisingly low, increasing from around 30 in 1766 to just over 50 in 1782. In 1788 this number stood at 40 in Essequibo and at 60 in Demerara.[72] Despite these relatively small numbers, it is of course still possible that British estates were larger than Dutch ones.

The data do not allow for a precise reconstruction, but it is clear that the British were among the biggest planters in Essequibo and Demerara. In 1764 there were ten plantations in Essequibo with more than one hundred enslaved people, and two were in British hands. In Demerara, only three plantations had more than one hundred slaves, as it was still developing, but all three were in non-Dutch hands, with Gedney Clarke's two estates being the largest.[73] Later, in 1777, in Essequibo 20 percent of the largest estates were in British hands, a rate that was similar in Demerara in 1779.[74] In 1785 again about a third of the biggest estates had British or North American owners in Essequibo, while in Demerara the proportion hovered around 20 percent in 1788.[75] Without an accurate number of foreign planters in the colonies, it is impossible to solidly determine whether British or North American planters were overrepresented in the colonies. Nevertheless, guesstimates based on surnames indicate they were indeed.[76] In other words, Bolingbroke was at least partially right when he explained the economic success of British planters by their more intensive exploitation.[77]

However, British planters had another advantage: a protected home market. If a planter succeeded in illicitly selling his produce in London, he would receive a much better price than on the open market of Amsterdam. This protected market resulted in higher prices, although the exact difference with other countries remains unclear. One historian has estimated that British sugars were priced between one-fourth and one-third higher than those in France. Another estimate put the price of London muscovado sugar at least 15 percent higher than in Amsterdam and probably around 23 percent in the years leading up to the American Revolution. Coffee and cotton, on the other hand, are said to have been around the same prices as on the European continent.[78] Smuggling sugar would thus pay off for British planters.

The British were perhaps also the more perceptive planters, recognizing the potential for cotton cultivation on the coast. In the early eighteenth century, most plantations were laid out upriver in order to be protected from privateers, foreign armies, and the tide. Gradually, the soil of these estates became depleted, and in 1740 it was discovered that land closer to the coast was much more fertile. Furthermore, Demerara was believed to be more fertile than Essequibo, and most British planters in fact settled in Demerara.[79] And although the coast was deemed too saline for sugar, coffee, or plantains, it proved suitable for cotton.[80]

The demand for cotton was likely higher in industrializing Britain than in the Dutch Republic, and most cotton planters were British. Figure 5.1 shows that cotton was generally surpassed by sugar and coffee in weight, but as figure 5.2 shows, it delivered the greatest value by the end of the century as it was a lighter crop and significantly more valuable per pound. Figure 5.1 also shows that after the British occupation a sudden boom in cotton exports occurred. While this development is partly the result of the general expansion in the colonies, the major factor must have been the rampant smuggling in previous years. In fact, that observation is the only reliable inference one could make from the figure.

This British dominance in coastal cotton planting is also clearly visible in maps 5.1, 5.2, and 5.3, which show the transition from the riverbanks banks to the coast. In map 5.1, of Demerara in 1759 (oriented roughly east-west), it is clear that virtually all plantations are laid out along the rivers. The most upstream plantations were abandoned already, but only a handful of plantations are established on the coast by this point in time. Furthermore, according to the legend there are only sugar, coffee, and bread estates, none growing cotton. Map 5.2, made in 1784 during the French occupation, reveals that Demerara's coastline is dotted with

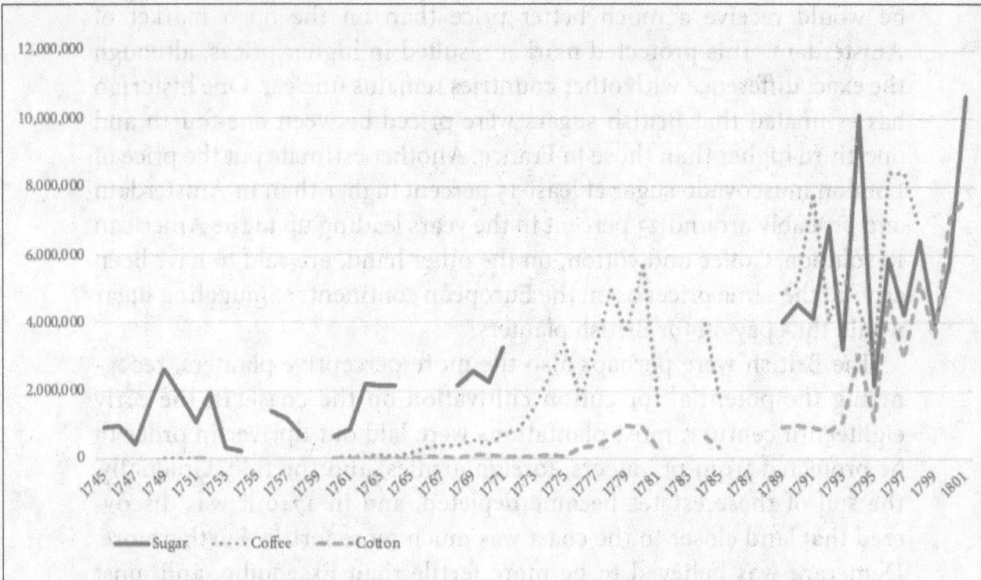

FIGURE 5.1. Exports from Essequibo and Demerara (1745–1801, in lbs). Source: Bolingbroke, A Voyage, 397; TNA, CO 111/3, f.209-213; TNA, Co 111/4, f.179.

plantations. Although crops are not mentioned, it is likely that most of those coastal estates produced cotton, as is revealed by map 5.3, from 1798. There one can see that both Demerara and Essequibo had sugar and coffee estates but that the majority of the plantations produced cotton. Especially Demerara's east coast and the westernmost coast of Essequibo were fully covered in cotton estates. The small sea fronts allowed a large number of plantations to be laid out, making maximum use of the fertile soil. Unfortunately, the colonial administration was so unorderly that for a very large number of estates the owners are unknown, particularly in Essequibo. For Demerara's east coast, however, the data are better and the names suggest that a large majority of the owners were non-Dutch.[81]

Finally, British (and other non-Dutch) planters had another important advantage: the ability to use multiple credit systems. On the one hand, they could use personal credit networks, borrowing large sums of money from individual merchant-bankers (a topic I discuss in the next chapter). On the other hand, a substantial number of British planters relied on the Dutch *negotiaties* to make their entry into the colonies. From Tulleken's original fourteen mortgages, five were granted to persons presumed to be British. For Boddaert, from his original thirty-seven plantations,

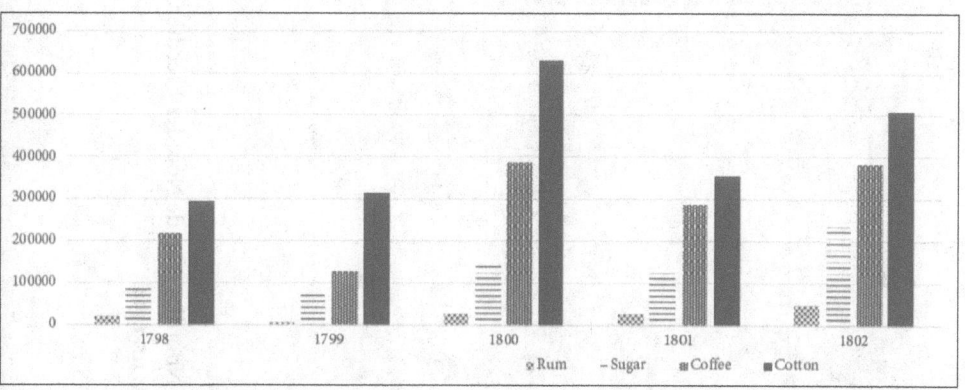

FIGURE 5.2. Registered exports from Essequibo and Demerara (1798–1802, in pounds sterling). Source: TNA, CO 111/4, f.179.

presumably fourteen planters were of British and one of French origin. Considering that around one-third of the planters in the two colonies were British at that point, they were overrepresented in the fund of Boddaert. In addition, when Dutch planters switched funds in the second phase of investments, British and French planters did exactly the same. We find four British couples with Van den Santheuvel, another two French and two British planters with Van Vloten, and Rijneveld & Zonen welcomed at least five foreign-owned plantations into his fund, including the lonely Italian, Octavio Sardi.[82]

While the *negotiaties* reached more Dutch than British planters, it likely gave British (and North American) colonists an additional advantage. In combination with the better smuggling opportunities, a keener eye for crop potential, and possibly more experience with larger estates (as many planters had previous experience elsewhere), it could explain why British colonists seemed to have repatriated richer than most Dutch colonists.

In the end, it proves very difficult to uncover the financial dealings of these planters, both because of the scarce source material and because of the complexities of the topic. It is striking that contemporaries themselves, even successful merchants and directors-general, did not understand the workings of the web of debt and were confronted with unexpected losses. This unpredictability was a consequence of the improvised nature of empire building in Essequibo and Demerara. Local actors had no incentive to untangle the web, while in the metropolis the

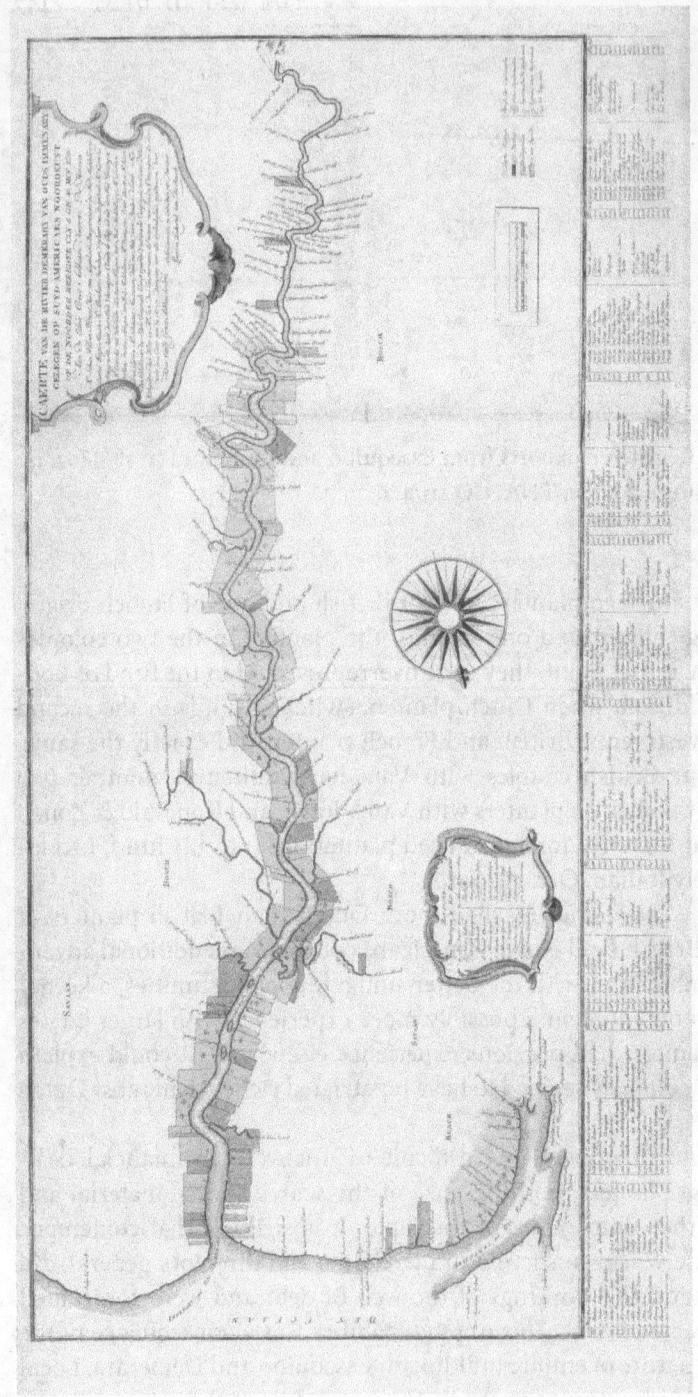

MAP 5.1. Caerte van de rivier Demerary van Ouds Immenary, gelegen op Suyd Americaes Noordkust op de Noorder Breedte van 6 Gr. 40 Min, Laurens Lodewyk van Berchyck, 1759. NL-HaNA, Kaarten Leupe, 4.VEL, inv. nr. 1494.

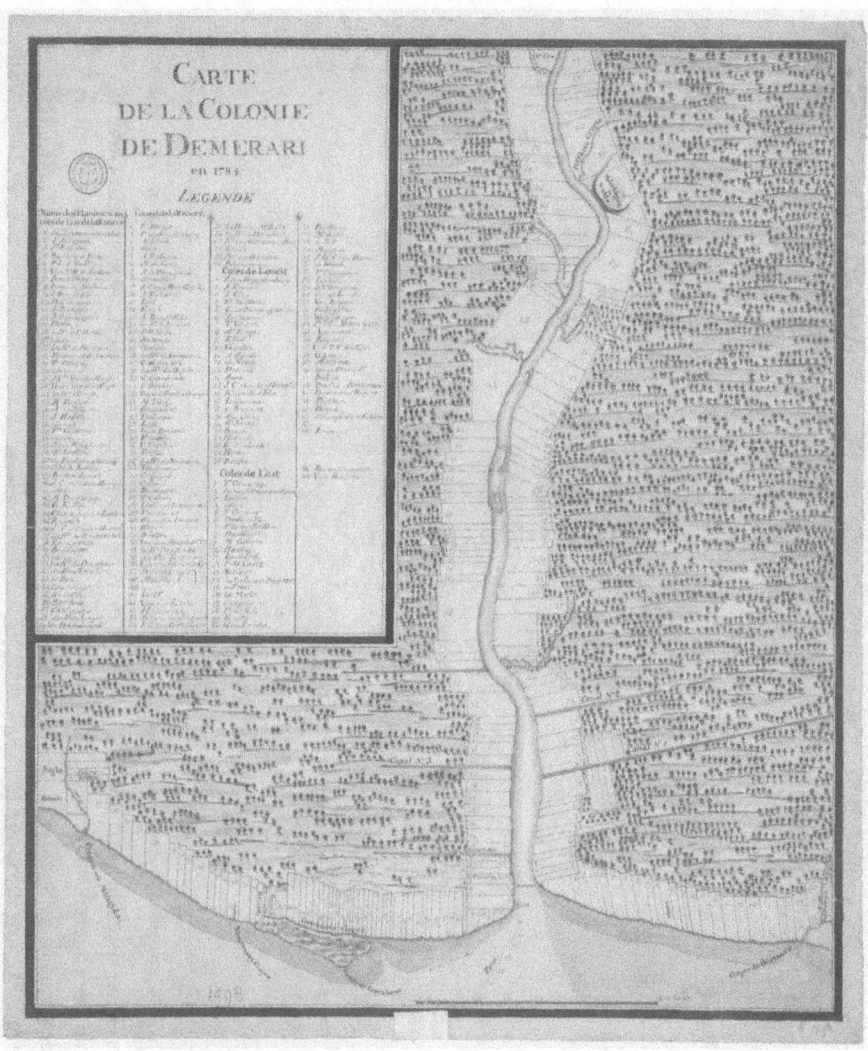

MAP 5.2. Carte de la Colonie de Demerary, unknown artist, 1784, NL-HaNA, Kaarten Leupe, 4.VEL, inv. nr. 1498.

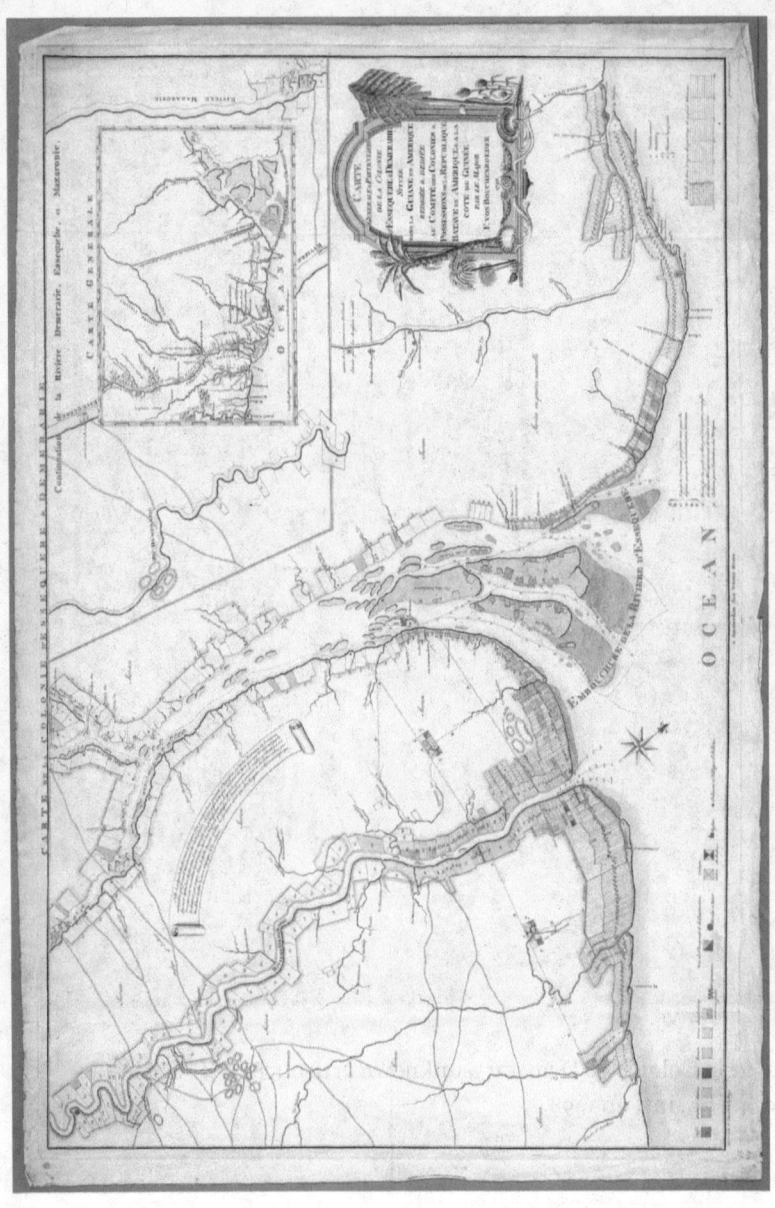

MAP 5.3. Generale en speciale kaart der Colonien van de republicq der Ver. Nederl., geleegen in Guyana, langs de Zeekust der rivieren Poumaron, Essequebo, Demerary; van de grensen van Berbice tot de rivier Morocco aan de grens in de Spaansche Bezitting Oronoco, Friederich von Bouchenröder, 1798, NL-HaNA, Kaarten Leupe, 4.VEL, inv. nr. 1490A1.

institutional structure proved too ineffective to balance the different interest groups in a way that led to a useful legal framework.

In fact, the judicial system was a source of confusion rather than clarity. Few members of the Court of Justice had a background in law, and most merely considered their position a "highly profitable metier" (*zeer voordelig metier*). According to Commissioners Grovestins and Boeij, the result was that many verdicts were close to worthless.[83] Verdicts could be inconclusive or overturned, to the apparent surprise of even the director-general. With a legal system that was based on the laws of Holland from the sixteenth century, the councillors had little relevant legal guidance. Yet they did not succeed in establishing a body of jurisprudence that could function as a basis for future insolvency settlements. Instead, each case proved to be a new battleground, where reputation, personal grudges, or the mood of the day could influence the outcome. While appeal to the States-General was possible, the long distance and protracted deliberation process of the States-General itself made this route a difficult one. Furthermore, access to the judicial system proved harder for those who did not speak Dutch—and this number of people only increased throughout the century. If an *ex post* debt settlement was hard to attain, it was also because so few rules existed *ex ante*.

Establishing a clear order of debt preference was a crucial issue, yet it remained unresolved by the actors involved. The WIC had expressed little interest in providing clear procedures and the States-General's efforts proved too little, too late. Only after the *negotiatie* bubble had burst did the States-General attempt to formulate an order of procedures in case of defaults. However, as the credit crunch plunged more and more planters into financial trouble, the rules remained opaque about who would get their money first. Again, the metropolis could not get a grip on developments in the colonies.

This web of debt likely prompted later investors to think twice before they invested their money in risky places like Essequibo and Demerara. In the long run, then, the colonies became less attractive to Dutch investors. However, the gap was filled by other investments, as numerous non-Dutch adventurers were eager enough to try their luck in these borderless societies. Many of them combined smuggling, regular trade, and plantation ownership in an effort to establish a profitable interimperial enterprise, as the individual stories in the next chapter show.

6 / Borderless Businessmen

Recently, historians have turned to studying individual lives to probe deeper into the functioning of empires. Such case studies can have three functions: they might draw attention to a person with a pivotal position, they may illustrate how an individual experienced larger developments, or they may show how a particular person was representative of a larger group.[1] This chapter relies on all of these motives to demonstrate how individual initiative was crucial in shaping the society of Essequibo and Demerara. It focuses on non-Dutch individuals, for reasons of source availability and because they showcase the borderlessness of these colonies.[2]

The first section shows that "nationality" hardly mattered in Essequibo and Demerara anyway, except during wartime. Subsequently, the chapter broadens its focus in three steps. It starts by analyzing regional connections, particularly with Barbados, by focusing on Gedney Clarke Sr., Gedney Clarke Jr., and William Croydon. It then investigates connections with North America, mainly looking at three Bostonians, John Hubbard and Gardiner Greene (brothers-in-law) and the merchant Theodore Barrell. Finally, the chapter turns to transatlantic networks, with a focus on Scottish ventures, by studying Thomas Cuming and the firm of Robertson, Parker, McInroy and Sandbach.[3]

Several of these figures occupied important positions in colonial society (Clarke, Cuming, and, to a lesser extent, Croydon). Others were more representative of a larger group: Croydon typified the migration of adventurous British planters from Barbados to Essequibo and Demerara; the

Bostonian merchants exemplify the involvement of North Americans in Atlantic trade networks; and the firm of Robertson, Parker, McInroy and Sandbach highlights the strong involvement of Scots in various other empires. Finally, studying these people sheds light on the development of Essequibo and Demerara during the eighteenth century. For example, they expanded their businesses by using trade as a springboard to establish themselves as planters. In addition, they were keen to enlarge their estates and participate in smuggling, as they refused to be bound by imperial borders. Indeed, through their initiatives, they contributed to transforming Essequibo and Demerara from Dutch possessions to borderless colonies that were firmly integrated in the Atlantic world.

A Planter Society?

The individuals mentioned above had different origins, but in practice this mattered little in the open colonial society of Essequibo and Demerara. Most of the time the planters saw themselves not as nationals of competing countries but more as colleagues in the struggle to succeed in the Atlantic economy. Of course, people belonged to multiple groups and emphasized different aspects depending on the circumstances, which is why this section employs the concept of identification rather than identity.[4] This process of identification merits study, for it begs the question to what extent we can speak of an integrated colonial community in Essequibo and Demerara.

Religion, the most obvious candidate to establish a shared understanding among planters, was far from prominent in Essequibo and Demerara. The smaller neighbor, Berbice, had its Moravian Brotherhood missionaries, but Essequibo and Demerara barely had a functioning church.[5] In the 1740s a church building existed on the Ampa plantation, but it had fallen into disrepair by 1750. In 1754 the church reopened and Storm asked the Company for five or six dozen simple chairs because it was so crowded. However, there is no mention of a functioning church afterward. Gedney Clarke Sr. wanted to establish one, to hold English services, and received permission from Storm to do so, as long as it was at Clarke's cost. The construction was supposed to take place together with the building of a village, yet neither of the projects materialized.[6]

Yet religion was not totally absent from planters' lives, as a minister performed marriages and baptisms on individual plantations when necessary. Furthermore, makeshift churches existed. In Essequibo services were held in the same building that housed the Secretariat and Council of Policy; in Demerara the lower floor of the Secretariat had a pulpit and a few benches. Apparently, it was good enough for the colonists. In theory Calvinism was the dominant religion, but in practice few people attended services, if only because the estates were widespread and could be days away by boat. Regardless, the colonies had a reputation of being godforsaken places. It even proved difficult to get reliable ministers: the Reverend Hermanus Lingius was allowed to serve for fourteen years, starting in 1763, despite his shortcomings. The council was aware of the minister's "unedifying behaviour" and his drunkenness, and Gedney Clarke Jr. asked Storm to prosecute Lingius for shooting and injuring one of "his most civilised Creoles." Nevertheless, it was not until 1777 that the reverend was fired for misconduct.[7]

For the WIC, religion was no priority. In theory, it should have had ample money for church buildings or the salary of a reliable reverend, for it levied special taxes (*kerk- en armengelden*) for the so-called Church and Poor Fund. While the proportion seems to have ranged from 0.5 to 2.5 percent over time, typically 1.5 percent of all public auctions was destined for this fund, as was one-third of all the fines. In addition, when a ship captain came to register for the necessary pass, he had to pay an extra 2.50 guilders for the fund. The Church and Poor Fund thus benefited from almost all financial transactions, so there ought to have been a substantial amount of money available. In fact, in 1795 it amounted to more than 21,177 guilders. However, the fund seemed to have been used mostly for other means. In 1775, for instance, the council wanted to compensate planters for the insurgents who had been executed after the 1772 Callaert rebellion (see chapter 3). It wanted to pay 400 guilders per rebel but did not have enough money at hand, so it decided to take the money from the Church and Poor Fund, with the aim of replenishing it later. Others stated that the Company instead used the money to speculate in VOC shares, and even the council recognized that the obligatory contributions to the fund were just an extra tax.[8] In colonies that were already underfunded, investment in religion was clearly not a priority.

Religion, then, did not have the potential to act as social glue, and social life took place mostly on individual estates rather than in churches or taverns. Whether taverns existed is unclear; perhaps there was one in Stabroek in Demerara and seemingly one on Fort Island and on Flag Island in Essequibo. Several unofficial drinking establishments existed, as demonstrated by the proclamations of the WIC against selling hard liquor to soldiers in such places.[9] Nevertheless, for planters drinking mainly took place at the plantations. Since the plantations were laid out along wide stretches of coastline and along rivers leading deep into the interior, distances within the two colonies were large. As a result, it was very time consuming to travel, especially since one had to be attentive of the tide. Consequently, it was perfectly acceptable to stop over on a plantation to wait for the right tide or to spend the night.[10]

Social cohesion was also limited by the lack of an urban center. In Suriname, in contrast, many planters had an additional house in Paramaribo and spend part of the year there, thus creating a planter community. This urban environment was an important social space for gossip, forming networks, or seeking marriage partners.[11] Since Stabroek was only established in the early 1780s, this process of local integration did not have deep roots in Essequibo or Demerara. Stabroek nevertheless grew substantially afterward. Rodway reported that it had 88 houses and 780 inhabitants in 1789, namely, 238 whites, 76 free coloreds, and 466 enslaved persons. The town continued to grow, though: in 1795 there were 1,594 enslaved people in Stabroek, together with 433 whites and 166 free coloureds. By then, the entire colony of Demerara had 1,241 white inhabitants; Essequibo, 753.[12] In other words, almost a quarter of the white population lived in Stabroek by the end of the century. Unfortunately, it is unknown how many of them were planters and how many were otherwise involved in the plantation economy as shopkeepers or commission agents, like Theodore Barrell.

One peculiar element in the makeup of the colonial society was the exclusion of Jewish inhabitants. Whereas Jewish settlers played a prominent role in Suriname, they were shunned from Essequibo and Demerara.[13] Individual requests to get permission went as high as the States-General but generally without success.[14] This ban provides a sharp contrast to the tolerant approach adopted previously and elsewhere.[15]

Regarding the political system, the Dutch also employed some mechanisms of exclusion, as visible in the patronage networks of Storm van 's Gravesande. Governing the colonies between 1743 and 1772, he managed to have his son, Jonathan, appointed commander of Demerara in 1750. When Jonathan died prematurely in 1761, he was replaced by Laurens Lodewijk van Bercheyk, who was Storm's wife's nephew and Jonathan's brother-in-law. And when Van Bercheyk died in 1764, his successor the following year was Jan Cornelis van den Heuvel, Storm's son-in-law.[16]

In this closed system it was hard for anyone, let alone non-Dutch planters, to get a foothold in the colonial bureaucracy. In 1770 Storm even told the WIC directors that it might be good to bar English planters from becoming members of the Council of Policy, although he noted that in practice one could not always be so strict.¹⁷ For the Council of Justice, Protestantism rather than origin was the most important requirement, although the fact that the meetings were in Dutch would have made direct participation by foreigners difficult. However, non-Dutch planters could be in the Electoral College that nominated possible councillors and thereby exercise some influence over colonial politics.¹⁸

Importantly, nationality did not become a tool for demanding privileges. Elsewhere, an "English Nation," a "Dutch Nation," or a "Swedish Nation" might claim certain privileges, usually after a foreign power took over. Examples include the right to choose their own officials, to hold their own church services, or to have their own court.¹⁹ Such divisions seem to have been absent from Essequibo and Demerara.

Personal connections were more important. So when Gedney Clarke Sr. received permission to build an English church, he may have acted on behalf of more British planters but succeeded because of his personal relationship with Storm. The fact that he had to pay for it himself might explain why it was never built. Similarly, when in 1769 William Croydon led an initiative of British planters asking to open the slave trade to foreigners, he did not ask for specific British privileges. Instead, his plans would benefit all colonists, and indeed a new version of the petition received wide support, as we shall see below.

The colonists certainly perceived differences in origins and sometimes attached stereotypes to them, but when it came to issues that affected their life as planters, they were quick to close ranks. Economic gain was the strongest common thread, prompting Bolingbroke to write, "All national enmity seems to be forgotten, while the pursuits of the motley group are directed unanimously to climbing the ladder of fortune."²⁰ Indeed, previous chapters demonstrated how quickly the "motley group" rallied together when their illegal trade activities were threatened. Even though informers could theoretically earn substantial sums for denouncing smugglers, in practice that never occurred. Furthermore, in the defining political issue of the 1780s—the division and election of councillors—the petition of 1785 showed the wide "cross-national" support (see chapter 2). Clearly, the planter community was unified enough to launch a major political protest against the WIC, and origin formed no barrier to political cooperation.

In fact, the only time planters felt the need to dust off their "national identities" was in times of war, as occurred twice: during the British and French occupation between 1781 and 1784 and after 1796.²¹ After the first takeover, in 1781, the British demanded an oath of allegiance of (at least) the Dutch planters before they would be allowed to access the British commercial network. This demand caused a stirring in the colonies, for it implied that the colonists would be obliged to take up arms against the Dutch Republic. The British tried to win support by stating that their only aim was to see the colonies prosper, so they recalled how much the French planters on Martinique and Guadeloupe had benefited after the British took possession of these islands. In the end, a compromise was reached and the model of Martinique was followed: the colonists were not obliged to take up arms against "the States of Holland" until the colonies were officially ceded to Great Britain.[22]

The British colonists were understandably pleased with Great Britain's intervention. Edward Thompson, the naval officer initially in charge of the occupation, claimed, "The Inhabitants have but one unanimous wish which is to be received under the Government of Britain, and never more to return to that of Holland."[23] In fact, British planters sent a petition to their king, asking him not to return the colonies to the Dutch. This petition was signed by 76 planters and spearheaded by William Croydon.[24] This idea was probably shared by other "nationalities" too, as the benefits of being part of the British commercial network were clear: high prices on the protected home market and easy access to the well-oiled machine of British slave trading. However, the French occupation in 1782 prevented this scenario from occurring.

The colonists were not just active in asking the British to stay; they allegedly also invited the British to invade in the first place. These rumors went around after both occupations and were not necessarily internally consistent. In 1781 the new British governor noted animosity between Dutch and British planters, as Dutch planters apparently believed British planters had asked for the invasion. On the other hand, it was the Dutch commander of Demerara, Paul van Schuylenburgh, who was forced to go back to the Dutch Republic in 1783 to defend himself against the same allegations of inviting the British. A similar situation occurred in 1796, when Anthony Beaujon, the governor at that point, was rumored to have solicited British intervention.[25]

In short, it was only in matters of war and peace that solidarity between the various groups of planters broke down and processes of national identification came to the fore again. In other circumstances—even though factions might have existed—the colonists identified largely as independent fortune seekers, developing their own initiatives but cooperating when needed. While the planter community cannot be called truly united or integrated, it was united enough to defend common interests and economic opportunities.

However, cooperation through petitions for a shared goal was different from cooperation in individual commercial networks. In establishing the necessary trust to start and maintain a business partnership, regions of origin actually played an important role. The next sections analyze the networks that were formed by individuals operating within different spheres, starting with regional networks.

Regional Connections

The diverse and loose-knit society of Essequibo and Demerara was not an ideal breeding ground for the trust required in long-distance trade. One needed to create a shared understanding not to cheat each other and honor obligations.[26] This trust could be based on familial ties (including the extended family), a shared religion (the Sephardim, for instance), a common region of origin (such as the Basques or the Scots), or even across cultures.[27] Many of the individuals who integrated Essequibo and Demerara in the Atlantic world relied both on their family networks and on partners from the same region of origin. Often they combined several branches of business, such as provisioning, slave trading, and plantation ownership.

The earliest foreigners who arrived in Essequibo and Demerara came from nearby British islands, particularly Barbados and Antigua. Within the British Caribbean and particularly on Barbados, soil erosion led to declining yields from a seventeenth-century peak.[28] Considering that sugar prices recovered from a low point in the 1730s, it became lucrative again to go into sugar planting, and Essequibo and Demerara offered good prospects.[29] Demerara in particular, after being opened up for colonization in 1746, would welcome a large number of non-Dutch settlers. This influx was the result of the policy of Storm van 's Gravesande, who offered prospective planters a ten-year tax exemption and granted land concessions without cost.[30] Even though the numerical importance of early non-Dutch settlers is difficult to ascertain, several historians have underlined that one family was particularly influential, namely, Gedney Clarke Sr. (1711–64) and his son, Gedney Clarke Jr. (1735–77).[31]

Clarke Sr. built a diverse interimperial business portfolio in the West Indies. Coming from an established family in North America, he moved to Barbados to begin his commercial career. He started as a sugar and rum trader but soon engaged in backward integration of the commodity chain by buying the Nieuw Walcheren and Pyra plantations in Demerara in 1746. To supply these plantations, as well as those of others, Clarke became active in the slave trade as well, together with his bankers, Lascelles and Maxwell.³²

In building his commercial network, Clarke Sr. was not afraid of illicit transactions. For example, he tried to brand Demerara sugar and rum as Barbadian to avoid the duties imposed by the Molasses Act. In addition, he was connected to a direct slave trading voyage between Demerara and Africa, to exchange rum for enslaved Africans.³³ Clarke also supplied Demerara planters with illegally imported slaves, acted as customs collector on Barbados, and engaged in victualing and privateering during the Seven Years' War. This broad range of activities initially paid off, and by the 1760s the Clarke family owned eleven plantations in Demerara. However, in the meantime debts had accumulated as well, and in 1764 Clarke Sr. died a heavily indebted man.³⁴

Yet Clarke Sr. had thought ahead and tried to facilitate the career of his sons by shielding them from his debts. For instance, he had transferred his Demerara property to his sons in 1755 and had sent one of his sons—Gedney Clarke Jr.—to the Dutch Republic to learn the language and naturalize. Naturalization was useful for a businessman, as it would offer the same trading rights as Dutchmen, and Clarke Jr. indeed exercised these rights afterward. Although Clarke Jr. sold all his Demerara property, he remained in arrears. Mortgages on his new estates, declining sugar prices, and the credit crisis of 1772 resulted in an increase in debt. Consequently, Clarke's banker foreclosed on the outstanding loans and took over his property.³⁵

The Clarkes relied on a combination of commerce, politics, and military might. Both maintained a good relationship with Storm van 's Gravesande, who even asked Clarke Jr. to be the godfather of his children.³⁶ This connection proved instrumental in saving Essequibo and Demerara from the 1763 slave uprising in neighboring Berbice. There, the enslaved had successfully taken over most of the colony, forcing the whites to abandon their plantations and retreat to a small fortress on the coast. The governor, Van Hoogenheim, engaged in negotiations with the insurgents' leader, Cuffy, who at some point proposed to divide the colony between blacks and whites. Van Hoogenheim's aim was mainly to delay until the reinforcements arrived from Suriname, the Dutch Republic, and St. Eustatius. Nevertheless, the deciding contribution came, as always, from the Amerindian soldiers. Storm van 's Gravesande had convinced Arawaks, Caribs, and Akawaios to go to Berbice to fight.³⁷ Without their involvement the insurgents probably would have formed maroon communities in the forest and hostilities would have continued for long afterward.³⁸

Gedney Clarke Sr., having been informed by Storm of the severity of the situation, took decisive action. Planters in Demerara were scared of the possible spread of this revolt and were unsure how to react. Yet Clarke Sr. arranged for four ships to be sent immediately from Barbados, followed by a fifth, carrying fifty militiamen as well as a hundred mariners and sailors lent to him from the British navy. Together with sailors from the merchant fleet, the total number of troops came to three hundred, scrambled together by "Threats, Arguments & the force of money." The historian Simon Smith aptly captured this situation: "In July 1763, then, a small, privately financed task force of armed men in both public and private employ crossed national boundaries, without any official sanction, solely to protect the property of a leading Barbados merchant [i.e., Clarke]."[39]

For the Clarkes, however, this private intervention became a financial nightmare. Clarke Sr. was surprised and annoyed that Dutch governors (both in Essequibo and on St. Eustatius) were so reluctant to employ private means for what he conceived as the public good. He soon found out the reason. Clarke Sr. claimed to have spent 8,000 pounds sterling (equivalent to some 90,000 guilders) on the colonies' protection and tried to reclaim this sum from the WIC. Storm agreed that Clarke's contributions had been vital, yet financial compensation was in the hands of the WIC directors. And they were not very sympathetic to the claims. Three years later Clarke Jr. was still arguing for compensation of his father's expenses, and the WIC stated that it and the colonists would each pay half. It is unclear whether the WIC paid its share, but it is clear that the colonists did not. An additional poll tax was instated to raise the money, but many planters flatly refused to pay.[40]

Dissatisfaction with the Company was likely a major reason for Clarke Jr. to quit Demerara in 1769. He decided to try his luck in other new developing areas, namely, Grenada and Tobago. Simon Smith notes that factionalism within the British community, with Clarke Jr. on the one hand and Lachlan McClane on the other, was the reason for Clarke's migration.[41] Yet frustration with the WIC also played a role. On several occasions he criticized Company rule and proposed that the States-General take the colonies into its own hands. He was particularly annoyed with the trade restrictions the Company maintained: he voiced a strong desire to be allowed to ship produce to Amsterdam, rather than just to Zealand, and foresaw a great future if Demerara would be made a free port.[42] Another thorny issue was the small scale of the slave trade, which—as Clarke explained—resulted in planters buying their enslaved laborers illegally via St. Eustatius, Barbados, or elsewhere.[43]

When, in 1766, the Company wanted to prohibit foreigners from bringing their "own" enslaved workers, smugglers like Clarke were annoyed. Storm informed Clarke that he was not allowed to import slaves to his plantations but also told the WIC that strict enforcement "would not be to the taste of Mr. Clarke, and many others."[44] In fact, closing the slaving loophole might have been the final straw for Gedney Clarke Jr., although some of his brothers remained.[45]

Storm was both sad and relieved to see Clarke Jr. go. On the one hand, he noted the great contributions that Clarke had made to the growth of Demerara; on the other, he complained about the English smuggling practices, in which Clarke was undoubtedly involved. In June 1768 Storm wrote:

> I should be very grieved if Mr Clarke were to leave the Colony; the reasons why he called in some of his outstanding monies are known to me and are very good ones. Mr Clarke in Demerara and W. Croydon in Essequibo are honest, upright men, of much profit and advantage to the Colony, the welfare of which they have at heart; but were we quit of all the other English and had Dutch or Germans instead the loss would not be great, but on the contrary, the Colony's progress and welfare would be much furthered and smuggling put an end to.[46]

This slave smuggling was indeed crucial to the two colonies, and William Croydon played a substantial role in it. Like Clarke, he came from Barbados and had established himself in Essequibo early on, but unlike Clarke, Croydon stayed. It is unclear when he arrived exactly, but Storm wrote that Croydon operated a timber plantation "with forty able-bodied slaves" already before 1750, placing him among the earliest migrants. Storm was irritated that in almost ten years Croydon had not shipped any cash crops and had only produced timber.[47] However, Croydon had likely discovered he was better off smuggling enslaved Africans. During the 1760s, Croydon, for example, advised his close friend (*boezemvriend*) Mr. Ferguson on how to best transfer sixty enslaved Africans from Antigua to Essequibo for Ferguson's newly bought plantation. Furthermore, a ship belonging to Croydon transported twenty-one of these people.[48]

In the 1760s Croydon also became a prominent planter. In 1764 he was one of the few British colonists to own an estate with more than a hundred enslaved laborers, and by 1777 his plantation Friendship (Vriendschap) exploited 211 enslaved Africans, which was the second largest slave population on an estate in Essequibo. Only the director-general had a bigger plantation.[49] And while Clarke was apparently put off by the WIC's renewed efforts to regulate the slave trade, Croydon sought the confrontation.

In 1768 he drafted a petition asking for permission for foreigners to participate in the slave trade. In this petition, addressed to the Council of Policy of Essequibo, ten British planters described their difficult situation: the price of sugar in the Dutch Republic was low, while slave prices were high, which prevented planters from buying the necessary number of enslaved laborers. Furthermore, they said, the slave supply was not even one-sixth of what was needed, with little prospect of improvement.[50]

The occasion for the petition was the recent ban on importing captives from non-Dutch areas in the Caribbean, which clearly undermined the standing practice among British planters. The prohibition applied to both new and "seasoned" slaves, including the ones already in the planter's possession elsewhere, and those acquired "by Legaces [sic] from their Relations or Friends." In fact, the petitioners wrote that the new rule was "depriving us from the Liberty of supplying of our Plantations with slaves from the English Islands." They emphasized how important "seasoned slaves" were, and that the colony would benefit if new planters were allowed to bring their own enslaved Africans with them. The petitioners did not desire a full opening of the slave trade, just to supply their own plantations, and were willing to subject themselves to "forfeiture of any Penalty" in case slaves would be sold onward.[51] While the petition had a small number of signers, all from Essequibo, it was later circulated in Demerara and translated, to be sent to the directors in the Dutch Republic. At that time Storm remarked that the English version was already signed by many of the foremost planters, both Dutch and non-Dutch, including councillors.[52] While the petition was denied, it demonstrates Croydon's leadership role as well as how accustomed British planters had become to importing captives through their own networks.

Croydon, like Clarke, made his fortune through a combination of smuggling and plantation exploitation. In 1775 he acquired a second plantation in Essequibo—a sugar estate called Schoonhoven—for the sum of 60,000 guilders (see map 6.1 below).[53] Subsequently, Croydon continued to enlarge his business, both in the number of estates and in the number of enslaved Africans who worked there. His will of 1799 shows he died a rich man. The Schoonhoven estate was valued at 118,573 guilders, including the 112 enslaved Africans. His main sugar plantation, Friendship, was worth even more: 470,544 guilders, including the 331 slaves. Together with a third smaller estate, Lunches, Croydon's assets came to 616,767 guilders, or 51,580 pounds sterling.[54]

Croydon did not finance all of this expansion himself, as—like Clarke Jr.—he used Dutch *negotiatie* credit as well. In 1788 both Schoonhoven and Friendship were mortgaged to the Zealand mortgage-cum-trading firm Spoors & Sprenger. At this time, the estates had 84 and 221 enslaved Africans respectively, so they were further intensified afterward, possibly using this *negotiatie* credit.[55]

As a long-term resident, Croydon became part of the colonial society in Essequibo but also remained strongly attached to his British and Barbadian networks. He apparently became a burgher of the colonies in 1786, probably because of trading privileges. Furthermore, he seemed to have had an Amerindian partner, Carolina Bedford Croydon, and had a son with her, John Croydon.[56] His will illustrates both his local and his wider connections. For instance, he wanted Francis Pile, the carpenter at Friendship, to be freed and receive 2,000 guilders and two slaves; he donated money to the free coloured Belgrave family in Barbados; he allocated 10,000 guilders for his godson John Blair who was in Holland for his education; and he donated money to nephews and nieces in the City of London.[57]

In conclusion, the cases of Croydon and the Clarkes were both unique and representative. On the one hand, they were leading individuals with particularly large estates; on the other, they were also part of a larger movement of British planters trying their luck in Essequibo and Demerara. In addition, their involvement in smuggling illustrates how illegal trade was part and parcel of the colonial fabric and facilitated the expansion of the two colonies.

While Croydon and the Clarkes were remarkable for the scale of their business operations, they were certainly not unique. In fact, they represented the three elements that characterized successful businessmen: they operated across imperial borders (including smuggling), combined different activities (trading and cash crop production), and employed large amounts of capital (from Dutch as well as other sources) to exploit large estates (relying on the work of hundreds of enslaved laborers). Subsequently, it becomes possible to compare the experiences of individuals from these regional networks to those from farther away, namely, North America.

Intra-American Networks

The two cases studied here further illustrate how Essequibo and Demerara became more integrated in the Atlantic world. First, the commercial venture of the brothers-in-law John Hubbard and Gardiner Greene shows how North Americans combined different business operations, much like Clarke and Croydon before them, to establish themselves in a foreign empire. They were active in the provisioning trade, engaged in smuggling cash crops, and managed plantations. Second, the merchant Thomas Barrell imported refined manufactures to the coarse colonial society of Demerara by combining business relationships with various sides of the Atlantic, thereby integrating the colonies in the wider Atlantic world.

The Bostonian Gardiner Greene (1753–1832) arrived in Demerara in 1774 and became a successful planter. In 1785 he owned the estate Saratoga in Essequibo, with forty-four enslaved Africans, but he likely also had possessions in Demerara, where he signed the 1785 petition against the WIC, like so many others.[58] In 1788 Greene was married for the second time, to Elizabeth Hubbard (1760–97). Subsequently, his brother-in-law John Hubbard (1765–1836) became an important business partner.[59] Initially, Greene resided in the colonies, while Hubbard remained in Boston to take care of trade. From around 1795 on, however, the roles were reversed and Greene assumed the position of absentee plantation owner. In Demerara, Hubbard looked after the growing number of plantations while also acquiring several estates of his own.[60] While the two men cooperated in importing and exporting goods to and from the two colonies, it is unclear to what extent they invested together in plantations and to what extent separately.

Regardless of the business arrangement, the two men were very successful in their—licit and illicit—exports of sugar, coffee, and cotton. For example, in 1789 they shipped cotton from Demerara to Boston (which was illegal under Dutch law) and in 1793 exported coffee to Amsterdam (which was legal).[61] By 1794 trade restrictions were loosened, on the initiative of the Council of Policy. To secure enough provisions, it decided that American traders were henceforth allowed to take in cash crops as return cargo, to the value of provisions they brought in. This opening would enable Hubbard and Greene to register their trades, although it is uncertain if they did: Hubbard mentioned in May 1795 that he shipped thirty-two bales of cotton to Barbados, but he did not discuss the legality of it.[62] The two men were probably aware of the rules, though: another Boston agent in Demerara, William Cowell, mentioned in 1791 that he was friends with Hubbard and Greene and that they had given him advice on shipping. Cowell wrote to his principals that he had loaded 50 hogsheads of rum, 30 hogsheads of sugar, and some cotton and coffee in a sloop. However, on the invoice he declared only 14 hogsheads of rum, explaining that the rest of the cargo was illegal to export from the two colonies.⁶³ Hubbard and Greene thus were well versed in how business was done there.

Hubbard and Greene also engaged in the provision trade, which contained risks of its own. They supplied fish and timber, which were in high demand. They considered these the most reliable articles in Essequibo and Demerara, which shows a keen eye for business.⁶⁴ Others, like Cowell, experienced firsthand how risky the trade in other articles could be. Horses, for example, were valuable draft animals but often did not survive the passage: Cowell reported having lost one, while another was "nothing but a sack of bones." Furthermore, flour could spoil and fish, when packed in bad weather, would rot. Beef was popular but rotten beef less so: Cowell wrote that some of his beef cargo smelled so awful he had to throw it overboard, a sight that would give him a hard time convincing people he had quality products on offer.⁶⁵

The letters of Jesse Breed, a correspondent for the firm of Lathrop & Luke, further illustrate why provisioning was risky. For example, the colonists wanted quality Dutch or Irish butter, not low-quality American produce. And while beef sold well, pork was unpopular, he noted in 1789. Breed also received finer goods, but while he recorded that men's shoes would always sell, he could find no market for the coarse women's shoes. Furthermore, the appetites of colonists could change quickly: in 1789 linen clothing proved a lucrative product, but a year later Breed wrote to his principals that they should stop sending linen and send coarse jeans and fustians instead.⁶⁶

Rather than provisioning, the biggest profits could be made producing and exporting plantation products, at which Hubbard and Greene excelled. Even during the French Revolutionary Wars (1792–1802), when shipping was difficult, their plantation business thrived. In 1795 Greene had at least three plantations, Greenfield, Saratoga, and the Union, and in 1799 Hubbard reported that the Union yielded 80,000 pounds of gross cotton. It seems he had sold and acquired new estates, for he also wrote that a plantation called Elizabeth Ann had produced 30,000 pounds, with the hope of another 10,000; and the estate Mainstay had yielded 17,000 pounds, with a potential second crop coming. Hubbard also planned to sell an estate called "No. 28," while he bought, together with a Mr. Thomas, another plantation referred to as "Brodus [perhaps Bourda's] Place."⁶⁷

In creating their wide-ranging commercial enterprise, family ties proved important for Hubbard and Greene. Hubbard married the daughter of Mr. Parkinson, another major business partner of Greene, and the two men shipped part of their produce to Greene's uncle, of the firm Daniel Greene & Sons.[68]

However, while the two men were generally on good terms, a sudden break seemed imminent in 1801. Hubbard, in Demerara at the time, wrote to Greene with some serious accusations. He had found that his credit with Mr. Robert and Mr. Pulsford, his financiers in London, was greatly diminished, apparently because of a letter that Greene had sent to them. Being forced to satisfy his creditors swiftly, Hubbard feared he had to accept a fire sale price for his plantation Mainstay: "I shall now be under the necessity of sell'g it for half its value & am reduced to this necessity by the Man who call'd himself my Friend & Brother & the Man for whom at one time I would have sacrificed my life for if necessary."[69]

Despite these strong words, the matter did not lead to a lasting break. The year after Hubbard wrote, "I hope you have destroyed the last letter I wrote you, I am sorry it was ever written! Forget that it ever was! 'tis my wish, should we ever meet again, to be on the same friendly footing we formerly were." Furthermore, he had named Greene as guardian of his son, without consulting Greene first, seemingly confident that the latter would agree.[70] Indeed, the men continued their correspondence, and in 1804 Hubbard expected his estates to produce a thousand hogsheads of sugar, which would be enough to settle his debts with his London creditors.[71]

While Hubbard and Greene in the end did not acquire the leadership roles that Clarke and Croydon did, their stories illustrate how the connections between North America and Essequibo and Demerara became stronger. Again, in this borderless world, smuggling proved easy and was important in order to stay in business. Yet it is also important to underline how provision trade and plantation ownership were not two separate activities but compatible options in a business portfolio. More control over the production process could furthermore reduce risk. Like many Atlantic businessmen, Hubbard and Greene therefore pursued "backward integration" from trade into plantation ownership.[72] However, the case of their fellow Bostonian Theodore Barrell (ca. 1770–after 1843) illustrates that the reverse path was also possible. Barrell came to the colonies as an adventurer, got involved in plantation administration, and later became a merchant in British manufactures.

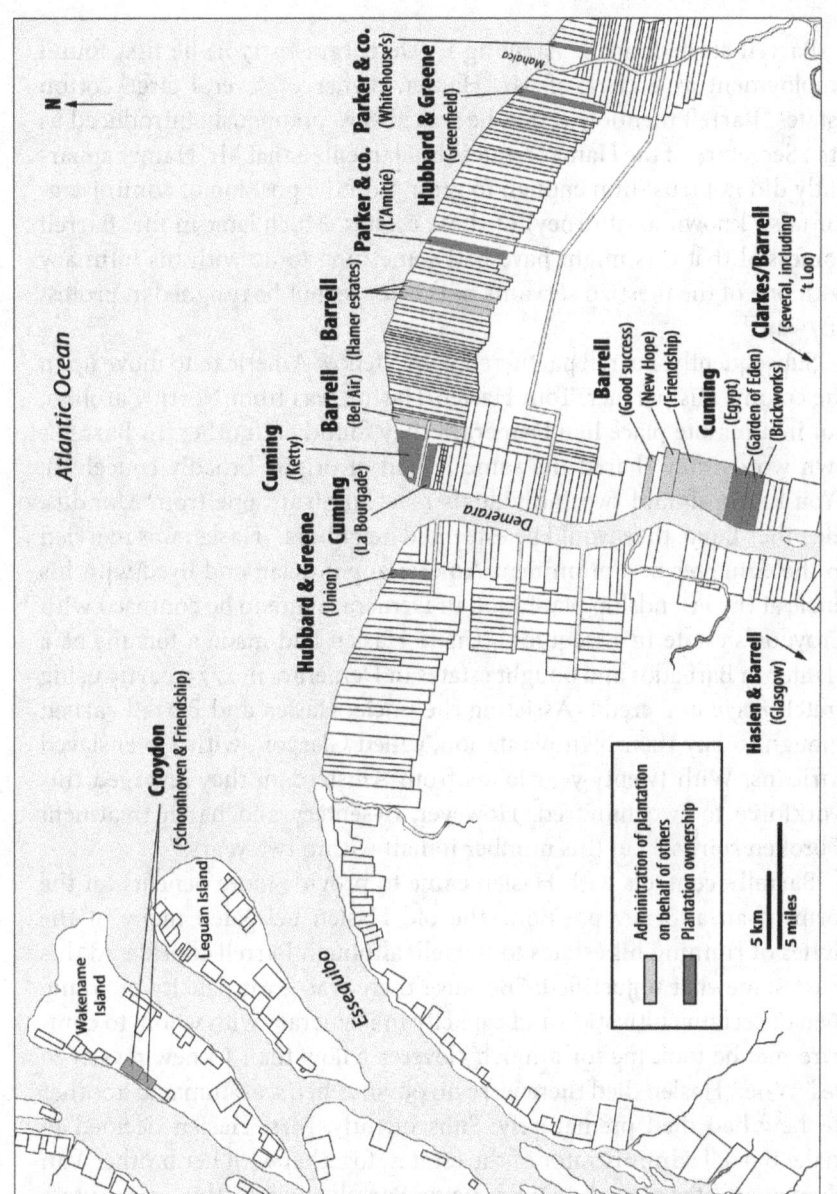

MAP 6.1. Estates of the individuals mentioned in the text

The Career of Theodore Barrell

Barrell started small. Arriving in Demerara in 1791, he first found employment as a clerk of Mr. Hamer, owner of several large cotton estates. Barrell mentioned that he was always pompously introduced as "the Secretary of the Hamer estates" but lamented that Mr. Hamer apparently did not trust him enough to grant him the position of administrator (also known as attorney) of these estates. Much later in life, Barrell confessed that this might have had something to do with his intimacy with one of the mestizo servants of the house, but he resigned in protest anyway.[73]

Subsequently, Barrell partnered with a fellow American to move up in the colony. His partner, Tom Haslen/Haslin, was from North Carolina, but in a remote place like Demerara they found each other. In Barrell's own words they shared the same region of origin, broadly conceived: "You know, should two individuals meet in Sirius, one from Mundus, the other Luna, they would be esteemed neighbors." Haslen was married to the daughter of a prominent American politician and lived with his uncle at the Friendship plantation in Demerara (not to be confused with Croydon's estate in Essequibo). Uncle Haslen had made a fortune as a planter in Barbados and bought estates in Demerara in 1773, partly using Dutch *negotiatie* credit. Assisting the uncle, Haslen and Barrell earned enough to buy their own plantation, called Glasgow, with 150 enslaved Africans. With twenty-year loans from Amsterdam they enlarged this workforce to two hundred. However, dysentery and harsh treatment ("broken spirits") cut this number in half within two years.[74]

Barrell's contacts with Haslen came to provide more benefits, in the form of an attorney position. The old Haslen delegated many of the duties of running his estates to Barrell, although Barrell considered this trust somewhat unjustified: "Because there was great paucity of young men of certain cultivation and capacity in Demerary with whom to compare me, he took me for a much cleverer fellow than I knew myself to be." When Haslen died there were no obvious heirs, as Tom and another nephew had died prematurely. Subsequently, Mrs. Haslen decided to make Barrell administrator of the estates, together with her brother Van Hamel, an officer in the Dutch navy. Barrell thought this was quite a responsibility, as he was just twenty-five years old, but he also believed he was the most reliable of the two, writing about Van Hamel, "He was totally unfit for business or trust of any kind . . . [but Mrs. Haslen wanted to keep him] so it became Van Hamel and Barrell: the latter to do the slavery, the former to carouse, get drunk, and enjoy himself." It seemed Van Hamel was found dead in a tavern in Boston after a gambling spree not long afterward, leaving Barrell to administer the estates by himself.[75]

From his work as an attorney, Barrell was able to start a merchant career. Through Mrs. Haslen he had the opportunity to present his wares to many of the prominent planters in the colony. He settled in Stabroek and started with securing and distributing supplies to various plantations and sending their produce to Europe. In addition, he claimed to have found a profitable way to deal with American traders: "[I] was the first who ventured to purchase whole cargoes. Vessels which formerly wasted two or three months to retail, were in this way, not often detained beyond eight or ten days."[76]

Around the same time (1798 or before) Barrell's business branched out to include the importation of British manufactures. He established regular trading connections with two London merchant-bankers, William Jones and Samuel Jones, and established a profitable niche in luxury products. Many of those related to the Industrial Enlightenment, such as copies of Adam's *Astronomical and Geographical Essays*, globes, telescopes, barometers, air pumps, pocket compasses, microscopes, camera obscuras, pantographers, goggles, concave and convex mirrors, "electrical machines," and copies of the *New Encyclopedia Brittannica*. In several cases he passed on special requests like engravings to satisfy his customers' desires, and he suggested that all scientific instruments be packed in mahogany boxes, so as to make even the cheap ones look appealing.[77]

By supplying all of these objects, Barrell gave planters the possibility to partake in the science-based entertainment popular at the time in educated metropolitan circles. Thereby, the colonists might try to shake off the rough image of a brutal frontier society, although some planters conducted cruel experiments on animals, Amerindians, and enslaved Africans with these electric machines.[78]

The diversity of goods imported was probably also a strategy of spreading risk, as Barrell was conservative in his choices. He imported only small numbers of items and shunned projects that seemed too risky. When his uncle Colborn needed to get rid of several pianofortes, Barrell urged him to go ahead only if the costs would remain below 50 pounds per piece. Others had sold pianos for that price, so more expensive ones would not sell. This condition resulted from the British takeover in 1796; previously pianos had sold well, but afterward the market became overstocked.[79] Being too adventurous could backfire, as Barrell discovered later. In 1799 Barrell deemed himself too inexperienced to deal in "articles for lady's," but later he was persuaded to sell "fashionable hats for ladies, shoes, slippers, gloves, very fine stockings." In 1802, however, he had to admit that the venture was a great financial loss, as he could not find a market for the goods.[80]

Both in business and in family matters, Barrell was a truly Atlantic figure. His uncle Colborn (a business partner), his father (who also took care of bills of exchange), and his sisters lived in London, and he lamented being away from them for so long. Therefore, he commissioned portraits of his sisters and sent them his own. Yet in 1798 it had been eleven years since they last saw each other, so he could not immediately recognize all of them.[81] Barrell regularly wrote to his sisters, sometimes in code language.[82] In addition to his London connections, Barrell had an uncle in Boston, Joseph, with whom he did business.[83] Finally, he had several business partners in Barbados, where his wife, some fifteen years his junior, also came from. On 29 March 1800, Barrell married "the innocent unsophisticated Elizabeth Beckles Gall," with whom he had two children in the next two years.[84]

Despite his business in scientific instruments and curiosities, Barrell had a preference for no-nonsense interactions. When his sister-in-law arrived from Barbados, he had little positive to say about her: "This phenomenon of elegance wonders how a sister of hers could condescend to marry a man of such a plain appearance as I have and so little solicitous to shine in the Beau Monde."[85] As she was used to a more luxurious lifestyle, she found life in Demerara rough and uncivilized: "She looks down with haughty disdain on the humble inhabitants of Guiana who have no such pretensions. I greatly suspect she will never meet her match in this country, and if she does not elsewhere, she must carry all her superexcellence with her, solitary to the grave."[86] More than Hubbard and Greene, then, Barrell became settled in Demerara, although in the end he would return to the United States.

Coincidentally, Barrell and Hubbard and Greene knew each other. For example, Barrell mentioned that Haslen and Greene went to Boston together, and on another occasion Barrell relied on Hubbard to send a letter to Boston.[87] Furthermore, in 1816 Barrell was still doing business in Demerara and one of his partners, a Mr. Benjamin, had apparently defrauded him, so Barrell had Benjamin arrested in Boston. The bail, set at 15,000 guilders, was posted by John Hubbard.[88] Barrell differed from Hubbard and Greene in his focus on acting on behalf of others rather than amassing a large number of estates himself. Barrell thus remained active mostly in trade rather than in plantation ownership, but he engaged in the specific trade of importing luxury goods. He was also less dependent on family relations for his trade; although his father took care of bills of exchange and his uncles sometimes sent some goods, his major partners were nonrelatives in Barbados and London. Similar to Hubbard and Greene, however, he followed an improvised path, along which he integrated Essequibo and Demerara more deeply in the Atlantic world.

Interestingly, Barrell had more connections with the other individuals studied in this chapter. He administered the estate 't Loo, which had previously belonged to Gedney Clarke Sr. Furthermore, a good friend of his, Samuel Sandbach, had housed him on his arrival in the colonies and also advised him in arranging his marriage.[89] When Sandbach went to Britain, he seems to have visited Barrell's family members to tell them about Barrell's recent marriage.[90] It turns out that Sandbach was involved in a major Scottish partnership, which forged a truly transatlantic business enterprise. It is to these people that I shall now turn.

Transatlantic Ties

Scots played a large role in the British West Indies, particularly the Windward Islands, and in Demerara as well. The historian David Hamilton suggested that the adaptation of older clan traditions accounted for Scottish commercial success in the Atlantic. By establishing an idea of relatedness based on kinship and shared local origins, the Scots had a powerful tool for establishing networks of trust. Although these networks remained open to outsiders, it provided an opening for insiders. Relatives or people from the same locality had a higher chance of entering a network or partnership through recommendations of fellow Scots.[91] Perhaps more than other groups, Scots tended to think of the Americas as a place of temporary residence. Rather than a place of settlement, the ideal was to get rich as quickly as possible, and to return home with as much of it as possible.[92] Demerara offered them exactly such a chance.

The Firm of Robertson, Parker, McInroy and Sandbach

The most successful Scots were probably the four men that formed the partnership of Robertson, Parker, McInroy and Sandbach. They succeeded in establishing an enterprise that connected all sides of the Atlantic: they had interests in Grenada and Demerara, sold enslaved persons from Africa, shipped provisions from Boston, exported cotton from

Demerara to Britain, and relied on financiers in Scotland to finance all of this.[93]

The firm started from small beginnings in both Demerara and Grenada. One of the partners, James McInroy, was apparently already settled in Demerara in 1782, although he left no archival trace as a plantation owner at any point in the century.[94] Most likely he was active as a trader only, which was how all his future partners started too. George Robertson might have been active at the same time, conducting business on Grenada, as Charles Stewart Parker began his career there. Parker arrived in Grenada in 1789, with great expectations but limited opportunities. However, he could rely on his fellow Scotsmen to get a position in one of the established trading firms, and he found a patron in James Campbell. Two of the main trading houses were already full of nephews and cousins, as Parker noted, but George Robertson was looking for a new partner who could bring in some capital. Parker took his chances and started as a clerk for Robertson. The firm focused on trade with the Spanish empire, probably Trinidad. Hence it proved convenient that Parker had been sent to Spain by his father to learn the language.[95]

The Grenada and Demerara branches of the future partnership were joined in 1790, when Parker, Robertson, and McInroy took in a fourth partner, Daniel Gordon. They likely had shared capital stock, yet decided to trade under separate names in Grenada and Demerara.[96] Gordon, however, soon turned out to be difficult to work with. In 1791 the partners planned that one of them would take residence in Demerara to oversee their estates rather than leave them to an overseer. Gordon was willing to take his turn but refused to accept another partner for this matter or settle in Demerara permanently, "nor shall I ever turn Dutchman for such a small object as my share in the profits in our Demerary concern."[97]

In 1792 a more serious conflict arose between Gordon and the other partners. Gordon's behavior remains unclear, but he went to Britain to explain himself to the creditors of the firm. Parker feared the scandal might ruin their credibility, but apparently only Gordon was blamed for his "underhand plots."[98] The other three dissolved the partnership and formed a new one—without Gordon but including Samuel Sandbach. The latter had been involved as a clerk since 1791, but now became a partner, although for a smaller share: Robertson, Parker, and McInroy contributed 4,000 pounds sterling, while Sandbach advanced 2,000 pounds. These were large sums—equivalent to more than 150,000 guilders, or the value of a substantial plantation—indicating the scale of their business, although it is likely that part of this money was borrowed.

The partnership had a duration of four years, although it could be dissolved after three, if desired.⁹⁹

At that time, 1792, the firm already had "a very respectable footing" in Demerara, partly resulting from the illicit export of cotton. The partners planned their shipments carefully, choosing between sending their cotton to England or to Scotland or to convert it to bills of exchange. At no point did they perceive its illicit nature as problematic, despite being clearly aware of it.¹⁰⁰ It appears they did not get caught, and after the British takeover in 1796, the trade became legal and the firm exported large amounts of cotton to Liverpool.¹⁰¹

Although it is impossible to quantify the contribution of smuggling to the firm's results, the Demerara ventures proved immensely profitable. In 1792 Parker noted that the firm had 148,000 guilders invested in Demerara and that he personally had a positive balance of 1,118 pounds sterling with the firm. He planned to "be worth" 3,000 pounds sterling at the end of the partnership. In 1795 earnings rose even higher, as the firm recorded a profit of 14,512 pounds over a twelve-month period on invested capital of 36,514 pounds.¹⁰² This was an enormous profit, which contrasts markedly with the financial difficulties of the *negotiaties* funds.

Despite this financial success, the firm experienced difficulties preserving their line of credit from their Scottish financiers. This Glasgow partnership of Robertson, McKay and Spears was the supplier for Parker & Co's Grenada and Demerara trade: they sent products to sell and extended credit to facilitate this trade. However, in 1793 the creditors were considering withdrawing from the West Indian business.¹⁰³ They offered to find new correspondents, but Parker was afraid of what might follow: changing correspondents meant that the balance would have to be settled, and Parker estimated his firm was 6,000 to 7,000 pounds sterling in debt. This money was tied up in plantations or credit to planters and could therefore not easily be recovered. The Caribbean was torn apart by war, explaining the creditors' caution, but Parker thought it exaggerated:

> How slender must their Credit be if they are distressed by [being?] out of 6 or £7000 Stg [sterling] for a few months, which I believe is all they are in actual advance for us, especially people that used to write us in such an Imperious tone, we at present in consequence of their distressed state study as our main point to pay them off & have done with them.¹⁰⁴

The firm planned to take the initiative and make the first move, by reducing debts as much as possible and finding other financiers that would take on the correspondence. Parker urged his father, a wealthy man who was himself active in maritime insurance, to ask around for interested financiers. When the firm's debt would be below 5,000 pounds, the partners would draw on the new fund and would then have to settle with the Glasgow creditors. The trick here was to use bills with long maturity dates, payable in twelve to eighteen months. The firm would send enough commodities in the meantime to cover the debt, meaning that the new financiers would be compensated before they would actually have to come up with the money. The original financiers quickly realized they had overplayed their hand and adopted a more conciliatory tone. Parker's partnership was a profitable one and therefore an asset worth keeping. Yet the relationship was damaged, and apparently Robertson and Parker went back to Britain in 1794 to act as correspondents themselves, leaving the Demerara management in the hands of McInroy and Sandbach.[105]

The firm continued to expand during the late eighteenth and early nineteenth century, increasing the number of estates in its portfolio. It is unclear when the first plantation was acquired, but it is known that in 1792 McInroy spent 42,000 guilders (or 3,400 pounds sterling) on a small cotton estate on Leguan Island in Essequibo. In addition, in 1795 the firm registered 50,000 pounds of cotton from two of their estates (probably in Demerara). One of these plantations was (likely) called Woodlands, and the partners tried to buy a new plantation close to it. In 1798 the firm bought "Whitehouses estate" for 217,500 guilders, including 70 enslaved workers. In 1800 they also acquired L'Amitié, and sometime before 1803 they also bought an estate called Coffee Grove.[106] Coincidentally, L'Amitié had previously belonged to John Haslen and was the site where the Dutch had signed the capitulation treaty with the French in 1782.[107]

Gradually, Parker & Co.'s firm created an integrated business, ranging from plantation ownership to provisioning to transporting cotton as well as slaves. In 1795, for example, McInroy bought 110 enslaved Africans from a fellow Scottish trading house and (illicitly) shipped them to Demerara. The partners had been active in the business of selling enslaved Africans for a while in Grenada but had abandoned it in 1793. However, it seems they reinvigorated it again for the Demerara market, for in 1803 a detailed account exists for 147 enslaved Africans sold to various persons. In addition to slave trading, the firm engaged in trade in provisions, shipping fish, planks, beef, pork, candles, and soap from Boston to Demerara. The partners also sent all sorts of manufactured goods and luxury articles from Britain, including playing cards, decanters, door hinges, and frying pans, as well as various spices.[108] Finally, the firm also owned several ships to transport its goods, making sure it controlled all aspects of the business, from production to sale.[109]

As in the cases discussed above, commercial and personal affairs were intertwined. In 1797 Parker married a niece of Robertson, Margareth Rainy. The partners further strengthened their ties when Sandbach married a niece of Robertson. Within this network of relationships, it was logical that the firm acted as a springboard for other relatives; when George Robertson died in 1799, his nephew Gilbert Robertson joined the firm and became a manager and investor in the Demerara estates.[110]

All in all, Robertson, Parker, McInroy, and Sandbach succeeded in establishing a wide-ranging and integrated enterprise that would expand further during the nineteenth century. In 1813 Liverpool became the headquarters of the firm, and Philip Frederick Tinne was taken in as partner. Tinne had worked for a long time as colonial secretary in Demerara, which likely made him a valuable contact. The firm would continue business under the name Sandbach, Tinne and Company and remained active in the sugar trade in Demerara until the twentieth century.[111]

Thomas Cuming: Between Prominence and Default

Not all Scots were successful in Demerara, however, and there was a great amount of market volatility. As Parker's firm experienced, credit conditions were crucial. In a society where virtually everyone was a debtor, calling in loans posed a serious threat even to wealthy individuals. One of the foremost figures in Demerara was Thomas Cuming. He was a long-term resident, arriving in Demerara around 1760 and only returning definitively to Europe in 1810. He was active in the *negotiatie* system as appraiser but also took out a mortgage from Changuion in 1770 and 1771, another one for his plantation Garden of Eden from Van Vloten (before 1788), and another one from Van Nooten Jansz. in 1792.[112] During the 1787 constitutional crisis he was one of the protest leaders, and his signature was said to be enough for other British planters to sign the petition for reform (see chapter 2). His possessions continued to grow, and in 1798 he owned at least four plantations: besides the Ketty and the Garden of Eden, he had the sugar estate Egypt and the coffee plantation La Bourgade. The latter was adjacent to the capital, Stabroek, and in the late 1790s would become part of the capital under the name Cummingsburg, which it carries to this day (see map 6.1).[113]

Nevertheless, Cuming's fortune was on the brink of collapse in 1799. By that time he was in Britain himself and had appointed Thomas Newburn as administrator. Cuming clearly needed crops from Demerara to cover his debts, writing to Newburn, "For G_ds sake make every exertion in sending me remittances." Not only had the agent of his mortgage fund come over to England, apparently pressing his daughter to get the finances in order, but Cuming had also borrowed the immense sum of 20,000 pounds sterling from a fellow Scotsman, George Baillie—a sum that was comparable to 200,000 to 240,000 guilders. In addition, he owed around 4,000 pounds to Mr. Tulloh, presumably his father-in-law, and was indebted to a Mr. Campbell, another Scotsman. In other words, Cuming was indebted about as much to Dutch as to British creditors, using both the *negotiatie* structure and his personal network. It is unclear whether his different creditors were aware of Cuming's other debts, nor do we know if Cuming mortgaged his estates twice.

To reduce his debts, Cuming aimed to sell one of his plantations. He preferred to sell the Garden of Eden but decided to put the Ketty up for sale as well to increase his chances.[114] The conditions for sale show the enormous sums involved. The Garden of Eden was offered for sale for 41,780 pounds sterling. The first 20,000 pounds had to be paid immediately in bills at three months' sight, the rest in four installments with interest. This remaining sum had to be secured by a mortgage, and Cuming and the buyer would jointly administer the plantation until it was paid in full. Included in the sale were 300 enslaved Africans, and with an average crop of 350,000 pounds of sugar the estate supposedly delivered 6,235 pounds in profit per year. According to Cuming's calculation, a buyer would have his investment back in just seven years. The Ketty was worth even more: the asking price was 70,000 pounds, the first 25,000 pounds payable immediately. Again, 300 enslaved workers were included in the price, even though Cuming employed 580, but many of them were transferred to another estate. The condition estimated a crop of 600,000 pounds of sugar, which would generate an annual profit of 10,234 pounds sterling, after subtracting expenses. Thus the prospective buyer would also have his money back after seven years.[115]

These were enormous sums and perhaps not realistic, considering the times. With Europe and the Caribbean caught up in the French Revolutionary Wars, shipping was highly uncertain. In addition, if the estates were indeed as profitable as the conditions sketched, Cuming would probably not have been as indebted as he was. Nevertheless, the conditions demonstrate the highly intensive production on Cuming's estate, employing a large number of enslaved people as well as an enormous financial investment.

Cuming likely did not succeed in selling his estate, for in 1804 he defaulted on his debt for the Garden of Eden to his Dutch creditors. In 1810 they took possession of the estate.[116] Despite this setback, Cuming was still among the most prominent planters in the colony. In 1812 the local newspaper published a list of 109 colonists in Demerara and another 50 from Berbice who expressed their gratitude to Cuming. They offered him an inscribed plate worth 500 guineas and emphasized the protective role Cuming had played for newly arrived planters, as well as for widows and orphans.[117]

The case of Thomas Cuming is illustrative of a larger process in which foreign planters took over the two colonies while also showing the fragility of colonial fortunes. While all of these men became wealthy at some point in their career, they often relied on credit to finance their business. Volatile markets and unexpected circumstances could lead to accumulating debts, and they were also vulnerable to changes in the credit conditions.

Nevertheless, this was a group of entrepreneurs who were willing to take risks and look across imperial borders to succeed. They established themselves in a foreign empire but relied on their personal networks to get ahead. While they followed political developments, the changes in official ownership of the colonies were not their greatest concern. Instead, they worried about their crops, their credit, flooded markets, or spoiled goods. Their trade networks remained largely the same under Dutch and under British rule, for most of them had made illicit trade a standard part of their business practice. In the borderless colonies of Essequibo and Demerara, this was a logical choice, as foreign markets offered higher profits.

Another element that stands out from their business practice was the scale and capital intensity of their operations. It seems that non-Dutch planters were more willing to scale up their projects. It helped that they could combine plantation mortgages from the Dutch Republic with personal credits from their own networks, as several of the individuals above did. Such gambles did not always pay off, as both the Clarkes and Thomas Cuming struggled to stay ahead of their debts. However, Theodore Barrell apparently was able to boost his career by buying a planation with an Amsterdam mortgage, and William Croydon seemed to have done well for himself too, despite his mortgages.

A final point arising from the stories above is the interrelated nature of provisioning, the trade in cash crop exports, and plantation management.

There was no strict division between suppliers, trading houses, and planters. Instead, one might lead to the other or a combination of different activities. Although one might start as a provision trader, the trade in cash crops would be tempting because of its high value. Plantation ownership was then a logical next step. Multiple estates allowed for differentiation in crops and thereby reduced price risks, while it also meant the managers could divide labor and food supplies between plantations in order to mitigate shortages.

In the end, these individuals demonstrate how the colonial economy in Essequibo and Demerara was created through improvised decisions by actors on the ground. Furthermore, they show how easily imperial borders were transgressed. Indeed, using their interimperial networks, these borderless businessmen facilitated the integration of Essequibo and Demerara in the wider Atlantic world.

Conclusion: The Shape of Empire

The colonies of Essequibo and Demerara were comparatively small and sparsely populated, located at the fringe of the Dutch empire. Nevertheless, they shed light on broader processes of migration, commerce, and slavery in the Americas. Transcending narratives about "linguistic Atlantics," the borderless history of Essequibo and Demerara reveals an Atlantic world that was more integrated than divisions into "national" empires would suggest.

With the metropolis literally and figuratively at a distance, in Essequibo and Demerara the most important decisions were taken on the ground. With hardly any institutional guidance, colonial actors were the ones that carved out the shape of empire, in which local improvisation and an Atlantic orientation worked in conjunction. This improvised shape, then, was distinctly cross-cultural and interimperial. Instead of counting on metropolitan soldiers, the colonists relied on Amerindian allies. Instead of waiting on slavers from Zealand, they bought captives from foreign smugglers. And instead of trying to populate the colonies with Dutchmen, the local authorities welcomed adventurers from throughout the Atlantic. While elsewhere in the Atlantic efforts to increase central control were ramped up, the case of Essequibo and Demerara shows that borderless societies could still exist by the end of the eighteenth century.

The borderless characteristics of Essequibo and Demerara resulted from a high degree of geographic openness and institutional weakness. The two reinforced each other. The open connection to the Atlantic

Ocean, with many plantations laid out on the coast, made smuggling particularly easy. Preventing such illicit exchanges would have required heavy expenses for patrol ships and forts, but the West India Company and its administrative successors were incapable of making such investments. However, the underdeveloped institutional structure also had an important enabling function, as it provided room for local initiatives.

Furthermore, the plantation society would have opposed any attempts at stricter imperial control anyway, as became clear in the 1780s. Lacking a suitable set of laws, by-laws were the most important form of colonial governance. Formulated in the local Council of Policy, these by-laws dealt with key topics such as taxes and the enforcement of mercantilist rules, and the colonists were keen on retaining their influence over them. Therefore, when the WIC tried to change the balance of power in the council in its favor, the colonists rose in opposition, by petitioning and by withholding their taxes. The WIC had no means to amend the situation, so a state of "anarchy" ensued. The planters were quite content with this anarchy, for they could comfortably engage in illegal trading, telling themselves there was no legitimate body to answer to for such behavior. The political battle only flared up again when the stubborn captain Frans Smeer arrived, sent to eradicate smuggling. His measures provoked renewed resistance, up to the point that a coup became a serious possibility.

This situation reflected the three Orwellian characteristics that capture Essequibo and Demerara's development: (institutional) weakness as strength, anarchy as stability, and smuggling as a right. The colonists in the two colonies were so dependent on illegal trade that they strongly resisted anyone who tried to put an end to it. In fact, they appealed to a moral economy of smuggling, as they deemed it defensible to buy enslaved Africans from foreigners as long as Dutch ships provided only few and expensive captives.[1]

Indeed, the majority of the enslaved Africans arrived in the colonies via unofficial ways, testifying to the fundamental importance of smuggling in Essequibo and Demerara. As the colonies were dependent on intra-American traders for much of their food and building materials, the clandestine export of cash crops gave those traders a reason to come. Molasses alone would not satisfy as a return cargo, and bills of exchange from the heavily indebted planters were too risky. Therefore, a substantial amount of cash crops ended up clandestinely in Britain, the United States, and elsewhere. Fully aware of the importance of these exchanges, the authorities had an incentive to look the other way. Officials often condoned the smuggling or were complicit themselves. Implicitly, they thereby consented to the loosening of the ties with the Dutch Republic and the further integration of the two colonies in the Atlantic world.

Illicit trade was thus of a different character from that in other parts of the Dutch empire. In Suriname, North American captains also flouted the rules by exporting cash crops, and the governor facilitated the systematic evasion of the British Molasses Act.[2] In addition, Curaçao and St. Eustatius were famous as contraband centers, to the extent that smuggling was their raison d'être.[3] Yet illegal trade was more fundamental to Essequibo and Demerara than to Suriname, whereas the place of the two colonies in the mercantilist system set them apart from the Antilles. In other words, smuggling at Curaçao was a mercantilist goal, but this was certainly not the case for Essequibo and Demerara. The two colonies did not exist to smuggle, but they survived because smuggling existed.

Contraband trade was but one example of entanglement within the Americas; the borderland interactions between the Essequibo and the Orinoco were another. There, the fates of Dutch, Spanish, Amerindian, and Africans actors were thoroughly intertwined. While the Dutch-Amerindian coalitions could threaten the Spanish presence in the region during the seventeenth century, the Spanish came to dominate the borderland in the eighteenth century. By then, the Amerindians had largely vacated the borderland to escape a life in missionary villages and had fostered closer ties with the Dutch. The latter increasingly needed Amerindian help to subdue maroons in Demerara and prevent slave refugees from Essequibo from escaping to Venezuela, where they might be freed.

The borderland thus greatly influenced the evolution of the slavery regime. The enslaved seemingly had few options to alleviate their situation, while in other societies throughout the Atlantic they enjoyed some legal protection (at least on paper, such as in the *Code Noir*), more opportunities for marronage (such as in Suriname), and more opportunities to pass as free in towns and cities (in the United States, for example). However, as the Spanish gained control over the region at the expense of the Caribs, the opportunities for slave refugees increased. Hoping to be declared free in Venezuela, many enslaved laborers tried to run away. As they might otherwise have resisted in more violent forms, these runaways inadvertently added an element of stability to the slavery system. However, as long as the Dutch could rely on their borderland allies, insurgencies hardly had a chance at succeeding. Amerindians from Carib, Arawak, Akawaio, and Warao groups often decided to help the colonists put down a revolt, tracking runaways or destroying small-scale maroon societies. Benefiting greatly from the Dutch dependence on them, these Amerindians were crucial in upholding the particularly cruel slave regime in Essequibo and Demerara.

While these key connections were thus established at the colonial level, a strong counterforce existed to keep the colonies tied to the Dutch Republic, in the form of finance. In a period of relative decline of the Dutch position on the world market, plantation mortgages promised to boost the volume of trade. Even though they turned out to be a bubble, these so-called *negotiaties* stimulated expansion of the plantation sector throughout the Guianas. Nevertheless, whereas in Suriname the unwinding of the debt circle took place in a relatively orderly fashion, in Essequibo and Demerara the opposite was the case. Debt collection proved highly challenging, and insecurity abounded because of the inadequate legislative framework, compounded by the self-interested behavior of agents, planters, and administrators. As long as the preference order remained opaque, creditors had an interest in maintaining the credit relationship. If a creditor believed that his debts were preferential, he had no need to order an execution; better to allow the struggling planter to improve his position than to face immediate losses after a forced liquidation. In a way, the planters thus managed to resist even this attempt at metropolitan control, although they also deterred future investors. However, enough foreign adventurers were ready to step in.

Borderless businessmen like William Croydon, Theodore Barrell, and the many small traders plying the intra-American trade gave shape to the Atlantic web in which Essequibo and Demerara participated. They typically made clever use of the borderless nature of these colonies. They might combine private British and Dutch *negotiatie* credit, they would ship legal provisions on one journey and contraband cargo on the next, and they could be involved in the slave trade as well as in plantation ownership. By crossing imperial borders, these actors helped to turn Essequibo and Demerara into profitable Atlantic colonies and determine the borderless shape of empire there. Consequently, the British were eager to take these colonies for themselves. Building upon the eighteenth-century fundamentals, they would turn the colonies into one of the most profitable, and one of the most intensively exploited societies, in the world of slavery.

Appendix 1

Missions of the Reverend Father Capuchins of Catalonia of the Province of Guiana, 1788

	Pueblos	Naciones	Indios existentes
1	Caroni	Guayanos y Guycas	764
2	Incita	Aruaca y Guacas	324
3	Sta Ana	Aruaca y Guarauno	457
4	Calvario	Salibas y Guaraunos	444
5	Marocure	Caribes	550
6	Caruani	Caribes	298
7	Sn Antonio	Guayanos	589
8	Guri	Caribes	235
9	Puétpa	Guayanos y Guaraunos	278
10	Sta. Clara	Guaycas	191
11	Sn. Seraphin	Guaycas	242
12	Bocas	Guaycas	618
13	Sta. Magdalena	Guaycas	138
14	Barceloneta	Barinagotas	254
15	Ayma	Guaycas	723
16	Arechica	Guaycas	177
17	Divina Pastora	Guayanos	431

Missions of the Reverend Father Capuchins of Catalonia of the Province of Guiana, 1788 (*continued*)

	Pueblos	*Naciones*	*Indios existentes*
18	Guaceypati	Caribes	706
19	Topoquen	Caribes	435
20	Angel Custodio	Guayanos	232
21	Cura	Guaycas	582
22	Canapo	Caribes	761
23	Miámo	Caribes	762
24	Cumamo	Caribes	712
25	Palmar	Caribes y Guayanos	589
26	Sta. Maria	Guayanos y Panacáyos	491
27	Cupapuy	Guayanos	715
28	Ipata	Españoles	477
29	Alta Gracia	Guayanos	837
		Total	14,012

Source: Overview sent by the Rev. Father Hermenegildo de Vich to Father Cervera, 31 August 1788, no. 627 in BGBB, BC app. vol. 5: 69.

Appendix 2

Goods ordered for 1,000 Amerindians (1803)

Amount	Product
18	Bucks' cotton (pieces) ["Bucks" used to refer to Amerindians]
18	checks (pieces)
18	hats with lace bands
18	sticks like those used by the drum major in Europe
500	guns
2,000	razors
1,500	lbs powder
2,000	wooden flint boxes
2,000	guns caps
2,000	pairs scissors
2,000	Jews' harps
6,000	bush knives
2,000	looking glasses
12,000	assorted fish-hooks
12,000	ells salemporis
50,000	needles
50,000	pins
2,000	coarse combs

Goods ordered for 1,000 Amerindians (1803) *(continued)*

Amount	Product
10,000	beads of all sorts and colors
12,000	flints
4,000	lbs assorted shot
2,000	Bucks' axes
2,000	cutlasses with yellow handles
48	cassava plates
1,500	thimbles
1,000	round hats
36	checked shirts
18	silver circular collars, engraved with the lion, bearing the inscription "Batavion Republic of Essequibo and Demerary" around and above it, with the necessary national ribbon
18	cases claret, of 18 bottles in each case
18	cases gin, of 6 flasks in each case
1,000	fish harpoons, from 4 to 5 inches long, as per annexed design
1,000	ditto

Source: Minutes of the Court of Policy of Essequibo, 22 February 1803, no. 679 in BGBB, BC app. vol. 5: 180.

Notes

Introduction

1. George Pinckard, *Notes on the West-Indies*, vol. 1 (London: Messrs. Baldwin, Cradock, and Joy, 1816), 328–29.

2. Unfortunately, no reliable figures exist to make a more precise statement. In 1800 the white population was apparently two-thirds British, but this was after four years during which many new British planters arrived (Gert Oostindie, "'British Capital, Industry and Perseverance' versus Dutch 'Old School'? The Dutch Atlantic and the Takeover of Berbice, Demerara and Essequibo, 1750–1815," *BMGN—Low Countries Historical Review* 127, no. 4 [2012]: 38). In 1788 a proxy exercise of looking at British-sounding names suggests less than half were British or North American (Dutch National Archives at The Hague [hereafter NL-HaNA], Tweede West-Indische Compagnie [hereafter WIC], 1.05.01.02, inv. nr. 192B). It thus seems reasonable to assume that in 1796 more than half of the white planters were British, although this included North Americans.

3. Pinckard, *Notes*, vol. 1: 330.

4. Seymour Drescher, *Econocide: British Slavery in the Era of Abolition* (Chapel Hill: University of North Carolina Press, 2010) 94–100.

5. Emilia Viotti Da Costa, *Crowns of Glory, Tears of Blood: The Demerara Slave Rebellion of 1823* (New York: Oxford University Press, 1994); Nicholas Draper, "The Rise of a New Planter Class? Some Countercurrents from British Guiana and Trinidad, 1807–33," *Atlantic Studies* 9, no. 1 (2012). Also see the related website: "Legacies of British Slave-ownership," www.ucl.ac.uk.lbs. In 1966 British Guiana gained independence as the Co-operative Republic of Guyana.

6. For the shocking mortality rates for the similar case of Berbice, see Randy M. Browne, *Surviving Slavery in the British Caribbean* (Philadelphia: University of Pennsylvania Press, 2017), 3.

7. For the number of colonists, see The National Archives, Kew (hereafter TNA), Colonial Office (hereafter CO), 111/4, f. 213 and 215. Van der Oest mentions 2,700

"Europeans" in 1796, see: E. W. Van der Oest, "The Forgotten Colonies of Essequibo and Demerara, 1700–1814," in *Riches from Atlantic Commerce: Dutch Transatlantic Trade and Shipping, 1585–1817*, ed. Victor Enthoven and Johannes Postma (Leiden: Brill, 2003), 329. See tables 2.1 and 3.1 for the figures for plantations and the enslaved population.

8. For Suriname's development, see Alex van Stipriaan, *Surinaams contrast: Roofbouw en overleven in een Caraïbische plantagekolonie, 1750–1863* (Leiden: KITLV, 1993), 33, 71, 311.

9. Anne Pérotin-Dumon, "Cabotage, Contraband, and Corsairs: The Port Cities of Guadeloupe and Their Inhabitants, 1650–1800," in Knight and Liss, *Atlantic Port Cities*; Kenneth Morgan, "Mercantilism and the British Empire, 1688–1815," in *The Political Economy of British Historical Experience, 1688–1914*, ed. Donald Winch and Patrick O'Brien (Oxford: Published for the British Academy by Oxford University Press, 2002); Silvia Marzagalli, "The French Atlantic and the Dutch, Late Seventeenth–Late Eighteenth Century," in *Dutch Atlantic Connections, 1680–1800: Linking Empires, Bridging Borders*, ed. Gert Oostindie and Jessica V. Roitman (Leiden: Brill, 2014) 105; Kenneth J. Banks, *Chasing Empire across the Sea: Communications and the State in the French Atlantic, 1713–1763* (Montreal: McGill-Queen's University Press, 2006).

10. Anthony R. Disney, *A History of Portugal and the Portuguese Empire: From Beginnings to 1807* (New York: Cambridge University Press, 2009), vol. 1: 245 and vol. 2: 277; Kenneth J. Andrien, "The Spanish Atlantic System," in *Atlantic History: A Critical Appraisal*, ed. Jack P. Greene and Philip D. Morgan (Oxford: Oxford University Press, 2009), 66–69; J. H. Elliott, *Empires of the Atlantic World: Britain and Spain in America, 1492–1830* (New Haven, CT: Yale University Press, 2006), 301–4.

11. J. P. van de Voort, *De Westindische plantages van 1720 tot 1795: Financiën en handel* (Eindhoven: Drukkerij de Witte, 1973).

12. See chaps. 1 and 3.

13. There is nevertheless a lot of attention to slavery in Berbice; see the work of Marjoleine Kars cited throughout this book and her upcoming volume on the 1763 rebellion. The nineteenth-century slavery regime is studied in: Browne, *Surviving Slavery*. For the openness of Berbice, see the 1802 map by F. van Bouchenrouder, which shows a situation very similar to Essequibo and Demerara (http://www.atlasofmutualheritage.nl/nl/Kaart-plantages-rond-rivier-Berbice.9437; accessed 6 August 2018).

14. Gert Oostindie and Alex van Stipriaan, "Slavery and Slave Cultures in a Hydraulic Society: Suriname," in *Slavery and Slave Cultures in the Americas*, ed. Stephan Palmié (Knoxville: University of Tennessee Press, 1996), 80–81.

15. K. Kramer, "Plantation Development in Berbice from 1753 to 1779: The Shift from Interior to the Coast," *New West Indian Guide* 65, no. 1–2 (1991).

16. For examples of smuggling in Suriname, see Karwan Fatah-Black, "Smokkelhandel en slavenhandel in Suriname gedurende de ondergang van de Nederlandse macht op zee, 1780–1795," *Tijdschrift voor Zeegeschiedenis* 32, no. 2 (2013).

17. See chapter 2.

18. Henk den Heijer, *Geschiedenis van de WIC: Opkomst, bloei en ondergang* (Zutphen: Walburg Pers, 2013), 177–91.

19. In 1683 the Society of Suriname divided its share in three: the WIC, the city of Amsterdam, and the private person Cornelis van Aerssen van Sommelsdijck. In 1770 the Van Sommelsdijck family sold its share to Amsterdam, which in 1773 sold half of

it to the WIC, so both now had 50 percent. Ibid., 186; Karwan Fatah-Black, *White Lies and Black Markets: Evading Metropolitan Authority in Colonial Suriname, 1650–1800* (Leiden: Brill, 2015), 5.

20. The three WIC plantations were located in Essequibo and called Agterkerke, Luyxbergen, and Duinenburg. The main source of revenue was the poll tax or head tax, which was based on the number of enslaved people on each estate. Generally, the rate was 2.50 guilders per slave over twelve years old. This money would go into the general WIC budget for the colonies. In addition, the Council of Policy could levy a "Colony Tax" (*Colonie Ongelden*), also based on the slave numbers. This revenue would go into the Colony Chest and could be spent locally, on infrastructure, defense repairs, or unforeseen expenses. There was also a tax on land (*akkergeld*), but it is unclear how consistently this was levied. See, e.g., J. Th. de Smidt, T. van der Lee, and H. J. M. van Dapperen, *Plakaatboek Guyana (Guyana Ordinance Book), 1670–1816* (The Hague: Huygens Instituut for Netherlands History, 2014), Essequibo and Demerara, 19 June 1778. A further source of income was the recognition fees that ships paid upon entering and clearing, which went into the WIC coffers. The rates varied throughout the century but were typically rather low in order not to discourage (foreign) traders from coming.

21. Henk den Heijer, "A Public and Private Dutch West India Interest," in Oostindie and Roitman, *Dutch Atlantic Connections*, 172–73.

22. For some good examples regarding the improvised nature of empire elsewhere, see Sanjay Subrahmanyam, *Improvising Empire: Portuguese Trade and Settlement in the Bay of Bengal, 1500–1700* (Delhi: Oxford University Press, 1990); Alejandra Irigoin and Regina Grafe, "Bargaining for Absolutism: A Spanish Path to Nation-State and Empire Building," *Hispanic American Historical Review* 88, no. 2 (2008); George Bryan Souza, *The Survival of Empire: Portuguese Trade and Society in China and the South China Sea, 1630–1754* (Cambridge: Cambridge University Press, 1986).

23. Lauren A. Benton, *A Search for Sovereignty: Law and Geography in European Empires, 1400–1900* (Cambridge: Cambridge University Press, 2010) 24; Irigoin and Grafe, "Bargaining for Absolutism," 179.

24. Eliga H. Gould, "Entangled Histories, Entangled Worlds: The English-Speaking Atlantic as a Spanish Periphery," *American Historical Review* 112, no. 3 (2007).

25. Ida Altman, "The Spanish Atlantic, 1650–1780," in *The Oxford Handbook of the Atlantic World c. 1450–1850*, ed. Nicholas P. Canny and Philip D. Morgan (Oxford: Oxford University Press, 2011); Xabier Lamikiz, *Trade and Trust in the Eighteenth-Century Atlantic World: Spanish Merchants and Their Overseas Networks* (Woodbridge: Boydell Press, 2010); Adrian J. Pearce, "British Trade with the Spanish Colonies, 1788–1795," *Bulletin of Latin American Research* 20, no. 2 (2001); Zacharias Moutoukias, "Power, Corruption, and Commerce: The Making of the Local Administrative Structure in Seventeenth-Century Buenos Aires," *Hispanic American Historical Review* 68, no. 4 (1988); Lance R. Grahn, "Cartagena and Its Hinterland in the Eighteenth Century," in Knight and Liss, *Atlantic Port Cities*; Daviken Studnicki-Gizbert, *A Nation upon the Ocean Sea: Portugal's Atlantic Diaspora and the Crisis of the Spanish Empire, 1492–1640* (Oxford: Oxford University Press, 2007). For an excellent contribution on how the *Carrera de Indias* actually reduced risk for merchants, see Jeremy Baskes, *Staying Afloat: Risk and Uncertainty in Spanish Atlantic World Trade, 1760–1820* (Stanford, CA: Stanford University Press, 2013).

26. Jesse Cromwell, "Illicit Ideologies: Moral Economies of Venezuelan Smuggling and Autonomy in the Rebellion of Juan Francisco de León, 1749–1751," *The Americas* 74, no. 3 (2017): 270–71, 290–94. Cromwell's book *The Smugglers' World: Illicit Trade and Atlantic Communities in Eighteenth-Century Venezuela* (Chapel Hill: University of North Carolina Press, 2018) unfortunately appeared after this book was completed but might portray a similar borderless society in Venezuela.

27. Casey S. Schmitt, "Virtue in Corruption: Privateers, Smugglers, and the Shape of Empire in the Eighteenth-Century Caribbean," *Early American Studies: An Interdisciplinary Journal* 13, no. 1 (2015): 109–10.

28. Christian J. Koot, "Anglo-Dutch Trade in the Chesapeak and the British Caribbean, 1621–1733," in Oostindie and Roitman, *Dutch Atlantic Connections*, esp. 91–92.

29. Christian J. Koot, *Empire at the Periphery: British Colonists, Anglo-Dutch Trade, and the Development of the British Atlantic, 1621–1713* (New York: New York University Press, 2011); Nuala Zahedieh, *The Capital and the Colonies: London and the Atlantic Economy, 1660–1700* (Cambridge: Cambridge University Press, 2010); April Lee Hatfield, *Atlantic Virginia: Intercolonial Relations in the Seventeenth Century* (Philadelphia: University of Pennsylvania Press, 2004), chaps. 7 and 8.

30. On New York during and after the war, see Thomas M. Truxes, *Defying Empire: Trading with the Enemy in Colonial New York* (New Haven, CT: Yale University Press, 2008). On loyalty, see Andrew Jackson O'Shaughnessy, *An Empire Divided: The American Revolution and the British Caribbean* (Philadelphia: University of Pennsylvania Press, 2000).

31. Koot, "Anglo-Dutch Trade," in Oostindie and Roitman, *Dutch Atlantic Connections*, 97; James Blaine Hedges, *The Browns of Providence Plantations: The Nineteenth Century* (Providence, RI: Brown University Press, 1968); Fatah-Black, *White Lies*, chap. 7, esp. 186; Lisa Sturm-Lind, *Actors of Globalization: New York Merchants in Global Trade, 1784–1812* (Leiden: Brill, 2018); Linda K. Salvucci, "Supply, Demand, and the Making of a Market: Philadelphia and Havana at the Beginning of the Nineteenth Century," in Knight and Liss, *Atlantic Port Cities*.

32. Wim Klooster, *The Dutch Moment: War, Trade, and Settlement in the Seventeenth-Century Atlantic World* (Ithaca, NY: Cornell University Press, 2016). For the idea of the Dutch as champions of free trade, see Pieter C. Emmer, "The Rise and Decline of the Dutch Atlantic, 1600–1800," in Oostindie and Roitman, *Dutch Atlantic Connections*, 353.

33. P. M. Netscher, *History of the Colonies Essequebo, Demerary & Berbice: From the Dutch Establishment to the Present Day* (Georgetown, Guyana: The Daily Chronicle, 1929 [orig. 1888]); James Rodway, *History of British Guiana: From the Year 1668 to the Present Time*, 2 vols. (Georgetown, Guyana: J. Thomson, 1891, 1893); Henry G. Dalton, *The History of British Guiana: Vol. 1* (London: Longman, Green, Brown, and Longmans, 1855). The only modern history, albeit based mainly on secondary sources, is Alvin O. Thompson, *Colonialism and Underdevelopment in Guyana: 1580–1803* (Bridgetown: Carib Research & Publications, 1987). Recent contributions are Johan van Langen, "De Britse overname van de Nederlandse koloniën Demerary, Essequebo en Berbice (Guyana) Van economische overvleugeling naar politieke overheersing (1740–1814)" (MA thesis, University of Amsterdam, 2003); Van der Oest, "Forgotten Colonies," in Enthoven and Postma, *Riches*; Oostindie, "British Capital, Industry and Perseverance."

34. Some landmark studies (not already cited above) are Gert Oostindie, *Roosenburg en Mon Bijou: Twee Surinaamse plantages, 1720–1870* (Dordrecht: Foris Publications, 1989); Alex van Stipriaan, *Surinaams contrast: Roofbouw en overleven in een Caraïbische plantagekolonie, 1750–1863* (Leiden: KITLV, 1993); Wim Klooster, *Illicit Riches: Dutch Trade in the Caribbean, 1648–1795* (Leiden: KITLV, 1998); Johannes Postma, *The Dutch in the Atlantic Slave Trade* (Cambridge: Cambridge University Press, 1990); Victor Enthoven and Johannes Postma, eds., *Riches from Atlantic Commerce: Dutch Transatlantic Trade and Shipping, 1585–1817* (Leiden: Brill, 2003).

35. Recent innovative studies include Michiel van Groesen, *Amsterdam's Atlantic: Print Culture and the Making of Dutch Brazil* (Philadelphia: University of Pennsylvania Press, 2017); Linda Marguerite Rupert, *Creolization and Contraband: Curaçao in the Early Modern Atlantic World* (Athens: University of Georgia Press, 2012); Browne, *Surviving Slavery*; Gert Oostindie and Jessica V. Roitman, eds., *Dutch Atlantic Connections, 1680–1800: Linking Empires, Bridging Borders* (Leiden: Brill, 2014); Fatah-Black, *White Lies*.

36. See chaps. 1 and 3 for a fuller discussion on this policy and the implementation.

37. Frank Dragtenstein, *"De ondraaglijke stoutheid der wegloopers": Marronage en koloniaal beleid in Suriname, 1667–1768* (Utrecht: Centrum voor Latijns-Amerikaanse en Caraïbische Studies; Instituut ter Bevordering van de Surinamistiek, 2002).

38. Michael Craton, *Testing the Chains: Resistance to Slavery in the British West Indies* (Ithaca, NY: Cornell University Press, 1982), 23, 62; Kevin Mulroy, *Freedom on the Border: The Seminole Maroons in Florida, the Indian Territory, Coahuila, and Texas* (Lubbock: Texas Tech University Press, 1993); Richard Price, *Maroon Societies: Rebel Slave Communities in the Americas*, 3rd ed. (Baltimore, MD: Johns Hopkins University Press, 1996), 15. For seventeenth-century cooperation between Amerindians and colonists, see Mark Meuwese, *Brothers in Arms, Partners in Trade: Dutch-Indigenous Alliances in the Atlantic World, 1595–1674* (Leiden: Brill, 2012); Mark Meuwese, "The Opportunities and Limits of Ethnic Soldiering: The Tupis and the Dutch-Portuguese Struggle for the Southern Atlantic, 1630–1657," in *Empires and Indigenes: Intercultural Alliance, Imperial Expansion, and Warfare in the Early Modern World*, ed. Wayne E. Lee (New York: New York University Press, 2011). For eighteenth-century Berbice, see Marjoleine Kars, "'Cleansing the Land': Dutch-Amerindian Cooperation in the Suppression of the 1763 Slave Rebellion in Dutch Guiana," in Lee, *Empires and Indigenes*. Future research might indicate that Amerindians also played a larger role than previously thought in Suriname.

39. Richard Drayton, "The Collaboration of Labour: Slaves, Empires, and Globalizations in the Atlantic World, c. 1600–1850," in *Globalization in World History*, ed. A. G. Hopkins (London: Pimlico, 2002), 100; Jeppe Mulich, "Microregionalism and Intercolonial Relations: The Case of the Danish West Indies, 1730–1830," *Journal of Global History* 8, no. 1 (2013): 79; Alison Games, "Conclusion: A Dutch Moment in Atlantic Historiography," in Oostindie and Roitman, *Dutch Atlantic Connections*, 358–59. On the need to focus on connections rather than borders, including some notable examples, see Alison Games, "Atlantic History: Definitions, Challenges, and Opportunities," *American Historical Review* 111, no. 3 (2006); Bernard Bailyn, *Atlantic History: Concept and Contours* (Cambridge, MA: Harvard University Press, 2005); Franklin W. Knight and Peggy K. Liss, eds., *Atlantic Port Cities: Economy, Culture, and Society in the Atlantic World, 1650–1850* (Knoxville: University of Tennessee Press, 1991);

Jorge Cañizares-Esguerra and Erik R. Seeman, eds., *The Atlantic in Global History, 1500–2000* (Upper Saddle River, NJ: Pearson Prentice Hall, 2007); Peter A. Coclanis, "Atlantic World or Atlantic/World?," *William and Mary Quarterly* 63, no. 4 (2006); Paul M. Pressly, *On the Rim of the Caribbean: Colonial Georgia and the British Atlantic World* (Athens: University of Georgia Press, 2013).

40. Matthew Mulcahy, *Hubs of Empire: The Southeastern Lowcountry and British Caribbean* (Baltimore, MD: Johns Hopkins University Press, 2014), 2; Ernesto Bassi, *An Aqueous Territory: Sailor Geographies and New Grenada's Transimperial Greater Caribbean World* (Durham, NC: Duke University Press, 2016), 11; Adrian Finucane, "Trade and Organization in the Colonial Caribbean," *History Compass* 16, no. 7 (2018): 2.

41. For the role of the intercolonial slave trade in connecting empires, see Gregory E. O'Malley, *Final Passages: The Intercolonial Slave Trade of British America, 1619–1807* (Chapel Hill: University of North Carolina Press, 2016).

42. M. A. P. Meilink-Roelofsz, "Archivalia betreffende de voormalige Nederlandse koloniën Essequebo, Demerary en Berbice in het Public Record Office te London," *Nieuwe West-Indische Gids* 41, no. 1 (1961).

43. For self-organization, see the following works by David Hancock: "Self-Organized Complexity and the Emergence of an Atlantic Market Economy, 1651–1815," in Coclanis, *The Atlantic Economy*; *Oceans of Wine: Madeira and the Emergence of American Trade and Taste* (New Haven, CT: Yale University Press, 2009); "Organizing Our Thoughts: Global Systems and the Challenge of Writing a More Complex History," *Journal of The Historical Society* 10, no. 3 (2010); "The Triumphs of Mercury: Connection and Control in the Emerging Atlantic Economy," in *Soundings in Atlantic History: Latent Structures and Intellectual Currents, 1500–1830*, ed. Bernard Bailyn and Patricia L. Denault (Cambridge, MA: Harvard University Press, 2011).

1 / The Borderland

1. Parts of this chapter have appeared in Bram Hoonhout and Thomas Mareite, "Freedom at the Fringes? Slave Flight and Empire-Building in the Early Modern Spanish Borderlands of Essequibo-Venezuela and Louisiana-Texas," *Slavery & Abolition* (2018). Reprinted with permission. https://www.tandfonline.com/doi/full/10.1080/01 44039X.2018.1447806

2. Robert Hermann Schomburgk, *A Description of British Guiana, Geographical and Statistical: Exhibiting Its Resources and Capabilities, Together with the Present and Future Condition and Prospects of the Colony* (London: A. M. Kelley, 1840; repr. 1970).

3. United States of Venezuela, *The Counter-Case of the United States of Venezuela before the Tribunal of Arbitration: To Convene at Paris under the Provisions of the Treaty between the United States of Venezuela and Her Britannic Majesty Signed at Washington February 2, 1897* (New York: Evening Post Job Printing House, 1898), quotation from 31.

4. Betty Jane Kissler, "Venezuela-Guyana Boundary Dispute: 1899–1966" (PhD diss., University of Texas at Austin, 1971), 14–36.

5. Jeremy Adelman and Stephen Aron, "From Borderlands to Borders: Empires, Nation-States, and the Peoples in between in North American History," *American Historical Review* 104, no. 3 (1999).

6. Account of the Commandante General de Orinoco, 20 December 1772, no. 513, in Great Britain, *British Guiana Boundary. Arbitration with the United States of Venezuela: Appendix to the Case on Behalf of the Government of Her Britannic Majesty. Volume IV. 1769–1781* (London: Harrison and Sons, 1898) (hereafter BGBB, BC app. vol. 4), 106–7.

7. For contact zones, see Mary Louise Pratt, *Imperial Eyes: Travel Writing and Transculturation*, 2nd ed. (London: Routledge, 2008), 7–8. For zones of transculturation, see Weber and Rausch, "Introduction," in *Where Cultures Meet: Frontiers in Latin American History*, ed. David J. Weber and Jane M. Rausch (Wilmington, DE: SR Books, 1994), xiii, xxxii–xxxiii. For entanglement, see Gould, "Entangled Histories." For the more specific concept of the middle ground, see Richard White, *The Middle Ground: Indians, Empires, and Republics in the Great Lakes Region, 1650–1815* (Cambridge: Cambridge University Press, 2011); and the discussion in *William and Mary Quarterly* in 2006, including Richard White, "Creative Misunderstandings and New Understandings," *William and Mary Quarterly* 63, no. 1 (2006): 9–14. I prefer to avoid the term "frontier," which carries different connotations across national contexts. For the classic version, see Frederick J. Turner, "The Significance of the Frontier in American History," in Weber and Rausch, *Where Cultures Meet*, 1–18. For the more nuanced Latin American connotations, see Fabricio Prado, "The Fringes of Empires: Recent Scholarship on Colonial Frontiers and Borderlands in Latin America," *History Compass* 10, no. 4 (2012): 318–19.

8. Dalton, *History of British Guiana*, 63–74; Thompson, *Colonialism and Underdevelopment*, 5–9.

9. Tamar Herzog, *Frontiers of Possession: Spain and Portugal in Europe and the Americas* (Cambridge, MA: Harvard University Press, 2015), 1–13, 117–30, 245–65.

10. Ibid., 70–74, 95–98; Brian P. Owensby, "Between Justice and Economics: 'Indians' and Reformism in Eighteenth-Century Spanish Imperial Thought," in *Legal Pluralism and Empires, 1500–1850*, ed. Lauren A. Benton and Richard J. Ross (New York: New York University Press, 2013).

11. Neil L. Whitehead, *Lords of the Tiger Spirit: A History of the Caribs in Colonial Venezuela and Guyana, 1498–1820* (Dordrecht: Foris Publications, 1988), 2, 36; Meuwese, *Brothers in Arms*, 106–8.

12. Whitehead, *Lords of the Tiger Spirit*, 87–91.

13. Ibid., 97–102.

14. Ibid., 110; Report of Commandant of Guayana to the King, 11 November 1773, no. 517, BGBB, BC app. vol. 4: 109.

15. Acting Commander of Essequibo to WIC, 6 March 1751, no. 263, in Great Britain, *British Guiana Boundary. Arbitration with the United States of Venezuela: Appendix to the Case on Behalf of the Government of Her Brittanic Majesty. Volume II. 1724–1763* (London: Harrison and Sons, 1898) (hereafter BGBB, BC app. vol. 2), 70; Director-General to WIC, 4 August 1752, no. 269, BGBB, BC app. vol. 2: 75–76.

16. Report of Commandant of Guayana to the King, 11 November 1773, no. 517, BGBB, BC app. vol. 4: 109.

17. Thompson, *Colonialism and Underdevelopment*, 192.

18. Report of judicial proceedings instituted and drawn up in reference to the complaints made by the Dutch minister concerning the proceedings of Spaniards of the

Orinoco against the Dutch colonies in Essequibo, 1769, no. 482, BGBB, BC app. vol. 4: 47–50.

19. A. R. F. Webber and Harry Perot Christiani, *Centenary History and Handbook of British Guiana* (Georgetown, Guyana: "The Argosy" Company, 1931) 75. Another remonstrance was sent in 1769 but to no effect.

20. Thompson, *Colonialism and Underdevelopment*, 192.

21. Whitehead, *Lords of the Tiger Spirit*, 129.

22. Ibid., 194, 197.

23. Table of the Missions of the Revered Father Capuchins of Catalonia of the Province of Guiana, 31 August 1788, no 627, Great Britain, *British Guiana Boundary. Arbitration with the United States of Venezuela: Appendix to the Case on Behalf of the Government of Her Britannic Majesty. Volume V. 1781–1814* (London: Harrison and Sons, 1898) (hereafter BGBB, BC app. vol. 5): 69.

24. Michael P. McKinley, *Pre-Revolutionary Caracas: Politics, Economy, and Society 1777–1811* (Cambridge: Cambridge University Press, 1985), 3–4, 10, 25, 29–30, 39–45. For a more pessimistic view of the cacao sector, see Robert J. Ferry, *The Colonial Elite of Early Caracas: Formation & Crisis, 1567–1767* (Berkeley: University of California Press, 1989), 6–9.

25. Férmin de Sincinenea to Count del Campo de Alange, 15 June 1790, no. 632 in BGBB, BC app. vol. 5: 76–77.

26. The British were invited by Prince William V of Orange to "protect" the Dutch colonies against a French invasion. The latter was likely in the revolutionary time period, as the Dutch Republic itself was overrun by French soldiers. See chap. 2 for more details.

27. United States, *Venezuela-British Guiana Boundary Arbitration. Digest of Evidence Arranged According to Subjects: Prepared for the Private Use of the Venezuelan Council* (New York: Evening Job Printing House, 1899), 51.

28. L. A. H. C. Hulsman, "Nederlands Amazonia: Handel met indianen tussen 1580 en 1680" (PhD diss., University of Amsterdam, 2009), 128, 137, 158.

29. Whitehead, *Lords of the Tiger Spirit*, 181–82.

30. Rodway, *History*, vol. 1: 226; Thompson, *Colonialism and Underdevelopment*, 179.

31. Thompson, *Colonialism and Underdevelopment*, 36.

32. United States, *Digest of Evidence*, 70–71.

33. Timothy J. Yeager, "Encomienda or Slavery? The Spanish Crown's Choice of Labor Organization in Sixteenth-Century Spanish American," *Journal of Economic History* 55, no. 4 (1995) 845; Whitehead, *Lords of the Tiger Spirit*, 2.

34. Brett Rushforth, *Bonds of Alliance: Indigenous and Atlantic Slaveries in New France* (Williamsburg, VA: University of Virginia Press, 2012), 356–71.

35. Whitehead, *Lords of the Tiger Spirit*, 188.

36. Report of Marquis de San Felipe y Santiago to the King of Spain, (?1739), no. 34, in Great Britain, *British Guiana Boundary. Arbitration with the United States of Venezuela: Appendix to the Counter Case on Behalf of the Government of Her Britannic Majesty* (London: Harrison and Sons, 1898) (hereafter BGBB, BCC appendix), 182.

37. C. A. Harris and J. A. J. de Villiers, *Storm van 's Gravesande: The Rise of British Guiana Compiled from His Despatches* (London: Hakluyt Society, 1911), vol. 2: 431.

38. Proclamation by the Commandeur of Essequibo, 2 April 1730, no. 182, in Great Britain, *British Guiana Boundary. Arbitration with the United States of Venezuela. Appendix to the Case on Behalf of the Government of Her Britannic Majesty. Volume II. 1724-1763*, (hereafter BGBB, BC app. vol. 2), 10.
39. De Smidt, Lee, and Van Dapperen, *Guyana Ordinance Book*, Essequibo, 28 April 1752.
40. United States, *Digest of Evidence*, 53.
41. Ibid., 54. The legal status of these black traders is not mentioned.
42. Ibid., 54–55.
43. Ibid., 59.
44. Ibid., 59, 64–66.
45. Whitehead, *Lords of the Tiger Spirit*, 153.
46. Great Britain, *Documents and Correspondence relating to the Question of Boundary between British Guiana and Venezuela* (London: Harrison and Sons, 1896), 9.
47. United States, *Digest of Evidence*, 49–50; Commandeur of Essequibo to WIC, 8 June 1734, no. 195 in BGBB, BC app. vol. 2: 17.
48. J. A. J. de Villiers, *Storm van 's Gravesande: Zijn werk en zijn leven uit zijne brieven opgebouwd* (The Hague: Martinus Nijhoff, 1920), 96.
49. Acting Commandeur of Essequibo to WIC, 8 September 1750, no. 260 in BGBB, BC app. vol. 2: 69.
50. Webber and Christiani, *Handbook of British Guiana*, 50.
51. Short account of the great river Orinoco . . . , ca. 1750, no. 38 in BGBB, BCC appendix, 195.
52. Ibid.
53. United States, *Digest of Evidence*, 68–70.
54. Director-General of Essequibo to WIC, 14 July 1772, no. 509 in BGB, app. vol. 4: 103.
55. Commander of Essequibo to WIC, 7 December 1746, no. 234 in BGBB, BC app. vol. 2: 46–48.
56. Thompson, *Colonialism and Underdevelopment*, 230–31; Judicial Report of the Attack made by the Spaniards upon the Dutch settled in Barima (1760), no. 351 in BGBB, BC app. vol. 2: 194–195.
57. Marjoleine Kars, "'Cleansing the Land': Dutch-Amerindian Cooperation in the Suppression of the 1763 Slave Rebellion in Dutch Guiana," in Lee, *Empires and Indigenes*, 265.
58. Damian Pargas, "Promised Lands: Seeking Freedom in the Age of American Slavery," Inaugural Lecture, Leiden University, 2018. "Slave refugee" places the focus on the person trying to seek freedom. The often-used term "fugitive," in contrast, is centered on the colonists and the law-breaking element of fleeing, whereas today we consider being free a basic human right. "Runaway" does not fully convey the idea that these people hoped to find "asylum" in Venezuela.
59. Linda M. Rupert, "'Seeking the Water of Baptism': Fugitive Slaves and Imperial Jurisdiction in the Early Modern Caribbean," in Benton and Ross, *Legal Pluralism*, 203.
60. De Smidt, Lee, and Van Dapperen, *Guyana Ordinance Book*, Essequibo, 4 December 1758.
61. Webber and Christiani, *Handbook of British Guiana*, 75.

62. Court of Policy in Essequibo to WIC, 10 July 1775, no. 538 in BGBB, BC app. vol. 4: 108–109.

63. Ambassador of the Dutch Republic in Madrid to the States-General, 12 February 1784, no. 595, in BGBB, BC app. vol. 5: 22.

64. Harris and Villiers, *Storm van 's Gravesande*, vol. 2: 430–31.

65. Director-General to WIC, 1 February 1774, no. 524 in BGBB, BC app. vol. 4: 123.

66. M. Van den Heuvel to Amsterdam Chamber, NL-HaNA, WIC, 1.05.01.02, inv. nr. 309, f. 455–461; Council of Policy in Essequibo to the WIC, 31 January 1773, no. 523 in BGBB, BC app. vol. 4: 123: Petition of colonists to States-General, 14 September 1784, no. 599 in BGBB, BC app. vol. 5: 23.

67. Original quotation: "door sachte middelen tot de betaling trachten te noodsaeken." De Smidt, Lee, and Van Dapperen, *Guyana Ordinance Book*, Essequibo, 14 August 1764.

68. *Resoluties van de directeur-generaal en raden van Demerary*, 1787–88, NL-HaNA, WIC, 1.05.01.02, inv. nr. 1033. See also De Smidt, Lee, and Van Dapperen, *Guyana Ordinance Book*, Essequibo, 4 October 1751; Essequibo, 9 May 1753; Essequibo and Demerara, 1 October 1764.

69. *Rapport bestemd voor erfstadhouder Willem V opgesteld door zijn commissarissen naar West-Indië, W.H. van Grovestins en W. Boeij*. 1790 juli 17, NL-HaNA, WIC, 1.05.01.02, inv. nr. 915; De Smidt, Lee, and Van Dapperen, *Guyana Ordinance Book*, Demerara, 8 January 1789.

70. Director-General to the WIC, 27 May 1775, no. 537 in BGBB, BC app. vol. 4: 136.

71. De Smidt, Lee and Van Dapperen, *Guyana Ordinance Book*, Demerara, 8 January 1789.

72. Ibid., Essequibo and Demerara, 1 May 1793.

73. For Amerindian's autonomy, see Kars, "'Cleansing the Land,'" in Lee, *Empires and Indigenes*, 253, 259, 265, 267.

74. Chris Schult, "Een noodzakelijk bondgenootschap: De rol van de indianen in de kolonies Essequibo en Demerary, 1770–1800" (MA thesis, Leiden University, 2014), 31.

75. In that case it was 25 guilders; see De Smidt, Lee, and Van Dapperen, *Guyana Ordinance Book*, Demerara, 8 January 1789. The reward for catching a runaway depended on the distance as well, for in 1784 it was 12.50 guilders "within the river," 25 guilders for farther upriver, up to 50 guilders for the plantations farthest away (Essequibo and Demerara, 29 July 1794).

76. De Smidt, Lee, and Van Dapperen, *Guyana Ordinance Book*, Demerara, 8 January 1789. Original quotation: "om eenige vereeringen vanweegens de Edele Compagnie en Colonie te ontfangen."

77. Rodway, *History*, vol. 1: 242–43; Webber and Christiani, *Handbook of British Guiana*, 88.

78. Council of Policy in Essequibo to WIC, 31 January 1774, no. 522, in BGBB, BC app. vol. 4: 122.

79. Council of Policy in Essequibo to WIC, 31 January 1774, no. 522, in BGBB, BC app. vol. 4: 92–93.

80. George Hendrik Trotz to Chamber Zeeland, 1 February 1774, TNA, CO 116/39, f. 111. Original quotation: "die niet wel onthaald sijn, als sij niet dronken vertrekken

en nog een pul of twee drank ook wel 1/2 dz. wijn en brood en bakkeljauw meede nemen."

81. Diary of the Director-General, 30 July 1785, no. 610 in BGBB, BC app. vol. 5: 35–36.

82. Director-General to WIC, 4 October 1785, no. 612 in BGBB, BC app. vol. 5: 38.

83. Diary of the Director-General, 30 July 1785, no. 610 in BGBB, BC app. vol. 5: 35–36.

84. Extracts from the government journal, 24 September 1785, no. 615 in BGBB, BC app. vol. 5: 40.

85. Storm van 's Gravesande to WIC, 22 June 1750, no. 66 in BGBB, BC app. vol. 2: 67.

86. Extracts from the government journal, 30 December 1785, no. 615 in BGBB, BC app. vol. 5: 40.

87. Extracts from the government journal, 2 October 1785, 7 October 1785, 11 October 1785, 8 December 1785, no. 615, in BGBB, BC app. vol. 5: 40.

88. Anonymous memorial (?1802), no. 686 in BGBB, BC app. vol. 5: 176–77.

89. Extract form Register of Meetings of the Ten, 26 March 1773, no. 514 in BGBB, BC app. vol. 4: 107–8; Extract from the Minutes of the Proceedings of the Court of Policy of Essequibo, 31 October 1803, no. 682 in BGBB, BC app. vol. 5: 183; Extract from the Minutes of the Proceedings of the Court of Policy of Essequibo, 1 May 1804, no. 684 in BGBB, BC app. vol. 5: 185.

90. The inflation calculator at www.measuringworth.com (accessed 24 May 2015) states that 192 pounds in 1773 (it does not convert guilders) was worth 419 pounds in 1804. The value of pounds to guilders was around 12 guilders during this entire period and thus cannot suffice as an explanation.

91. Extract from the Minutes of the Proceedings of the Court of Policy of Essequibo, 22 February 1803, no. 680 in BGBB, BC app. vol. 5: 179–81.

92. Instruction for the Postholders with the Indians in Essequibo and Demerary, 15 may 1803, enclosed in no. 717 in BGBB, BC app. vol. 5: 216–17.

93. Extract from the Minutes of the Proceedings of the Court of Policy of Essequibo, 29 May 1804, no. 685 in BGBB, BC app. vol. 5: 185.

94. Extract from the Minutes of the Proceedings of the Court of Policy of Essequibo, 30 April 1805, no. 689 in BGBB, BC app. vol. 5: 187.

95. Extract from the Minutes of the Proceedings of the Court of Policy of Essequibo and Financial Representatives, 20 November 1812, no. 713 in BGBB, BC app. vol. 5: 202.

96. Acting Governor Codd to Earl Bathurst, 26 September 1813, no. 717 in BGBB, BC app. vol. 5: 216.

97. Extract from the Minutes of the Proceedings of the Court of Policy of Essequibo, 22 February 1803, no. 680 in BGBB, BC app. vol. 5: 179–181.

98. Extract from the Minutes of the Proceedings of the Court of Policy of Essequibo, 29 October 1810, no. 701 in BGBB, BC app. vol. 5: 194–95.

99. Extract from the Minutes of the Proceedings of the Court of Policy of Essequibo, 29 October 1810, no. 701 in BGBB, BC app. vol. 5: 194–95; Questions and answers by acting governor Codd to D. van Sirtema, 30 August 1813, enclosed in no. 713 in BGBB, BC app. vol. 5: 215.

100. Extract from the Minutes of the Proceedings of the Court of Policy of Essequibo, 2 July 1812, no. 712 in BGBB, BC app. vol. 5: 199–200; Governor Carmichael to Earl Bathurst, 18 January 1813, no. 714 in BGBB, BC app. vol. 5: 203.

101. Acting governor Codd to Earl of Bathurst, 26 September 1813, no. 717 in BGBB, BC app. vol. 5: 216.

102. Acting governor Codd to Earl of Bathurst, 6 September 1813, no. 716 in BGBB, BC app. vol. 5: 214–15.

103. Thompson, *Colonialism and Underdevelopment*, 201.

2 / Political Conflicts

1. TNA, CO 116/61, f. 217–18. Original quotation: "Wat wilt gij doen met uw handje vol volk, teegens 40000 Negers die wij alle ogenblikken gewapend kunnen hier brengen, zijnde meest alle reeds in gereedheid, en aan wiens hooft, wij ons met een aanzienelijk getal blanken zullen stellen, die dan u en uw 80 zoldaten bij de minsten tegenweer tot sir . . . kappen, indien gij ons de toegang tot de Raeden niet wilde openen."

2. This was captain Drebber, who died shortly after this event. There are no indications that he indeed would have supported the dissenting planters.

3. The leader of the dissenters was Bernhard Albinus (former Councillor), together with three others, G. J. Riem, Bartholomeus van den Santheuvel (who formerly ran a mortgage investment fund; see chapter 4), and Hermanus Jonas. TNA, CO 116/61, f. 220–358, esp. reply to L'Espinasse, 19-9-1787, f. 261–62.

4. Declaration Lasberg, 5-1-1788, TNA, CO 116/61, f. 216–19.

5. As will be discussed in more detail below, Essequibo and Demerara were officially just one colony, termed "Essequibo and dependent rivers." However, since Demerara developed and received its own council in 1773, I prefer to speak of two colonies.

6. Hendrik Spruyt, *The Sovereign State and Its Competitors: An Analysis of Systems Change* (Princeton, NJ: Princeton University Press, 1994); Irigoin and Grafe, "Bargaining for Absolutism," 177–82; Grafe, *Distant Tyranny*, 13, 219; Joseph R. Strayer, *On the Medieval Origins of the Modern State* (Princeton, NJ: Princeton University Press, [1973] 2005); Jack P. Greene, *Negotiated Authorities: Essays in Colonial Political and Constitutional History* (Charlottesville: University of Virginia Press, 1994).

7. A. J. R. Russell-Wood, "Center and Peripheries in the Luso-Brazilian World, 1500–1808," in *Negotiated Empires: Centers and Peripheries in the Americas, 1500–1820*, ed. Christine Daniels and Michael V. Kennedy (London: Routledge, 2002); J. H. Elliott, *Empires of the Atlantic World: Britain and Spain in America, 1492–1830* (New Haven, CT: Yale University Press, 2006), 310–12.

8. Christine Daniels and Michael V. Kennedy, eds., *Negotiated Empires: Centers and Peripheries in the Americas, 1500–1820* (London: Routledge, 2002).

9. Regina Grafe and Alejandra Irigoin, "A Stakeholder Empire: The Political Economy of Spanish Imperial Rule in America," *Economic History Review* 65, no. 2 (2012): 609–51.

10. Francisco Bethencourt, "Political Configurations and Local Powers," in *Portuguese Oceanic Expansion, 1400–1800*, ed. Francisco Bethencourt and Diogo Ramada Curto (New York: Cambridge University Press, 2007), 199.

11. Regina Grafe, "Polycentric States: The Spanish Reigns and the 'Failures' of Mercantilism," in *Mercantilism Reimagined: Political Economy in Early Modern Britain*

and its Empire, ed. Philip J. Stern and Carl Wennerlind (New York: Oxford University Press, 2014); Pedro Cardim et al., "Polycentric Monarchies: How Did Early Modern Spain and Portugal Achieve and Maintain a Global Hegemoney?," in *Polycentric Monarchies: How did Early Modern Spain and Portugal Achieve and Maintain a Global Hegemony?*, ed. Pedro Cardim et al. (Eastborne: Sussex Academic Press, 2012); Lauren A. Benton, *Law and Colonial Cultures: Legal Regimes in World History, 1400–1900* (Cambridge: Cambridge University Press, 2002), 33.

12. For discussions regarding legal pluralism, see Lauren A. Benton, *A Search for Sovereignty: Law and Geography in European Empires, 1400–1900* (Cambridge: Cambridge University Press, 2010); Paul Halliday, "Laws' Histories: Pluralisms, Pluralities, Diversity," in *Legal Pluralism and Empires*, ed. Lauren A. Benton and Richard J. Ross (New York: New York University Press, 2013), 262, 273; Richard J. Ross and Philip J. Stern, "Reconstructing Early Modern Notions of Legal Pluralism," in Benton and Ross, *Legal Pluralism and Empires*; Jane Burbank and Frederick Cooper, "Rules of Law, Politics of Empire," in Benton and Ross, *Legal Pluralism and Empires*; Lauren A. Benton and Richard Jeffrey Ross, "Empires and Legal Pluralism: Jurisdiction, Sovereignty, and Political Imagination in the Early Modern World," in Benton and Ross, *Legal Pluralism and Empires*; Philip J. Stern, *The Company-State: Corporate Sovereignty and the Early Modern Foundations of the British Empire in India* (New York: Oxford University Press, 2011).

13. Den Heijer, "Dutch West India Company," in Enthoven and Postma, *Riches*, 114; Jan Luiten van Zanden and Arthur van Riel, *Nederland 1780–1914: Staat, instituties en economische ontwikkeling* (Amsterdam: Balans, 2000), 52.

14. Netscher, *History of the Colonies*, 14–16, 29; Harris and Villiers, *Storm van 's Gravesande*, vol. 1: 8–25.

15. Harris and Villiers, *Storm van 's Gravesande*, vol. 1:144.

16. Jan Jacob Hartsinck, *Beschryving van Guiana, of de wilde kust in Zuid-America* (Amsterdam: Gerrit Tielenburg, 1770), 228–56.

17. Ibid.

18. Den Heijer, "Dutch West India Interest," in Oostindie and Roitman, *Dutch Atlantic Connections*, 171–74.

19. NL-HaNA, States-General (hereafter S-G), 1.01.02, inv. nr. 3827, at 40–42.

20. Sources for table 2.1: Winston F. McGowan, "The French Revolutionary period in Demerara-Essequibo, 1793–1802," *History Gazette* 55 (1993): 18; Rodway, *History*, vol. 1: 258–60; Harris and Villiers, *Storm van 's Gravesande*, vol. 2: 398–400; Van der Oest, "Forgotten Colonies," in Enthoven and Postma, *Riches*, 329; *Rekening en verantwoording van de kolonie-ongelden van Essequebo in de vorm van een grootboek; met achterin 3 losse lijsten van achterstallige ongelde, over het jaar 1777*, NL-HaNA, WIC, 1.05.01.02, inv. nr. 189; "*Generaale staat van de Rivier Demerary, en onderhoorige districten over het jaar 1788". Overzicht van de plantages van Demerary, en onderhorige districten, 1788*, NL-HaNA, WIC, 1.05.01.02, inv. nr. 192B; "*Generaal tableau van de Colonie Essequebo en onderhoorige districten van 1788". Overzicht van de plantages van Essequebo en onderhorige districten*, NL-HaNA, WIC, 1.05.01.02, inv.nr. 193A; *Memorie over de verbeteringen in Essequebo en Demerary ingevoerd ten aanzien van het rechtswezen en de cultures, over den gelimiteerden handel met de Noord-Amerikanen, het wezen van den smokkelhandel, de defensie, de vriendschappelijk betrekkingen met de Indiaansche inboorlingen en de middelen tot verhooging van de welvaart aldaar,*

NL-HaNA, Raad der Amerikaanse Bezittingen (hereafter RAB), 2.01.28.02, inv. nr. 168M; TNA, CO 111/3, f. 214–15, 294, 295, 298; TNA, CO 116/36, f. 205, 446. Both colonies also had plantations dedicated to producing timber: 41 in Essequibo in 1798 and 31 in Demerara in the same year. These are not added to the total figures here.

21. Rodway, *History*, vol. 1: 223.

22. Hartsinck, *Beschryving van Guiana*, 278.

23. The judicial council thereafter consisted of the member of the Court of Policy, except for the plantation director, and four citizens—two from each colony. The election procedure was rather complicated: the Court of Justice would nominate a College of Electors from the members of the Burgher Militia. In turn the College of Electors could put forward two candidates to fill the seats, and the current councillors would then choose one of them. Rodway, *History*, vol. 1: 223.

24. Harris and Villiers, *Storm van 's Gravesande*, vol. 2: 648.

25. The titles Commandant and Commander are somewhat confusing: the former was the head of the military, the latter the highest official in Demerara, answering to the director-general in Essequibo.

26. Harris and Villiers, *Storm van 's Gravesande*, vol. 1: 33, 46, 52.

27. Again, just for clarification, the Zealand Chamber considered Essequibo and Demerara one colony.

28. Three planters from each colony were delegated, but since the meeting was presided over by the director-general and took place in Essequibo, that colony retained the upper hand. Rodway, *History*, vol. 1: 241.

29. G. H. Trotz to WIC, 23-12-1773, TNA, CO 116/39, f. 45–55.

30. J. L. C. van Baerle, report, 1774, TNA, CO 116/39, f. 402–3.

31. Trotz to WIC, 27-9-1773, TNA, CO, 116/39, f. 11–12. Original quotation: "droevig, slegt logement."

32. Frederick Roetering to Zealand Chamber, 13-12-1773, TNA, CO 116/39, f. 76–78; 14-1-1774, TNA, CO 116/39 f. 79–80; 1-3-1774, TNA, CO 116/39 f. 322–328. Original quotation, from folio 77: "was er nooyt geen Secretarye geweest ik sag beter kans om alles in zijn ordre te brengen dan nu."

33. Schuylenburg to WIC, 6-6-1776, TNA, CO 116/44; f. 212–13.

34. Harris and Villiers, *Storm van 's Gravesande*, vol. 1: 258; W.C. Boeij to WIC, 7-4-1774, TNA, CO 116/39, f. 184–85; Trotz to WIC, 5-7-1774, TNA, CO 116/36, f. 427–30.

35. Harris and Villiers, *Storm van 's Gravesande*, vol. 1: 257. The commandant, J. C. Severijn, was fired afterward, but the WIC directors ordered he be reinstated in his role.

36. J. C. de Winter to WIC, 22-5-1774, TNA, CO 116/39, f. 308–10; Council of Policy to Zealand Chamber, 2-7-1774, TNA, CO 116/39, f. 406–7.

37. Journal of Schuylenburg, 4-3-1780 to 9-4-1780, TNA, CO 116/44, f. 49.

38. W. C. Boeij to WIC, 23-6-1774, TNA, CO 116/39, f. 292–94; Councillors to G. H. Trotz, 30-4-1774, TNA, CO 116/39, f. 400–401; G. H. Trotz to Zealand Chamber, 8-12-1776, TNA, CO 116/44, f. 316–37.

39. In 1762 in Essequibo it was 6 guilders for every English barque entering. In 1774 in Essequibo it was 7.50 guilders for the director-general for a pass, 2.50 guilders for the secretary, 5 guilders for the surgeon, and 2.50 guilders for the Poor Fund. Harris and Villiers, *Storm van 's Gravesande*, vol. 2: 396–97; TNA, CO 116/39, f. 427–30, Trotz to WIC, 5-7-1774; TNA, CO 116/55, f. 76–78, D.H. Macaré to WIC, 6-7-1780.

40. NL-HaNA, WIC, 1.05.01.02, inv. nr. 915, Rapport bestemd voor erfstadhouder Willem V opgesteld door zijn commissarissen naar West-Indië, W. H. van Grovestins en W. Boeij, 1790 juli 17.

41. Netscher, *History of the Colonies*, 122–23; NL-HaNA, S-G, 1.01.02, inv. nr. 3842, 16 June 1784, at 510.

42. Banks, *Chasing Empire*, 42; Matthew Parker, *The Sugar Barons: Family, Corruption, Empire, and War in the West Indies* (New York: Walker & Co., 2011), 303–30; Altman, "The Spanish Atlantic," in Canny and Morgan, *The Oxford Handbook*; Baskes, *Staying Afloat*, 70; Herbert S. Klein, *African Slavery in Latin America and the Caribbean* (Oxford: Oxford University Press, 1986), 87; Allan J. Keuthe, "Havana in the Eighteenth Century," in Knight and Liss, *Atlantic Port Cities*.

43. Lieutenant-Colonel Kingston to General Vaughan, 26-10-1781, TNA, CO 111/1, f. 41–45.

44. Proclamation by Kingston to the inhabitants of Essequibo, Demerara and Berbice, TNA, CO 111/1, f. 50–54.

45. Thompson, *Colonialism and Underdevelopment*, 53; Rodway, *History*, vol. 2: 1–8. Company plantations were taken for the king, and the auction master and tax receiver were replaced.

46. Rodway, *History*, vol. 2: 7.

47. Ibid., 20; Netscher, *History of the Colonies*, 124; C. C. Kanne to Amsterdam Chamber, 12-2-1784, TNA, CO 116/55, f. 236–40.

48. Rodway, *History*, vol. 2: 34.

49. The director-general's salary was 12,000 guilders, plus 2,000 as president of thecCouncil, plus 2,000 as councillor, plus 1,500 as commissary, plus 1,200 as bookkeeper. This was next to an additional 5 percent on receipts as receiver. Previously he also had 1,200 guilders in "table money" (Netscher, *History of the Colonies*, 66; Rodway, *History*, vol. 2: 27).

50. Aristodemus and Sincerus, *Brieven over het bestuur der colonien Essequebo en Demerary, gewisseld tusschen de Heeren Aristodemus en Sincerus nevens bylagen, tot deeze briefwisseling: Vol. 3*, 12 vols. (Amsterdam: W. Holtrop, 1786), 75–76.

51. The director-general would choose six Protestant members to form the court. These would be chosen from eighteen nominees put forward by the Burgher Militia. Rodway, *History*, vol. 2: 24–28.

52. Sources differ on who these were, either the president of the court, the fiscal, the receiver of taxes, and the commissioner of supplies or the fiscal, auctioneer, receiver of taxes, and a fourth man.

53. Oostindie, "Dutch Atlantic Decline," in Oostindie and Roitman, *Dutch Atlantic Connections*; P. C. Emmer, "The Dutch and the Making of the Second Atlantic System," in *The Dutch in the Atlantic Economy, 1580–1880: Trade, Slavery and Emancipation*, ed. P. C. Emmer (Aldershot: Ashgate, 1998), 29; Emmer, *Nederlandse slavenhandel*, 171.

54. Jonathan I. Israel, *The Dutch Republic: Its Rise, Greatness and Fall, 1477–1806* (Oxford: Clarendon Press, 1998), 1098–1103.

55. Ibid., 1105–14.

56. G. J. Schutte, *De Nederlandse patriotten en de koloniën: Een onderzoek naar hun denkbeelden en optreden, 1770–1800* (Groningen: H. D. Tjeenk Willink, 1974), 43, 55–56, 103.

57. Ibid., 43, 58–69; Aristodemus and Sincerus [pseudonym], *Brieven over het bestuur der colonien Essequebo en Demerary, gewisseld tusschen de Heeren Aristodemus*

en Sincerus nevens bylagen, tot deeze briefwisseling, en eene voorreden van den Nederlandschen uitgeever: Volume 1 (Amsterdam: W. Holtrop, 1785), 41–83.

58. Aristodemus and Sincerus, *Brieven*, vol 1: Appendix A.

59. Ibid., Appendixes A and B; Aristodemus and Sincerus, *Brieven over het bestuur der colonien Essequebo en Demerary, gewisseld tusschen de Heeren Aristodemus en Sincerus nevens bylagen, tot deeze briefwisseling: Volume 2* (Amsterdam: W. Holtrop, 1786), 101–9.

60. Aristodemus and Sincerus, *Brieven*, vol. 3: 106–10; Aristodemus and Sincerus, *Brieven over het bestuur der colonien Essequebo en Demerary, gewisseld tusschen de Heeren Aristodemus en Sincerus nevens bylagen, tot deeze briefwisseling* (Amsterdam: W. Holtrop, 1786) vol. 4: 104–5.

61. Aristodemus and Sincerus, *Brieven over het bestuur*, vol. 5: 67–83; Aristodemus and Sincerus, *Brieven*, vol. 3: appendixes L and N.

62. Rodway, *History*, vol. 2: 34–35.

63. The prewar councillors were Cornelis Overbroek (who died), Joseph Bourda, and Pieter van Helsdingen. The men who refused were, respectively, H. Riem, H. Jonas, and H. H. Post. Rodway, *History*, vol. 2: 34–35.

64. These were C. J. Hecke, A. Lonck (or Loncq), and J. Bastiaanse. Rodway, *History*, vol. 2: 35.

65. Ibid., vol. 2: 35; "Nationalities" found in *Naamlijst van de eigenaars van plantages in Demerary, Juli 1785*, NL-HaNA, Verspreide West-Indische Stukken (hereafter VWIS), inv. nr. 59.

66. Rodway, *History*, vol. 2: 35.

67. Albinus was appointed council member in Demerara in 1773, Jonas was appointed president of the Orphan and Estate Chamber in 1784, Hartsinck was receiver and councillor in Demerara in 1785, Grovestins was president of the Orphan and Estate Chamber (Boedelkamer) and was captain of one of the civil militias and fiscal between 1776 and 1782 (NL-HaNA, WIC, 1.05.01.02, inv nr. 39; TNA, CO 116/44, f. 397; CO 116/39, f. 393; Rodway, *History*, vol. 1: 309; Rodway, *History*, vol. 2: 34).

68. TNA, CO 116/57, f. 291–98, 313.

69. Aristodemus and Sincerus, *Brieven*, vol. 3: 12th letter, appendix K.

70. In fact, there were more planters in the colonies, and around sixty of them did not sign the petition (see CO 116/61, f.280–81).

71. The document made no distinction between English, Scottish, Irish, people from "the islands" (the British Caribbean, mostly from Barbados), and North Americans, although my suspicion is that the latter group was rather small. NL-HaNA, VWIS, 1.05.06, inv. nr. 59.

72. Aristodemus and Sincerus, *Brieven*, vol. 3: 47, app. K.

73. Ibid., vol. 3: appendix M.

74. Netscher, *History of the Colonies*, 124.

75. Rapport Grovestins en Boeij, NL-HaNA, WIC, 1.05.01.02, inv. nr. 915.

76. Very few plantations had more than a hundred enslaved laborers, meaning that most people paid less than 250 guilders per year in poll tax. While certainly not negligible, this was a small sum compared to the many thousands of guilders in profits that some attained. For those in debt, however, a few hundred guilders would still matter. See chap. 5 for a more detailed discussion of debts and profits.

77. *Stukken betreffende de onderzoekingen in opdracht van de Admiraliteit op de Maze door de luitenant ter zee Frans Smeer aangaande de sluikhandel in Essequebo, Demerary en Berbice, 1787,* NL-HaNA, Admiraliteitscolleges XXA Paulus-Olivier (hereafter Admiraliteitscolleges / Paulus-Olivier), 1.01.47.13, inv. nr. 44; *Resoluties van de directeur-generaal en raden van Demerary. 1787 jan. 15—1788 aug. 21,* NL-HaNA, WIC, 1.05.01.02, inv. nr. 1033. See also chap. 4.

78. See the introduction of this chapter.

79. Original quotations: "men is hier niet meer gewoon dan anarchie, & men wil niet geregeerd weeze"; "aller hachelijkst"; "U moet zich niet verwonderen, wat er ook gebeure." L'Espinasse to Zeeland Chamber, 12-9-1787, TNA, CO 116/61, f. 5–6.

80. L'Espinasse to WIC, 7-10-1787, TNA, CO 116/61, f. 40–41; L'Espinasse to WIC, 7-10-1787, TNA, CO 116/61, f. 244; L'Espinasse to WIC, 31-12-1787, TNA, CO 116/61, f. 176.

81. J. Bastiaanse and Eyre Butler to L'Espinasse, 26-10-1787, TNA, CO 116/61, f. 264–65; J. Bastiaanse and Eyre Butler et al. to L'Espinasse, 31-10-1785, TNA, CO 116/61, f. 278–81.

82. L'Espinasse to WIC, 31-12-1787, TNA, CO 116/61, f. 172, 189.

83. To be more precise, the advice was to have only one Council of Policy in Demerara, consisting of the director-general, the commander of Essequibo, the fiscal from each colony, and two colonists from each river. In Essequibo a College of Electors (*Kiezers*) already existed but was to be enlarged from 5 to 7, while Demerara would establish its own. Rodway, *History,* vol. 2: 48–51.

84. *Brief van de Kamer Amsterdam aan de Staten-Generaal betreffende de bewering door enige ingezetenen van Demerary uitgesproken, dat Essequebo en Demerary met geen mogelijkheid langer onder de behering der West- Indische Compagnie konden blijven, 22 januari 1788,* NL-HaNA, VWIS, 1.05.06, inv. nr. 128. Original quotations: "hunne vrije halsen gewillig neder leggen op 't blok van arbitraire heerszucht"; "starker, en voor een jeder onaangenamers middel te gebruyken."

85. L'Espinasse to WIC, 31-12-1787, TNA, CO 116/61 f. 209–10.

86. These were J. L. C. van Baerle and François Changuion (Extract from the minutes of the Council of Policy of Demerara, 15-10-1787, TNA, CO 116/61, f. 225–33).

87. A few weeks later Meertens would ask permission to take up his post again, saying it had not been his intention to desert the government (Meertens to L'Espinasse, 27-10-1787, TNA, CO 116/61, f. 272–74).

88. Rodway, *History,* vol. 2: 35–37.

89. Publication by L'Espinasse, 17-10-1787, TNA, CO 116/61, f. 256–60.

90. Answer L'Espinasse to 31-10-1787, petition, 2-11-1787, TNA, CO 116/61, f. 294–95.

91. TNA, CO 116/61, f. 298–338.

92. Rapport Grovestins and Boeij, NL-HaNA, WIC, 1.05.01.02, inv. nr. 915, f. 5–7. (The archival entry contains two versions of the report, the original and the duplicate. For reasons of legibility I have consulted the duplicate, so the cited page numbers refer to the duplicate.) Original quotations: "resolutien en beveelen, met een blinden ijver hadden willen ten uytvoer brengen"; "die zich als Colonie Raaden kenmerkende, het Sistema van de Planters tegen het gouvernement begunstigden"; "een volkoomen staat van regeeringloosheid was gebracgt, en dat uytgezonders de publique rust en veyligheid, welke nog altijd gelijkkig bewaard is gebleeven, niemand zig verplicht

rekende, aan eenige vastgestelde wetten of ordres te voldoen of eenige lasten op te brengen."

93. Webber and Christiani, *Handbook of British Guiana*, 132.

94. Previously councillors were appointed for life, with the college comprising five members. This number was thus increased to seven, and every two years the most senior councillor had to retire. The Plan of Redress would remain in force as a basis for Guiana's government until 1928. One of the electors was the Bostonian Gardiner Greene, while the Scot Thomas Cuming served as one of the temporary heads of government; both of them are discussed in chap. 6. Rapport Grovestins en Boeij, NL-HaNA, WIC, 1.05.01.02, inv. nr. 915, f. 106, 108; *Journaal, dagboek van het gouvernement in Demerary*, NL-HaNa, Raad der Koloniën (hereafter RdK), 1.05.02, inv. nr. 75, 27 May 1795, 31 May 1795.

95. Alicia Schrikker, *Dutch and British Colonial Intervention in Sri Lanka, 1780–1815: Expansion and Reform* (Leiden: Brill, 2007), 131–32.

96. McGowan, "The French Revolutionary Period," 1–4.

97. Rodway, *History*, vol. 2: 72.

98. Ibid., 74; Bound volume of correspondence of Peter Fairbairn, Seaforth's secretary, National Records of Scotland (hereafter NRS), Edinburgh, inv. nr. GD46/17/14, f. 813, 817, 821.

99. The commander of Essequibo was Albert Backer and the acting fiscal of Demerara was Frans Wolff (the official fiscal was probably away). McGowan, "The French Revolutionary Period," 5.

100. Anthony Beaujon's brother, Jan Jacob, was sent in 1796 by the Batavian Republic to Curaçao to become the new governor. There, Jan Jacob, although a Patriot himself, was accused of having convinced his brother to seek English support. Karwan Fatah-Black, "The Patriot Coup d'État in Curaçao, 1796," in *Curaçao in the Age of Revolutions, 1795-1800*, ed. Wim Klooster and Gert Oostindie (Leiden: KITLV, 2011), 137.

101. Webber and Christiani, *Handbook of British Guiana*, 114.

102. The appointment of Beaujon comes across as rather strange, considering that a few weeks earlier he had been accused of selling out to the English. McGowan, "The French Revolutionary period," 5–7.

103. Edward L. Cox, "The British Caribbean in the Age of Revolution," in *Empire and Nation: The American Revolution in the Atlantic world*, ed. Eliga H. Gould and Peter S. Onuf (Baltimore, MD: Johns Hopkins University Press, 2005) 276–279; Beverley A. Steele, *Grenada: A History of Its People* (Oxford: Macmillan Caribbean, 2003), 101; David Geggus, "Slave Rebellion during the Age of Revolution," in Klooster and Oostindie, *Curaçao in the Age of Revolutions*, 29–31; Ramón Aizpurua, "Revolution and Politics in Venezuela and Curaçao, 1795–1800," in Klooster and Oostindie, *Curaçao in the Age of Revolutions*, 103–5; Fatah-Black, "Patriot Coup," in Klooster and Oostindie, *Curaçao in the Age of Revolutions*, 132; Michael Craton, *Testing the Chains: Resistance to Slavery in the British West Indies* (Ithaca, NY: Cornell University Press, 1982) 182–83, 211.

104. NL-HaNA, RdK, 1.05.02, inv. nr. 75, 19 May 1795.

105. See the website of David Alston: http://www.spanglefish.com/slavesandhighlanders/index.asp?pageid=164658 (retrieved 19 June 2016).

106. Dalton, *History of British Guiana*, 245–47.

107. McGowan, "The French Revolutionary Period," 11; Oostindie, "British Capital."

108. Webber and Christiani, *Handbook of British Guiana*, 106.

3 / Rebels and Runaways

1. Interrogation of Maddelon, 18 August 1772, TNA, CO 116/38, f. 287. Original quotation: "de nieuwe meester behandelt ons zo slegt, laat ons hem een mes in zijn keel steeken."

2. Obeah is "an Afro-Caribbean complex of spiritual healing, harming, and divination" (Randy M. Browne, "The 'Bad Business' of Obeah: Power, Authority, and the Politics of Slave Culture in the British Caribbean," *William and Mary Quarterly* 68, no. 3 [2011]: 453). The word she used was *Fetiche* (Diana Paton, *The Cultural Politics of Obeah: Religion, Colonialism and Modernity in the Caribbean World* (Cambridge: Cambridge University Press, 2015), 20 n. 4; TNA, CO 116/38, f. 285-87; Journal of the command post at plantation Zeelugt, TNA, CO 116/38, f. 266-77.

3. TNA, CO 116/36, f. 285-87 (quotation). Further interrogations of Callaert, 30 December 1773, TNA, CO 116/38, f. 236-43. Original quotation: "dat Callaard bij haar is geweest en haar heeft gebruikt, in zijn slaapkamer op een plank voor dat zij verkogt waren."

4. Minutes of the Court of Civil and Criminal Justice of Essequibo, 16 October 1772, National Archives of Guyana (hereafter NAG), AB 3, inv. nr. 12, f. 178-82; Minutes of the Court of Civil and Criminal Justice of Essequibo, 4 and 5 November 1772, NAG, AB 3, inv. nr. 13, f. 1-5.

5. She was tied to a pole, with a chain, so that she could walk around, putting her in the position of an animal. Subsequently, a fire was pushed closer and closer, to burn her alive. Proceedings of the Court of Justice, 15 December 1772, NAG, AB 3, inv. nr. 13, f. 38.

6. Da Costa, *Crowns of Glory*, 170-71.

7. Extract from Minutes of Court of Justice, 3 January 1774, TNA, CO 116/39, f. 246-49. Original quotation: "niet minder dan de ruine van deze gansche Colonie en de verhaaste dood van zoo veele Blanken Christenen."

8. TNA, CO 116/38, f. 236-43; Confession of Callaert, 8 January 1774, CO 116/39, f. 266-67.

9. Marjoleine Kars, "Dodging Rebellion: Politics and Gender in the Berbice Slave Uprising of 1763," *American Historical Review* 121, no. 1 (2016): 41.

10. Parts of this chapter have been previously published as Hoonhout and Mareite, "Freedom at the Fringes?" Reprinted with permission.

11. Steele, *Grenada*, chap. 4; Laird W. Bergad, *The Comparative Histories of Slavery in Brazil, Cuba, and the United States* (New York: Cambridge University Press, 2007), 16-17; Banks, *Chasing Empire*, 42; Klein, *African Slavery*, 87.

12. Klein, *African Slavery*, 83-88; Bergad, *Comparative Histories*, 23-63; Disney, *History of Portugal*, chap. 24.

13. Van Stipriaan, *Surinaams contrast*.

14. Mohammed Shahabuddeen, *From Plantocracy to Nationalisation: A Profile of Sugar in Guyana* (Georgetown: University of Guyana, 1984), 16-17; Oostindie and Van Stipriaan, "Hydraulic Society," 80-81.

15. Van Stipriaan, *Surinaams contrast*, 318.
16. Gert Oostindie, "Voltaire, Stedman and Suriname Slavery," *Slavery & Abolition* 14, no. 2 (1993); Van Stipriaan, *Surinaams contrast*, 372–75. Barry Higman gives the figures between 0.5 and 1.5 percent negative growth in the period 1817–32, and David Eltis also notes how the enslaved population declined after 1817 when the slave trade between British colonies was ended (B. W. Higman, *Slave Populations of the British Caribbean 1807–1834* [Baltimore, MD: Johns Hopkins University Press, 1984], 310; Eltis, "Traffic in Slaves").
17. Philip D. Morgan, "The Black Experience in the British Empire, 1680–1810," in *Black Experience and the Empire*, ed. Philip D. Morgan and Sean Hawkins (New York: Oxford University Press, 2004), 90–91.
18. Gert Oostindie, "The Economics of Slavery," in *Economic and Social History in the Netherlands*, vol. 5, ed. Peter Boomgaard et al. (Amsterdam: Nederlands Economisch-Historisch Archief, 1993), 15.
19. Gert Oostindie, "Slavenleven," in *Ik ben eigendom van—: Slavenhandel en plantageleven*, ed. Bea Brommer (Wijk en Aalburg: Pictures Publishers, 1993), 101; Van Stipriaan, *Surinaams contrast*, 168–69.
20. Database "Global Commodities, Trade Exploration and Cultural Exchange," www.globalcommodities.amdigital.co.uk; accessed 5 July 2016.
21. Ibid.; Bergad, *Comparative Histories*, chap. 4; Giorgio Riello, *Cotton: The Fabric That Made the Modern World* (New York: Cambridge University Press, 2013), chap. 9; Da Costa, *Crowns of Glory*, 28.
22. Klein, *African Slavery*, 86; Angelina Pollak-Eltz, "La esclavitud en Venezuela," in *Influencias africanas en las culturas tradicionales de los países andinos: Il encuentro para la promoción y difusión del patrimonio folclórico de los países andinos* (Santa Ana de Coro: Ministerio de Educación, Cultura y Deportes, 2001); Roland Dennis Hussey, *The Caracas Company 1728–1784: A Study in the History of Spanish Monopolistic Trade* (Cambridge, MA: Harvard University Press, 1934).
23. Bergad, *Comparative Histories*, 194; Morgan, "The Black Experience," in Morgan and Hawkins, *Black Experience*, 94; Gert Oostindie, "Slave Resistance, Colour Lines, and the Impact of the French and Haitian Revolutions in Curaçao," in Klooster and Oostindie, *Curaçao in the Age of Revolutions*, 3; Karwan Fatah-Black, "Slaves and Sailors on Suriname's Rivers," *Itinerario* 36, no. 3 (2012).
24. Van Langen, "Britse overname," 91; Henry Bolingbroke, *A Voyage to Demerary, Containing a Statistical Account of the Settlement There, and of Those on the Essequebo, the Berbice, and Other Contiguous Rivers of Guyana* (London: M. Carey, 1807) 40. The British reported in 1802 that 2,669 (5 percent) of the 49,451 slaves were registered in Stabroek (CO 111/4 f. 179).
25. Oostindie, "Voltaire, Stedman and Suriname Slavery," 21.
26. Rodway, *History*, vol. 2: 173.
27. Most of these numbers are based on tax figures and therefore represent a lower boundary: many planters underreported the number of enslaved workers in order to pay less taxes, and quite a few did not report any number at all. Furthermore, not all enslaved people were included in the taxes (such as young children and possibly elderly, sick, or disabled people). Eltis, "Traffic in Slaves," 60; Rodway, *History*, vol. 2: 11; Thompson, *Colonialism and Underdevelopment*, 93; Harris and Villiers, *Storm van 's Gravesande*, vol. 2: 398–99; *Gedrukte extract-resolutiën van de*

Staten-Generaal en andere stukken . . . , 1769–76, NL-HaNA, Laurens Pieter van de Spiegel [levensjaren 1737–1800] (hereafter Raadpensionaris Van de Spiegel), 3.01.26, inv. nr. 450, H18, f. 91–94; TNA, CO 116/34, f. 205–8, 330–34; TNA, CO 116/36, f. 205,.446; *Overzicht inwoners en plantages Essequibo 1777, 1778*, NL-HaNA, WIC, 1.05.01.02, inv. nr. 189; *"Generaal tablea van de Colonie Essequebo"* . . . , 1789, NL-HaNA, WIC, 1.05.01.02, inv. nr. 192A; *"Generaale staat van de Rivier Demerary"* . . . , 1789, NL-HaNA, WIC, 1.05.01.02, inv. nr. 192B; TNA, CO 111/3, f. 97, 213, 214, 231; TNA, CO 111/4, f. 8; TNA, CO 111/4, f. 179.

28. Rodway, *History*, vol. 2: 36–37; Van Langen, "Britse overname," 88.

29. Thomas Pierronet, "Remarks Made during a Residence at Stabroek Rio Demerary (Lat. 6. 10. N.) in the Latter Part of the Year 1798," in *Collections of the Massachusetts Historical Society for the Year 1799*, ed. Massachusetts Historical Society (Boston: Charles C. Little and James Brown, 1799), 9.

30. Nigel Worden and Gerald Groenewald, *Trials of Slavery: Selected Documents Concerning Slaves from the Criminal Records of the Council of Justice at the Cape of Good Hope, 1705–1794* (Cape Town: Van Riebeeck Society for the Publication of South African Historical Documents, 2005) xxi n. 65.

31. Harris and Villiers, *Storm van 's Gravesande*, vol. 2: 638.

32. Original phrasing: "niet onverdiend sullen mogen straffen, doen straffen ofte mishandelen"; "christelijk gemoed." De Smidt, Lee, and Van Dapperen, *Guyana Ordinance Book*, Essequibo, 12 October 1771.

33. Ibid., Demerara, 2 November 1773.

34. Ibid., Essequibo and Demerara, 1 October 1784.

35. As discussed in Vincent Brown, *The Reaper's Garden: Death and Power in the World of Atlantic Slavery* (Cambridge, MA: Harvard University Press, 2008), 133–37.

36. De Smidt, Lee, and Van Dapperen, *Guyana Ordinance Book*, Essequibo and Demerara, 1 October 1784.

37. Da Costa, *Crowns of Glory*, 45; Browne, *Surviving Slavery*, 35–36, 58, 62, 67–69.

38. Karwan Fatah-Black, "Desertion by Sailors, Slaves and Soldiers in the Dutch Atlantic, ca. 1600–1800," in *Desertion in the Early Modern World: A Comparative History*, ed. Matthias Van Rossum and Jeanette Kamp (London: Bloomsbury Press, 2016), 105.

39. Sylviana A. Diouf, *Slavery's Exiles: The Story of the American Maroons* (New York: New York University Press, 2014), 5.

40. For the concepts, see Pargas, "Promised Lands," 5.

41. Jeanette Kamp and Matthias van Rossum, "Introduction: Leaving Work across the World," in Van Rossum and Kamp, *Desertion*, 5.

42. Jared Hardesty, *Unfreedom: Slavery and Dependence in Eighteenth-Century Boston* (New York: New York University Press, 2016), 2.

43. Matthias van Rossum, "'Working for the Devil': Desertion in the Eurasian Empire of the VOC," in Van Rossum and Kamp, *Desertion*, 134.

44. Fatah-Black, "Slaves and Sailors"; Fatah-Black, "Desertion by Sailors, Slaves and Soldiers," in Van Rossum and Kamp, *Desertion*.

45. Miles Ogborn, *Global Lives: Britain and the World, 1550–1800* (Cambridge: Cambridge University Press, 2008), 253.

46. Diouf, *Slavery's Exiles*, chap. 8.

47. Pargas, "Promised Lands."

48. Hoonhout and Mareite, "Freedom at the Fringes," 11–17; Jane Landers, *Atlantic Creoles in the Age of Revolutions* (Cambridge, MA: Harvard University Press, 2010) 4, 9, 11, 98–99.

49. Neville A. T. Hall, "Maritime Maroons: Grand Marronage," in *Slave Society in the Danish West Indies: St. Thomas, St. John, and St. Croix*, ed. B. W. Higman (Baltimore, MD: Johns Hopkins University Press, 1992).

50. Linda M. Rupert, "Marronage, Manumission and Maritime Trade in the Early Modern Caribbean," *Slavery & Abolition* 30, no. 3 (2009); Rupert, "'Seeking the Water of Baptism,'" in Benton and Ross, *Legal Pluralism and Empires*; Rupert, *Creolization and Contraband*, chap. 4.

51. Craton, *Testing the Chains*, 23, 190–94.

52. Landers, *Atlantic Creoles*, 102–9.

53. Kate Ekama, "Just Deserters: Runaway Slaves from the VOC Cape, c. 1700–1800," in Van Rossum and Kamp, *Desertion*, 178.

54. Richard Price and Sally Price, *Les Marrons* (Châteauneuf-le-Rouge: Vents d'ailleurs, 2003), 15–21.

55. Robert Cohen, *Jews in Another Environment. Surinam in the Second Half of the Eighteenth Century* (Leiden: Brill, 1991), 79–80; Oostindie, "Voltaire, Stedman and Suriname Slavery," 5.

56. Fatah-Black, "Desertion by Sailors, Slaves and Soldiers," in Van Rossum and Kamp, *Desertion*, 130.

57. Wim Klooster and Gert Oostindie, *Realm between Empires: The Second Dutch Atlantic, 1680–1815* (Ithaca, NY: Cornell University Press, 2018), 143; Dragtenstein, *Ondraaglijke stoutheid*, 55, 236.

58. Thompson, *Colonialism and Underdevelopment*, 141; Thompson, *Maroons of Guyana: Problems of Slave Desertion in Guyana, c. 1750–1814* (Georgetown, Guyana: Free Press, 1999), 15.

59. NL-HaNA, WIC, 1.05.01.02, inv. nrs. 192A and 192B.

60. Berta E. Pérez, "The Journey to Freedom: Maroon Forebears in Southern Venezuela," *Ethnohistory* 47, no. 3–4 (2000): 611–34.

61. Director-General to WIC, 6 January 1772, no. 505 in BGBB, BC app. vol. 4: 100–101.

62. The titles of these men changed, depending on the place of the Guayana province within the Spanish empire. At first it fell under the governor of Trinidad, which later became the governor of Cumaná. The highest official in Orinoco is called "commandant" in the sources, but Storm van 's Gravesande often used the term "governor." He complained several times that the quick turnover of governors in Orinoco (three to five years) made the establishment of long-term agreements impossible (Court of Policy to WIC, 4 July 1731, no. 187 in BGBB, BC, app. vol. 2: 13–14; Director-General to WIC, 9 February 1769, addendum K1 to no. 469 in BGBB, BC app. vol. 4: 34).

63. Commandeur to Director's Committee of Ten, 27 March 1749, no. 249 in BGBB, BC app. vol. 2: 60–61.

64. Storm to WIC, 19 February 1754, no. 292 in BGBB, BC app. vol. 2: 91; Storm to WIC, 12 December 1759, no. 345 in BGBB, BC app. vol. 2: 182. Yet in 1789 a cartel was established with France for the mutual exchange of deserters to and from Cayenne; see De Smidt, Lee, and Van Dapperen, *Guyana Ordinance Book*, Essequibo and Demerara, 1 March 1789.

NOTES TO CHAPTER 3 / 219

65. Storm to WIC, 9 February 1762, no. 365 in BGBB, BC app. vol. 2: 211–12.
66. Storm to WIC, 6 September 1767, no. 431 in BGBB, BC app. vol. 3: 150–52.
67. Declaracion of Benito de Garriga (and others who repeated his statement almost verbatim), no. 482 in BGBB, BC app. vol. 4: 47–50.
68. Discripcion Corografico-mixta de la Provincia de Guayana..., no date [around 1770], no. 70 in BGBB, VCC app., 3: 120; Diary of Matheo Beltran, commander of the revenue cutter in the Orinoco, 1785, no. 438 in BGBB, VCC app. 3: 332–33.
69. Personal correspondence with Thomas Mareite, based on his research in the Archivo de Indias, Sevilla, folder Indiferente 2787.
70. Declaration of Benito de Garriga (and others who repeated his statement almost verbatim), no. 482 in BGBB, BC app. vol. 4: 47–50.
71. Court of Policy in Essequibo to WIC, 1 March 1727, no. 177 in BGBB, BC app. vol. 2: 6. However, in 1776 Trotz reported that the desertion of "creoles and Indian slaves" had increased significantly later. See Trotz to Chamber Zeeland, 28 August 1776, TNA, CO 116/44, f. 430.
72. Resolutions of the Court of Policy of Demerara, 16 July 1786, NL-HaNA, WIC, 1.05.01.02, inv. nr. 1032.
73. In 1788 there were 120 people listed as enslaved Amerindians in Essequibo (NL-HaNA, WIC, 1.05.01.02, 188A).
74. Storm to WIC, 3 March 1769, no. 454 in BGBB, BC app. vol. 4: 4–5.
75. Storm to WIC, 8 September 1760, no. 350 in BGBB, BC app. vol. 2: 186.
76. Trotz to WIC, 30 September 1774, no. 529 in BGBB, BC app. vol. 4: 127–28.
77. Courts of Policy and Justice of Essequibo to WIC, 31 January 1773, no. 523 in BGBB, BC app. vol. 4: 122–23; Courts of Policy and Justice of Essequibo to WIC, 10 July 1775, no. 538 in BGBB, BC app. vol. 4: 137; Memorial of Burgher Officers to the Court of Policy in Essequibo, 2 January 1772, no. 531 in BGBB, BC app. vol. 4: 129.
78. Minutes of the Court of Policy of Essequibo, 5 November 1784, no. 602 in BGBB, BC app. vol. 5:27.
79. Director-General to WIC, 20 October 1786, no. 620 in BGBB, BC app. vol. 5: 44–46; Declaration by J. Bertholy, 7 October 1788, no. 628 in BGBB, BC app. vol. 5: 70.
80. *Memorie van de bewindhebbers van de West-Indische Compagnie Willem August Syrtema van Groevestins en Willem Cornelis Boey op het rapport van de commissarissen van prins Willem V naar de koloniën van de Staat in West-Indië inzake het veranderen van de regeringsvorm aldaar, 1790,* NL-HaNA, S-G, 1.01.02, inv. nr. 9425, at 49–53; NL-HaNA, S-G, 1.01.02, inv .nr. 3832, 8 April 1777, at 225–26.
81. Court of Policy to WIC, 1 March 1727, no. 177 in BGBB, BC app. vol. 2: 6; Storm to WIC, 9 February 1762, no. 365 in BGBB, BC app. vol. 4: 211–12; Storm to WIC, 6 September 1767, no. 431 in BGBB, BC app. vol. 3: 150–152; Storm to WIC, 15 June 1770, no 484 in BGBB, BC app. vol. 3: 76; Trotz to WIC, 6 April 1773, no. 516 in BGBB, BC app. vol. 3: 100–101; Commander of Demerara to WIC's Amsterdam Chamber, 3 April 1784, no. 596 in BGBB, BC app. vol. 5: 22–23; Director-General ad interim to WIC, 12 May 1790, no. 630 in BGBB, BC app. vol. 5: 73–74.
82. Storm to WIC, 6 January 1772, no. 505 in BGBB, BC app. vol. 4:100–101.
83. Trotz to WIC, 6 April 1773, no. 516 in BGBB, BC app. vol. 4: 108–9; Court of Policy to WIC, 31 January 1773, no. 523 in BGBB, BC app. vol. 4: 123; Trotz to WIC, 30 September 1774, no. 529 in BGBB, BC app. vol 4: 127–28; Trotz to WIC, 30 June 1784, no. 598 in BGBB, BC app. vol. 5: 23.

84. Aristodemus and Sincerus, *Brieven*, vol. 3: 82–83.
85. Proceedings of the Ten, 30 September 1784, no. 601 in BGBB, BC app. vol. 5: 24.
86. Ibid., 25.
87. Storm to WIC, 6 September 1767, no. 431 in BGBB, BC app. vol. 3: 150–152; WIC's Chamber of Zeeland to Director-General, 18 July 1768, no. 446 in BGBB, BC app. vol. 3: 179–81.
88. In 1776 an official remarked that it took three weeks to mobilize Amerindian troops, but he was talking about uprisings (Van den Heuvel to Chamber Amsterdam, 16 December 1776, TNA, CO 116/44, f. 455–61). As shown below for 1789, within several days various Amerindian soldiers came forward.
89. Director-General to WIC, 4 October 1785, no. 612 in BGBB, BC app. vol. 5: 38.
90. Schult, "Een noodzakelijk bondgenootschap," 37.
91. Rodway, *History*, vol. 2: 56–57.
92. Fatah-Black, "Desertion by Sailors, Slaves and Soldiers," in Van Rossum and Kamp, *Desertion*, 104–6.
93. Thompson, *Colonialism and Underdevelopment*, chap. 8.
94. Marjoleine Kars, "Transgressing and Policing Borders: Soldiers, Slave Rebels, and the Early Modern Atlantic," *New West Indian Guide* 83, no. 3–4 (2009) 187–213 (quotation 196).
95. Ibid., 188, 207.
96. Anthony Brown to Amsterdam Chamber, 2 October 1773, TNA, CO 116/39, f. 9–10; Trotz to WIC, 2 Augustus 1773, TNA, CO 116/39, f. 11–12; Mr. Boeij to WIC, 7 April 1774, TNA, CO 116/39, f. 184–85.
97. Trotz to Chamber Zeeland, 1 February 1774, TNA, CO 116/39, f. 90–96; NL-HaNA, S-G, 1.01.02, inv. nr. 9425; J. C. de Winter to WIC, 19 March 1774, TNA, CO 116/39, f. 186–89; J.C. de Winter to WIC, 22 May 1774, TNA, CO 116/39, f. 308–10.
98. Storm to WIC, 1 June 1768, no. 444 in BGBB, BC app. vol. 3: 176–78.
99. Commander of Demerara to WIC, 18 February 1768, no. 440 in BGBB, BC app. vol. 3: 162–63 (quotation); Storm to WIC, 8 December 1766, no. 420 in BGBB, BC app. vol. 3: 138–40.
100. Storm to WIC, 9 April 1769, no. 442 in BGBB, BC app. vol. 3: 163–66. Why exactly the Amerindians so resented French postholders is unclear; it seems unlikely they were much worse than the Dutch ones.
101. Storm to WIC, 9 November 1768, no. 449 in BGBB, BC app. vol. 3: 182–83.
102. Storm to WIC, 8 December 1766, no. 420 in BGBB, BC app. vol. 3: 138–40; Zeeland Chamber to Storm, 18 July 1768, no. 446 in BGBB, BC app. vol. 3: 179–81.
103. Minutes of the court martial, 14 August 1786, TNA, CO 116/61, f. 77–80.
104. Eugene D. Genovese, *From Rebellion to Revolution: Afro-American Slave Revolts in the Making of the Modern World* (Baton Rouge: Louisiana State University Press, 1979), xiv–xxii, 3.
105. Craton, *Testing the Chains*, 99–101, 161–65, 241–49.
106. Trevor Burnard, *Planters, Merchants, and Slaves: Plantation Societies in British America, 1650–1820* (Chicago: University of Chicago Press, 2015), 6, chap. 2.
107. Browne, *Surviving Slavery*, 3; Kars, "Dodging Rebellion," 41.
108. It is possible that more revolts will be discovered in future research.
109. When the Company had plans to sell its own plantations in 1774, the local authorities advised against it, fearing that the enslaved might not accept a new director

and might rise up or turn to marronage (Director-General G. H. Trotz to WIC, 13 September 1773, TNA, CO 116/39, f. 23-26; Council of Policy to Gentlemen Ten, 31 January 1774, TNA, CO 116/39, f. 168-71).

110. Interrogation of Pierro, 18 August 1772, TNA, CO 116/38, f. 288; Interrogations of Andries, TNA, CO 116/38, f. 300; Interrogation of Sam, TNA, CO 116/38, f. 306.

111. Petition of Callaert to Court of Justice, 27 May 1771, NAG, AZ 1, inv. nr 68, f. 157-59.

112. TNA, CO 116/38, f.300; Confirmation of Callaert's confession, 8 January 1774, TNA, CO 116/39, f. 266-67; Interrogation of Pieter Callaert by Fiscal Anthony Brown, 30 December 1773, TNA, CO 116/39, f. 236-43; Interrogation of Snel and Sam, 28 August 1772, TNA, CO 116/38, f. 308; Interrogation of Febus, 1 September 1772, CO 116/38, f. 315.

113. Harris and Villiers, *Storm van 's Gravesande*, vol. 2: 666.

114. Testimony of Lea, 20 August 1772, TNA, CO 116/38, f. 298. Original quotations: "wij hebben tegen de Blanken oorlog & van nu af zult gij onzen Slaaven zijn"; "Wij zijn uw slaven niet, wij zullen bij de Blanken blijven."

115. Interrogations, TNA, CO 116/38, f. 285-318. In the Dutch context, "Amina" or "Elmina" (Coromantee in the British context) was used for Akan and Ga speakers from the Gold Coast area (Kars, "Dodging Rebellion," 47).

116. As there are no maps for this period, the demarcations of the plantations are based on earlier and later maps, so it is for example not known how many estates were already established along the canals or on Demerara's east coast.

117. Interrogations, TNA, CO 116/38, f. 285-318; Interrogation of Pieter Callaert by Fiscal Anthony Brown, 30 December 1773, TNA, CO 116/39, f. 236-43.

118. Report by J.F. Boode to Director-General, 24 August 1772, TNA, CO 116/38, f. 278-82.

119. Harris and Villiers, *Storm van 's Gravesande*, vol. 2: 665-66.

120. For more on cross-cultural brokers, see: Simon Schaffer et al., "Introduction," in *The Brokered World: Go-Betweens and Global Intelligence, 1770-1820*, ed. Simon Schaffer et al. (Sagamore Beach, MA: Science History Publications, 2009); Sanjay Subrahmanyam, "Between a Rock and a Hard Place: Some Afterthoughts," in Schaffer et al., *The Brokered World*.

121. Journal of the post at the plantation Zeelugt, 15 August-6 September 1772, TNA, CO 116/38, f. 266-77.

122. Harris and Villiers, *Storm van 's Gravesande*, vol. 2: 667.

123. Minutes of the Court of Justice, 20 October 1772, NAG, AB 3, inv. nr. 12, f. 183; Resolution of the States-General, NL-HaNA, S-G, 1.01.02, inv. nr. 3828, at 3-4.

124. Minutes of the Court of Justice of Essequibo, 16 and 20 October 1772, NAG, AB 3, inv. nr. 12, f. 178-83. The punishment of Louis was altered to a harsh flogging, burning, and lifelong chain labor because the councillors thought his testimonies would be too valuable to execute him.

125. Council of Policy to the Ten, 31 January 1774, TNA, CO 116/39, f. 172-73.

126. *Duplicaat-missive van P.G. Duker te Stabroek aan de Kamer Amsterdam betreffende een opstand der negerslaven in Demerary, 27 November 1789*, NL-HaNA, VWIS, 1.05.06, inv. nr. 130; *Ingekomen brieven met bijlagen uit Essequebo, 1787 July 14-1791 August 25*, NL-HaNA, WIC, 1.05.01.02, inv. nr. 534, f. 1180-94; NL-HaNA, WIC, 1.05.01.02, inv. nr. 915.

127. NL-HaNA, VWIS, 1.05.06, inv. nr. 130; NL-HaNA, WIC, 1.05.01.02, inv. nr. 534, f. 1180–94.

128. The sources mention "mulatto" but make no distinction between mulattoes (of white and black descent) and mestizos (of white and Amerindian descent). It is likely that in many cases these were in fact people of white-Amerindian descent.

129. NL-HaNA, VWIS, 1.05.06, inv. nr. 130; NL-HaNA, WIC, 1.05.01.02, inv. nr. 534, f. 1180–94.

130. NL-HaNA, WIC, 1.05.01.02, inv. nr. 534, f. 1180–94. Seventy-nine persons received presents as a reward for their service in the revolt: 41 Caribs, 33 Arawaks, 4 Akawaios, and 5 Waraos. See Schult, "Een noodzakelijk bondgenootschap," app. 2.

131. De Smidt, Lee, and Van Dapperen, *Guyana Ordinance Book*, Demerara, 8 October 1789.

132. NL-HaNA, VWIS, 1.05.06, inv. nr. 130; NL-HaNA, WIC, 1.05.01.02, inv. nr. 534, f. 1180–94; NL-HaNA, WIC, 1.05.01.02, inv. nr. 915.

133. Craton, *Testing the Chains*, chaps. 15 and 17.

134. Aizpurua, "Revolution and Politics," in Klooster and Oostindie, *Curaçao in the Age of Revolutions*, 99–101.

135. Oostindie, "Slave Resistance," in Klooster and Oostindie, *Curaçao in the Age of Revolutions*, 8–9.

136. Alex Borucki, "Trans-Imperial History in the Making of the Slave Trade to Venezuela, 1526–1811," *Itinerario* 36, no. 2 (2012): 43; Landers, *Atlantic Creoles*, 51.

137. Cox, "The British Caribbean."

138. Craton, *Testing the Chains*, 243–44; David Geggus, "Slavery, War, and Revolution in the Wider Caribbean, 1789–1815," in *A Turbulent Time: The French Revolution and the Greater Caribbean*, ed. David B. Gaspar and David P. Geggus (Bloomington: Indiana University Press, 1997), 10; David Geggus, "Slave Rebellion during the Age of Revolution," in Klooster and Oostindie, *Curaçao in the Age of Revolutions*, 35; Wim Klooster, "The Rising Expectations of Free and Enslaved Blacks in the Greater Caribbean," in Klooster and Oostindie, *Curaçao in the Age of Revolutions*, 60, 65; Da Costa, *Crowns of Glory*, 78.

139. Wim Klooster, "Slave Revolts, Royal Justice, and a Ubiquitous Rumor in the Age of Revolutions," *William and Mary Quarterly* 71, no. 3 (2014).

140. Gert Oostindie, "Slave Resistance, Colour Lines, and the Impact of the French and Haitian Revolutions in Curaçao," in Klooster and Oostindie, *Curaçao in the Age of Revolutions* , 9; Rodway, *History*, vol. 2: 71. In 1794 the States-General had warned against the subversive influence of the French revolution; see De Smidt, Lee and Van Dapperen, *Guyana Ordinance Book*, Essequibo and Demerara, 29 April 1794.

141. Rodway, *History*, vol. 2: 77.

142. "Journaal," dagboek van het gouvernement in Demerary, NL-HaNA, RdK, 1.05.02, inv. nr. 75, 14 May to 13 June 1795.

143. Ibid., 13 June to 19 June 1795.

144. Ibid., 20 June to 30 June 1795.

145. Rodway, *History*, vol. 2: 78.

146. NL-HaNa, RdK, 1.05.02, inv. nr. 75, 1 to 11 July 1795.

147. Ibid., 17 to 22 July; De Smidt, Lee, and Van Dapperen, *Guyana Ordinance Book*, Demerara, 1 July 1795.

148. De Smidt, Lee and Van Dapperen, *Guyana Ordinance Book*, Demerara, 24 July 1795. Original quotation: "verpligt zoude worden, dat gedeelte van deeze Colonie geheel te moeten verlaaten."

149. NL-HaNa, RdK, 1.05.02, inv. nr. 75, 19 to 31 July.

150. Rodway, *History*, vol. 2: 78. The price for the enslaved soldiers of the black corps was not to exceed 1,000 guilders per person. See also Craton, *Testing the Chains*, 169–70; Dragtenstein, *Ondraaglijke stoutheid*, 35; Philip D. Morgan and Andrew J. O'Shaughnessy, "Arming Slaves in the American Revolution," in *Arming Slaves: From Classical Times to the Modern Age*, ed. Christopher L. Brown and Philip D. Morgan (New Haven, CT: Yale University Press, 2006).

151. Rodway, *History*, vol. 2: 79–80, quotation at 79.

152. Thompson, *Colonialism and Underdevelopment*, 150.

153. Schult, "Een noodzakelijk bondgenootschap," 40.

154. Report to the Court of Policy in Demerara, 26 October 1795, no. 657 in BGBB, BC app. vol. 5: 159–61.

155. For a short account, see Craton, *Testing the Chains*, chap. 21. For an excellent and more detailed study, see Da Costa, *Crowns of Glory*.

4 / The Centrality of Smuggling

1. Director-General and Council to Heren X in Amsterdam, 31 January 1774, TNA, CO 116/39, f. 176. Original quotation: "Dat wat betreft, om op de aankomende vaartuijgen Schildwagten te plaatsen om fraude voor te komen, ons soude voorkomen, van die spreekwijse gebruijk makende een blint paard vastbinden dewijl alhier geen Clandestine invoer van ongepermitteerde producten plaats heeft, nog iets werd in gebragt, dat inkomende regten betaald, dat ook soo diende te blijven, om den invoer van provisien het geen hun eenigste Carga is, niet te stremmen en ons en onse slaven aan gebrek bloot te stellen, en schoon zulks al geschiede soo soude een Schildwagt al sliep hij nimmer zulks niet in staat zijn te beletten."

2. Van der Oest, "Forgotten Colonies," in Enthoven and Postma, *Riches*, 357.

3. For "antithesis," see Eli F. Heckscher, *Mercantilism*, vol. 1, trans. Mendel Shapiro (London: George Allen & Unwin, 1955), 353. For "champions," see Victor Enthoven, "Neutrality: Atlantic Shipping in and after the Anglo-Dutch Wars," in Stern and Wennerlind, *Mercantilism Reimagined*, 330; Pieter C. Emmer, "The Rise and Decline of the Dutch Atlantic, 1600–1800," in Oostindie and Roitman, *Dutch Atlantic Connections*, 353.

4. Klooster, *Dutch Moment*, 1–2.

5. Ibid., 112.

6. Silvia Marzagalli, "The French Atlantic," in Oostindie and Roitman, *Dutch Atlantic Connections*; Kenneth Morgan, "Anglo-Dutch Economic Relations in the Atlantic World, 1688–1783," in Oostindie and Roitman, *Dutch Atlantic Connections*, 122; Kenneth Morgan, "Mercantilism and the British Empire, 1688–1815," in *The Political Economy of British Historical Experience, 1688–1914*, ed. Donald Winch and Patrick O'Brien (Oxford: Published for the British Academy by Oxford University Press, 2002), 171; P. C. Emmer, "'Jesus Christ Was Good but Trade Was Better': An Overview of the Transit Trade of the Dutch Antilles, 1634–1795," in Emmer, *The Dutch in the Atlantic Economy*, 107–9.

7. De Vries, "Dutch Atlantic Economies," in Coclanis, *The Atlantic Economy*.

8. Klooster, *Illicit Riches*, 1 (quotation); Borucki, "Slave Trade to Venezuela"; Rupert, *Creolization and Contraband*; Victor Enthoven, "'That Abominable Nest of Pirates': St. Eustatius and the North Americans, 1680–1780," *Early American Studies: An Interdisciplinary Journal* 10, no. 2 (2012): 239–301; Wim Klooster, "Inter-Imperial Smuggling in the Americas, 1600–1800," in Bailyn and Denautl, *Soundings in Atlantic History*; Wim Klooster, "Curaçao as a Transit Center to the Spanish Main and the French West Indies," in Oostindie and Roitman, *Dutch Atlantic Connections*; Jordaan and Wilson, "Danish, Dutch and Swedish Free Ports," in Oostindie and Roitman, *Dutch Atlantic Connections*.

9. Victor Enthoven, "As Assessment of Dutch Transatlantic Commerce, 1585–1817," in Enthoven and Postma, *Riches*, 444; Wim Klooster, "An Overview of Dutch Trade with the Americas, 1600–1800," in Enthoven and Postma, *Riches*.

10. Chris Nierstrasz, *Rivalry for Trade in Tea and Textiles: The English and Dutch East India Companies (1700–1800)* (Houndmills, Basingstoke: Palgrave Macmillan, 2015), 37; Johannes Hovy, *Het voorstel van 1751 tot instelling van een beperkt vrijhavenstelsel in de Republiek (propositie tot een gelimiteerd port-franco)* (Groningen: J. B. Wolters, 1966), 120–48.

11. Johannes Postma, "Breaching the Mercantile Barriers of the Dutch Colonial Empire: North American Trade with Surinam during the Eighteenth Century," in *Merchant Organization and Maritime Trade in the North Atlantic, 1660–1815*, ed. Olaf U. Janzen (St. John's, Newfoundland: International Maritime Economic History Association, 1998), 118; Van der Oest, "Forgotten Colonies," in Enthoven and Postma, *Riches*, 356.

12. For the battles over free trade and monopolies regarding Brazil and the lack of resistance to chartered companies afterward, see Arthur Weststeijn, "Dutch Brazil and the Making of Free Trade Ideology," in *The Legacy of Dutch Brazil*, ed. Michiel van Groesen (New York: Cambridge University Press, 2014).

13. For a good discussion of the various VOC monopolies, see Chris Nierstrasz, *In the Shadow of the Company: The Dutch East India Company and Its Servants in the Period of Its Decline (1740–1796)* (Leiden: Brill, 2012), chap. 4. Of course, in practice individual traders and VOC officials tried to circumvent the monopolies. The WIC had a one-third share in the Suriname Company until 1770 and a half share afterward; see Fatah-Black, *White Lies*, 4–5.

14. Ruud Paesie, "Van monopolie naar vrijhandel: De illegale slavenhandel tijdens het octrooi van de Tweede West-Indische Compagnie, 1674–1730," *Oso: Tijdschrift voor Surinamistiek en het Caraïbisch gebied* 28, no. 2 (2009): 103–21.

15. Den Heijer, *Geschiedenis van de WIC*, 140–43; Den Heijer, "Dutch West India Company," in Enthoven and Postma, *Riches*, 102–3.

16. J. R. Bruijn, *The Dutch Navy of the Seventeenth and Eighteenth Centuries* (Columbia: University of South Carolina Press, 1993), 133–36; J. R. Bruijn, *De admiraliteit van Amsterdam in rustige jaren, 1713–1751: Regenten en financiën, schepen en zeevarende* (Amsterdam: Schelteman & Holkema, 1970), 165–68.

17. David Ormrod, *The Rise of Commercial Empires: England and the Netherlands in the Age of Mercantilism, 1650–1770* (Cambridge: Cambridge University Press, 2008), 307–9, 351; Van Zanden and Van Riel, *Nederland*, 19, 52–61.

18. Fatah-Black, *White Lies*, 188.

19. Gert Oostindie, "Economics of Slavery," in Peter Boomgaard et al., *Economic and Social History*.

20. Joseph Horan, "The Colonial Famine Plot: Slavery, Free Trade, and Empire in the French Atlantic, 1763–1791," *International Review of Social History* 55, Supplement S18 (2010); Truxes, *Defying Empire*; Klooster, "Inter-Imperial Smuggling"; Silvia Marzagalli, "Was Warfare Necessary for the Functioning of Eighteenth-Century Colonial Systems? Some Reflections on the Necessity of Cross-Imperial and Foreign Trade in the French Case," in *Beyond Empires: Global, Self-Organizing, Cross-Imperial Networks, 1500–1800*, ed. Cátia Antunes and Amélia Polónia (Leiden: Brill, 2016).

21. Fatah-Black, *White Lies*, 166, 204.

22. De Smidt, Lee, and Van Dapperen, *Guyana Ordinance Book*, Essequibo and Demerara, 2 December 1788.

23. *Lijsten van de in Demerary binnengekomen en uitgeloopen schepen, 1791 Augustus 25–1792 Maart 20, 1791–1792*, Admiraliteitscolleges XIII Hinxt, 1763–95 (hereafter Admiraliteiten / Hinxt), 1.01.47.09, inv. nr. 11.

24. Michael Jarvis, *In the Eye of All Trade: Bermuda, Bermudians, and the Maritime Atlantic World, 1680–1783* (Chapel Hill: University of North Carolina Press, 2010), 120–29.

25. Amsterdam City Archives, Amsterdam (hereafter ACA), Notaries, inv. nr. 5075, f. 13917/253.

26. TNA, CO 116/42, f. 234–43. Although I do realize that the unfolding American War of Independence probably had a disturbing effect on the sample, possibly reducing the number of British and North American vessels in fear of privateers.

27. TNA, CO 116/42, f. 234–43.

28. Bolingbroke, *Voyage to Demerary*, 216.

29. TNA, CO 116/42, f. 234–43.

30. NL-HaNA, S-G, 1.01.02, inv. nr. 915.

31. TNA, CO 116/42, f. 234–43.

32. Harris and Villiers, *Storm van 's Gravesande*, vol. 1: 209–10, 214 (quotation).

33. Villiers, *Storm van 's Gravesande*, 279. Original quotation: "Is het mogelijk 25 maende toe te komen met het gene voor een jaer gesonden word? De plantagien en slaeven hebben daer het meest door geleden."

34. Harris and Villiers, *Storm van 's Gravesande*, vol. 2: 625.

35. A planter had to provide one acre (0.43 hectare) for every five enslaved workers. In 1784 a fine of 90 guilders for each lacking acre was instated, indicating that previous rules had not been sufficient (Thompson, *Colonialism and Underdevelopment*, 121; Rodway, *History*, vol. 2: 43).

36. Journal Commander Van Schuylenburg, 4 March 1780 to 9 April 1780, TNA, CO 116/ 55, f. 45–50.

37. J. C. Severijn to Heren X, 28-8-1778, NL-HaNA, WIC, 1.05.01.02, inv. nr. 309; Trotz to WIC's Zeeland Chamber, 8 December 1776, TNA, CO 116/44, f. 316–37.

38. TNA, CO 116/42, f. 234–43.

39. TNA, CO 116/42, f. 234–43.

40. Cf. TNA, Records of the Boards of Customs, Excise, and Customs and Excise, and HM Revenue and Customs (hereafter CUST), 16/1 (North America), CO 33/18 (Barbados), CO 76/4 (Dominica), CO 106/2 (Grenada), Board of Trade (hereafter BT) 6/188 (St. Vincent), CO 10/2 (Antigua), and CO 243/1 (St. Christopher).

41. Author's database, based on CO 33, inv. nr. 18, 19, 20 (Barbados), CO 76, inv. nr. 4, 5, 6 (Dominica), CO 106, inv. nr. 2, 3 (Grenada), Board of Trade (BT) 6, inv. nr.

188 (St. Vincent), CO 10, inv. nr. 2 (Antigua), CO 243, inv. nr. 1 (St. Christopher). The excellent book by Gregory O'Malley uses the same methodology to investigate the intercolonial slave trade; see O'Malley, *Final Passages*, 17.

42. For the connection between the slave and other commerce, see O'Malley, *Final Passages*, 10.

43. TNA, CO 10/2, 29 January 1785.

44. TNA, CO 243/1, 28 April 1785 and 28 July 1785.

45. TNA, CO 76/5, 1 January 1788.

46. TNA, CO 33/19. The weight of one cotton bale varied between 240 and 300 pounds (TNA, CO 111/4 f. 179).

47. NL-HaNA, VWIS, 1.05.06, inv. nr. 151.

48. The exports to the Dutch Republic were listed in barrels (sugar), barrels and bales (coffee), and bales (cotton). I converted these to kilograms at the rate of 800 pounds for sugar barrels, 350 pounds for coffee barrels, 120 pounds for coffee bales, and 300 pounds for cotton bales.

49. NL-HaNA, Admiraliteitscolleges / Paulus-Olivier, 1.01.47.13, inv. nr. 44.

50. The following sections reuse parts of a chapter previously published as "Smuggling for Survival: Self-Organized, Cross-Imperial Colony Building in Essequibo and Demerara, 1746–1796," in *Beyond Empires: Global, Self-Organizing, Cross-Imperial Networks, 1500–1800*, ed. Cátia Antunes and Amélia Polónia (Leiden: Brill, 2016), 212–35. Reprinted with permission.

51. De Smidt, Lee and Van Dapperen, *Guyana Ordinance Book*, Essequibo and Demerara, 7 January 1766; 5 October 1771; Demerara, 2 November 1773.

52. Van der Oest, "Forgotten Colonies," in Enthoven and Postma, *Riches*, 359.

53. *Journaal van den luitenant, O. Wiggerts, door den kapitein D. E. Hinxt belast zijnde geweest met het bevel van een hulpkruiser, tot wering van den smokkelhandel langs de kust van Demerary en Berbice (1792 Maart 9–1792 Mei 28)*, NL-HaNA, Admiraliteitscolleges / Hinxt, 1.01.47.09, inv. nr. 8.

54. NL-HaNA, S-G, 1.01.02, inv. nr. 3849, 13 Juli 1787, 749–750; NL-HaNA, Admiraliteiten / Van Paulus, 1.01.47.13, inv. nr. 44.

55. NL-HaNA, WIC, 1.05.01.02, inv. nr. 1033, 19 February 1787.

56. NL-HaNA, WIC, 1.05.01.02, inv. nr. 1033, 19, 20, and 23 February 1787; NL-HaNA, Admiraliteiten / Van Paulus, 1.01.47.13, inv. nr. 44.

57. NL-HaNA, WIC, 1.05.01.02, inv. nr. 1033; NL-HaNA, Admiraliteiten / Van Paulus, 1.01.47.13, inv. nr. 44.

58. NL-HaNA, WIC, 1.05.01.02, inv. nr. 1033, 15 March, 24 April, and 30 April 1787; De Smidt, Lee, and Van Dapperen, *Guyana Ordinance Book*, Demerara, 25 January 1787.

59. NL-HaNA, Admiraliteiten / Hinxt, 1.01.47.09, inv.nr. 11; De Smidt, Lee, and Van Dapperen, *Guyana Ordinance Book*, Demerara, 25 January 1787.

60. NL-HaNa, Admiraliteiten / Van Paulus, 1.01.47.13, inv. nr. 44.

61. De Smidt, Lee and Van Dapperen, *Guyana Ordinance Book*, Essequibo and Demerara, 7 February 1785.

62. NL-HaNA, WIC, 1.05.01.02, inv. nr. 1033, 15 March 1787.

63. L'Espinasse to Zealand Chamber, 12 September 1787, TNA, CO 116/61, f. 4–7; NL-HaNA, WIC, 1.05.01.02, inv. nr. 1033, 22 August 1787; NL-HaNA, Admiraliteiten / Van Paulus, 1.01.47.13, inv. nr. 44.

64. NL-HaNA, WIC, 1.05.01.02, inv. nr. 1033, 15 April 1787; NL-HaNA, Admiraliteiten / Van Paulus, 1.01.47.13, inv. nr. 44.

65. NL-HaNA, WIC, 1.05.01.02, inv. nr. 1033, 15 April 1787; *Registers van resoluties*, 13 November 1787, NL-HaNA, WIC, 1.05.01.02, inv. nr. 442, f. 252–56; NL-HaNA, S-G, 1.01.02, inv .nr. 3849, 5 December 1787, f. 1277.

66. NL-HaNA, Admiraliteiten / Van Paulus, 1.01.47.13, inv. nr. 44. Origintal quotation: "Slandts officieren (met zoo een last als de onse) zijn hier zoo welkom als een zwijn in een Joodse kueke [sic]."

67. Bolingbroke, *Voyage to Demerary*, 283–84 (quotation 284).

68. NL-HaNA, Admiraliteiten / Van Paulus, 1.01.47.13, inv. nr. 44.

69. NL-HaNA, S-G, 1.01.02, inv. nr. 3849, 14 December 1787, f. 1320.

70. *Stukken betreffende de verrichtingen van de luitenant Frans Smees* [sic], *kommandant van 's lands brigantijn De Maasnymph, tot wering van de sluikhandel in Demerary., 10 april 1787–18 december 1787*, Nl-HaNA, VWIS, 1.05.06, inv. nr. 126; NL-HaNA, WIC, 1.05.01.02, inv. nr. 1033, 22 August 1787; TNA, CO 116/61, no date, f. 86.

71. Shipping Returns, 1786–1806 (Barbados), TNA, CO 33/20.

72. NL-HaNA, VWIS, 1.05.06, inv. nr. 126.

73. Alan L. Karras, *Smuggling: Contraband and Corruption in World History* (Lanham, MD: Rowman & Littlefield, 2010), 11; Jarvis, *Eye of All Trade*, 176–77; Truxes, *Defying Empire*, prologue.

74. The Trans-Atlantic Slave Trade Database (hereafter TASTD), www.slavevoyages.org; accessed 4 August 2016.

75. Van de Voort, *Westindische plantages*, 53.

76. De Smidt, Lee, and Van Dapperen, *Guyana Ordinance Book*, Essequibo, 12 October 1771.

77. Postma, *The Dutch*, 170, 268, 273–75; Karwan Fatah-Black, "Suriname and the Atlantic World, 1650–1800" (PhD diss., Leiden University and KITLV, 2013), 171; Zeeuws Archief (hereafter ZA), MCC, 20, inv. nr. 1772.5.

78. De Smidt, Lee, and Van Dapperen, *Guyana Ordinance Book*, Essequibo and Demerara, 2 May 1776; 11 February 1785; Demerara, 24 November 1789.

79. P. C. Emmer, *De Nederlandse slavenhandel 1500–1850* (Amsterdam: Arbeiderspers, 2000), 171.

80. Postma, *The Dutch*, 219–20; Van der Oest, "Forgotten Colonies," in Enthoven and Postma, *Riches*, 338.

81. NL-HaNA, Raadpensionaris Van de Spiegel, 3.01.26, inv. nr. 450; Van der Oest, "Forgotten Colonies," in Enthoven and Postma, *Riches*, 339; *Stukken betreffende de slavenhandel in Essequebo en Demerary, 1767–1776*, NL-HaNA, VWIS, 1.05.06, inv. nr. 48; NL-HaNA, 1.05.01.02, inv. nr. 915; NL-HaNA, RAB, 2.01.28.02, inv. nr. 168M.

82. NL-HaNA, Raadpensionaris Van de Spiegel, 3.01.26, inv. nr. 450.

83. NL-HaNA, Raadpensionaris Van de Spiegel, 3.01.26, inv. nr. 450, H1 Loco B; *Secrete resoluties*, 4 June 1764, NL-HaNA, WIC, 1.05.01.02, inv. nr. 765.

84. Bram Hoonhout, "De noodzaak van smokkelhandel in Essequebo en Demerary, 1750–1800," *Tijdschrift voor Zeegeschiedenis* 32, no. 2 (2013): 68.

85. NL-HaNA, Raadpensionaris Van de Spiegel, 3.01.26, inv. nr. 450, H4 Loco A. Original quotation: "egter zien ik niet wel Kans, om d'Eigearen in Demerary te beletten, Slaaven voor haar eige Plantagiën te zenden; niet allen die van Barbados

staan daar volstrekt op, maar zelver van St. Eustatius . . . ik hebben moeten zulks provisioneel toelaaten."

86. NL-HaNA, Raadpensionaris Van de Spiegel, 3.01.26, inv. nr. 450, H5. Original quotation: "Myne Exactitude, in het Verhinderen van den invoer van eenige vreemde Slaaven, veroozaakt een algemeene Murmureering in de beide Rivieren en een opentlyk Misnoegen; (en, in Gemoede gesprooken, vinde d'Ingezeetenen juist geen groot Ongelyk hebben), zy zeggen, in Barbados kosten de Slaaven omtrend 320 Guldens, in St. Christoffel kan men zoo veel men wil, voor 250 à 280 Gulden bekomen, en hier moet men een exorbitante Prys betalen, en kan men de Helvt niet bekomen, die men noodig heeft."

87. De Smidt, Lee and Van Dapperen, *Guyana Ordinance Book*, Essequibo and Demerara, 23 October 1766.

88. NL-HaNA, Raadpensionaris Van de Spiegel, 3.01.26, inv. nr. 450, D2, H4 Loco B.

89. NL-HaNA, Raadpensionaris Van de Spiegel, 3.01.26, inv. nr. 450, D3.

90. NL-HaNA, Raadpensionaris Van de Spiegel, 3.01.26, inv. nr. 450; *Repertorium op de resoluties*, 27-2-1769, NL-HaNA, WIC, inv. nr. 747.

91. NL-HaNA, Raadpensionaris Van de Spiegel, 3.01.26, inv. nr. 450. Original quotation: "of de Zeeuwsche Schepen hebben een voegsaam Getal Slaaven aangebragt, en vry grooter als de Supplianten opgeeven, of men heeft zig aan ons scherp Verbod van Invoer weinig gekreund, en zoo veel Engelsche Slaaven, als men maar magtig konde worden, ter Sluik of wel bij Conniventie ingevoerd."

92. Villiers, *Storm van 's Gravesande*, 364, 374. Original quotations: "openbaerlyk & zonder de minsten achterhoudentheyt de slaeven van d' Engelsche koopen"; "Den invoer van vreemde slaeven houd niet op . . . wanneer ik het verneem is 't te laet off de regte voldoende bewysen ontbreken my."

93. Demerara Council of Policy to WIC, 21 April 1774, TNA, CO 116/39, f. 333–77.

94. Postma, *The Dutch*, 165, 284–85.

95. These are the origins discerned by O'Malley, see O'Malley, *Final Passages*, 369–71.

96. The counterfactuals are based on the reported slave population in 1762 for Essequibo and 1764 for Demerara, for reasons of data availability. Subsequently, the average annual number of imported captives was used from Postma, *The Dutch*, 220–21, which includes adjustments for nonregistered ships. Subsequently, I compiled two estimates, a high rate of demographic decline (4.7 percent per year, as during Suriname's expansion phase) and a low rate (2.4 percent, as in Suriname's consolidation phase). The actual slave population figures can be found in table 3.1 in chap. 3.

97. Borucki, "Slave Trade to Venezuela."

98. Johannes Postma, "The Dispersal of African Slaves in the West by Dutch Slave Traders, 1630–1803," in *The Atlantic Slave Trade: Effects on Economies, Societies, and Peoples in Africa, the Americas, and Europe*, ed. Joseph E. Inikori and Stanley L. Engerman (Durham, NC: Duke University Press, 1992), 294.

99. For examples in Suriname, see: Fatah-Black, *White Lies*, 58–61, 182, 187.

100. Wim Klooster calculated that in many production places a particular crop was for the most part exported clandestinely, such as in Venezuela, Louisiana and Saint-Domingue. Klooster, "Inter-Imperial Smuggling," 179.

101. De Smidt, Lee, and Van Dapperen, *Guyana Ordinance Book*, Essequibo and Demerara, 22 September 1794.

102. Ibid., Essequibo and Demerara, 26 July 1795.

103. Answers of Governor Beaujon to questions by the new British rulers, 15 June 1799, TNA, CO 111/3, f. 239.

104. The British would instate their own mercantilist restrictions, allowing only exports to Britain and in British ships once they took over the colonies in 1796, see: De Smidt, Lee and Van Dapperen, *Guyana Ordinance Book*, Essequibo and Demerara, 14 July 1796. However, their merchant network proved much stronger than the Dutch one.

5 / The Web of Debt

1. Russell R. Menard, "Law, Credit, the Supply of Labour, and the Organization of Sugar Production in the Colonial Greater Caribbean: A Comparison of Brazil and Barbados in the Seventeenth Century," in *The Early Modern Atlantic Economy*, ed. John J. McCusker and Kenneth Morgan (Cambridge: Cambridge University Press, 2000), 157–61.

2. Beverley A. Steele, *Grenada: A History of Its People* (Oxford: Macmillan Caribbean, 2003), 70; S. D. Smith, *Slavery, Family, and Gentry Capitalism in the British Atlantic: The World of the Lascelles, 1648-1834* (Cambridge: Cambridge University Press, 2006), 133.

3. Smith, *World of the Lascelles*, 147, 152–53, 159. Lenders engaged in credit rationing: if a banker could not ask the rate that would realistically compensate for the risk, he would deny the loan. On the other hand, if one had to ask an interest rate of 10 percent to a planter, then the loan was probably too risky anyway. These interest rate caps could thus contribute to economic stability by preventing risky loans. See Peter Temin and Hans-Joachim Voth, "Credit Rationing and Crowding Out during the Industrial Revolution: Evidence from Hoare's Bank, 1702–1862," *Explorations in Economic History* 42, no. 3 (2005): 329; Peter Temin and Hans-Joachim Voth, "Hoare's Bank in the Eighteenth Century," in *The Birth of Modern Europe: Culture and Economy, 1400–1800. Essays in Honor of Jan de Vries*, ed. Laura Cruz and Joel Mokyr (Leiden: Brill, 2010), 86–87.

4. Fatah-Black, "Suriname and the Atlantic World," 165.

5. Price, "Credit," in Solow, *Slavery and the Rise of the Atlantic System*, 296.

6. Russell R. Menard, *Sweet Negotiations: Sugar, Slavery, and Plantation Agriculture in Early Barbados* (Charlottesville: University of Virginia Press, 2006), 55–56, 97.

7. Steele, *Grenada*, 70.

8. Richard Pares argued for an "ontology of debt," in which overdraft facilities gradually led to the establishment of a mortgage, as creditors demanded more security. See Richard Pares, *Merchants and Planters* (New York: Cambridge University Press, 1960), 49–50. Others have nuanced this view, arguing that Pares's argument is confined to specific periods and places. See Jacob M. Price, "Credit in the Slave Trade and Plantation Economies," in *Slavery and the Rise of the Atlantic System*, ed. Barbara L. Solow (Cambridge: Cambridge University Press, 1991), 324–27; Smith, *World of the Lascelles*, 140–42, 220.

9. Wantje Fritschy, *Public Finance of the Dutch Republic in Comparative Perspective: The Viability of an Early Modern Federal State (1570s–1795)* (Leiden: Brill, 2017), 159; Marjolein 't Hart, "Mutual Advantages: State Bankers as Brokers between the City of Amsterdam and the Dutch Republic," in *The Political Economy of the Dutch Republic*, ed. Oscar Gelderblom (Farnham: Ashgate, 2009), 116.

10. Oostindie, *Roosenburg en Mon Bijou*, 291; Van de Voort, *Westindische plantages*, 84, 91–94; *Negotiatie ten behoeve van eenige planters in de colonie van Essequebo en Demerary*, International Institute of Social History (hereafter IISH), Collectie Effecten en loterijbriefjes (Bijzondere Collecties 266), inv. nr. ARCH03766, box 1, final folder, marked "was KA 68.1-I." For British commission fees, see Zahedieh, *Capital and the Colonies*, 101; Smith, *World of the Lascelles*, 81, 163.

11. The conversion rate between guilders and pounds was somewhere between 10:1 and 12:1; see Enthoven and Postma, *Riches*, 463. The estimates were 109,175 guilders for a sugar estate of 1,005 acres with 119 enslaved Africans and 111,350 guilders for a 500-acre coffee plantation with 124 enslaved people; see Van de Voort, *Westindische plantages*, 83.

12. In case of marriage on equal terms, the wife was obliged go to the secretary and declare that she had no other debt relations and that she would commit to repayment of the mortgage (*willige condemnatie*). Otherwise, if the plantation was shared, the husband might default on his part while his wife's part would prevent execution of the estate.

13. IISH, Collectie Effecten en loterijbriefjes, inv. nr. ARCH03766. Sometimes an exception was made for items like furniture, as those did not contribute to the production.

14. Van de Voort, *Westindische plantages*, 109.

15. Ibid., 184. The rest was divided among other West Indian destinations, particularly the Danish West Indies. The figures are likely to be revised upward by the ongoing research into this subject by Peter Koudijs and Abe de Jong.

16. See table 2.1, chap. 2. The expansion was not just the result of the *negotiaties*, as foreign planters also established themselves in the two colonies. While they sometimes relied on Dutch credit, many would have had their own financing.

17. Another problem was that payments to investors were fixed instead of related to the plantation's profits.

18. Harris and Villiers, *Storm van 's Gravesande*, vol. 2: 624.

19. NL-HaNA, S-G, 1.01.02, inv.nr. 3826, 26 July 1771, f. 488–89.

20. Neal, *Rise of Financial Capitalism*, 168–71.

21. Alex van Stipriaan, "Debunking Debts. Image and Reality of a Colonial Crisis: Suriname at the End of the 18th Century," *Itinerario* 19, no. 1 (1995). Piet Emmer, however, maintains that the crisis was caused by defaulting planters, even though most loans were extended after 1765, so repayment of the principal was not due until 1775. See P. C. Emmer, "Capitalism Mistaken? The Economic Decline of Surinam and the Plantation Loans, 1773–1850: A Rehabilitation," *Itinerario* 20, no. 1 (1996).

22. W. W. van der Meulen, "Beschrijving van eenige Westindische plantage leeningen. Bijdrage tot de kennis der geldbelegging in de achttiende eeuw," *Bijdragen en Mededeelingen van het Historisch Genootschap* 25 (1904): 616–18.

23. Van de Voort mentions 33 plantations in the original *negotiatie* (Van de Voort, *Westindische plantages*, 272–73), but CO 116/36 f. 206 and f. 480 list the estates Jerusalem and Zuidbeeveland as well. The capital was probably close to the above-mentioned sum of one million guilders already in 1766, as the average calculated over 18 plantations was 27,354 guilders per plantation, so 35 plantations would amount to closer to a million (CO 116/36, f. 206, 480).

24. Van de Voort, *Westindische plantages*, 269–323. For a fascinating account of how irregularities with mortgages harmed Tulleken's finances, see *Copie-brieven van Ambrosius Tulleken te Demerary aan de griffier der Staten-Generaal, Fagel*, NL-HaNA, VWIS, 1.05.06, inv. nr. 478.

25. ACA, Notarissen, 5075, Notary Thierry D. de Marolles, 11474/177; 11479/93; *Conditien van Negotiatie tot een Fonds waar uit, onder Directie van Daniel Changuion, aan eenige Planters in Rio Essequebo en Rio Demmerary, tot voortzetting en verbeetering hunner Plantagien een Somma van f400.000 voor 10 Jaaren zal werden gefourneerd, teegens den Intrest van 6 Pct. 's jaars*, IISH, Collectie Effecten (tweede aanvulling), ARCH04145, inv. nr 1.

26. Van de Voort, *Westindische plantages*, 162.

27. Ibid., 160, 185, 203. The revenue of a sold plantation could be used to redeem the principal to a bondholder, after which the bond effectively ended and no future interest payments would have to be made.

28. Van Stipriaan, *Surinaams contrast*, 41, 199, 294; J. Marten W. Schalkwijk, *The Colonial State in the Caribbean: Structural Analysis and Changing Elite Networks in Suriname, 1650–1920* (The Hague: Amrit, 2011), 157, 181.

29. Van de Voort, *Westindische plantages*, 194–95.

30. Van Langen, "Britse overname," 123; Paul Koulen, "Slavenhouders en geldschieters: Nederlandse belangen in Berbice, Demerara en Essequebo, 1815–1819," *Gen.* 21, no. 5 (2015): 46. The list of mortgages is located in TNA, CO 111/28 and transcribed by Paul Koulen: http://www.cbg.nl/upload/Berbice-Demerara-Essequebo.pdf, accessed 26 August 2016.

31. IISH, Collectie P. A. Brugmans, ARCH03525, inv. nr. 12 (but in folder labeled 13–14).

32. ACA, Archief van de Firma Ketwich & Voomberg en Wed. W. Borski (hereafter Ketwich), 600, inv. nr. 606; inv. nr. 605.

33. Netscher, *History of the Colonies*, 124; *Dossiers betreffende het proces voor de Staten-Generaal van Pieter Brotherson, eigenaar van de plantage 'Haynieroenie' in Rio Demerary, impetrant bij mandement van revisie contra François Changuion jr., gedaagde, 1786*, NL-HaNA, S-G, 1.01.02, inv. nr. 9602; *Stukken betreffende de hypothecatie van The Behive bij D.W.van Vloten voor—112.000. 1776 januari 10–1777 december 6*, ACA, Ketwich, 600, inv. nr. 654; *Inventarissen van Le Repentir en een stuk land van 25 akkers. 1772 april 18, 1773 oktober 18, 1773 december 4 en 9. Met prisaties en bijlagen*, ACA, Ketwich, 600, inv. nr. 663; *Inventarissen van The Coventgarden, met prisaties. 1772 juli 1 en 1774 maart 29*, ibid., inv. nr. 672; ACA, Notarissen, 5075, inv. nr. 15326/788; *Registratie—van hypotheekakte groot f 27.790,- gepasseerd door Thomas Grandt en Jenette van Baarle, echtelieden en Thomas Cuming ten behoeve van Daniel Changuion op 26-7-1770 in Rio Demerary*, Utrechts Archief (hereafter UA), 34-4, Notarissen in de Stad Utrecht 1560–1905, D.W. van Vloten, inv. nr. U247a010, akte 232, 21 December 1771.

34. ACA, Ketwich, 600, inv. nr. 607. In 1777 Cornelis Overbroek was a member of the Council of Justice (TNA, CO 116/48, f. 59). Cuming was probably not a councillor yet (he was only known as such for certain in 1796; see Bolingbroke, *Voyage to Demerary*, 276). Yet he was one of the most prominent British planters (see chaps. 2 and 6), while Joseph Bourda started as councillor of justice in 1774, would become commandeur ad interim in 1784 and became one of the wealthiest planters in the

colony (TNA, CO 116/48; CO 116/39 f. 359, 393). Grovestins served as captain in the militia up to 1774, was fiscal from 20 May 1776 to January 1782, and in 1776 was also the president of the Wees- en Desolate Boedelkamer (NL-HaNA, WIC, 1.05.01.02, inv. nr. 309, missives Grovestins, 4 August 1779: TNA, CO 116/48, f.87; Rodway, *History*, vol. 1: 309; CO 116/44, f. 397).

35. For Bourda, see ACA, Ketwich, 600, inv. nr. 607; for Cuming, see ACA, Notarissen, 5075, 15252/1218; for Grovestins see ACA, Notarissen, 5075, 15231/286 and 11474/177.

36. *Codex Eng 52, Accounts and Ledger of Weilburg Plantation, Demerara, 1767–1770*, John Carter Brown Library, Providence, RI. See also *Day book and ledger of Prospect Estate, 1791–1796*, NRS, inv. nr. CS96/4483.

37. Villiers, *Storm van 's Gravesande*, 368. Original quotation: "had . . . voldoenend bewys in handen en konde die trekkers gerust aantasten; dan had ik den draad & 't kluwen soude haest volgen, want deese moeten bloeden soo draa andere beklappen & zoude de geheele zaak voor den dag koomen."

38. Ibid., 372.

39. De Smidt, Lee, and Van Dapperen, *Guyana Ordinance Book*, Essequibo and Demerara, 30 May 1771. Original quotation: "totale ruine deser Colonie."

40. Villiers, *Storm van 's Gravesande*, 386.

41. Ibid., 379–80.

42. Trotz to Chamber Zealand, 24 April 1774, TNA, CO 116/39, f. 200–201. Original quotation: "sulke ruineuse middelen sijn, dat is er van schrik als ik gaan optellen de menigte onser burgers der welke op dat doot vonnis genomineerd staan, door 't allgemeen discredit en verslapping der prijsen onser producten 't geen hier thans een chaos van verwarring begint te geven."

43. Van de Voort, *Westindische plantages*, 205–13.

44. The sources differ on whether it was 2 or 5 percent of the value (in 1777 it was 2 percent), and how much was to go back to the WIC coffers is unclear. Nevertheless, it is telling that the office of *vendumeester* was generally considered one of the most rewarding in the colony, requiring little effort. NL-HaNA, S-G, 1.01.02, inv. nr. 9424, f. 107; NL-HaNA, Raadpensionaris van de Spiegel, 3.01.26, inv. nr 450; Trotz to Zeeland Chamber, 1-1-1774, TNA, CO 116/39 f. 113; De Smidt, Lee, and Van Dapperen, *Guyana Ordinance Book*, Essequibo and Demerara, 20 May 1777.

45. Harris and Villiers, *Storm van 's Gravesande*, vol. 2: 449–50.

46. Ibid., vol. 2: 546. Rousselet de la Jarie had been appointed salesmaster after Adriaan Spoors became unable to fulfill his duties due to eye problems. Rousselet de la Jarie died on 24 June 1767.

47. Extract from the minutes of the Court of Justice, 3 June 1771, TNA, CO 116/39, f. 206.

48. Extract from the minutes of the Court of Justice, 3 June 1771, TNA, CO 116/39, f. 206–10; NL-HaNA, WIC, 1.05.01.02, inv. nr. 748, 3 September 1773.

49. Trotz to WIC, 13 September 1773, TNA, CO 116/39, f. 23–26.

50. Trotz to WIC, 13 September 1773, TNA, CO 116/39, f. 23–26; NL-HaNA, S-G, 1.01.02, inv. nr. 3831, 25 July 1776, f. 453–54. In 1783 another investigation was started into the Insolvency Chamber, which placed the blame for its ill functioning on the planters, who did not come to the Chamber to either approve or contest the handling of an insolvency case. It was therefore decided that in the future debts were deemed

accepted if a planter did not contest them. See De Smidt, Lee, and Van Dapperen, *Guyana Ordinance Book*, Demerara, 1 May 1783.

51. *Brief met bijlagen van directeur-generaal en raden van Rio Essequebo en Rio Demerary aan de Staten-Generaal betreffende de afdoening van de boedels van Pieter Callard en Pieter Christiaan Hooft, eigenaars van de plantages 'Cornelia' en 'Ida' alsmede Cornelia Cattiari, 1776*, NL-HaNA, S-G, 1.01.02, inv. nr. 9552; NL-HaNA, S-G, 1.01.02, inv. nr. 3831, 21 June 1776, f. 381; NL-HaNA, S-G, 1.01.02, inv. nr. 1506. For a digital version of the 1774 regulations, see De Smidt, Lee, and Van Dapperen, *Guyana Ordinance Book*, Essequibo and Demerara, 4 October 1774.

52. NL-HaNA, S-G, 1.01.02, inv. nr. 3829, 4 October 1774, f. 590–98.

53. NL-HaNA, S-G, 1.01.02, inv. nr. 3829, 4 October 1774, f. 590–98.

54. In these new rules, advertisements also had to be placed in the Utrecht newspapers. NL-HaNA, S-G, 1.01.02/1506. For examples of second and third mortgages that could become preferential in Suriname, see Oostindie, *Roosenburg en Mon Bijou*, 293.

55. NL-HaNA, S-G, 1.01.02, inv. nr. 3832, 28 August 1777, f. 606–7.

56. NL-HaNA, S-G, 1.01.02, inv. nr. 3832, 28 August 1777, f. 606–7.

57. NL-HaNA, S-G, 1.01.02, inv. nr. 3833, 6 February 1788, f. 77; 13 May 1778, f. 361–65. In 1777 a move toward more standardized settlement procedures was visible in the metropolis as well, when the Insolvency Chamber became responsible for handling insolvencies (rather than relying on private settlements). See Christiaan van Bochove and Heleen Kole, "Uncovering Private Credit Markets: Amsterdam, 1660–1809," *Tijdschrift voor Sociale en Economische Geschiedenis* 11, no. 3 (2014): 50. In the colonies, however, the council remained the one to establish the preference order, as outlined in new rules in 1777; see De Smidt, Lee, and Van Dapperen, *Guyana Ordinance Book*, Essequibo and Demerara, 20 May 1777.

58. NL-HaNA, S-G, 1.01.02, inv. nr. 9552; ACA, Notarissen, 5075, Notary Kier van der Piet, 13917/25.

59. Nicholas Crawford, "'In the Wreck of a Master's Fortune': Slave Provisioning and Planter Debt in the British Caribbean," *Slavery & Abolition* 37, no. 2 (2016): 11–13.

60. NL-HaNA, S-G, 1.01.02, inv. nr. 3833, 16 July 1778, f. 529–34; 27 August 1778, f. 621–24. It nevertheless does not appear in the *Guyana Ordinance Book*.

61. Johan Bremer to Jan Rousman, 28 February 1780, *Brieven als Buit*, http://brievenalsbuit.inl.nl/zeebrieven/page/article?doc=87&query=; accessed 26 August 2016.

62. Theodore Barrell to Walter Barrell, 15 September 1800, New York Historical Society (hereafter NYHS), Theodore Barrel Letter Book, MS 859, f. 130 (quotation); Theodore Barrell to Samuel Sandbach, 24 September 1800, NYHS, Theodore Barrel Letter Book, f. 132–33; Crawford, "Master's Fortune," 14.

63. The Ordinance Book does not list any further attempts to clarify the preference order, although in 1779 an alteration was made to previous rules that "death taxes" (for the doctor, surgeon, and pharmacist) were preferential over other WIC debts. The WIC directors also gained preference over the debts of Company officials to them, yet with several clauses that betrayed the fact that the preference order remained vague. See De Smidt, Lee, and Van Dapperen, *Guyana Ordinance Book*, Essequibo, Demerara and Berbice, 18 March 1779.

64. NL-HaNA, WIC, 1.05.01.02, inv. nrs. 188A and 188B.

65. David Alston, "'Very Rapid and Splendid Fortunes'? Highland Scots in Berbice (Guyana) in the Early Nineteenth Century," *Transactions of the Gaelic Society of Inverness* 63 (2006): 208-36; Burnard, *Planters, Merchants, and Slaves*, 122-25.

66. Draper, "New Planter Class." This is not the place to take up the discussion on whether the plantation complex was still profitable after 1776 or if it was self-defeating. For some important contributions, see Eric Williams, *Capitalism and Slavery* (Chapel Hill: University of North Carolina Press, [1944] 1994); Drescher, *Econocide*; Ryden, *West Indian Slavery*; Justin Roberts, "Uncertain Business: A Case Study of Barbadian Plantation Management, 1770-93," *Slavery & Abolition* 32, no. 2 (2011); Barbara L. Solow and Stanley L. Engerman, eds., *British Capitalism and Caribbean Slavery: The Legacy of Eric Williams* (Cambridge: Cambridge University Press, 2004); Inikori, *Africans and the Industrial Revolution*.

67. Harris and Villiers, *Storm van 's Gravesande*, vol. 1: 390.

68. See chap. 6.

69. Bolingbroke, *Voyage to Demerary*, 37.

70. See tables 2.1 and 3.1.

71. Da Costa, *Crowns of Glory*, 47.

72. NL-HaNA, WIC, 1.05.01.02 inv. nr. 192A and 193A; NL-HaNA, WIC, 1.05.01.02, inv. nr. 192B. See also tables 2.1 and 3.1. The figures are rounded, as giving the exact number would suggest a precision that is unattainable considering the uncertainties in the data. In fact, this is a lower-bound estimate, as planters underreported their enslaved laborers, and sometimes the colonial authorities were only interested in the number of people for whom "head taxes" had to be paid, which excluded children under 12 and partially excluded sick or disabled people.

73. TNA, CO 116/34, f. 205-8.

74. NL-HaNA, WIC, 1.05.01.02, inv. nr. 189; TNA, CO 116/55, f. 156-76.

75. For Essequibo this is regardless of whether one looks at the top twenty biggest estates or those with more than 100 enslaved laborers; see NL-HaNA, WIC, 1.05.01.02, inv. nr. 188B. For Demerara, see NL-HaNA, WIC, 1.05.01.02, inv. nr. 192B.

76. See, e.g., the names in the lists in TNA, CO 116/55, f. 156-76; NL-HaNA, WIC, 1.05.01.02, inv. nrs. 188B and 189.

77. Which is not to say that all British people became rich or that Dutch planters did not. Bolingbroke exaggerated the differences between Dutch and British. See also Da Costa, *Crowns of Glory*, 41-42.

78. Menard, *Sweet Negotiations*, 68; Nierstrasz, *Rivalry for Trade*, 37; O'Shaughnessy, *An Empire Divided*, 58, 61-66, 73.

79. Thompson, *Colonialism and Underdevelopment*, 45.

80. Dalton, *History of British Guiana*, 224; for a similar movement in Berbice, see K. Kramer, "Plantation Development in Berbice from 1753 to 1779: The Shift from Interior to the Coast," *New West Indian Guide* 65, no. 1-2 (1991).

81. See the list of names in map 5.3: http://dpc.uba.uva.nl/cgi/i/image/image-idx?sid=227d1a6701d2d90bff84cf510d2057e3;q1=Friederich%20von%20Bouchenr%F6der;rgn1=surinamica_all;size=20;c=surinamica;lasttype=boolean;view=entry;lastview=thumbnail;subview=detail;cc=surinamica;entryid=x-627;viewid=SURI01_KAARTENZL-105-23-05-1.SID;start=1;resnum=2, accessed 27 August 2016 (part 1); http://www.geheugenvannederland.nl/?/zoom/index/&language=nl&i=

http%3A%2F%2Fresolver.kb.nl%2Fresolve%3Furn%3Durn%3Agvn%3ASURI01%3A KAARTENZL-105-23-05-2%26size%3Dlarge; accessed 27 August 2016 (part 2).

82. Van de Voort, *Westindische plantages*, 269–23; Harris and Villiers, *Storm van 's Gravesande*, vol. 2: 399–400; TNA, CO 116/36, f. 206, 480; *Ingekomen brieven met bijlagen van Essequebo*, NL-HaNA, WIC, 1.05.01.02, inv. nr. 533, f. 441–49; NL-HaNA, Van de Spiegel, 3.01.26, inv. nr. 450, H14, 1 juni 1769.

83. Council of Policy of Demerara to WIC, 21 April 1774, TNA, CO 116/39, f. 372; *Rapport bestemd voor erfstadhouder Willem V opgesteld door zijn commissarissen naar West-Indië, W.H. van Grovestins en W. Boeij. 1790 juli 17*, NL-HaNA, 1.05.01.02, inv. nr. 915.

6 / Borderless Businessmen

1. Emma Rothschild, *The Inner Life of Empires: An Eighteenth-Century History* (Princeton, NJ: Princeton University Press, 2011), 7. Other recent examples are Ogborn, *Global Lives*; Linda Colley, *The Ordeal of Elizabeth Marsh: A Woman in World History* (New York: Anchor Books, 2008); Sarah Pearsall, *Atlantic Families: Lives and Letters in the Later Eighteenth Century* (Oxford: Oxford University Press, 2008); Alison Games, *The Web of Empire: English Cosmopolitans in an Age of Expansion, 1560–1660* (Oxford: Oxford University Press, 2008); Claudia Schnurmann, "A Scotsman in Hamburg: John Parish and His Commercial Contribution to the American War of Independence, 1776–1783," in *Small Is Beautiful? Interlopers and Smaller Trading Nations in the Pre-Industrial Period: Proceedings of the XVth World Economic History Congress in Utrecht (Netherlands) 2009*, ed. Markus A. Denzel, Jan de Vries, and Philipp R. Rössner (Stuttgart: Franz Steiner Verlag, 2011). For broader histories, see Cathy D. Matson, *Merchants and Empire: Trading in Colonial New York* (Baltimore, MD: Johns Hopkins University Press, 1998); David Hancock, *Citizens of the World: London Merchants and the Integration of the British Atlantic Community, 1735-1785* (Cambridge: Cambridge University Press, 1995).

2. Evidently, the most important non-Dutch actors were the enslaved Africans, as their labor made the colonies into what they were. In this chapter, however, I focus on the white non-Dutch actors in their capacities as planters, merchants, and agents in the Atlantic economy. For lack of a better term, I use "non-Dutch" to describe all the people of European descent, both creoles and European born.

3. Unfortunately, the sources make the study of influential women much harder, but for a remarkable story of a highly successful free colored woman, see Kit Candlin, *The Last Caribbean Frontier, 1795–1815* (Houndmills, Basingstoke: Palgrave Macmillan, 2012), chap. 2; Kit Candlin and Cassandra Pybus, *Enterprising Women: Gender, Race, and Power in the Revolutionary Atlantic* (Athens: University of Georgia Press, 2015), chap. 5.

4. Frederick Cooper, *Colonialism in Question: Theory, Knowledge, History* (Berkeley: University of California Press, 2005), 67–73. In this chapter, Cooper and Brubaker argue for the use of "identification" over "identity." The latter, in its strong sense, is static and universal, something an individual or a group has to discover and can even be wrong about. The weak conceptualization of identity, on the other hand, stipulates that identities are always malleable, constructed, and negotiated and thereby loses its analytical power. Identification is a viable alternative, giving agency to individuals

and groups in the self-fashioning of their image while still allowing for different images under different circumstances.

5. Netscher, *History of the Colonies*, 85; Hartsinck, *Beschryving van Guiana*, 285–90.

6. Harris and Villiers, *Storm van 's Gravesande*, vol. 1: 271, 301, 308; vol. 2: 378.

7. NL-HaNA, WIC, 1.05.01.02, inv. nr. 915; Council of Policy to WIC, 24 April 1774, TNA, CO 116/39, f. 361; Secretary to Chamber Zealand, 1 March 1774, ibid., f. 186–89; TNA, CO 116/38, f. 225; Rodway, *History*, vol. 1: 258; L. J. D. Grovestins to WIC, 2 May 1779, NL-HaNA, WIC, 1.05.01.02, inv. nr. 309.

8. Extract from the Council of Ten, 15 May 1776, NAG, Letter book 1776 (February–May), AG 1, inv. nr. 15, f. 163; Council of Policy to WIC, 24 April 1774, TNA, CO 116/39, f. 361; Director-General to WIC, 5 July 1774, TNA, CO 116/39, f. 427–30; Van Schuylenburg to WIC, 17 January 1774, TNA, CO 116/39, f. 66–67; Schuylenburg to Zealand Chamber, 16 December 1776, TNA CO 116/44, f. 408; Extract of Council Minutes, 21 June 1775, TNA CO 116/44, f. 418–20; Account of emoluments, TNA, CO 116/55, f. 79; De Smidt, Lee, and Van Dapperen, *Guyana Ordinance Book*, 8 January 1746; De Smidt, Lee, and Van Dapperen, *Guyana Ordinance Book*, Essequibo and Demerara, 6 October 1784; NL-HaNA, Staten-Generaal, 1.01.02, inv. nr. 9424, f. 107; *Publicatien van directeur-generaal en raden van Civiele- en Criminele Justitie in Essequebo betreffende de levering van wapenen aan de slaven en de invoer van slaven uit naburige kolonien*, NL-HaNA, VWIS, inv. nr. 140, 6 July 1772; NL-HaNA, WIC, 1.05.01.02, inv.nr. 1032, 19 May 1786; NRS, GD46/17/14, f. 817–21.

9. Bolingbroke, *Voyage to Demerary*, 37, 41; Rodway, *History*, vol. 2: 161. Theodore Barrell to Abby Winslow, 8 February 1843, University Archives, Rare Book & Manuscript Library, Columbia University Libraries (hereafter Columbia RBML), Barrell Family Papers, 1751–1929, MS 0082, box 3, folder 12, f. 21; *Essequebo en Demerarische Courant*, no. 26, 27 April 1794, http://www.vc.id.au/edg/17940427edc.html, accessed 31 August 2016; De Smidt, Lee, and Van Dapperen, *Guyana Ordinance Book*, Essequibo, 5 July 1756; Essequibo, 19 August 1768; Essequibo, 30 May 1771; Essequibo and Demerara, 30 July and 20 August 1793.

10. Bolingbroke, *Voyage to Demerary*, 37.

11. Fatah-Black, "Slaves and Sailors," 62.

12. Rodway, *History*, vol. 2: 45–46; TNA, CO 111/3, f. 213, 215.

13. Cohen, *Jews in Another Environment*,; Jonathan I. Israel, "The Jews of Dutch America," in *The Jews and the Expansion of Europe to the West, 1450–1800*, ed. Paolo Barnardini and Norman Fiering (New York: Berghahn, 2001); Jonathan I. Israel, *Diasporas within a Diaspora: Jews, Crypto-Jews and the World Maritime Empires (1540-1740)* (Leiden: Brill, 2009) 527; Council of Policy to WIC, 21 April 1774, TNA, CO 116/39, f. 361; NAG, AG 1, inv. nr. 11, 20 October 1774. In the mid-seventeenth century, however, Jews received permission to start a colony in Essequibo, which was stimulated by the Amsterdam parnassim; see Klooster, *Dutch Moment*, 225–27.

14. NL-HaNA, S-G, 1.01.02, inv. nr. 3829, 13 October 1774, f. 615; NL-HaNA, S-G, 1.01.02, inv. nr. 3831, 24 April, 19 July, and 6 December 1774, f. 235, 437, and 777–78; NL-HaNA, S-G, 1.01.02, inv. nr. 3852, 13 February 1789, f. 118; NL-HaNA, S-G, 1.01.02, inv. nr. 3857, 4 December 1792, f. 946. Paul Koulen, however, has identified several estates with Jewish owners in the nineteenth century who probably were there already in the eighteenth century. See Koulen, "Slavenhouders en geldschieters," 50–51.

15. Haefeli, *Dutch Origins*; Klooster, *Dutch Moment*, 230.

16. Netscher, *History of the Colonies*, 63–64, app. 1; Webber and Christiani, *Handbook of British Guiana*, 49, 56.

17. Villiers, *Storm van 's Gravesande*, 364.

18. De Smidt, Lee, and Van Dapperen, *Guyana Ordinance Book*, Essequibo and Demerara, 19 March 1787.

19. Mark L. Thompson, *The Contest for the Delaware Valley: Allegiance, Identity, and Empire in the Seventeenth Century* (Baton Rouge: Louisiana State University Press, 2013), 7–9.

20. Bolingbroke, *Voyage to Demerary*, 50.

21. In 1802 the colonies were briefly returned to the Dutch as part of the Treaty of Amiens, but as soon as war resumed the British took Essequibo and Demerara as well as Berbice into their possession again.

22. Correspondence of Lieutenant Colonel Robert Kingston, TNA, CO 111/1, f. 4–5, 41–54, 57, 84–88, 92–93.

23. Correspondence of Edward Thompson, 22 April 1781, TNA, CO 111/1, f. 1–2.

24. Ingekomen brieven met bijlagen van Essequebo, NL-HaNA, WIC, 1.05.01.02, inv. nr. 533, f. 441–49.

25. Thompson to George Germaine, 18 June 1781, TNA, CO 111/1, f. 24–25, 101; Fatah-Black, "Patriot Coup," in Klooster and Oostindie, *Curaçao in the Age of Revolutions*, 137.

26. Douglass C. North, "Institutions, Transaction Costs, and the Rise of Merchant Empire," in *The Political Economy of Merchant Empires*, ed. James D. Tracy (Cambridge: Cambridge University Press, 1991); Douglass C. North and Barry R. Weingast, "Constitutions and Commitment: The Evolution of Institutional Governing Public Choice in Seventeenth-Century England," *Journal of Economic History* 49, no. 4 (1989): 803–32; Douglass C. North, *Understanding the Process of Economic Change* (Princeton, NJ: Princeton University Press, 2005); Avner Greif, "Cultural Beliefs and the Organization of Society: A Historical and Theoretical Reflection on Collectivist and Individualist Societies," *Journal of Political Economy* 102, no. 5 (1994): 912–50; Avner Greif, "The Maghribi Traders: A Reappraisal?," *Economic History Review* 65, no. 2 (2012): 445–69; Oscar Gelderblom, *Cities of Commerce: The Institutional Foundations of International Trade in the Low Countries, 1250–1650* (Princeton, NJ: Princeton University Press, 2015). For an insightful discussion on the continuum between institutions and networks, see Regina Grafe, "On the Spatial Nature of Institutions and the Institutional Nature of Personal Networks in the Spanish Atlantic," *Culture & History Digital Journal* 3, no. 1 (2014): 4–11.

27. Daviken Studnicki-Gizbert, *A Nation upon the Ocean Sea: Portugal's Atlantic Diaspora and the Crisis of the Spanish Empire, 1492–1640* (Oxford: Oxford University Press, 2007); Xabier Lamikiz, *Trade and Trust in the Eighteenth-Century Atlantic World: Spanish Merchants and Their Overseas Networks* (Woodbridge: Boydell Press, 2010); Cátia Antunes, "Cross-Cultural Business Cooperation in the Dutch Trading World, 1580–1776: A View from Amsterdam's Notarial Contracts," in *Religion and Trade: Cross-Cultural Exchanges in World History, 1000–1900*, ed. Francesca Trivellato, Leor Halevi, and Cátia Antunes (New York: Oxford University Press, 2014); Francesca Trivellato, *The Familiarity of Strangers: The Sephardic Diaspora, Livorno, and Cross-Cultural Trade in the Early Modern Period* (New Haven, CT: Yale University Press, 2009); Nuala Zahedieh, "Making Mercantilism Work: London Merchants

and Atlantic Trade in the Seventeenth Century," *Transactions of the Royal Historical Society* 9 (1999): 143–58; Nuala Zahedieh, "Economy," in *The British Atlantic World, 1500–1800*, ed. David Armitage and M. J. Braddick (Houndmills, Basingstoke: Palgrave Macmillan, 2002), 51–68; Douglas J. Hamilton, *Scotland, the Caribbean and the Atlantic World, 1750–1820* (Manchester: Manchester University Press, 2010).

28. Parker, *Sugar Barons*, 314; Vincent K. Hubbard, *A History of St Kitts: The Sweet Trade* (Oxford: Macmillan, 2002), 80. Antigua's production continued to grow: Richard B. Sheridan, "The Rise of a Colonial Gentry: A Case Study of Antigua, 1730–1775," *Economic History Review* 13, no. 3 (1961): 344.

29. S. D. Smith, "Gedney Clarke of Salem and Barbados: Transatlantic Super-Merchant," *New England Quarterly* 76, no. 4 (2003): 512.

30. Van der Oest, "Forgotten Colonies," in Enthoven and Postma, *Riches*, 328.

31. For mentions of the Clarkes, see Mulcahy, *Hubs of Empire*, 176–77; Thompson, *Colonialism and Underdevelopment*, 163; Oostindie, "British Capital," 38–39; and particularly the excellent article by Simon Smith, which forms the basis of the following section, "Gedney Clarke."

32. Smith, "Gedney Clarke," 508–11.

33. NL-HaNA, Raadpensionaris Van de Spiegel, 3.01.26, inv. nr. 450, H1 Loco B; *Secrete resoluties*, 4 June 1764, NL-HaNA, WIC, 1.05.01.02, inv. nr. 765.

34. Smith, "Gedney Clarke," 511–14.

35. Ibid., 533–35.

36. Ibid., 522.

37. Rodway, *History*, vol. 1: 219.

38. Kars, "'Cleansing the Land,'" in Lee, *Empires and Indigenes*; Thompson, *Colonialism and Underdevelopment*, chap. 8.

39. Smith, "Gedney Clarke," 519–20.

40. BL, Egerton Ms. 1720, f. 21, 43–44, 53–54, 75–76, 77; Harris and Villiers, *Storm van 's Gravesande*, vol. 1: 43, vol. 2: 599; Rodway, *History*, vol. 1: 228.

41. Smith, "Gedney Clarke," 536.

42. BL, Egerton Ms. 1720, f. 4, 10–11, 13, 43–44, 72–73.

43. BL, Egerton Ms. 1720, f. 4.

44. Harris and Villiers, *Storm van 's Gravesande*, vol. 2: 525; NL-HaNA, Raadpensionaris Van de Spiegel 3.01.26, appendix D2, f. 56 (quotation), H4A, f. 70. Original quotation: "dat dit de Hr. Clarke, en veele andere weinig smaaken zal."

45. Some of the other Clarkes remained in the colonies. Chapter 3 already told how a J. Clarke was killed in the 1795 uprisings, and a map of 1795 mentions a P. Clarke (York estate), a William Clarke (Richmond), and a Gedney Clarke Sr. (Blenheim), although the latter probably reflects that Clarke Sr. used to own the estate before his death in 1764. (See the list of names belonging to map 5.3: http://dpc.uba.uva.nl/cgi/i/image/image-idx?sid=227d1a6701d2d90bff84cf510d2057e3;q1=Friederich%20von%20Bouchenr%F6der;rgn1=surinamica_all;size=20;c=surinamica;lasttype=boolean;view=entry;lastview=thumbnail;subview=detail;cc=surinamica;entryid=x-627;viewid=SURI01_KAARTENZL-105-23-05-1.SID;start=1;resnum=2, accessed 27 August 2016).

46. Harris and Villiers, *Storm van 's Gravesande*, vol. 2: 555, 582–83 (quotation).

47. Ibid., vol. 1: 352. Storm wrote in 1757 but stated that Croydon already owned his timber states before Storm went to Europe, which was in 1750–52. However, Croydon

does not appear on the 1748 map of Essequibo, nor does the estate De Vriendschap which he owned in 1769 (ibid., vol. 2: 399; http://www.davidrumsey.com/luna/servlet/detail/RUMSEY~8~1~204055~3001779:Essequibo-by-Storm-Van-s-Gravesande, accessed 6 November 2015).

48. NL-HaNA, Raadpensionaris Van de Spiegel, 3.01.26, inv.nr. 450, appendix H17, f. 90-91.

49. TNA, CO 116/34, f. 205-8; NL-HaNA, WIC, 1.05.01.02, inv. nr. 189.

50. NL-HaNA, Raadpensionaris Van de Spiegel, 3.01.26, inv. nr. 450, appendix H14 Loco B, f. 83-85.

51. Ibid. The signatories were William Croydon, Thomas Wiltshire, Cornelis Leary, William Matthews, Geo: Charter, Peter Cornelis Donovan, John Raper, Samuel Zeagers, William Mansfield, and William Rowe. Of those, only Croydon, Leary, and Rowe can be positively identified as planters in 1769 (Harris and Villiers, *Storm van 's Gravesande*, vol. 2: 399-400).

52. NL-HaNA, Raadpensionaris Van de Spiegel, 3.01.26, inv. nr. 450, appendix I, f. 95.

53. *Croyden [sic], William Ms.D.S. Account for purchase of Schoonhoven plantation; Essequebo, 22 August 1775*, Boston Public Library (hereafter BPL), Boston, English (British) Civilization Collection, 1573-1970, Ms. Eng 249, inv. nr. 2; *Essequebo (Colony) Directeur Generaal en Raaden. Ms.D.S. (illegible); Essequebo, 05 March 1777 Certification of sale of Schoonhoven plantation to William Croyden [sic]*, ibid., inv. nr. 4.

54. *Croyden [sic], William Ms.D.S. (Robert W. Hall; H. W. Knolman): Valuation of Friendship estate and Schoonhoven plantation; Essequebo, 13 February 1800*, BPL, English (British) Civilization Collection, 1573-1970, Ms. Eng 249, inv. nr. 9. The enslaved on Schoonhoven were listed as 50 men, 38 women, 15 boys, and 9 girls. On Friendship there were 120 men, 118 women, 54 boys, 14 girls, and 24 "small girls."

55. NL-HaNA, WIC, 1.05.01.02, inv. nr. 192A. Gedney Clarke's estate De Vriendschap was mortgaged to Boddaert in 1766 (Van de Voort, *Westindische plantages*, 273).

56. BPL, English (British) Civilization Collection, 1573-1970, Ms. Eng 249, inv. nr. 9; Extract of minutes of the Council of Policy, 3 May 1786, NL-HaNA, WIC, 1.05.01.02, inv. nr. 533, f. 437-38. This finding is consistent with the 1788 tax survey, where a "free mulattoe or negro woman," a "free mulatto or negro," and a free Amerindian woman were registered together with Croydon (NL-HaNA, WIC, 1.05.01.02, inv. nrs. 192A and 193A).

57. *Croyden [sic], William A.L.S. to Alexander Tulloh; Essequebo, 17 April 1799*, BPL, English (British) Civilization Collection, 1573-1970, Ms. Eng 249, inv. nr. 5.

58. *Lijst van de slaven in Essequebo in 1785*, NL-HaNA, WIC, 1.05.01.2, inv. nr. 188B; Aristodemus and Sincerus, *Brieven*, vol. 3: 12th letter, appendix K.

59. Data about birthdates and places for John Hubbard retrieved from http://www.geni.com/people/John-Hubbard/308256371220003848; for Gardiner Greene, from http://www.geni.com/people/Gardiner-Greene/5309362592380040381; and for Elizabeth Greene, from http://www.geni.com/people/Elizabeth-Hubbard/5309344737510077451 (all accessed 3 September 2016).

60. Massachusetts Historical Society (hereafter MHS), Boston, Hubbard-Greene Papers, Ms. N-312, folder 1.

61. John Hubbard to Gardiner Greene, 28 October 1789, MHS, Hubbard-Greene Papers, Ms. N-312; John Hubbard to Gardiner Greene, 29 August 1793, MHS, Hubbard-Greene Papers, Ms. N-312.

62. John Hubbard to Gardiner Greene, 20 May 1795, MHS, Hubbard-Greene Papers, Ms. N-312.

63. William Cowell to Stephan Gorham and William Smith, 21 February 1791, MHS, Smith-Carter Family Papers, Ms. N-2170.

64. John Hubbard to Gardiner Greene, 18 August 1795, MHS, Hubbard-Greene Papers, Ms. N-312.

65. William Cowell to Stephen Gorham and William Smith, 4 January 1791, MHS, Smith-Carter Family Papers, Ms. N-2170; William Cowell to Stephen Gorham and William Smith, 27 January 1791, MHS, Smith-Carter Family Papers, Ms. N-2170.

66. Letters of Jesse Breed to Simon Breed, 1788–1791, Fairfield Museum and History Center, Fairfield, CT, Breed and Mumford Family Papers/Susquehannah Company Papers 1754–1966, Ms. B4.

67. John Hubbard to Gardiner Greene, 20 May 1795, MHS, Hubbard-Greene Papers, Ms. N-312; John Hubbard to Gardiner Greene, 18 August 1795, MHS, Hubbard-Greene Papers, Ms. N-312; John Hubbard to Gardiner Greene, 7 February 1799, MHS, Hubbard-Greene Papers, Ms. N-312. In 1788 Greenfield (or Greenfields) was listed as owned by Parkinson & Greene and free from Dutch mortgages; see NL-HaNA, WIC, 1.05.01.02, 192B.

68. John Hubbard to Gardiner Greene, 18 November 1802 and 17 May 1804, MHS, Hubbard-Greene Papers, Ms. N-312.

69. John Hubbard to Gardiner Greene, 12 May 1801, MHS, Hubbard-Greene Papers, Ms. N-312.

70. John Hubbard to Gardiner Greene, 18 November 1802, MHS, Hubbard-Greene Papers, Ms. N-312.

71. John Hubbard to Gardiner Greene, 5 June 1804, MHS, Hubbard-Greene Papers, Ms. N-312.

72. Hancock, *Citizens of the World*; Sheryllynne Haggerty, *"Merely for Money"? Business Culture in the British Atlantic, 1750–1815* (Liverpool: Liverpool University Press, 2012), 63; Studnicki-Gizbert, *Nation upon the Ocean Sea*, 107–8.

73. Theodore Barrell to Abby Winslow, 8 February 1843, Columbia RBML, Barrell Family Papers, MS 0082, box 3, folder 12, f. 1–3.

74. Theodore Barrell to Abby Winslow, 8 February 1843, Columbia RBML, Barrell Family Papers, MS 0082, box 3, folder 12, f. 3–4; Theodore Barrell to Joseph Barrell, 15 June 1798, New York Historical Society (hereafter NYHS), New York, Theodore Barrell Letter book, 1798–1803, MS 859, f. 16–19. In 1788 Haslin's estates Friendship and Het Loo were mortgaged to Van den Helm Boddaert, while Bel-Air did not have a registered Dutch mortgage, and the situation of New Hope is not noted; see NL-HaNA, WIC, 1.05.01.02, 192B. In 1814 the mortgage for Friendship to Boddaert was still standing; see the transcription by Paul Koulen of TNA, CO 111/28, p. 23 (https://cbg.nl/documents/55/Berbice-Demerara-Essequebo.pdf, accessed 31 July 2018).

75. Theodore Barrell to Abby Winslow, 8 February 1843, Columbia RBML, Barrell Family Papers, MS 0082, box 3, folder 12, f. 4–7 (quotations); Theodore Barrell to Walter Barrell, 21 April 1798, NYHS, Theodore Barrell Letter book, f. 9–11.

76. Theodore Barrell to Abby Winslow, 8 February 1843, Columbia RBML, Barrell Family Papers, MS 0082, box 3, folder 12, f. 21–22 (quotation).

77. Theodore Barrell to William and Samuel Jones, 20 March 1798, NYHS, Theodore Barrell Letter book, f. 1–5; Theodore Barrell to William and Samuel Jones, 9 April 1798, NYHS, Theodore Barrell Letter book, f. 6–7; Theodore Barrell to William and Samuel Jones, 30 April 1798, NYHS, Theodore Barrell Letter book, f. 12; Theodore Barrell to William and Samuel Jones,, 9 June 1798, NYHS, Theodore Barrell Letter book, f. 14–16; Theodore Barrell to Colborn Barrell, 22 July, NYHS, Theodore Barrell Letter book, f. 24. For the Industrial Enlightenment, see Joel Mokyr, *The Enlightened Economy: An Economic History of Britain, 1700–1850* (New Haven, CT: Yale University Press, 2009).

78. Koulen, "Slavenhouders en geldschieters," 50.

79. Theodore Barrell to Joseph Barrell, 30 May 1798, NYHS, Theodore Barrell Letter book, f. 12–14; Theodore Barrell to Colborn Barrell, 5 July 1798, NYHS, Theodore Barrell Letter book, f. 20–24.

80. Theodore Barrell to Polly Barrell, 6 March 1798, NYHS, Theodore Barrell Letter book, f. 55–59; Theodore Barrell to Francis Wilson, 9 October 1799, NYHS, Theodore Barrell Letter book, f. 100; Theodore Barrell to Walter Barrell, 10 December 1801, NYHS, Theodore Barrell Letter book, f. 155–57.

81. Theodore Barrell to Charlotte Forbes, 25 November 1798, NYHS, Theodore Barrell Letter book, f. 37–40; Theodore Barrell to Sayward Barrell, 9 March 1799, NYHS, Theodore Barrell Letter book, f. 54–55; Theodore Barrell to Polly Barrell, 6 March 1799, NYHS, Theodore Barrell Letter book, f. 55–59.

82. Theodore Barrell to Abigail Barrell, included in a letter to William and Samuel Jones, 13 April 1800, f. 109–19.

83. Theodore Barrell to Joseph Barrell, 15 June 1798, NYHS, Theodore Barrell Letter book, f. 16–19; Theodore Barrell to Joseph Barrell, 19 November 1799, NYHS, Theodore Barrell Letter book, f. 105.

84. Theodore Barrell to Abby Winslow, 8 February 1843, Columbia RBML, Barrell Family Papers, MS 0082, box 3, folder 12, f. 40 (quotation); Theodore Barrell to Sarah Gall, 12 January 1801, NYHS, Theodore Barrell Letter book, f. 149; Theodore Barrell to John Alleyne Beckles, 31 August 1802, NYHS, Theodore Barrell Letter book, f. 168. Some of his business partners in Barbados listed in his letter book were Le Gay Evens & Reid, Robert Gibbons, William Barton, John Went, and Samuel Went.

85. Theodore Barrell to Abigail Barrell, 4 October 1800, NYHS, Theodore Barrell Letter book, f. 135–37.

86. Theodore Barrell to John Gill, 30 October 1800, NYHS, Theodore Barrell Letter book, f. 144–45.

87. Theodore Barrell to Joseph Barrell, 30 May 1798, NYHS, Theodore Barrell Letter book, f. 12–14; Theodore Barrell to Benjamin Joy, 21 July 1800, NYHS, Theodore Barrell Letter book, f. 120.

88. New York Public Library (hereafter NYPL), New York, Theodore Barrell Letter book, 1816–17, MssCol 218, 13 December 1816.

89. Theodore Barrell to Abby Winslow, 8 February 1843, Columbia RBML, Barrell Family Papers, MS 0082, box 3, folder 12, f. 7, 39–40.

90. Theodore Barrell to Polly Barrell, 17 August 1800, NYHS, Theodore Barrell Letter book, f. 121–24; Theodore Barrell to Samuel Sandbach, 24 September 1800, NYHS, Theodore Barrell Letter book, f. 132–33.

91. Hamilton, *Scotland, the Caribbean and the Atlantic World*, 55–57.

92. Alan L. Karras, *Sojourners in the Sun: Scottish Migrants in Jamaica and the Chesapeake, 1740–1800* (Ithaca, NY: Cornell University Press, 1992), 3, 6.

93. The Parker Family Papers in the Liverpool Archives have been central to reconstructing the firm's story, which means that it is rather Parker-centered.

94. Broadsheet over Three Centuries, 1790–1952, Liverpool Record Office (hereafter LRS), Liverpool, Parker Family Papers, 920 PAR V 2/1.

95. Charles Stewart Parker to Patrick Parker, 3 December 1789, LRS, Parker Family Papers, 920 PAR I/46.

96. The later firm had shared capital at least. In Grenada the name was Robertson, Parker & Co., and while in Demerara it was McInroy & Gordon. George Robertson to George Rainy, 15 December 1790, LRS, Parker Family Papers, 920 PAR I/50/1.

97. Daniel Gordon to George Robertson, 24 November 1791, LRS, Parker Family Papers, 920 PAR I/50/2.

98. Charles Stewart Parker to James Parker, 12 June 1792, LRS, Parker Family Papers, 920 PAR I/50/10; Charles Stewart Parker to James Parker, 19 July 1792, LRS, Parker Family Papers, 920 PAR I/47/11.

99. Charles Stewart Parker to James Parker, 3 October 1792, LRS, Parker Family Papers, 920 PAR I/47/13.

100. Charles Stewart Parker to James Parker, 19 July 1792, LRS, Parker Family Papers, 920 PAR I/47/12; Charles Stewart Parker to James Parker, 3 October 1792, LRS, Parker Family Papers, 920 PAR I/47/13 (quotation); Charles Stewart Parker to James Parker, 27 January 1793, LRS, Parker Family Papers, 920 PAR I/47/15; Charles Stewart Parker to James Parker, 10 August 1793, LRS, Parker Family Papers, 920 PAR I/47/20; Charles Stewart Parker to James Parker, 15 January 1794, LRS, Parker Family Papers, 920 PAR I/47/23.

101. The firm was the sixth-largest cotton importer from the Guianas to Liverpool, exporting 2,822,002 lbs to the city between 1796 and 1815 (Alexey Krichtal, "Liverpool and the Raw Cotton Trade: A Study of the Port and its Merchant Community, 1770–1815" [MA Thesis, Victoria University of Wellington, 2013], 45).

102. Charles Stewart Parker to James Parker, 29 December 1792, LRS, Parker Family Papers, 920 PAR I/47/14 (quotation); James McInroy to Robertson & Parker, 4 February 1795, LRS, Parker Family Papers, 920 PAR I/50/4.

103. Charles Stewart Parker to James Parker, 3 October 1792, LRS, Parker Family Papers, 920 PAR I/47/13. The creditors were Robertson, McKay and Spears. Mr. Spears wanted to continue the correspondence, but as he was the junior partner of the three, with little money and few connections, Parker wrote him that he better find some monied men first.

104. Charles Stewart Parker to James Parker, 10 August 1793, LRS, Parker Family Papers, 920 PAR I/47/20.

105. Charles Stewart Parker to James Parker, 19 July 1792, LRS, Parker Family Papers, 920 PAR I/47/12; Charles Stewart Parker to James Parker, 10 August 1793, LRS, Parker Family Papers, 920 PAR I/47/20; Charles Stewart Parker to James Parker, 7 September 1793, LRS, Parker Family Papers, 920 PAR I/47/21; Charles Stewart Parker to James Parker, 13 November 1793, LRS, Parker Family Papers, 920 PAR I/47/22; LRS, Parker Family Papers, 920 PAR V 2/1.

106. James McInroy to Robertson & Parker, 4 February 1795, LRS, Parker Family Papers, 920 PAR I/50/4; Charles Stewart Parker to James Parker, 3 October 1792, LRS, Parker Family Papers, 920 PAR I/47/13; Charles Stewart Parker to James Parker, 10 March 1797, LRS, Parker Family Papers, 920 PAR I/47/31; James McInroy to Samuel Sandbach, 6 March 1803, LRS, Parker Family Papers, 920 PAR IV/1/1/1; Charles Stewart Parker to James McInroy, 8 June 1798, LRS, Parker Family Papers, 920 PAR III/26/4.

107. Webber and Christiani, *Handbook of British Guiana*, 97.

108. James McInroy to Robertson and Parker, 4 February 1795, LRS, Parker Family Papers, 920 PAR I/50/4; McInroy, Sandbach and McBean to James McInroy, 10 April 1803, LRS, Parker Family Papers, 920 PAR IV 1/2/2; Charles Stewart Parker to James Parker, 10 April 1793, LRS, Parker Family Papers, 920 PAR I/47/16; Charles Stewart Parker to James Parker, 7 September 1793, LRS, Parker Family Papers, 920 PAR I/47/21; McInroy, Sandbach, McBean & Co to Samuel Sandbach, , LRS, Parker Family Papers, 920 PAR IV 1/1/4 and 1/1/5.

109. McInroy, Sandbach, McBean & Co to Samuel Sandbach, LRS, Parker Family Papers, 920 PAR IV 1/1/4; LRS, Parker Family Papers, 920 PAR V 2/1.

110. LRS, Parker Family Papers, 920 PAR V 2/1; Charles Steward Parker to James Parker, LRS, Parker Family Papers, 17 June 1800, 920 PAR I/47/40. Gilbert Robertson was married to a daughter of Dolly Thomas, a wealthy woman of color; see Candlin, *Last Caribbean Frontier*, 38.

111. LRS, Parker Family Papers, 920 PAR V 2/1.

112. Van de Voort, *Westindische plantages*, 306; UA, 34-4 Notarissen, D. W. van Vloten, inv. nr. U247a010, akte 232, 21 December 1771; *Procuratie—om plantage De Goede Intentie te Demerary uit verband te ontslaan ingevolge aflossing van schuld door door Cornelis van den Helm Boddaert te Middelburg voor rekening van Thomas Cuming en de erven Thomas Grand*, UA, 34-4 Notarissen, C. van Beest, inv. nr. U235a004, akte 97, 15 December 1771. In 1788 the Garden of Eden was mortgaged to Van Vloten, while the Ketty had no mortage. His brickworks were mortgaged locally to B. Albinus. See NL-HaNA, WIC, 1.05.01.02, 192B.

113. David Alston, *Slaves and Highlanders*,
http://www.spanglefish.com/slavesandhighlanders/index.asp?pageid=164658, accessed 5 January 2016.

114. Thomas Cuming to Thomas Newburn, 11 September 1799, NRS, Letter book of Thomas Cuming, inv. nr. GD23/6/364, f. 1–4; Thomas Cuming to Thomas Newburn, 14 October 1799, ibid., f.4–8.

115. Thomas Cuming to Thomas Newburn, 11 September 1799, NRS, Letter book of Thomas Cuming, inv. nr. GD23/6/364, f. 1–4; Thomas Cuming to Thomas Newburn, 14 October 1799, ibid., f. 4–8. For conditions on which the Garden of Eden was offered for sale, ibid., f. 10; for conditions for sale of plantation Ketty, ibid., f. 11.

116. History Associates Incorporated, "Predecessors of ABN AMRO Bank N.V. and Connections to African Slavery in the United States and the Americas" (2006) 7–8, http://files.shareholder.com/downloads/ABN/452437691x0x147069/6aadc21e-e7e4-482c-9ced-13ce9dc70161/hai_report.pdf, accessed 13 September 2016. Furthermore, in 1818, when he was already deceased, the estates La Bourgade and Thomas were still

listed as mortgaged to Turing & co and P. J. Boddaert, respectively. See Paul Koulen's transcription of TNA, CO 111/28, pp. 17, 23, and 24.

117. Essequebo and Demerary Royal Gazette, 18 April 1818, http://www.vc.id.au/edg/18120418edrg.html, accessed 13 September 2016.

Conclusion

1. For the idea of a moral economy of smuggling, see Cromwell, "Illicit Ideologies."
2. Fatah-Black, *White Lies*, 60.
3. Klooster, *Illicit Riches*, 1.

Bibliography

Manuscript Sources

Guyana

NATIONAL ARCHIVES OF GUYANA (NAG), GEORGETOWN
AB 3, inv. nrs. 12, 13
AZ 1, inv. nrs. 11, 68
AG 1, inv. nr. 15

The Netherlands

AMSTERDAM CITY ARCHIVES (ACA), AMSTERDAM
Notarial archives, Notaries, inv. nr. 5075
Firma Ketwich & Voomberg en Wed. W. Borski, 600, inv. nrs. 605, 606, 607, 654, 663

INTERNATIONAL INSTITUTE OF SOCIAL HISTORY (IISH), AMSTERDAM
Collectie Effecten en loterijbriefjes, ARCH03766
Collectie Effecten (tweede aanvulling), ARCH04145, inv. nr. 1
Collectie P. A. Brugmans, ARCH03525, inv. nr. 12

NATIONAL ARCHIVES (NL-HANA), THE HAGUE
Admiraliteiten / Hinxt, 1.01.47.19, inv. nrs. 8, 11
Admiraliteitscolleges / Paulus-Olivier, 1.01.47.13, inv. nr. 44
Kaarten Leupe, 4.VEL, nrs. 1494, 1490A1, 1498
Raadpensionaris van de Spiegel, 3.01.26, inv. nr. 450
Raad der Amerikaanse Bezittingen, 2.01.28.02, inv. nr. 168M
Raad der Koloniën, 1.05.02, inv. nr. 75

Staten-Generaal, 1.01.02, inv. nrs. 1506, 3826, 3827, 3829, 3831–33, 3842, 3849, 3852, 3856, 3857, 9424, 9425, 9552

Tweede West-Indische Compagnie, 1.05.01.02, nrs. 39, 189, 140, 188B, 192A, 192B, 193A, 309, 442, 533, 534, 747, 748, 765, 915, 1032, 1033, 1275C

Verspreide West-Indische stukken, 1.05.06, inv. nrs. 48, 59, 126, 128, 130, 150, 151, 478

UTRECHTS ARCHIEF (UA), UTRECHT
Notarissen in de Stad Utrecht 1560–1905, 34–4, inv. nrs. U247a010, U235a004

ZEEUWS ARCHIEF (ZA), MIDDLEBURGH
Middelburgse Commercie Compagnie, 20, inv.nr. 1772.5

United Kingdom

BRITISH LIBRARY (BL), LONDON
Egerton Ms. 1720

LIVERPOOL RECORD OFFICE (LRO), LIVERPOOL
Parker Family Papers, 920: PAR I/46, I/47, I/50, PAR III/26, PAR IV/1, PAR V 2/1

NATIONAL RECORDS OF SCOTLAND (NRS), EDINBURGH
Bound volume of correspondence of Peter Fairbairn, Seaforth's secretary, inv. nr. GD46/17/14
Day book and ledger of Prospect Estate, 1791–96, inv. nr. CS96/4483
Letter book of Thomas Cuming, inv. nr. GD23/6/364

THE NATIONAL ARCHIVES (TNA), KEW
BT, 6, inv. nr. 188
CO, 10, inv. nr. 2
CO, 33, inv. nr. 18, 19, 20
CO, 76, inv. nr. 4, 5, 6
CO, 106, inv. nr. 2
CO, 111, inv. nrs. 1, 3, 4
CO, 116, inv. nrs. 36, 38, 39, 42, 44, 48, 55, 57, 61
CO, 243, inv. nr. 1
CUST 16, inv. nr. 1

United States

BOSTON PUBLIC LIBRARY (BPL), BOSTON
English (British) Civilization Collection, 1573–1970, Ms. Eng 249, inv. nrs. 2, 4, 5, 9

COLUMBIA RARE BOOK AND MANUSCRIPT LIBRARY (RBML), NEW YORK
Barrell Family Papers, 1751–1929, MS 0082

FAIRFIELD MUSEUM AND HISTORY CENTER, FAIRFIELD, CT
Breed and Mumford Family Papers/Susquehannah Company Papers 1754–1966, Ms B4

JOHN CARTER BROWN LIBRARY, PROVIDENCE, RI
Codex Eng 52, Accounts and Ledger of Weilburg Plantation, Demerara, 1767–70

MASSACHUSETTS HISTORICAL SOCIETY (MHS), BOSTON
Hubbard-Greene Papers, Ms. N-312
Smith-Carter Family Papers, Ms. N-2170

NEW YORK HISTORICAL SOCIETY (NYHS), NEW YORK
Theodore Barrell Letter book, 1798–1803, MS 859

NEW YORK PUBLIC LIBRARY, NEW YORK
Theodore Barrell Letter Book, 1816–17, MssCol 218

Published Primary Sources

Aristodemus and Sincerus [pseudonym]. *Brieven over het bestuur der colonien Essequebo en Demerary, gewisseld tusschen de Heeren Aristodemus en Sincerus nevens bylagen, tot deeze briefwisseling, en eene voorreden van den Nederlandschen uitgeever.* 12 vols. Amsterdam: W. Holtrop, 1785–86.

Bolingbroke, Henry. *A Voyage to Demerary, Containing a Statistical Account of the Settlement There, and of Those on the Essequebo, the Berbice, and Other Contiguous Rivers of Guyana.* 1st ed. London: M. Carey, 1807.

Great Britain. *Documents and Correspondence relating to the Question of Boundary between British Guiana and Venezuela.* London: Harrison and Sons, 1896.

———. *British Guiana Boundary. Arbitration with the United States of Venezuela: Appendix to the Case on Behalf of the Government of Her Britannic Majesty. Volume II. 1724–1763.* London: Harrison and Sons, 1898.

———. *British Guiana Boundary. Arbitration with the United States of Venezuela: Appendix to the Case on Behalf of the Government of Her Britannic Majesty. Volume III. 1763–1768.* London: Harrison and Sons, 1898.

———. *British Guiana Boundary. Arbitration with the United States of Venezuela: Appendix to the Case on Behalf of the Government of Her Britannic Majesty. Volume IV. 1769–1781.* London: Harrison and Sons, 1898.

———. *British Guiana Boundary. Arbitration with the United States of Venezuela: Appendix to the Case on Behalf of the Government of Her Britannic Majesty. Volume V. 1781–1814.* London: Harrison and Sons, 1898.

———. *British Guiana Boundary. Arbitration with the United States of Venezuela: Appendix to the Counter Case on Behalf of the Government of Her Britannic Majesty.* London: Harrison and Sons, 1898.

Harris, C. A., and J. A. J. de Villiers. *Storm van 's Gravesande: The Rise of British Guiana Compiled from His Despatches.* 2 vols. London: Hakluyt Society, 1911.

Hartsinck, Jan J. *Beschryving van Guiana, of de wilde kust in Zuid-America.* Amsterdam: Gerrit Tielenburg, 1770.
Pierronet, Thomas. "Remarks Made during a Residence at Stabroek Rio Demerary (Lat. 6. 10. N.) in the Latter Part of the Year 1798." In *Collections of the Massachusetts Historical Society for the Year 1799.* Edited by Massachusetts Historical Society, 1–15. Boston: Charles C. Little and James Brown, 1799.
Schomburgk, Robert H. *A Description of British Guiana, Geographical and Statistical: Exhibiting its Resources and Capabilities, Together with the Present and Future Condition and Prospects of the Colony.* London: A. M. Kelley, 1840; repr. 1970.
Villiers, J. A. J. de. *Storm van 's Gravesande: Zijn werk en zijn leven uit zijne brieven opgebouwd.* The Hague: Martinus Nijhoff, 1920.
United States. *Venezuela-British Guiana Boundary Arbitration. Digest of Evidence Arranged According to Subjects: Prepared for the Private Use of the Venezuelan Council.* New York: Evening Job Printing House, 1899.
United States of Venezuela. *The Counter-Case of the United States of Venezuela before the Tribunal of Arbitration: To Convene at Paris under the Provisions of the Treaty between the United States of Venezuela and Her Britannic Majesty Signed at Washington February 2, 1897.* Vol.1. New York: Evening Post Job Printing House, 1898.

Online Sources

Atlas of Mutual Heritage, www.atlasofmutualheritage.nl
Brieven als Buit, www.brievenalsbuit.inl.nl
Database "Global Commodities, Trade Exploration and Cultural Exchange," www.globalcommodities.amdigital.co.uk
David Rumsey Map Collection, www.davidrumsey.com
Geheugen van Nederland, www.geheugenvannederland.nl
Geni, www.geni.com
Hathi Trust, babel.hathitrust.org
Measuring Worth, www.measuringworth.com
Plakaatboek Guyana (Guyana Ordinance Book), 1670–1816, Huygens Institute, http://resources.huygens.knaw.nl/retroboeken/guyana
Slaves and Highlanders, David Alston, http://www.spanglefish.com/slavesandhighlanders
The Trans-Atlantic Slave Trade Database (TASTD), www.slavevoyages.org
University of Amsterdam Suriname 1599–1975 map collection, http://dpc.uba.uva.nl/suriname
Guyana Colonial Newspapers, http://www.vc.id.au/edg/

Secondary Sources

Adelman, Jeremy, and Stephen Aron. "From Borderlands to Borders: Empires, Nation-States, and the Peoples in between in North American history." *American Historical Review* 104, no. 3 (1999): 814–41.

Aizpurua, Ramón. "Revolution and Politics in Venezuela and Curaçao, 1795–1800." In Klooster and Oostindie, *Curaçao in the Age of Revolutions, 1795–1800*, 97–122.

Allen, Douglas W. *The Institutional Revolution: Measurement and the Economic Emergence of the Modern World*. Chicago: University of Chicago Press, 2012.

Alston, David. "'Very Rapid and Splendid Fortunes'? Highland Scots in Berbice (Guyana) in the Early Nineteenth Century." *Transactions of the Gaelic Society of Inverness* 63 (2006): 208–36.

Altman, Ida. "The Spanish Atlantic, 1650–1780." In Canny and Morgan, *The Oxford Handbook of the Atlantic World c. 1450–1850*, 183–200.

Andrien, Kenneth J. "The Spanish Atlantic System." In Greene and Morgan, *Atlantic History*, 55–79.

Antunes, Cátia. "Cross-Cultural Business Cooperation in the Dutch Trading World, 1580–1776: A View from Amsterdam's Notarial Contracts." In *Religion and Trade: Cross-Cultural Exchanges in World History, 1000–1900*. Edited by Francesca Trivellato, Leor Halevi, and Cátia Antunes, 150–68. New York: Oxford University Press, 2014.

Antunes, Cátia, and Amélia Polónia. *Beyond Empires: Global, Self-Organizing, Cross-Imperial Networks, 1500–1800*. Leiden: Brill, 2016.

Armitage, David. "Three Concepts of Atlantic History." In Armitage and Braddick, *The British Atlantic World, 1500–1800*, 11–27.

Armitage, David, and M. J. Braddick, eds. *The British Atlantic World, 1500–1800*. Houndmills, Basingstoke: Palgrave Macmillan, 2002.

Armytage, Frances. *The Free Port System in the British West Indies: A Study in Commercial Policy, 1766–1822*. London: Published for the Royal Empire Society by Longmans, Green and Co., 1953.

Bailyn, Bernard. *Atlantic History: Concept and Contours*. Cambridge, MA: Harvard University Press, 2005.

Bailyn, Bernard, and Patricia L. Denault. "Introduction: Reflections on some Major Themes." In Bailyn and Denault, *Soundings in Atlantic History*, 1–43.

———, eds. *Soundings in Atlantic History: Latent Structures and Intellectual Currents, 1500–1830*. 1st ed. Cambridge, MA: Harvard University Press, 2011.

Banks, Kenneth J. *Chasing Empire across the Sea: Communications and the State in the French Atlantic, 1713–1763*. Montreal: McGill-Queen's University Press, 2006.

Barth, Jonathan. "Reconstructing Mercantilism: Consensus and Conflict in British Imperial Economy in the Seventeenth and Eighteenth Centuries." *William and Mary Quarterly* 73, no. 2 (2016): 257–90.

Baskes, Jeremy. *Staying Afloat: Risk and Uncertainty in Spanish Atlantic World Trade, 1760–1820*. Stanford, CA: Stanford University Press, 2013.
Benton, Lauren A. *Law and Colonial Cultures: Legal Regimes in World History, 1400–1900*. Cambridge: Cambridge University Press, 2002.
———. *A Search for Sovereignty: Law and Geography in European Empires, 1400–1900*. Cambridge: Cambridge University Press, 2010.
Benton, Lauren A., and Richard J. Ross. "Empires and Legal Pluralism: Jurisdiction, Sovereignty, and Political Imagination in the Early Modern World." In Benton and Ross, *Legal Pluralism and Empires*, 1–17.
———, eds. *Legal Pluralism and Empires, 1500–1850*. New York: New York University Press, 2013.
Bergad, Laird W. *The Comparative Histories of Slavery in Brazil, Cuba, and the United States*. New York: Cambridge University Press, 2007.
Bethencourt, Francisco. "Political Configurations and Local Powers." In *Portuguese Oceanic Expansion, 1400–1800*. Edited by Francisco Bethencourt and Diogo Ramada Curto, 197–254. New York: Cambridge University Press, 2007.
Bochove, Christiaan van, and Heleen Kole. "Uncovering Private Credit Markets: Amsterdam, 1660–1809." *Tijdschrift voor Sociale en Economische Geschiedenis* 11, no. 3 (2014): 39–72.
Borucki, Alex. "Trans-Imperial History in the Making of the Slave Trade to Venezuela, 1526–1811." *Itinerario* 36, no. 2 (2012): 29–54.
Brown, Vincent. *The Reaper's Garden: Death and Power in the World of Atlantic Slavery*. Cambridge, MA: Harvard University Press, 2008.
Browne, Randy M. "The 'Bad Business' of Obeah: Power, Authority, and the Politics of Slave Culture in the British Caribbean." *William and Mary Quarterly* 68, no. 3 (2011): 451–80.
———. *Surviving Slavery in the British Caribbean*. Philadelphia: University of Pennsylvania Press, 2017.
Bruijn, J. R. *De admiraliteit van Amsterdam in rustige jaren, 1713–1751: Regenten en financiën, schepen en zeevarende*. Amsterdam Schelteman & Holkema, 1970.
———. *The Dutch Navy of the Seventeenth and Eighteenth Centuries*. Columbia: University of South Carolina Press, 1993.
Burbank, Jane, and Frederick Cooper. "Rules of Law, Politics of Empire." In Benton and Ross, *Legal Pluralism and Empires*, 279–93.
Burnard, Trevor. "The British Atlantic." In Greene and Morgan, *Atlantic History*, 111–36.
———. *Planters, Merchants, and Slaves: Plantation Societies in British America, 1650–1820*. Chicago: University of Chicago Press, 2015.
Bushnell, Amy T. "Gates, Patterns, and Peripheries: The Field of Frontier Latin America." In Daniels and Kennedy, *Negotiated Empires*, 15–28.

Candlin, Kit. *The Last Caribbean Frontier, 1795–1815*. Houndmills, Basingstoke: Palgrave Macmillan, 2012.

Candlin, Kit, and Cassandra Pybus. *Enterprising Women: Gender, Race, and Power in the Revolutionary Atlantic*. Athens: University of Georgia Press, 2015.

Cañizares-Esguerra, Jorge and Erik R. Seeman, eds. *The Atlantic in Global History, 1500–2000*. Upper Saddle River, NJ: Pearson Prentice Hall, 2007.

Canny, Nicholas P., and Philip D. Morgan, eds. *The Oxford Handbook of the Atlantic World c. 1450–1850*. Oxford: Oxford University Press, 2011.

Cardim, Pedro, Tamar Herzog, Ruiz Ibáñez, José Javier, and Gaetano Sabatini. "Polycentric Monarchies: How Did Early Modern Spain and Portugal Achieve and Maintain a Global Hegemony?" In *Polycentric Monarchies: How did Early Modern Spain and Portugal Achieve and Maintain a Global Hegemony?* Edited by Pedro Cardim et al., 3–8. Eastbourne: Sussex Academic Press, 2012.

Chaplin, Joyce E. "The British Atlantic." In Canny and Morgan, *The Oxford Handbook of the Atlantic World c. 1450–1850*, 219–33.

Coclanis, Peter A., ed. *The Atlantic Economy during the Seventeenth and Eighteenth Centuries: Organization, Operation, Practice, and Personnel*. Columbia: University of South Carolina Press, 2005.

———. "Atlantic World or Atlantic/World?" *William and Mary Quarterly* 63, no. 4 (2006): 725–42.

Cohen, Robert. *Jews in Another Environment: Surinam in the Second Half of the Eighteenth Century*. Leiden: Brill, 1991.

Colley, Linda. *The Ordeal of Elizabeth Marsh: A Woman in World History*. New York: Anchor Books, 2008.

Cooper, Frederick. *Colonialism in Question: Theory, Knowledge, History*. Berkeley: University of California Press, 2005.

Cox, Edward L. "The British Caribbean in the Age of Revolution." In *Empire and Nation: The American Revolution in the Atlantic World*. Edited by Eliga H. Gould and Peter S. Onuf, 275–94. Baltimore, MD: Johns Hopkins University Press, 2005.

Craton, Michael. *Testing the Chains: Resistance to Slavery in the British West Indies*. Ithaca, NY: Cornell University Press, 1982.

Crawford, Nicholas. "'In the Wreck of a Master's Fortune': Slave Provisioning and Planter Debt in the British Caribbean." *Slavery & Abolition* 37, no. 2 (2016): 1–22.

Cromwell, Jesse. "Illicit Ideologies: Moral Economies of Venezuelan Smuggling and Autonomy in the Rebellion of Juan Francisco de León, 1749–1751." *The Americas* 74, no. 3 (2017): 267–97.

Da Costa, Emilia V. *Crowns of Glory, Tears of Blood: The Demerara Slave Rebellion of 1823*. New York: Oxford University Press, 1994.

Dalton, Henry G. *The History of British Guiana: Vol. 1.* London: Longman, Green, Brown, and Longmans, 1855.

Daniels, Christine, and Michael V. Kennedy, eds. *Negotiated Empires: Centers and Peripheries in the Americas, 1500–1820.* London: Routledge, 2002.

Diouf, Sylviana A. *Slavery's Exiles: The Story of the American Maroons.* New York: New York University Press, 2014.

Disney, Anthony R. *A History of Portugal and the Portuguese Empire: From Beginnings to 1807.* New York: Cambridge University Press, 2009.

Dragtenstein, Frank. *"De ondraaglijke stoutheid der wegloopers": Marronage en koloniaal beleid in Suriname, 1667–1768.* Utrecht: Centrum voor Latijns-Amerikaanse en Caraïbische Studies; Instituut ter Bevordering van de Surinamistiek, 2002.

Draper, Nicholas. "The Rise of a New Planter Class? Some Countercurrents from British Guiana and Trinidad, 1807–33." *Atlantic Studies* 9, no. 1 (2012): 65–83.

Drayton, Richard. "The Collaboration of Labour: Slaves, Empires, and Globalizations in the Atlantic World, c. 1600–1850." In *Globalization in World History.* Edited by A. G. Hopkins, 98–114. London: Pimlico, 2002.

Drescher, Seymour. *Econocide: British Slavery in the Era of Abolition.* 2nd ed. Chapel Hill: University of North Carolina Press, 2010.

Dubois, Laurent. "The French Atlantic." In Greene and Morgan, *Atlantic History*, 137–61.

Ekama, Kate. "Just Deserters: Runaway Slaves from the VOC Cape, c. 1700–1800." In Van Rossum and Kamp, *Desertion in the Early Modern World*, 160–84.

Elliott, J. H. *Empires of the Atlantic World: Britain and Spain in America, 1492–1830.* New Haven, CT: Yale University Press, 2006.

Eltis, David. "The Traffic in Slaves between the British West Indian Colonies, 1807–1833." *Economic History Review* 25, no. 1 (1972): 55–64.

Emmer, P. C. "Capitalism Mistaken? The Economic Decline of Surinam and the Plantation Loans, 1773–1850: A Rehabilitation." *Itinerario* 20, no. 1 (1996): 11–18.

———. "The Dutch and the Making of the Second Atlantic System." In Emmer, *The Dutch in the Atlantic Economy*, 11–32.

———, ed. *The Dutch in the Atlantic Economy, 1580–1880: Trade, Slavery and Emancipation.* Aldershot: Ashgate, 1998.

———. "'Jesus Christ Was Good but Trade Was Better': An Overview of the Transit Trade of the Dutch Antilles, 1634–1795." In Emmer, *The Dutch in the Atlantic Economy*, , 91–109.

———. *De Nederlandse slavenhandel 1500–1850.* Amsterdam: Arbeiderspers, 2000.

———. "The Rise and Decline of the Dutch Atlantic, 1600–1800." In Oostindie and Roitman, *Dutch Atlantic Connections*, 339–56.

Enthoven, Victor. "'That Abominable Nest of Pirates': St. Eustatius and the North Americans, 1680–1780." *Early American Studies: An Interdisciplinary Journal* 10, no. 2 (2012): 239–301.
———. "Neutrality: Atlantic Shipping in and after the Anglo-Dutch Wars." In Stern and Wennerlind, *Mercantilism Reimagined*, 328–47.
Enthoven, Victor, and Johannes Postma, eds. *Riches from Atlantic Commerce: Dutch Transatlantic Trade and Shipping, 1585–1817*. Leiden: Brill, 2003.
Fatah-Black, Karwan. "Desertion by Sailors, Slaves and Soldiers in the Dutch Atlantic, ca. 1600–1800." In Van Rossum and Kamp, *Desertion in the Early Modern World*, 97–124.
———. "The Patriot Coup d'État in Curaçao, 1796." In Klooster and Oostindie, *Curaçao in the Age of Revolutions, 1795–1800*, 123–40.
———. "Slaves and Sailors on Suriname's Rivers." *Itinerario* 36, no. 3 (2012): 61–82.
———. "Smokkelhandel en slavenhandel in Suriname gedurende de ondergang van de Nederlandse macht op zee, 1780–1795." *Tijdschrift voor Zeegeschiedenis* 32, no. 2 (2013): 38–53.
———. "Suriname and the Atlantic World, 1650–1800." PhD diss., Leiden University and KITLV, 2013.
———. *White Lies and Black Markets: Evading Metropolitan Authority in Colonial Suriname, 1650–1800*. Leiden: Brill, 2015.
Ferry, Robert J. *The Colonial Elite of Early Caracas: Formation & Crisis, 1567–1767*. Berkeley: University of California Press, 1989.
Finucane, Adrian. "Trade and Organization in the Colonial Caribbean." *History Compass* 16, no. 7 (2018): 1–11.
Fritschy, Wantje. *Public Finance of the Dutch Republic in Comparative Perspective: The Viability of an Early Modern Federal State (1570s–1795)* Leiden: Brill, 2017.
Games, Alison. "Atlantic History: Definitions, Challenges, and Opportunities." *American Historical Review* 111, no. 3 (2006): 741–57.
———. "Conclusion: A Dutch Moment in Atlantic Historiography." In Oostindie and Roitman, *Dutch Atlantic Connections*, 357–74.
———. *The Web of Empire: English Cosmopolitans in an Age of Expansion, 1560–1660*. Oxford: Oxford University Press, 2008.
Geggus, David. "Slave Rebellion during the Age of Revolution." In Klooster and Oostindie, *Curaçao in the Age of Revolutions*, 23–56.
———. "Slavery, War, and Revolution in the Wider Caribbean, 1789–1815." In *A Turbulent Time: The French Revolution and the Greater Caribbean*. Edited by David B. Gaspar and David P. Geggus, 1–50. Bloomington: Indiana University Press, 1997.
Gelderblom, Oscar. *Cities of Commerce: The Institutional Foundations of International Trade in the Low Countries, 1250–1650*. Princeton, NJ: Princeton University Press, 2015.

Genovese, Eugene D. *From Rebellion to Revolution: Afro-American Slave Revolts in the Making of the Modern World*. Baton Rouge: Louisiana State University Press, 1979.
Gould, Eliga H. "Entangled Histories, Entangled Worlds: The English-Speaking Atlantic as a Spanish Periphery." *American Historical Review* 112, no. 3 (2007): 764–86.
Grafe, Regina. *Distant Tyranny: Markets, Power, and Backwardness in Spain, 1650–1800*. Princeton, NJ: Princeton University Press, 2012.
———. "On the Spatial Nature of Institutions and the Institutional Nature of Personal Networks in the Spanish Atlantic." *Culture & History Digital Journal* 3, no. 1 (2014): 4–11.
———. "Polycentric States: The Spanish Reigns and the 'Failures' of Mercantilism." In Stern and Wennerlind, *Mercantilism Reimagined*, 241–62.
Grafe, Regina, and Alejandra Irigoin. "A Stakeholder Empire: The Political Economy of Spanish Imperial Rule in America." *Economic History Review* 65, no. 2 (2012): 609–51.
Grahn, Lance R. "Cartagena and Its Hinterland in the Eighteenth Century." In Knight and Liss, *Atlantic Port Cities*, 168–95.
Greene, Jack P. *Negotiated Authorities: Essays in Colonial Political and Constitutional History*. Charlottesville: University of Virginia Press, 1994.
———. "Transatlantic Colonization and the Redefinition of Empire in the Early Modern Era: The British-American Experience." In Daniels and Kennedy, *Negotiated Empires*, 267–82.
Greene, Jack P., and Philip D. Morgan, eds. *Atlantic History: A Critical Appraisal*. Oxford: Oxford University Press, 2009.
Greif, Avner. "Cultural Beliefs and the Organization of Society: A Historical and Theoretical Reflection on Collectivist and Individualist Societies." *Journal of Political Economy* 102, no. 5 (1994): 912–50.
———. "The Maghribi Traders: A Reappraisal?" *Economic History Review* 65, no. 2 (2012): 445–69.
Groesen, Michiel van. *Amsterdam's Atlantic: Print Culture and the Making of Dutch Brazil*. Philadelphia: University of Pennsylvania Press, 2017.
Haefeli, Evan. *New Netherland and the Dutch Origins of American Religious Liberty*. Philadelphia: University of Pennsylvania Press, 2012.
Haggerty, Sheryllynne. *"Merely for Money"? Business Culture in the British Atlantic, 1750–1815*. Liverpool: Liverpool University Press, 2012.
Hall, Neville A. "Maritime Maroons: Grand Marronage." In *Slave Society in the Danish West Indies: St. Thomas, St. John, and St. Croix*. Edited by B. W. Higman, 124–38. Baltimore, MD: Johns Hopkins University Press, 1992.
Halliday, Paul. "Laws' Histories: Pluralisms, Pluralities, Diversity." In Benton and Ross, *Legal Pluralism and Empires*, 261–77.
Hamilton, Douglas J. *Scotland, the Caribbean and the Atlantic World, 1750–1820*. Manchester: Manchester University Press, 2010.

Hancock, David. *Citizens of the World: London Merchants and the Integration of the British Atlantic Community, 1735–1785*. Cambridge: Cambridge University Press, 1995.

———. *Oceans of Wine: Madeira and the Emergence of American Trade and Taste*. New Haven, CT: Yale University Press, 2009.

———. "Organizing Our Thoughts: Global Systems and the Challenge of Writing a More Complex History." *Journal of the Historical Society* 10, no. 3 (2010): 319–35.

———. "Self-Organized Complexity and the Emergence of an Atlantic Market Economy, 1651–1815." In Coclanis, *The Atlantic Economy*, 30–71.

———. "The Triumphs of Mercury: Connection and Control in the Emerging Atlantic Economy." In Bailyn and Denault, *Soundings in Atlantic History*, 112–40.

Hardesty, Jared. *Unfreedom: Slavery and Dependence in Eighteenth-Century Boston*. New York: New York University Press, 2016.

Hart, Marjolein 't. "Mutual Advantages: State Bankers as Brokers between the City of Amsterdam and the Dutch Republic." In *The Political Economy of the Dutch Republic*. Edited by Oscar Gelderblom, 115–42. Farnham: Ashgate, 2009.

Hatfield, April L. *Atlantic Virginia: Intercolonial Relations in the Seventeenth Century*. Philadelphia: University of Pennsylvania Press, 2004.

Heckscher, Eli F. *Mercantilism: Volume One*. Translated by Mendel Shapiro. 2 vols. London: George Allen & Unwin Ltd., 1955.

Hedges, James B. *The Browns of Providence Plantations*. 2 vols. Providence: Brown University Press, [1952] 1968.

Heijer, Henk den. "The Dutch West India Company, 1621–1791." In Enthoven and Postma, *Riches from Atlantic Commerce*, 77–112.

———. *Geschiedenis van de WIC: Opkomst, bloei en ondergang*. Zutphen: Walburg Pers, 2013.

———. "A Public and Private Dutch West India Interest." In Oostindie and Roitman, *Dutch Atlantic Connections*, 159–82.

Herzog, Tamar. *Frontiers of Possession: Spain and Portugal in Europe and the Americas*. Cambridge, MA: Harvard University Press, 2015.

Higman, B. W. *Slave Populations of the British Caribbean 1807–1834*. Baltimore, MD: Johns Hopkins University Press, 1984.

Hoonhout, Bram. "Subprime Plantation Mortgages in Suriname, Essequibo and Demerara, 1750–1800." MA thesis, Leiden University, 2012.

———. "De noodzaak van smokkelhandel in Essequebo en Demerary, 1750–1800." *Tijdschrift voor Zeegeschiedenis* 32, no. 2 (2013): 54–79.

Hoonhout, Bram, and Mareite, Thomas. "Freedom at the Fringes? Slave Flight and Empire-Building in the Early Modern Spanish Borderlands of Essequibo–Venezuela and Louisiana–Texas." *Slavery & Abolition* 40, no. 1 (2018): 1–26.

Horan, Joseph. "The Colonial Famine Plot: Slavery, Free Trade, and Empire in the French Atlantic, 1763–1791." *International Review of Social History*, Supplement S18 (2010): 103–21.

Hovy, Johannes. *Het voorstel van 1751 tot instelling van een beperkt vrijhavenstelsel in de Republiek (propositie tot een gelimiteerd port-franco)*. Groningen: J. B. Wolters, 1966.

Hubbard, Vincent K. *A History of St Kitts: The Sweet Trade*. Oxford: Macmillan, 2002.

Hulsman, L. A. H. C. "Nederlands Amazonia: Handel met indianen tussen 1580 en 1680." PhD diss., University of Amsterdam, 2009.

Hussey, Roland D. *The Caracas Company 1728–1784: A Study in the History of Spanish Monopolistic Trade*. Cambridge, MA: Harvard University Press, 1934.

Hyles, Joshua R. *Guiana and the Shadows of Empire: Colonial and Cultural Negotiations at the Edge of the World*. Lanham, MD: Lexington Books, 2014.

Inikori, J. E. *Africans and the Industrial Revolution in England: A Study in International Trade and Economic Development*. New York: Cambridge University Press, 2002.

Irigoin, Alejandra, and Regina Grafe. "Bargaining for Absolutism: A Spanish Path to Nation-State and Empire Building." *Hispanic American Historical Review* 88, no. 2 (2008): 173–209.

Ishmael, Odeen. *The Guyana Story from the Earliest Times to Independence*. Bloomington, IN: Xlibris, 2013.

Israel, Jonathan I. *Diasporas within a Diaspora: Jews, Crypto-Jew and the World Maritime Empires (1540–1740)*. Leiden: Brill, 2009.

——. *The Dutch Republic: Its Rise, Greatness and Fall, 1477–1806*. Oxford: Clarendon Press, 1998.

——. "The Jews of Dutch America." In *The Jews and the Expansion of Europe to the West, 1450–1800*. Edited by Paolo Barnardini and Norman Fiering, 335–49. New York: Berghahn, 2001.

Jarvis, Michael. *In the Eye of All Trade: Bermuda, Bermudians, and the Maritime Atlantic World, 1680–1783*. Chapel Hill: University of North Carolina Press, 2010.

Jordaan, Han, and Victor Wilson. "The Eighteenth-Century Danish, Dutch and Swedish Free Ports in the Northeastern Caribbean: Continuity and Change." In Oostindie and Roitman, *Dutch Atlantic Connections*, 275–308.

Kamp, Jeanette, and Matthias Van Rossum. "Introduction: Leaving Work across the World." In Van Rossum and Kamp, *Desertion in the Early Modern World*, 3–14.

Karras, Alan L. *Smuggling: Contraband and Corruption in World History*. Lanham, MD: Rowman & Littlefield, 2010.

——. *Sojourners in the Sun: Scottish Migrants in Jamaica and the Chesapeake, 1740–1800*. Ithaca, NY: Cornell University Press, 1992.

Kars, Marjoleine. "'Cleansing the Land': Dutch-Amerindian Cooperation in the Suppression of the 1763 Slave Rebellion in Dutch Guiana." In *Empires and Indigenes: Intercultural Alliance, Imperial Expansion, and Warfare in the Early Modern World*. Edited by Wayne E. Lee, 251–75. New York: New York University Press, 2011.

———. "Dodging Rebellion: Politics and Gender in the Berbice Slave Uprising of 1763." *American Historical Review* 121, no. 1 (2016): 39–69.

———. "Transgressing and Policing Borders: Soldiers, Slave Rebels, and the Early Modern Atlantic." *New West Indian Guide* 83, no. 3–4 (2009): 187–213.

Keuthe, Allan J. "Havana in the Eighteenth Century." In *Atlantic Port Cities: Economy, Culture, and Society in the Atlantic World, 1650–1850*. Edited by Franklin W. Knight and Peggy K. Liss, 13–39. Knoxville: University of Tennessee Press, 1991.

Kissler, Betty J. "Venezuela-Guyana Boundary Dispute: 1899–1966." PhD diss., University of Texas at Austin, 1971.

Klein, Herbert S. *African Slavery in Latin America and the Caribbean*. Oxford: Oxford University Press, 1986.

Klooster, Wim. "Curaçao as a Transit Center to the Spanish Main and the French West Indies." In Oostindie and Roitman, *Dutch Atlantic Connections*, 25–51.

———. *The Dutch Moment: War, Trade, and Settlement in the Seventeenth-Century Atlantic World*. Ithaca, NY: Cornell University Press, 2016.

———. *Illicit Riches: Dutch Trade in the Caribbean, 1648–1795*. Leiden: KITLV, 1998.

———. "Inter-Imperial Smuggling in the Americas, 1600–1800." In Bailyn and Denault, *Soundings in Atlantic History*, 141–80.

———. "An Overview of Dutch Trade with the Americas, 1600–1800." In Enthoven and Postma, *Riches from Atlantic Commerce*, 365–83.

———. "The Rising Expectations of Free and Enslaved Blacks in the Greater Caribbean." In Klooster and Oostindie, *Curaçao in the Age of Revolutions*, 57–74.

Klooster, Wim and Gert Oostindie, eds. *Curaçao in the Age of Revolutions, 1795–1800*. Leiden: KITLV, 2011.

———. *Realm between Empires: The Second Dutch Atlantic, 1680–1815*. Ithaca, NY: Cornell University Press, 2018.

Knight, Franklin W., and Peggy K. Liss, eds. *Atlantic Port Cities: Economy, Culture, and Society in the Atlantic World, 1650–1850*. Knoxville: University of Tennessee Press, 1991.

Koot, Christian J. "Anglo-Dutch Trade in the Chesapeake and the British Caribbean, 1621–1733." In Oostindie and Roitman, *Dutch Atlantic Connections*, 72–99.

———. *Empire at the Periphery: British Colonists, Anglo-Dutch Trade, and the*

Development of the British Atlantic, 1621–1713. New York: New York University Press, 2011.

Koulen, Paul. "Slavenhouders en geldschieters: Nederlandse belangen in Berbice, Demerara en Essequebo, 1815–1819." *Gen.* 21, no. 5 (2015): 46–52.

Kramer, K. "Plantation Development in Berbice from 1753 to 1779: The Shift from Interior to the Coast." *New West Indian Guide* 65, no. 1–2 (1991): 51–65.

Krichtal, Alexey. "Liverpool and the Raw Cotton Trade: A Study of the Port and Its Merchant Community, 1770–1815." MA thesis, Victoria University of Wellington, 2013.

Lamikiz, Xabier. *Trade and Trust in the Eighteenth-Century Atlantic World: Spanish Merchants and their Overseas Networks.* Woodbridge: Boydell Press, 2010.

Landers, Jane. *Atlantic Creoles in the Age of Revolutions.* Cambridge, MA: Harvard University Press, 2010.

Langen, Johan van. "De Britse overname van de Nederlandse koloniën Demerary, Essequebo en Berbice (Guyana) Van economische overvleugeling naar politieke overheersing (1740–1814)." MA thesis, University of Amsterdam, 2003.

Marzagalli, Silvia. "The French Atlantic and the Dutch, Late Seventeenth–Late Eighteenth Century." In Oostindie and Roitman, *Dutch Atlantic Connections*, 103–18.

———. "The French Atlantic in the Seventeenth and Eighteenth Centuries." In Canny and Morgan, *The Oxford Handbook of the Atlantic World c. 1450–1850*, 234–51.

———. "Was Warfare Necessary for the Functioning of Eighteenth-Century Colonial Systems? Some Reflections on the Necessity of Cross-Imperial and Foreign Trade in the French Case." In *Beyond Empires: Global, Self-Organizing, Cross-Imperial Networks, 1500–1800.* Edited by Cátia Antunes and Amélia Polónia, 253–77. Leiden: Brill, 2016.

Matson, Cathy D. *Merchants and Empire: Trading in Colonial New York.* Baltimore, MD: Johns Hopkins University Press, 1998.

McCusker, John J., and Kenneth Morgan, eds. *The Early Modern Atlantic Economy.* Cambridge: Cambridge University Press, 2000.

McGowan, Winston F. "The French Revolutionary Period in Demerara-Essequibo, 1793–1802." *History Gazette* 55 (1993): 2–18.

McKinley, Michael P. *Pre-Revolutionary Caracas: Politics, Economy, and Society 1777–1811.* Cambridge: Cambridge University Press, 1985.

Meilink-Roelofsz, M. A. P. "Archivalia betreffende de voormalige Nederlandse koloniën Essequebo, Demerary en Berbice in het Public Record Office te London." *Nieuwe West-Indische Gids* 41, no. 1 (1961): 127–40.

Menard, Russell R. "Law, Credit, the Supply of Labour, and the Organization of Sugar Production in the Colonial Greater Caribbean: A Comparison of Brazil and Barbados in the Seventeenth Century." In McCusker and Morgan, *The Early Modern Atlantic Economy*, 154–62.

———. *Sweet Negotiations: Sugar, Slavery, and Plantation Agriculture in Early Barbados*. Charlottesville: University of Virginia Press, 2006.

Meulen, W. W. van der. "Beschrijving van eenige Westindische plantage leeningen. Bijdrage tot de kennis der geldbelegging in de achttiende eeuw." *Bijdragen en Mededeelingen van het Historisch Genootschap* 25 (1904): 490–580.

Meuwese, Mark. *Brothers in Arms, Partners in Trade: Dutch-Indigenous Alliances in the Atlantic World, 1595–1674*. Leiden: Brill, 2012.

———. "The Opportunities and Limits of Ethnic Soldiering: The Tupis and the Dutch-Portuguese Struggle for the Southern Atlantic, 1630–1657." In Lee, *Empires and Indigenes*, 193–220.

Mokyr, Joel. *The Enlightened Economy: An Economic History of Britain, 1700–1850*. New Haven, CT: Yale University Press, 2009.

Morgan, Kenneth. "Mercantilism and the British Empire, 1688–1815." In *The Political Economy of British Historical Experience, 1688–1914*. Edited by Donald Winch and Patrick O'Brien, 165–91. Oxford: Published for the British Academy by Oxford University Press, 2002.

———. "Anglo-Dutch Economic Relations in the Atlantic World, 1688–1783." In Oostindie and Roitman, *Dutch Atlantic Connections*, 119–38.

Morgan, Philip D. "The Black Experience in the British Empire, 1680–1810." In *Black Experience and the Empire*. Edited by Philip D. Morgan and Sean Hawkins, 86–110. New York: Oxford University Press, 2004.

Morgan, Philip D., and Andrew J. O'Shaughnessy. "Arming Slaves in the American Revolution." In *Arming Slaves: From Classical Times to the Modern Age*. Edited by Christopher L. Brown and Philip D. Morgan, 180–208. New Haven, CT: Yale University Press, 2006.

Moutoukias, Zacharias. "Power, Corruption, and Commerce: The Making of the Local Administrative Structure in Seventeenth-Century Buenos Aires." *Hispanic American Historical Review* 68, no. 4 (1988): 771–801.

Mulcahy, Matthew. *Hubs of Empire: The Southeastern Lowcountry and British Caribbean*. Baltimore, MD: Johns Hopkins University Press, 2014.

Mulich, Jeppe. "Microregionalism and Intercolonial Relations: The Case of the Danish West Indies, 1730–1830." *Journal of Global History* 8, no. 1 (2013): 72–94.

Mulroy, Kevin. *Freedom on the Border: The Seminole Maroons in Florida, the Indian Territory, Coahuila, and Texas*. Lubbock: Texas Tech University Press, 1993.

Neal, Larry. *The Rise of Financial Capitalism: International Capital Markets in the Age of Reason*. New York: Cambridge University Press, 1990.

Netscher, P. M. *History of the Colonies Essequebo, Demerary & Berbice. From the Dutch Establishment to the Present Day*. Georgetown, Guyana: Daily Chronicle, 1929. Originally published 1888, translated by W. E. Roth.

Nierstrasz, Chris. *In the Shadow of the Company: The Dutch East India Company and its Servants in the Period of Its Decline (1740–1796)*. Leiden: Brill, 2012.

———. *Rivalry for Trade in Tea and Textiles: The English and Dutch East India Companies (1700–1800)*. Houndmills, Basingstoke: Palgrave Macmillan, 2015.

North, Douglass C. "Institutions." *Journal of Economic Perspectives* 5, no. 1 (1991): 97–112.

———. "Institutions, Transaction Costs, and the Rise of Merchant Empires." In Tracy, *The Political Economy of Merchant Empires*, 22–40.

———. *Understanding the Process of Economic Change*. Princeton, NJ: Princeton University Press, 2005.

North, Douglass C., and Barry R. Weingast. "Constitutions and Commitment: The Evolution of Institutional Governing Public Choice in Seventeenth-Century England." *Journal of Economic History* 49, no. 4 (1989): 803–32.

O'Malley, Gregory E. *Final Passages: The Intercolonial Slave Trade of British America, 1619–1807*. Chapel Hill: University of North Carolina Press, 2016.

Oest, E.W. van der. "The Forgotten Colonies of Essequibo and Demerara, 1700–1814." In Enthoven and Postma, *Riches from Atlantic Commerce*, 323–61.

Ogborn, Miles. *Global Lives: Britain and the World, 1550–1800*. Cambridge: Cambridge University Press, 2008.

Oostindie, Gert. "'British Capital, Industry and Perseverance' versus Dutch 'Old School'? The Dutch Atlantic and the Takeover of Berbice, Demerara and Essequibo, 1750–1815." *BMGN—Low Countries Historical Review* 127, no. 4 (2012): 28–55.

———. "The Economics of Slavery." In *Economic and Social History in the Netherlands*. Vol. 5. Edited by Peter Boomgaard et. al., 1–24. Amsterdam: Nederlands Economisch-Historisch Archief, 1993.

———. *Roosenburg en Mon Bijou: Twee Surinaamse plantages, 1720–1870*. Dordrecht: Foris Publications, 1989.

———. "Slavenleven." In *Ik ben eigendom van—: Slavenhandel en plantageleven*. Edited by Bea Brommer, 95–113. Wijk en Aalburg: Pictures Publishers, 1993.

———. "Slave Resistance, Colour Lines, and the Impact of the French and Haitian Revolutions in Curaçao." In Klooster and Oostindie, *Curaçao in the Age of Revolutions*, 1–22.

———. "Voltaire, Stedman and Suriname Slavery." *Slavery & Abolition* 14, no. 2 (1993): 1–34.

Oostindie, Gert, and Jessica V. Roitman, eds. *Dutch Atlantic Connections, 1680–1800: Linking Empires, Bridging Borders*. Leiden: Brill, 2014.

———. "Introduction." In Oostindie and Roitman, *Dutch Atlantic Connections*, 1–21.

Oostindie, Gert, and Alex van Stipriaan. "Slavery and Slave Cultures in a Hydraulic Society: Suriname." In *Slavery and Slave Cultures in the Ameri-*

cas. Edited by Stephan Palmié, 78–99. Knoxville: University of Tennessee Press, 1996.

Ormrod, David. *The Rise of Commercial Empires: England and the Netherlands in the Age of Mercantilism, 1650–1770*. Cambridge: Cambridge University Press, 2008.

O'Shaughnessy, Andrew J. *An Empire Divided: The American Revolution and the British Caribbean*. Philadelphia: University of Pennsylvania Press, 2000.

Owensby, Brian P. "Between Justice and Economics: 'Indians' and Reformism in Eighteenth-Century Spanish Imperial Thought." In Benton and Ross, *Legal Pluralism and Empires*, 143–69.

Paesie, Ruud. "Van monopolie naar vrijhandel: De illegale slavenhandel tijdens het octrooi van de Tweede West-Indische Compagnie, 1674–1730." *Oso: Tijdschrift voor Surinamistiek en het Caraïbisch gebied* 28, no. 2 (2009): 103–21.

Pares, Richard. *Merchants and Planters*. New York: Cambridge University Press, 1960.

Pargas, Damian A. "Promised Lands: Seeking Freedom in the Age of American Slavery." Inaugural Lecture, Leiden University, 2018.

Parker, Matthew. *The Sugar Barons: Family, Corruption, Empire, and War in the West Indies*. New York: Walker & Co., 2011.

Paton, Diana. *The Cultural Politics of Obeah: Religion, Colonialism and Modernity in the Caribbean World*. Cambridge: Cambridge University Press, 2015.

Pearce, Adrian J. "British Trade with the Spanish Colonies, 1788–1795." *Bulletin of Latin American Research* 20, no. 2 (2001): 233–60.

Pearsall, Sarah M. S. *Atlantic Families: Lives and Letters in the Later Eighteenth Century*. Oxford: Oxford University Press, 2008.

Pérez, Berta E. "The Journey to Freedom: Maroon Forebears in Southern Venezuela." *Ethnohistory* 47, 3–4 (2000): 611–34.

Pérotin-Dumon, Anne. "Cabotage, Contraband, and Corsairs: The Port Cities of Guadeloupe and Their Inhabitants, 1650–1800." In Knight and Liss, *Atlantic Port Cities*, 58–86.

Pinckard, George. *Notes on the West-Indies: Vol. 1*. 1st ed. 2 vols. London: Messrs. Baldwin, Cradock, and Joy, 1816.

Pollak-Eltz, Angelina. "La esclavitud en Venezuela." In *Influencias africanas en las culturas tradicionales de los países andinos: Il encuentro para la promoción y difusión del patrimonio folclórico de los países andinos*, 29–35. Santa Ana de Coro: Ministerio de Educación, Cultura y Deportes, 2001.

Postma, Johannes. "Breaching the Mercantile Barriers of the Dutch Colonial Empire: North American Trade with Surinam during the Eighteenth Century." In *Merchant Organization and Maritime Trade in the North Atlantic, 1660–1815*. Edited by Olaf U. Janzen, 107–31. St. John's, Newfoundland: International Maritime Economic History Association, 1998.

———. "The Dispersal of African Slaves in the West by Dutch Slave Traders, 1630–1803." In *The Atlantic Slave Trade: Effects on Economies, Societies, and*

Peoples in Africa, the Americas, and Europe. Edited by Joseph E. Inikori and Stanley L. Engerman, 283–99. Durham, NC: Duke University Press, 1992.

——. *The Dutch in the Atlantic Slave Trade*. Cambridge: Cambridge University Press, 1990.

Prado, Fabricio. "The Fringes of Empires: Recent Scholarship on Colonial Frontiers and Borderlands in Latin America." *History Compass* 10, no. 4 (2012): 318–33.

Pressly, Paul M. *On the Rim of the Caribbean: Colonial Georgia and the British Atlantic World*. Athens: University of Georgia Press, 2013.

Price, Jacob M. "Credit in the Slave Trade and Plantation Economies." In *Slavery and the Rise of the Atlantic System*. Edited by Barbara L. Solow, 293–339. Cambridge: Cambridge University Press, 1991.

Price, Richard. *Maroon Societies: Rebel Slave Communities in the Americas*. 3rd ed. Baltimore, MD: Johns Hopkins University Press, 1996.

Price, Richard, and Sally Price. *Les Marrons*. Châteauneuf-le-Rouge: Vents d'ailleurs, 2003.

Riello, Giorgio. *Cotton: The Fabric That Made the Modern World*. New York: Cambridge University Press, 2013.

Roberts, Justin. "Uncertain Business: A Case Study of Barbadian Plantation Management, 1770–93." *Slavery & Abolition* 32, no. 2 (2011): 247–68.

Rodway, James. *History of British Guiana: From the Year 1668 to the Present Time. Volume 1: 1668–1781*. 2 vols. Georgetown, Demerara: J. Thomson, 1891.

——. *History of British Guiana: From the Year 1668 to the Present Time. Volume 2: 1782–1833*. 2 vols. Georgetown, Guyana: J. Thomson, 1893.

Ross, Richard J., and Philip J. Stern. "Reconstructing Early Modern Notions of Legal Pluralism." In Benton and Ross, *Legal Pluralism and Empires*, 109–41.

Rossum, Matthias van. "'Working for the Devil': Desertion in the Eurasian Empire of the VOC." In Van Rossum and Kamp, *Desertion in the Early Modern World*, 127–58.

Rossum, Matthias van, and Jeanette Kamp, eds. *Desertion in the Early Modern World: A Comparative History*. London: Bloomsbury Press, 2016.

Rothschild, Emma. *The Inner Life of Empires: An Eighteenth-Century History*. Princeton, NJ: Princeton University Press, 2011.

Rupert, Linda M. *Creolization and Contraband: Curaçao in the Early Modern Atlantic World*. Athens: University of Georgia Press, 2012.

——. "Marronage, Manumission and Maritime Trade in the Early Modern Caribbean." *Slavery & Abolition* 30, no. 3 (2009): 361–82.

——. "'Seeking the Water of Baptism': Fugitive Slaves and Imperial Jurisdiction in the Early Modern Caribbean." In Benton and Ross, *Legal Pluralism and Empires*, 199–231.

Rushforth, Brett. *Bonds of Alliance: Indigenous and Atlantic Slaveries in New France*. Chapel Hill: University of North Carolina Press, 2012.

Russell-Wood, A. J. R. "Center and Peripheries in the Luso-Brazilian World, 1500–1808." In Daniels and Kennedy, *Negotiated Empires*, 105–42.

Ryden, David. *West Indian Slavery and British Abolition, 1783–1807*. Cambridge: Cambridge University Press, 2009.

Salvucci, Linda K. "Supply, Demand, and the Making of a Market: Philadelphia and Havana at the Beginning of the Nineteenth Century." In Knight and Liss, *Atlantic Port Cities*, 40–57.

Schaffer, Simon, Lissa Roberts, Kapil Raj, and James Delbourgo. "Introduction." In Schaffer, Roberts, Raj, and Delbourgo, *The Brokered World*, ix–xxxviii.

———, eds. *The Brokered World: Go-Betweens and Global Intelligence, 1770–1820*. Sagamore Beach, MA: Science History Publications, 2009.

Schalkwijk, J. M. W. *The Colonial State in the Caribbean: Structural Analysis and Changing Elite Networks in Suriname, 1650–1920*. The Hague: Amrit, 2011.

Schmitt, Casey S. "Virtue in Corruption: Privateers, Smugglers, and the Shape of Empire in the Eighteenth-Century Caribbean." *Early American Studies: An Interdisciplinary Journal* 13, no. 1 (2015): 80–110.

Schnurmann, Claudia. "A Scotsman in Hamburg: John Parish and His Commercial Contribution to the American War of Independence, 1776–1783." In *Small Is Beautiful? Interlopers and Smaller Trading Nations in the Pre-Industrial Period: Proceedings of the XVth World Economic History Congress in Utrecht (Netherlands), 2009*. Edited by Markus A. Denzel, Jan de Vries and Philipp R. Rössner, 157–76. Stuttgart: Franz Steiner Verlag, 2011.

Schrikker, Alicia. *Dutch and British Colonial Intervention in Sri Lanka, 1780–1815: Expansion and Reform*. Leiden: Brill, 2007.

Schult, Chris. "Een noodzakelijk bondgenootschap: De rol van de indianen in de kolonies Essequibo en Demerary, 1770–1800." MA thesis, Leiden University, 2014.

Schutte, G. J. *De Nederlandse patriotten en de koloniën: Een onderzoek naar hun denkbeelden en optreden, 1770–1800*. Groningen: H. D. Tjeenk Willink, 1974.

Shahabuddeen, Mohammed. *From Plantocracy to Nationalisation: A Profile of Sugar in Guyana*. Georgetown: University of Guyana, 1984.

Sheridan, Richard B. "The Rise of a Colonial Gentry: A Case Study of Antigua, 1730–1775." *Economic History Review* 13, no. 3 (1961): 342–57.

Smidt, J. Th. d., T. van der Lee, and H. J. M. van Dapperen. *Plakaatboek Guyana (Guyana Ordinance Book), 1670–1816*. The Hague: Huygens Instituut for Netherlands History, 2014.

Smith, S. D. "Gedney Clarke of Salem and Barbados: Transatlantic Super-Merchant." *New England Quarterly* 76, no. 4 (2003): 499–549.

———. *Slavery, Family, and Gentry Capitalism in the British Atlantic: The World of the Lascelles, 1648–1834*. Cambridge: Cambridge University Press, 2006.

Solow, Barbara L., and Stanley L. Engerman, eds. *British Capitalism and Carib-*

bean Slavery: The Legacy of Eric Williams*. Cambridge: Cambridge University Press, 2004.

Souza, George Bryan. *The Survival of Empire: Portuguese Trade and Society in China and the South China Sea, 1630–1757*. Cambridge: Cambridge University Press, 1986.

Spruyt, Hendrik. *The Sovereign State and Its Competitors: An Analysis of Systems Change*. Princeton, NJ: Princeton University Press, 1994.

Steele, Beverley A. *Grenada: A History of Its People*. Oxford: Macmillan Caribbean, 2003.

Stern, Philip J. *The Company-State: Corporate Sovereignty and the Early Modern Foundations of the British Empire in India*. New York: Oxford University Press, 2011.

Stern, Philip J., and Carl Wennerlind. "Introduction." In Stern and Wennerlind, *Mercantilism Reimagined*, 3–22.

———, eds. *Mercantilism Reimagined: Political Economy in Early Modern Britain and its Empire*. New York: Oxford University Press, 2014.

Stipriaan, Alex van. *Surinaams contrast: Roofbouw en overleven in een Caraïbische plantagekolonie, 1750–1863*. Leiden: KITLV, 1993.

———. "Debunking Debts. Image and Reality of a Colonial Crisis: Suriname at the End of the 18th Century." *Itinerario* 19, no. 1 (1995): 69–85.

Strayer, Joseph R. *On the Medieval Origins of the Modern State*. Princeton, NJ: Princeton University Press, [1973] 2005.

Studnicki-Gizbert, Daviken. *A Nation upon the Ocean Sea. Portugal's Atlantic Diaspora and the Crisis of the Spanish Empire, 1492–1640*. Oxford: Oxford University Press, 2007.

Subrahmanyam, Sanjay. *Improvising Empire: Portuguese Trade and Settlement in the Bay of Bengal, 1500–1700*. Delhi: Oxford University Press, 1990.

———. "Between a Rock and a Hard Place: Some Afterthoughts." In Schaffer et al., *The Brokered World*, 429–40.

Sturm-Lind, Lisa. *Actors of Globalization: New York Merchants in Global Trade, 1784–1812*. Leiden: Brill, 2018.

Temin, Peter, and Hans-Joachim Voth. "Credit Rationing and Crowding Out during the Industrial Revolution: Evidence from Hoare's Bank, 1702–1862." *Explorations in Economic History* 42, no. 3 (2005): 325–48.

———. "Hoare's Bank in the Eighteenth Century." In *The Birth of Modern Europe: Culture and Economy, 1400–1800. Essays in Honor of Jan de Vries*. Edited by Laura Cruz and Joel Mokyr, 81–108. Leiden: Brill, 2010.

Thompson, Alvin O. *Colonialism and Underdevelopment in Guyana: 1580–1803*. Bridgetown: Carib Research & Publications, 1987.

———. *Maroons of Guyana: Problems of Slave Desertion in Guyana, c. 1750–1814*. Georgetown, Guyana: Free Press, 1999.

Thompson, Mark L. *The Contest for the Delaware Valley: Allegiance, Identity,*

and Empire in the Seventeenth Century. Baton Rouge: Louisiana State University Press, 2013.
Tracy, James D., ed. *The Political Economy of Merchant Empires*. Cambridge: Cambridge University Press, 1991.
Trivellato, Francesca. *The Familiarity of Strangers: The Sephardic Diaspora, Livorno, and Cross-Cultural Trade in the Early Modern Period*. New Haven, CT: Yale University Press, 2009.
Trivellato, Francesca, Leor Halevi, and Cátia Antunes, eds. *Religion and Trade: Cross-Cultural Exchanges in World History, 1000-1900*. New York: Oxford University Press, 2014.
Truxes, Thomas M. *Defying Empire: Trading with the Enemy in Colonial New York*. New Haven, CT: Yale University Press, 2008.
Turner, Frederick J. "The Significance of the Frontier in American History." In Weber and Rausch, *Where Cultures Meet*, 1-18.
Turner Bushnell, Amy, and Jack P. Greene. "Peripheries, Centers, and the Construction of Early Modern American Empires. An Introduction." In Daniels and Kennedy, *Negotiated Empires*, 1-14.
Voort, J. P. van de. *De Westindische plantages van 1720 tot 1795: Financiën en handel*. Eindhoven: Drukkerij de Witte, 1973.
Vries, Jan de. "Dutch Atlantic Economies." In Coclanis, *The Atlantic Economy*, 1-29.
Vries, Jan de, and Ad Van der Woude. *The First Modern Economy: Success, Failure, and Perseverance of the Dutch Economy; 1500—1815*. Cambridge: Cambridge University Press, 1997.
Webber, A. R. F., and Harry P. Christiani. *Centenary History and Handbook of British Guiana*. Georgetown, Guyana: The Argosy Company, 1931.
Weber, David J., and Jane M. Rausch. "Introduction." In Weber and Rausch, *Where Cultures Meet*, xii-xli.
———, eds. *Where Cultures Meet: Frontiers in Latin American History*. Wilmington, DE: SR Books, 1994.
Weststeijn, Arthur. "Dutch Brazil and the Making of Free Trade Ideology." In *The Legacy of Dutch Brazil*. Edited by Michiel van Groesen, 187-204. New York: Cambridge University Press, 2014.
White, Richard. *The Middle Ground: Indians, Empires, and Republics in the Great Lakes Region, 1650-1815*. 2nd ed. Cambridge: Cambridge University Press, [1991] 2011.
Whitehead, Neil L. *Lords of the Tiger Spirit: A History of the Caribs in Colonial Venezuela and Guyana, 1498-1820*. Dordrecht: Foris Publications, 1988.
Williams, Eric E. *Capitalism and Slavery*. Chapel Hill: University of North Carolina Press, 1994. Originally published 1944.
Worden, Nigel, and Gerald Groenewald. *Trials of Slavery: Selected Documents Concerning Slaves from the Criminal Records of the Council of Justice at the*

Cape of Good Hope, 1705–1794. Cape Town: Van Riebeeck Society for the Publication of South African Historical Documents, 2005.

Yeager, Timothy J. "Encomienda or Slavery? The Spanish Crown's Choice of Labor Organization in Sixteenth-Century Spanish American." *Journal of Economic History* 55, no. 4 (1995): 842–59.

Zahedieh, Nuala. *The Capital and the Colonies: London and the Atlantic Economy, 1660–1700*. Cambridge: Cambridge University Press, 2010.

———. "Economy." In Armitage and Braddick, *The British Atlantic World, 1500–1800*, 51–68.

———. "Making Mercantilism Work: London Merchants and Atlantic Trade in the Seventeenth Century." *Transactions of the Royal Historical Society* 9 (1999): 143–58.

Zanden, Jan Luiten van, and Arthur van Riel. *Nederland 1780–1914: Staat, instituties en economische ontwikkeling*. Amsterdam: Balans, 2000.

Index

Agents (mortgage funds), 66, 144, 150, 152, 186, 191
Akawaio, 22, 29, 36, 100, 102, 169, 191
Albinus, Bernard, 61, 64, 144, 212n67, 243n112
American (US), 58, 78–80, 155, 163, 175; colonists, 2, 154, 157, 178; traders, 11, 34, 113–18, 123–24, 126, 135, 163, 173–74, 179, 191
Amerindians, 13, 24, 39–41, 93; abuse of, 36, 39–40; as allies 3, 11, 15, 34, 98, 100–102, 105–10, 191; destroying maroon settlements, 13, 77, 92, 108, 191; enslavement, 21, 26, 28–30, 36, 40–42, 87–88; guns for, 38–39, 106, 109, 195; in missionary villages, 14, 21, 25–27, 34, 88, 191; on plantations, 29, 88, 97; rewards for, 37–42, 107, 109; trade with, 14, 22, 34, 35–36. *See also* Akawaio; Arawak; Carib; Warao
Amsterdam, 9–10, 52, 115, 121, 139–40, 155, 170, 174, 178; rivalry with Zealand, 10, 16, 45, 47–49, 52, 115, 140, 147, 170
Anarchy, 45, 64–65, 68, 73, 190
Anna Catharina (plantation), 97, 149
Annatto, 28–29, 31, 35
Antigua, 2, 78, 119, 121, 131–32, 168, 171
Arawak, 22, 28–29, 33, 36, 41, 102, 169, 191
Arinda River, 29, 35–36

Aristodemus, 59; *Brieven*, 66
Auction, 50, 87, 101, 127–29, 136–37, 146–49, 151, 153, 164

Barbados, 2, 9, 16, 69, 77–78, 118–19, 127, 130–31, 137–38, 150, 162, 168–70, 178, 180
Barrell, Theodore, 162, 165, 172, 174, 176–81, 187, 192
Basden, Henry, 126–27
Beaujon, Anthony, 70–71, 167
Belvedere (plantation), 126
Berbice, 2–4, 93–94, 97, 100, 107, 109, 130, 144, 169, 187
Bermingham, Edward Martin, 98
Black Corps, 108, 223n150
Boddaert, Kornelis van den Helm, 140, 142, 144, 156–57
Bolingbroke, Henry, 125, 154, 166
Bomba, 74–75, 97, 101–3
Boode, Johann, 98, 101–2
Borderland, 3–4, 11, 15, 19–43, 85, 88, 91, 191; dispute between Britain and Venezuela, 14, 19–20
Borsselen Island, 6, 55
Boston, 120, 125, 152, 162–63, 174, 176, 179–81, 184
Bourda, Joseph, 63, 145
British, 11, 39–42, 77, 112–13, 137–39, 152, 181–84; commerce, 118, 131, 157–58,

268 / INDEX

185, 190; credit, 77 137–38, 153, 156, 176, 183–84, 186, 192; Guiana, 2, 19–20, 153; planters, 1–2, 17, 61, 65, 68–69, 72, 114, 129, 134, 136–37, 145, 153–57, 162, 166–67, 171–73, 185, 197n2; slave traders, 2, 9, 131, 146, 154, 167; takeover in 1781, 53–54, 120, 166–67; takeover in 1796, 1–2, 15, 28, 45, 69–72, 80, 126, 167, 179, 183; takeover in 1803, 2, 39–40, 45, 72, 126, 129; takeover in 1814, 2, 19, 45. *See also* Smuggling
By-laws, 10, 15, 63, 75, 81, 190

Callaert, Pieter, 75–76, 96–98, 101, 142, 147, 149, 164
Capuchins, 24–27, 32, 87, 193–94
Caribs, 22, 25–28, 34, 38, 40, 85, 88, 94, 191; allies, 15, 22, 37, 88, 90–91, 100, 102, 110, 169; slave traders, 15, 26, 28–30, 36, 40–42, 87–88
Cartel, 35, 86–87, 90
Catholicism, 15, 34, 87, 94
Changuion, Daniel, 140, 142, 144–45, 185
Changuion, Francois, Jr., 61, 144, 149, 213n86
Clarke, Gedney, Jr., 153–54, 162, 168–71, 173, 187
Clarke, Gedney, Sr., 162–63, 166, 168–70, 181, 187
Coffee, 1, 78, 110–11, 120, 139, 155; cultivation, 78, 155; smuggling, 16, 119–24, 174
Contraband. *See* Smuggling
Convict labour, 52–53, 95, 101, 104
Council of Colonies, 68
Council of Justice, 10, 49, 57, 62, 66, 68, 149–50, 161, 166
Council of Policy, 10, 15, 40, 49–50, 57, 60, 66–68, 70, 165–66, 172, 190; attempts to overthrow, 43–45; civil councillors, 43, 45, 49–50, 57, 60–62, 67–68; decisions, 80–82, 122, 130, 148, 151, 164, 174
Cotton, 1, 28–29, 78, 91, 110–11, 118, 155; cultivation, 78–79, 87, 155–56, 178, 184; smuggling, 9, 16, 118–19, 122, 174, 183
Credit, 16–17, 48, 65, 97, 128–29, 136, 139–40, 151, 156. *See also* British; Plantation mortgages
Creolization, 78–79
Croydon, William, 162, 166–67, 171–73, 177, 187, 192
Cuba, 54, 77, 79

Cuche, J.P., 65
Cuming, Thomas, 65, 72, 145, 162, 177, 185–87
Curaçao, 9, 12, 59, 104–5, 112–13, 130, 134, 191
Cuyuni River, 4, 6, 22, 26, 30–32, 35, 86, 88, 91

Debt. *See* Credit; Default; Plantation mortgages
Default, 115, 136–37, 141, 144–45, 153, 161, 187, 230n12
Demography, 78–79, 131–32
Desertion: governor, 15, 70, 105–6; soldiers, 11, 76, 78, 90, 93–95. *See also* Runaways
Dominica, 77, 85, 119, 121
Drunkenness, 38, 42, 45, 95, 125, 164, 179, 233
Dutch Moment, 12, 112
Dutch Republic, 3–4, 11–12, 42, 47, 54, 57–60, 64, 66–70, 72, 81, 93, 97, 105, 111, 113–14, 119–21, 129, 134–35, 145, 155, 167, 169, 172, 187, 191–92

Electors College, 66, 68, 166
Elmina, 9
Espinasse, Jean L', 60–68
Essequeebsche kwestie. *See* Amsterdam, rivalry with Zealand
Eustatius. *See* St. Eustatius

Factions, 15, 45, 58, 65–66, 69–71, 105, 167, 170
Fines, 30, 61, 81, 106, 122, 127, 164
Fiscal, 10, 66, 68, 70, 83, 123–26, 128; position of, 10, 50, 57, 62
Fourth Anglo-Dutch War, 6, 53, 57–58, 122
Forts, 6, 9, 93, 95, 102, 107, 146, 190
Fourth Anglo-Dutch War, 6, 53, 58, 120
Franciscans, 24, 26–27
Free people of color, 80, 106
French 25, 95, 113, 133; factions, 70–71; Guiana, 71, 105; mercenaries, 93–95; occupation in 1782, 2, 6, 45, 53–56, 63, 91, 120, 166–67, 184; planters, 61, 65, 68, 157; Revolutionary Wars, 69–71, 104–5, 175, 186
Friendship (plantations), 171–73, 178

Garden of Eden (plantation), 185–87
Georgetown, 6
Gordon, Daniel, 182
Greene, Gardiner, 162, 173–77, 180–81
Greenfield (plantation), 175

Grenada, 71, 77, 104, 119, 134, 138, 170, 181–84
Grovestins, Willem August Sirtema, baron of, 68–70, 129, 161

Haarlem (plantation), 106–7
Hartsinck, Maurits Balthasar, 43–44, 57, 60–61, 64, 124, 212n67
Hecke, Christopher Johan, 61, 98, 212n64
Heyden, Stephanus Gerardus van der, 100, 102
Heyden, Daniel van der, 102, 107, 109
Hooft, Pieter Cornelis, 74–75, 96–97, 110, 149–51
Hubbard, John, 162, 173–77, 180–81

Illegal trade. See Smuggling
Intra-American network, 16, 115–17, 120–21, 173, 190, 192
Improvisation, 3, 10, 15, 67, 70–71, 73, 76, 148–51, 157, 181, 188–89
Insurgencies. See Revolts
Institutions, 9, 15, 49–52, 72–73, 189–90
Investors. See Plantation mortgages

Jacob (bomba), 74–75, 96–98
Jesuits, 24–27
Jews, 165

Ketty (plantation), 185–86
Kyk-over-al, fort, 6, 29, 31

Legal framework, 10, 16, 62–63, 66, 150–51, 161
London, 2, 14, 70–71, 126, 137, 154–55, 173, 176, 179–80
Loo, 't (plantation), 153, 181

Maddelon (enslaved woman), 74–76, 96–97
Mainstay (plantation), 175–75
Manumission, 80, 85
Marronage, 13, 15, 34, 77, 83–86, 91–93, 96, 105, 109–10, 140, 191–92; during uprisings, 76, 93, 102, 106–8, 110, 169
Martinique, 54, 70, 77, 118, 120–21, 167
Mazaruni River, 6, 22, 29–30, 32, 100
McInroy, James, 182–84
Meertens, Anthony, 66, 123–26, 128, 134, 213n87
Mellet, Major de, 107, 109
Mercantilism, 4, 11–12, 64, 111–15, 120, 126, 129, 134, 138, 190–91

Merchant-banker, 115, 138, 156, 179
Middleburgh, 47, 140, 142–43
Middleburgse Commercie Compagnie (MCC), 127–28
Militia, 35, 61, 98, 102, 106
Molasses, 32, 111, 114, 120, 124, 169, 191
Moral economy of smuggling, 11, 190
Mortgages. See Plantation mortgages
Moruka, 27, 35, 90–91, 95

Native Americans. See Amerindians
Negotiaties. See Plantation mortgages
Negotiation, 45–46, 73
New York, 118, 120

Oath of allegiance, 54, 166
Obeah, 74, 101
Occupation. See British; French
Orangists, 58, 66–70
Orinoco, 19–26, 28–34, 76, 86, 90–91, 93–95, 117
Outposts, 22, 26–27 29, 35–38, 88, 90, 93–95

Parker, Charles Stewart, 182–85
Patriots, 58–59, 66–68, 70
Petitions, 44–45, 61–66, 70, 128–29, 167–68, 172
Pieterse, Jacobus, 100, 102, 106
Plantation, 81–84, 88, 92–93, 100, 106, 115, 169, 174, 179; location, 4, 6, 9, 65, 74, 99, 103, 122–23, 155,158–60, 177, 190; number, 2–3, 48, 50, 144, 152–54, 157; ownership, 9–10, 17, 49, 90, 98, 100, 102, 130, 154, 168–69, 171–78, 180, 182, 184–88, 192; produce, 11, 16, 28, 37, 59–60, 111, 123–24, 156, 175; relation with water, 4,6, 36, 78, 107; scale, 154; sector/complex, 13, 16, 22,32–34, 42, 47–49, 61, 73, 76–80, 83–84, 93, 95–96, 103, 105, 110, 112–13, 134, 137–39, 147, 192; society, 61, 163, 190. See also Revolts
Plantation mortgages, 4, 16, 100, 115, 128, 135–53, 156–57, 161, 169, 173, 178, 183, 185–87, 192
Polder, 4, 78
Postholder, 22, 35–40, 90, 94–95
Princenhof (plantation), 100
Priseur, 139, 144–45
Proclamations. See By-laws
Provisioning. See Trade
Punishments, 75, 81–82, 95, 100–101, 104, 109

Rebellions. *See* Revolts
Religion, 13, 94, 163–64, 166; Catholicism, 15, 34, 87, 94; religious sanctuary, 4, 15, 22, 34, 83, 87, 191
Revolts, 15, 71, 85, 96, 104–5, 110, 169; of 1772, 74, 96–101; of 1789, 96, 101–4; of 1795, 96, 104–9
Robertson, George, 182, 184–85
Robertson, Parker, McInroy and Sandbach (firm), 162–63, 182–85
Rum, 32, 37, 45, 52 60, 91, 145, 168; export, 119–20, 124, 135, 169, 174
Runaways, 3–4, 13, 15, 21–22, 26–27, 32, 34–37, 39, 42, 74, 76, 80, 83–95, 109, 191, 205n58

Santheuvel, Bartholomeus van den, 61, 64, 141–43, 157
Sandbach, Samuel, 181–82, 184
Saratoga (plantation), 174–75
Schuylenburg, Paul van, 52, 167
Scots, 162–63, 181–86
Self-organisation, 17, 72, 125
Seven Years' War, 12, 33, 77, 137
Slave testimonies, 74–76
Slave refugees. *See* Runaways
Slave trade: 58, 111, 169, 189; auctions, 127–28, 147; illegal, 2–3, 9, 11, 16, 60, 72 78, 119, 126–32, 145–46, 169–71, 184, 190; legal, 9, 16, 59–60, 114, 127, 132, 135, 184; payment, 147–48; reform of, 59–60, 126, 129, 172
Smeer, Frans, 64, 122–27, 190
Smuggling, 134, 187, 190–91; of cash crops, 3–4, 6, 9, 11, 16, 25, 60, 64, 112, 118–20, 122–24, 146. *See also* Slave trade
Soldiers, 3, 11, 22, 52, 76, 93–94, 102. *See also* Desertion
Spanish Empire, 11, 14–15, 21–28, 31, 33, 42, 46, 87, 90, 191. *See also* Venezuela
Stabroek, 6, 38, 55, 65, 83, 106, 179, 185; population, 80, 165
St. Christopher, 118–19, 130, 132
St. Domingue, 55, 79, 104
St. Eustatius, 9, 12, 93, 112–13, 117–18, 130–31, 133–34, 169–70, 191
St. Vincent, 71, 77, 84–85, 104, 119, 121, 137
States-General, 46, 57, 59, 100, 114, 126, 148–52, 161, 165, 170
Storm van 's Gravesande, Laurens, 26, 49, 50–51, 81, 87–88, 90, 94–95, 98, 100, 117, 129–31, 134, 139, 145–47, 149, 163–65, 168–72

Sugar, 1, 78, 110–11, 113, 117, 120; cultivation, 78–80, 155, 168, 186; smuggling, 16, 120–26, 155, 169, 174
Suriname, 3–4, 6, 55, 77, 80, 84, 93, 100, 107, 113–14, 165, 169; demography, 78, 132; governance, 9–10, 62, 114; investments, 16, 137–39, 141, 152, 192; marronage,13, 15. 77, 85–86, 93, 109–10, 140, 191; slave trade, 16, 114, 127–28, 130, 133; smuggling, 6, 134, 191

Taxation, 2, 55, 59, 63–64, 109, 111, 133, 150, 164, 168, 170, 190
Trade: with Amerindians, 14, 22, 34, 35–36; bricks, 116; candles, 113, 118, 184; cash crops, 16, 81, 111–14, 117–20, 124, 126, 128–29, 134–35, 138, 146–47, 171, 174, 188, 190–91; fish, 117–18, 152, 175, 184; horses, 29, 31–32, 113, 118, 175; manufactures, 179–80, 184–85; meat, 117–19, 145, 175, 184; planks, 116–17, 134; provisions, 3, 9–10, 16, 110–19, 122, 125, 135–36, 148, 151–53, 168, 174–76, 179, 181, 184, 187–88, 192; tonnage, 115–16. *See also* Coffee; Cotton; Slave trade; Smuggling; Sugar
Trotz, George Hendrik, 51–52, 144, 146, 148–49

Uitvlugt (plantation), 98, 101
Union (plantation), 107, 175
Uprisings. *See* Revolts

Velserhoofd (plantation), 92
Venezuela, 3, 11, 14, 19–21, 27, 42, 80, 86, 89, 104, 110, 133, 191. *See also* Borderland; Orinoco
Vlissingen (plantation), 93
Vloten, Dirk Wernard van, 141–45, 157, 185

War of the Spanish Succession, 25, 57
Warao, 22, 29, 94, 102, 191
WIC (Dutch West India Company), 3, 9, 14, 29–31, 35, 37–38, 47, 76, 90, 98, 100, 104, 111, 140, 145, 163, 165–66; finances, 10, 36, 53, 55–59, 63, 114, 117, 122, 126, 151–53, 164, 170, 190; governance structure, 9–10, 15, 36, 42–53, 55–68, 73, 102, 114–15, 118, 123, 128, 149–51, 161, 170, 174, 190; plantations, 10, 37, 49, 52, 87, 90, 98, 199n20; policies, 29–33, 36, 38, 81, 91, 111, 122, 164; seventeenth century,

9, 29, 31, 47–49; slave trade, 29–30, 114, 126–27, 129–31, 147, 171–72

Zealand, 10, 47, 49, 114, 117, 127, 129, 131, 140–41, 147, 170, 173; rivalry with

Amsterdam, 10, 16, 45, 47–49, 52, 115, 140, 147, 170; slave trade: 127, 129, 131, 147, 189
Zeelandia, fort, 6, 52–53, 55
Zeelugt (plantation), 97–98, 100

Early American Places

On Slavery's Border: Missouri's Small Slaveholding Households, 1815–1865
by Diane Mutti Burke

Sounds American: National Identity and the Music Cultures of the Lower Mississippi River Valley, 1800–1860
by Ann Ostendorf

The Year of the Lash: Free People of Color in Cuba and the Nineteenth-Century Atlantic World
by Michele Reid-Vazquez

Ordinary Lives in the Early Caribbean: Religion, Colonial Competition, and the Politics of Profit
by Kirsten Block

Creolization and Contraband: Curaçao in the Early Modern Atlantic World
by Linda M. Rupert

An Empire of Small Places: Mapping the Southeastern Anglo-Indian Trade, 1732–1795
by Robert Paulett

Everyday Life in the Early English Caribbean: Irish, Africas, and the Construction of Difference
by Jenny Shaw

Natchez Country: Indians, Colonists, and the Landscapes of Race in French Louisiana
by George Edward Milne

Slavery, Childhood, and Abolition in Jamaica, 1788–1838
by Colleen A. Vasconcellos

Privateers of the Americas: Spanish American Privateering from the United States in the Early Republic
by David Head

Charleston and the Emergence of Middle-Class Culture in the Revolutionary Era
by Jennifer L. Goloboy

Anglo-Native Virginia: Trade, Conversion, and Indian Slavery in the Old Dominion, 1646–1722
by Kristalyn Marie Shefveland

Slavery on the Periphery: The Kansas-Missouri Border in the Antebellum and Civil War Eras
by Kristen Epps

In the Shadow of Dred Scott: St. Louis Freedom Suits and the Legal Culture of Slavery in Antebellum America
by Kelly M. Kennington

Brothers and Friends: Kinship in Early America
by Natalie R. Inman

George Washington's Washington: Visions for the National Capital in the Early American Republic
by Adam Costanzo

Borderless Empire: Dutch Guiana in the Atlantic World, 1750–1800
by Brian Hoonhout

Complexion of Empire in Natchez: Race and Slavery in the Mississippi Borderlands
by Christian Pinnen

Toward Cherokee Removal: Land, Violence, and the White Man's Chance
by Adam J. Pratt

A Weary Land: Slavery on the Ground in Arkansas
by Kelly Houston Jones

Generations of Freedom: Gender, Movement, and Violence in Natchez, 1779–1865
by Nik Ribianszky

www.ingramcontent.com/pod-product-compliance
Lightning Source LLC
Chambersburg PA
CBHW011755220426
43672CB00018B/2966